MINISTERING
GRACIOUSLY
TO THE GAY AND LESBIAN
COMMUNITY

LEARNING TO RELATE AND UNDERSTAND

MINISTERING GRACIOUSLY

TO THE GAY AND LESBIAN COMMUNITY

POURING IN *the* OIL *and the* WINE

DR. BRIAN KEITH WILLIAMS

Destiny Image® Publishers, Inc.
P.O. Box 310
Shippensburg, PA 17257-0310

*"Speaking to the Purposes of God for This Generation
and for the Generations to Come"*

ISBN 0-7684-2268-X

For Worldwide Distribution
Printed in the U.S.A.

This book and all other Destiny Image, Revival Press, MercyPlace,
Fresh Bread, Destiny Image Fiction, and Treasure House books are available
at Christian bookstores and distributors worldwide.

1 2 3 4 5 6 7 8 9 10 / 09 08 07 06 05

For a U.S. bookstore nearest you, call
1-800-722-6774.

For more information on foreign distributors, call
717-532-3040.

Or reach us on the Internet:
www.destinyimage.com

Dedicated in Graciousness

Ministering Graciously to the Gay and Lesbian Community is a liberating, emancipating, love-demonstrating word. It is not an *accommodating, accepting,* or *agreeing* word. It is a word of *change* and *exchange* that will *rearrange* one's entire existence. It is a word of *transformation* by the power of God, *translation* from a life of sin and *transplantation* from the kingdom of lewdness into the Kingdom of light (see Col. 1:13).

I dedicate this writing to the *weeping women,* whose exposure to sexuality came at the hands of *trauma,* thereby producing a life of *drama* and thereby stifling a life of worship. A lady once sat across from me and acknowledged that she *never had a desire* to be with a man in her life. Her entire attraction was for women only. She asked painfully, "What am I to do about this? Is this who I am?" However, because of the efficacy of the blood of Christ, the sanctity of His Word, and the power of His Holy Spirit, she was completely delivered; and today she is living a victorious life above and beyond reproach to the glory of God. Not only do miracles happen, but miracles can last a lifetime. *Where there is a willing soul, there is a waiting Savior. Where there is an open mind, there is an opportune miracle.*

I dedicate this writing to all persons who have struggled or are currently experiencing crisis with their *sexual identity* issues. Surely, nobody, but Jesus, knows the trouble that they have seen. In my ministry of 30 years, I have seen many individuals delivered and made whole from the disorder of dysfunction or malady of maladjustment. Unfortunately, I have also seen the diseased, dying, or dead carcasses of *wayward* and sin-sick souls litter the wayside of life's *highway.* Jesus said, "*Wherever there is a carcass, there the vultures will gather*" (Mt. 24:28 NIV). Having traveled several million miles in three decades of ministry and speaking to multitudes throughout the planet, I have dealt firsthand with the horrific effects of lives that are lived outside the will of God. The scene is never a pretty one until God's grace is applied by faith and deliverance is accomplished. The "oil and wine" Church in

America, indeed throughout the world, must be ready to give an answer to life's toughest questions—questions like, "Why am I this way?" and "Does God love me and accept me as I am?"

I dedicate this writing to the young man who sat across from me some years ago, weeping his eyes sore, because although he had discontinued his homosexual lifestyle, he still had the inclination and the daily temptation to return. He told me of a relationship that he had broken off that seemed to him as true love. How could something that felt so right be so wrong? He questioned me, "Why am I like this? Is there deliverance for me?" Our conversation lasted all evening. Deliverance takes time. Therapy takes even more time. While he and I talked, the Lord showed me an open vision of this young man when he was but an adolescent boy.

He was on the playground. The other boys were laughing at him, because he was not chosen by anyone to play on their team. His look was one of shame, humiliation, and rejection. I saw his domineering mother and his passive father, and I heard his siblings call him "sissy, fag, and queer"; and the Holy Spirit said to me, "That is when the curse began. That is when the predisposition began." I ministered the word of knowledge and wisdom to him forthrightly. He received it in the spirit of brokenness. He did not resist the truth, and consequently that young man began a journey to justification or in other words, *just as if* he had never sinned. Today, that young man is delivered and made whole, because of the *truth spoken in love* that answered his lifelong question of self-condemnation. The late Kathryn Kuhlman said that she "believed in miracles." Well, I do too!

I dedicate this writing to the countless young men who have been raised in the church and introduced to a life of homosexuality, because of a spiritual authority figure's transference of their preference for young boys upon them, thus, relegating their impressionable minds to a lifetime of sexual bonds with the spirit of perversion. As everyone knows, hurting little boys grow up to be hurting men, and as John Maxwell says, "Hurting people often hurt other people." The cycle of violation and victimization is thus perpetuated trans-generationally. Our heartfelt prayer is that the healing power of Jeremiah's balm of Gilead will reverse the curse and stay the plague in any second– or third-generation victim of violation. It is never too late for a miracle. It is never too late for a breakthrough. It is never too late for the breaking of day.

In closing, to those antagonists of the *truth* who have dedicated themselves to dissertations that wrest the Scriptures from their clear meanings to confused ones, I simply say, may God be merciful unto you and grant you repentance to the saving of your soul. It is a dangerous and damnable thing to alter the Word of God. The Scripture states, *"But there were false prophets also among the people, even as there shall be false teachers among you, who privily shall bring in damnable heresies, even denying the Lord that bought them, and bring upon themselves swift destruction"* (2 Pet. 2:1). May you recover yourself out of the snare of deception. The justification of homosexuality in the name of God is nearly equivalent to blasphemy, which is undoubtedly one of the worst sins imaginable. In ancient times, the penalty for blasphemy was extermination. Surely, Jesus taught that all manner of sin shall be forgiven, including blasphemy against the Father and the Son, but blasphemy against the Holy Spirit shall not be forgiven (see Mt. 12:31). Those who profess the ecstatic experience of being Spirit-baptized and Spirit-filled and yet endorse anything that defies Pentecost and mocks the truth need *to be aware* that they are treading on *blasphemous ground* (see Mt. 12:31).

To the beloved Church of the Firstborn, whom I love and whose God I serve, may Christ grant His Body a *new spirit* and a *new understanding* that will cause a greater appreciation and an affectionate appeal to those ensnared in the ravages of sexual dysfunction and malpractice. The wages of *all* sin is the same, but the sin of homosexuality has terrible consequences, even in this lifetime. May this writing bring all *seekers* of *truth* to a place where they see the *Truth* and *seize this moment of truth. Ministering Graciously to the Gay and Lesbian Community* declares the message that God loves the homosexuals, but He loathes homosexuality. There are strong reasons for this, and this writing will explore them. The *"oil and wine"* Church of the apostles must speak now, because later on, there will not be a peace to hold. For those who need to see the truth, to believe it, I invite you to read along, until you visit the heavenly website and untangle the web that has been spun with the purpose of destroying an entire nation. Hence, the journey to uncovering, discovery, and recovery begins.

Bishop Brian Keith Williams, D.D.
All Nations Church and Charlotte Immanuel Church
of All Nations in the year of our Lord 2005
Presiding Prelate and a Minister of God for Righteousness

Acknowledgments

It has been said that the "pen is mightier than the sword." I would add that family and friends are more formidable than any foes. First, I wish to thank my darling wife for life. Donna, your encouragement, endearment, and understanding of the enormous amount of time that it takes away from home made this task easier and possible. Without your love, this book would not exist. I thank my three children, Achea, Brian, and Brandon for always showing a personal interest and always encouraging me to pursue the destiny of being a writer.

I thank my mother and father, Dr. Jannie B. Williams and Brother Franklin C. Williams, for raising me the right way and providing the childhood atmosphere that was conducive to learning. Thank you for starting my book collection in the eleventh grade.

I thank my siblings, Rick, Dirrick, Kevin, and my late brother, Eric, for being supportive and strengthening. I am honored that we share the same DNA.

I thank the members of All Nations Church for their incredible support over the past 20 years. You have believed in the purpose of God upon my life and you have stood with me through it all. Without you, I could not imagine where my life and ministry would be. You are the greatest congregation in the world.

I thank my associate pastors, Everette L. Spencer and Evelyn Turnbull, for saying "go ahead," at all the right times. Your loyalty to me is unsurpassed.

I thank my extended staff, Susan Petruska, Melanie Diggs, Shanda Harris, Ramona Whitehurst, Yolanda Lyons, and Joy Thomas for their valuable assistance in research, typing, editing, and critiquing, as well as in the framing of positions.

I thank my executive assistant, Min. Vivian Herron. Two years ago, you left a promising career to come and work alongside of me as I initiated my writing ministry. I have never met anyone with a more detailed, dedicated, and dutiful demeanor than you. You are brilliant, blessed, and bold. You are intelligent, intense, and inspiring. Your future in ministry is certain. From the beginning to the end, your assistance has been all-encompassing. Again, I thank you.

I thank Bishop Carlton D. Pearson, the most unselfish man that I have ever known. You epitomize "graciousness." Many years ago, you opened Azusa to me and from it, God opened the world.

I thank my lifelong friend, Dr. E. McDonald Wortham, for his stellar example of excellence. You were the first to prophecy to me that I would preach and write. Thirty years later, your prophecy has come to past.

I thank Bishop Dennis Leonard, Bishop Henry Hearns, Apostle Michael Pitts, and Dr. John Wilson for their endorsement of this book. You are the generals amongst us and I esteem you highly for your works' sake.

I thank my dear friends, Dean John Jenkins and Elder Ettwann Baytops. You are two of the brightest and best stars shining in the light of my life.

Lastly, I thank all the pastors and artists with whom I have graced the pulpit for many times of ministry. May God grant us more of them.

In memory of:

My Grandmother, Mother Nannie Boydner

My Youngest Brother, Minister Eric Williams

My Spiritual Father, Bishop Presley J. Wortham

My Hero, Bishop Q. L. Wilson, Sr.

Table of Contents

Preface

GOD'S GRACIOUS WORD TO THE
GAY AND LESBIAN COMMUNITY

*And He came to Nazareth, where He had been brought up: and, as His custom was, He went into the synagogue on the sabbath day, and stood up for to read. And there was delivered unto Him the book of the prophet Esaias. And when He had opened the book, He found the place where it was written, The Spirit of the Lord is upon Me, because He hath anointed Me to preach the gospel to the poor; He hath sent Me to heal the brokenhearted, to preach deliverance to the captives, and recovering of sight to the blind, to set at liberty them that are bruised, to preach the acceptable year of the Lord. And He closed the book, and He gave it again to the minister, and sat down. And the eyes of all them that were in the synagogue were fastened on Him. And He began to say unto them, This day is this scripture fulfilled in your ears. And all bare Him witness, and wondered at the **gracious words which proceeded out of His mouth**...* (Luke 4:16-22, emphasis added).

The contextual setting of the above message is in the synagogue at the outset of Jesus' earthly ministry. It was just after His 40-day wilderness encounter. He had successfully overcome temptations of the spirit, soul, and body and had summarily overcome the pride of life, the lust of the eye, and the lust of the flesh. Satan's dismissal from Him was as immediate as it would be ultimate.

Upon reading the scroll of Isaiah 61:1-2, He boldly declared, "*This day is this scripture fulfilled in your ears.*" He then proceeded to close the book and immediately take the seat that was reserved for Messiah, who was to come and whom He now asserted Himself to be.

The initial reaction of the congregants was *wonderment*. His reading of the Scripture and subsequent declaration had summoned their ears to full attention. They called His words "gracious."

This implies that although His words were powerful, they were not pompous. They were insistent, but not insensitive. They were arresting, but not arrogant. They were *gracious*; that is, they were compassionate, concerned, caring, and considerate in their clarion pronouncement. The tenor of His voice possessed the genetic code of the Everlasting Father whose goings forth are from eternity, thereby affording Him the unparalleled ascription, as "Ancient of Days." The DNA of divinity resounded in His rich baritone, and His bravery evidenced gentility and civility. Surely, never a man had spoken like this before. The text says that they *"all bare Him witness, and wondered at the gracious words which proceeded out of His mouth"* (emphasis added).

In most instances, first impressions are lasting ones, but in the case of Christ, oftentimes, the crowds turned on a *proverbial* dime. They went from shouts of "Hosanna," to cries of "Crucify Him"; from embracing Him to seeking to erase Him; from calling Him popular to crudely persecuting Him. This initial encounter with Christ served as a cruel awakening to the religious zealots and all others in the audience. If there were any misconceptions concerning His ministry of truth and testimony to the truth, they would soon be radically dismissed.

The text says, *"And they said, Is not this Joseph's son?"* (Lk. 4:22b) Normally, a reference to one's earthly "Abba" would not have a negative ramification, but in this context it is quite obvious that it was the beginning of the harsh reality of the resistant hardness of their hearts and also their fierce determination to preserve the ecclesiastical power structure of "things as they had always been."

Within moments of their initial "wonderment," Jesus was engaged in a straightforward diatribe of the prophetic ministry and its unpopular succession. He boldly informed them of His awareness of their refusal to accept Him and His advance preparation for rejection at the hands of the proponents of particular perspectives and religious persuasions. His predictive conclusion unnerved them. Their secondary response was vehemently different from the initial one.

> *And He said unto them, Ye will surely say unto Me this proverb, Physician, heal Thyself: whatsoever we have heard done in Capernaum, do also here in Thy country. And He said, Verily I say unto you, No prophet is accepted in His own country. But I tell you of a truth, many widows*

were in Israel in the days of Elias, when the heaven was shut up three years and six months, when great famine was throughout all the land; but unto none of them was Elias sent, save unto Sarepta, a city of Sidon, unto a woman that was a widow. And many lepers were in Israel in the time of Eliseus the prophet; and none of them was cleansed, saving Naaman the Syrian. And all they in the synagogue, when they heard these things, were filled with wrath (Luke 4:23-28).

The story concludes with the word "all" being used again in reference to their response. Remember, that "all" of them had borne Him witness and wondered at His gracious words, and now "all" of them heard these things and were filled with wrath or exceedingly indignant anger and perturbation. They immediately decided that the best first-page way to deal with this new-breed, non-credentialed professor of "prophetology" was to eliminate His influence before He could ever gain any. The thoughts of their hearts manifested in this faction's reaction. The assassination of this self-proclaimed Christ seemed to be the appropriate course of counteraction. Therefore, bodily harm became the only amen they would give Him on this or any subsequent day. His gracious words were reciprocated with unmitigated ingratitude.

And rose up, and thrust Him out of the city, and led Him unto the brow of the hill whereon their city was built, that they might cast Him down headlong. But He passing through the midst of them went His way (Luke 4:29-30).

Their execution exercise and assassination attempt was futile, because His time had not yet come. He could not die until the predestined date determined by the counsel of the eternal Godhead. He was inspired and He could not expire until He had borne witness of the truth before an "ungrateful nation," a Jewish kangaroo court, and a vacillating Roman governor.

Foreword

A Vision Concerning the State of the Church

I once had a dream in which three other people and I were sitting at a table. One of the individuals was crying profusely. The other two were engaged in dialogue about the reason for this person's stress. One of them said, "There they go again feeling sorry for themselves." The other said, "No, they are just going through some hard times, but they'll be okay." I began to try to convince them of his need for deliverance. In the meantime, the person who had been crying immediately began to emit smoke from his nostrils, mouth, and two ears. Within moments, he literally dwindled into a dwarf-like creature, and eventually he disappeared before my eyes. I awakened from the dream, obviously shaken by the vividness of it. I sought God for its interpretation. Within days, He released it to me. Of the four individuals at the table, the one crying represented the person who had serious personal problems. One represented the "accuser" who found fault with him. Another represented the "excuser," who simply released him from any responsibility. I represented the "diffuser" who had the answer, but who was engaged in argument with the accuser and the excuser. The person's death took place because I had focused on my convincing *them* rather than helping *him*. This is the problem of the Church today. There are accusers, excusers, and diffusers. While the Church argues concerning doctrine and deviance, the devil destroys souls. Enough is enough. We must get on with "deliverance to the captives" because the King's business requires haste. *Ministering Graciously to the Gay and Lesbian Community* is a God-breathed effort to erase the spirit of the accuser and excuser from the 21st-century Church. A thorough perusal of the Scriptures provides the model for "pouring out the" oil and applying the wine" to contemporary society. For this to happen, the believer today must learn to relate and to understand.

The words of a contemporary Christian chorus speak to the *"oil and the wine."*

> *He poured in the oil and the wine,*
>
> *The kind that restoreth my soul.*
>
> *I was bleeding and dying*
>
> *On the Jericho Road and*
>
> *He poured in the oil and the wine.*

Throughout the sacred writ, "oil" is a type and shadow of the Holy Spirit. "Wine" is representative of love. Another popular chorus says,

> *I will rejoice in you and be glad,*
>
> *I will extol your love more than wine.*
>
> *Draw me unto you and let us run together,*
>
> *I will rejoice in you and be glad.*

The oil and the wine were applied by the Good Samaritan to the wounds of the dying man in the Master Teacher's famous parable. Throughout two millennia, this teaching has served as a guidepost to the Church in its treatment "of the least of these." In light of the current conditions of culture, the incessant controversy concerning gays and lesbians in the church, and the same-sex marriage debate, the Church needs to pour in the "oil" and apply the "wine" to the bleeding and dying on life's Jericho Road.

In the annals of military history, one of the most legendary battles took place at Jericho. The old spiritual says, "Joshua fit the bat'l of Jericho and the walls came a tumblin' down." Ironically, they came down with a powerful shout. When the people of God opened their mouths, they released matter that contained the DNA of God. DNA speaks of the Dynamic New Anointing. The walls had to fall.

When the Church recognizes that the battle is not against the gay and lesbian revisionists, apologists, and activists, but rather against the power of the spirit(ualist)s, it will prevail, though the night seems at its darkest. The "oil" of the Holy Spirit's anointing and the "wine" of the Spirit's love will restore the fallen, rescue the perishing, and revive the dying.

18

May you, the reader, receive the "oil and wine" for the 21st century upon your soul as you ponder God's heart toward the gay and lesbian community. Selah.

Introduction

WHY THIS BOOK AND WHY NOW?

Ministering Graciously to the Gay and Lesbian Community is a compassionate treatise that directly addresses one of the most controversial and divisive issues of today. The issue of homosexuality cannot simply be discussed in private and dismissed in public.

First, I am writing this book because *I am concerned and I care.* As a minister of the gospel of Jesus Christ for the past 30 years, I am very concerned for the state of the Church in America and throughout the world. It greatly and gravely concerns me that Christianity is growing at the rate of 30,000 converts per day in China, 20,000 converts a day in Sub-Saharan Africa, and 10,000 per day in Latin America; while in the United States as many as 60 churches a week are being closed.[1] It concerns me that while the gospel is spreading throughout the world, so is the epidemic of AIDS and other deadly sexually transmitted diseases. Today's generation's teeth are set on edge because the fathers have eaten sour grapes (see Ezek. 18:2). The fathers, that is, the baby boomers of yesterday, have grossly disadvantaged the baby busters of today. The previous generations have sown the wind of promiscuity, and the children of today are reaping the cost in a whirlwind and cesspool of perversion. Brothers and Sisters, we have a problem.

Second, I am writing this book to *counteract the confusion.* Ours is a generation of gender blender, AC/DC, he-she mentality that has hijacked hope and carjacked clarity. In the 50's there was the Elvis Pelvis; in the 60's there were the Beatles and the Beatniks; in the 70's there was Disco and Dance Fever; in the 80's there was *Billy Jean* and *Beat It*; in the 90's there was Rap and the Rave; and in the 21st century we have a *sound* that totally *confounds* and lyrics that are *implicitly* and *explicitly* sexually situated and motivated.

In ancient Greek literature, a shipping vessel carried soldiers who were seduced by a serenading sound that proceeded from the island of the Sirens. Unable to simply pass by, they were allured, much like a fish is enticed, by the lure of bait. As they beached upon the shore it was not long before the men were overcome and killed. This is precisely how satan operates. *He shows the bait, but he hides the hook.* He propagates and promotes his evil agenda for one purpose only and that is *"to lure that which God loves"* away from Him. He cannot equal God in any way, shape, or form, but he attempts to injure God's heart by his seduction of the sons and daughters of men. He could not stop God from loving Adam, but he could work through the one whom Adam loved in an attempt to draw his heart away from God. The Bible says in Second Corinthians 12:10 that the weakness of God is stronger than the strength of men. Of course, the truth is, that since God is almighty and all-powerful, there is no inherent weakness in Him or with Him. However, in a figurative sense, if there is a weakness, a vulnerability, a soft underbelly and a tender spot with God, it is His unquenchable love for mankind. The age-old tactic of a person attacking someone you love in order to indirectly hurt you is indeed the enemy's method of operation against God. Needless to say, this plot has never worked, and it will not work this time either. The Church will triumph, and there is nothing the gates of hell can do to thwart it.

Third, I am writing this book because the *zeal of the Lord has consumed me.* This writing will rely heavily on the biblical record, and it will be interfaced with modern scientific research and societal data. I will endeavor to answer in a limited sense the major questions concerning the subject of male homosexuality. I will speak to the issue of lesbianism in a somewhat lesser sense. Therefore, this book will engage the "gay debate" head-on, but it is not to be considered as a scientific, scholarly, or systematic treatment of the subject. It is more of a prophetic perusal penned by a preacher. Even as *"the word of the Lord"* came unto the prophet Elijah, and the prophet Malachi began his writing with the statement, "The *burden* of the word of the Lord" (emphasis added), I also am *speaking*, because I have been *spoken* to. I have no bones to pick, no axes to grind, and no chips on my shoulder. All I have is a burden on my back and a hot coal on my tongue (see Is. 6). In writing this book I have felt the brush of angels' wings, and at times I have seen the glory on my face. It became apparent to me that the powerful presence of the *Paracletos*, the Comforter, the one called alongside to help—the Holy Spirit—was helping me as I endeavored to help His people, the household of faith. I am consumed with zeal, like Jehu of old.

...And he gave him his hand; and he took him up to him into the chariot. And he said, Come with me, and see my zeal for the Lord. So they made him ride in his chariot (2 Kings 10:15-16).

Zeal is ardent desire; it is passion in action. It is when the Word of God burns within your soul. Hopefully, this writing will cause you to say, *"Did not our heart burn within us, while He talked with us by the way...?"* (Lk. 24:32b)

Fourth, I am writing this book to bring *clarity to the Church. The world needs to return to the Book of books. It contains a gracious word for the gay and lesbian community.* It is a word of compassion and sensitivity. Some Bible exponents will not fully appreciate this exposition of truth because it is not hard or harsh enough. Those of a diametrically different interpretation quite possibly will depreciate it because it provides *no placation* or *evacuation* from the clear *pronunciations* of Scripture. *Ministering Graciously to the Gay and Lesbian Community* leaves no wiggle room for those whose loose lives require a loose liturgy and license to live in a state that is against *the current order.* Therefore this writing may be targeted by the terrorists of *truth.* To others, it may serve as a "certain sound" concerning homosexuality in an "uncertain setting" known as the church.

Essentially, the "gay debate" boils down to this: Is the gay/lesbian born or made? Are they welcome in the church, and if so, what roles do they play? If they are not welcome, then why are they not? Should two people of the same sex be sanctioned in marriage? Should gays and lesbians be ordained in the ministry? Is the gay/lesbian lifestyle a sin? Can a gay/lesbian person truly be changed? Should they seek to be changed or to "come out of the closet," or should they seek to be at peace with themselves and remain the way they are? Is the gay church a legitimate church, or is it an illegitimate one? Is it possible to be a gay/lesbian Christian? Will gay and lesbian people go to Heaven? Is the homosexual who claims to be created with same-sex attraction cursed or caused to be that way? Is homosexuality a sin, or is it simply a fault? If it is a fault, is it their fault? The question must be asked and prophetically answered: *"Is the homosexual at home in the church?"* To the individuals involved or engrossed in episodes of the gay lifestyle, may this explanation and brief exegesis enable you to find a path of peace in the recovery of your soul and self-esteem. These are a few of the questions that the Church needs to get clarity on. Hopefully, this writing will help you. In the process of research, over 60 different sources of data have been sought out, consulted, and combined with a burning desire to speak the word of the Lord; I am confident that this is our best effort.

Fifth, I am writing this book out of a *compassion for the gay and lesbian community*. Charles Colson, the former legal counsel of the Nixon administration, was subsequently converted to Christ after going to jail for his role in the Watergate cover-up. He founded the greatest prison ministry in the history of the Church, and he wrote a book entitled *Born Again*. In it, he spoke concerning the subject of compassion. He said:

> We must defend the truth lovingly, winsomely, letting others see in all we do the excellence of him who has called us from darkness into light.[2]

Throughout this book, time and again, we will endeavor to do exactly that. Richard J. Mouw, the former president of the National Association of Evangelicals, says:

> The whole point of the Biblical perspective is to promote a sexuality that is kind and reverent. So it's important that we present the Biblical viewpoint kindly and reverently to those with whom we disagree about sexual standards. Not to do so is to undermine our own message. Sexual civility is an important way of living out our commitment to the gospel.[3]

The late Pastor John Osteen called *compassion*, "The divine flow." Throughout the New Testament the expression "moved with compassion" is used no less than six recorded instances. In each instance, the compassion of Christ preceded a miraculous move of God. Effective ministry must follow the Master Teacher's model if it is to represent Christ in excellence. *The Passion of the Christ* was a movie that depicted the suffering of Christ par excellence. The sequel should be entitled *The Compassion of the Christ* and illustrate the singular theme of the Master's message and method of ministry.

1. *"But when He saw the multitudes, He was **moved with compassion** on them, because they fainted, and were scattered abroad, as sheep having no shepherd"* (Mt. 9:36, emphasis added). Christ's compassion caused Him to extend a gracious hand.

2. *"And Jesus went forth, and saw a great multitude, and was **moved with compassion** toward them, and He healed their sick"* (Mt. 14:14, emphasis added). Christ's compassion graciously felt their pain.

3. *"Then the lord of that servant was **moved with compassion**, and loosed him, and forgave him the debt"* (Mt. 18:27, emphasis added). Christ's compassion graciously cleared the slate.

4. *"And Jesus, **moved with compassion**, put forth His hand, and touched him, and saith unto him, I will; be thou clean"* (Mk. 1:41, emphasis added). Christ's compassion graciously cleansed a soul.

5. *"Then Jesus called His disciples unto Him, and said, I have **compassion** on the multitude, because they continue with Me now three days, and have nothing to eat: and I will not send them away fasting, lest they faint in the way"* (Mt. 15:32, emphasis added). Christ's compassion graciously provided fulfillment.

6. *"So Jesus had **compassion on them**, and touched their eyes: and immediately their eyes received sight, and they followed Him"* (Mt. 20:34, emphasis added). Christ's compassion graciously provided hope for a brighter future.

Concerning the gay and lesbian community I have great compassion. This is the fathering heart of God in operation. "[He is] *not willing that any should perish, but that all should come to repentance"* (2 Pet. 3:9b), despite whatever they have done or are currently doing. I absolutely detest the gay and lesbian deception. I also am adamantly persuaded that it is completely contrary to God's will for a human being, but I believe in a God who does not discriminate or turn His back on anyone who sincerely seeks His face.

Some years ago, I went into a seven-day shut-in with God, and I experienced enormous visitation and revelation while I was in His presence. The first sermon that I preached afterward was entitled, "Salvation and Not Condemnation." The text was found in John 3:17, following its more well-known and often quoted counterpart, John 3:16. It says, *"For God sent not His Son into the world to condemn the world; but that the world through Him might be saved."* My secretary at that time commented that on the particular day that the sermon was preached, I possessed a glory on

> COMPASSION IS THE MASTER KEY THAT UNLOCKS THE HEARTS OF THE HAPLESS, THE HELPLESS, AND THE HOPELESS.

my face and a fire in my eyes that she had never witnessed before. I believe that during the time of consecration God had imprinted my spirit with an impression that would serve as an insignia for all the time that I am allowed to occupy the holy office and mount the holy platform.

Compassion is the master key that unlocks the hearts of the hapless, the helpless, and the hopeless. It is also the master key to the heart of the homosexual person. Dean Merrill, author of *Sinners in the Hands of an Angry Church* says it best, "We represent a God who doesn't bludgeon sinners into submission."[4]

Sixth, I am writing this book because *as an apostle, I can*. In Philippians 4:13, St. Paul declares, "*I can do all things through Christ which strengtheneth me*." This applies to anybody willing to be apostolic. One should never apologize for being a commissioned one or for writing a defense for the faith. Without holy hermeneutic (exegesis and exposition) the church will plummet into heresy and the apostolic mandate will become apostate. It is indeed much better to light a candle than it is to curse the darkness. When a glass is half empty, confession does not change the fact. Calling it half full may be positive, but it is still half empty, nonetheless. The fact is, every adult at some time in their life has had to personally deal with the "gay issue," whether in their life or someone else's life. In the book, *Craving for Love*, Briar Whitehead quotes Reverend Dr. Jack Hayford, one of the greatest apologists in church history as saying,

> There's not a Christian man alive, who has never had a homosexual idea come to his mind, as repulsed as you may have been.[5]

Though I am a *straight* man, married at the time of this writing to my wife for 25 years, and though I have always been *straight*, I have members of my extended family who have struggled with same-sex attraction. I also have many very dear friends in ministry and in business who either were or are gay or lesbian. I have many parishioners whom I have pastored whose lives have been checkered with this proclivity, and I am acquainted with a number of public, civic, and church leaders who daily lead a duplicitous lifestyle. If the truth be told, this sad fact is a more common occurrence than most people are ready to acknowledge and admit. I believe that whenever you tell the truth that you shame the devil. In the book, *The Bible and Homosexual Practice*, Robert A.J. Gagnon writes:

> ...to feel homosexual impulses does not make one a bad person. I deplore attempts to demean the humanity of homosexuals. Whatever one thinks about the immorality of homosexual behavior, or about the obnoxiousness of elements within the homosexual lobby, homosexual impulses share with all other sinful impulses the feature of being an attack on the "I" or inner self experiencing the impulses (Romans 7:14-25).[6]

The key phrase in the above quote is that the "impulse" toward homosexuality "does not make one a bad person." Those who struggle with gay and lesbian issues are not of themselves repugnant and repulsive. Those who have experimented with it are not necessarily homosexuals, but they are not better than the homosexual either.

The seventh and final answer to the question, "Why This Book and Why Now?" is because *I am called as an apologist*. An apologist is one who defends the faith. It is very true that *desperate times require desperate measures*. Days of apostasy require deeds of apologists. The difference between a major prophet and a minor prophet was not the size of the ministry, the depth of their word, the preciseness of their predictions, or their poetic/prophetic penmanship. Rather, it was the length of their books that qualified them with the "major or minor" ascription. *Ministering Graciously to the Gay and Lesbian Community* is not simply a word that addresses the debate, but a word that contains the blessing of Gad, given by Moses (see Deut. 33:20).

Gad represents God's Army of Deliverers, the end-time company that is being raised up to become history makers, kingdom shakers, and world changers. It is time for *Gad* to rise. The Church, like *Gad,* has been overcome, but we shall overcome in the last. Moses blessed him, saying: "Gad, a troop shall overcome him: but he shall overcome at the last" (Gen. 49:19).

Furthermore, one of the intercessors an elder of my ministry had a prophetic dream shortly after I began this book. It gives spiritual insight to why I was chosen for such a task. In the prophetic dream, I had just finished preaching. I was walking down a long hall. There were many people running after me, but I did not see them. I turned the corner and suddenly saw the people and said, "*What are you doing? Why are you following me?*" They answered, "*You told us to follow you.*" Then I said, "*I didn't tell you to follow me—Go back.*" The individuals reversed direction and came back down a long hall where a person was standing, who appeared to be a woman, but was actually a man. Then the people began throwing money as the wall opened and I was sitting in a throne chair with gold cloth over my head and face. The chair rolled forward and a voice declared, "*They think they are being delivered, set free, but they are not.*" There was so much light coming off my face that it was covered like that of Moses. A demon spirit appeared on my right shoulder. It said, "*I'm still here,*" in a mocking laughter.

The following interpretation was suggested. The man dressed like a woman represented the church turned in on itself in a perverse way. The people running after me were demonstrating inordinate affection, idolizing, and trying to pay for their deliverance by throwing money at my feet. The perverse spirit in front of me was not saying a word, but he was present. The demon on my shoulder and the man dressed like a woman were representing an assignment and deliverance. The burden of the exposure of homosexuality/inordinate affection in the church had been placed on my shoulders to deal with in this season. This book is an effort to "understand the times."

ENDNOTES

1. Dean Merrill, *Sinners in the Hands of an Angry Church* (Grand Rapids, MI: Zondervan Publishing House, 1997), 59-60.

2. Charles Colson, "From a Moral Majority to a Persecuted Minority," *Christianity Today* (May 14, 1990): 80.

3. Richard J. Mouw, *Uncommon Decency* (Downers Grove, Illinois: InterVarsity Press, 1992), 94.

4. Dean Merrill, *Sinners in the Hands of an Angry Church* (Grand Rapids: Zondervan Publishing House, 1997), 56.

5. Briar Whitehead, *Craving for Love* (London, England: Monarch Books, 2003), 115.

6. Robert A. J. Gagnon, *The Bible and Homosexual Practice* (Nashville: Abingdon Press, 2001), 31.

CHAPTER
ONE

It is the sad tendency of modern men to either do the right thing in the wrong way or to do the wrong thing in the right way. We either hold to the truth obnoxiously, or we hold to a lie graciously. We are either a rude angel, or a polite devil. Often what poses as a cruel orthodoxy is defeated by what poses as a kind heresy. [1]

George Grant and Mark Horne

God gives us the will wherewith to will, and the power to use it, and the help needed to supplement the power...but we ourselves must will the truth, and for that the Lord is waiting. [2]

George Macdonald

When Jesus said that he was hungry and thirsty and naked in those around us, he was referring to more than mere corporal needs. We're surrounded by people who are hungry and thirsty and naked in their souls, and they come to us hungry for understanding, thirsty for affirmation, naked with loneliness, and wanting to be covered with the mantle of our genuine tenderness. [3]

Brennan Manning
The Wisdom of Tenderness

It is contrary to reason for a thirsty person to turn from a pure, sparkling mountain stream to quench his thirst at a stale, putrid cistern—yet that is what the human race does when it rejects God's truth and standards in favor of the devil's impure philosophies. [4]

Dr. Billy Graham

The Confrontive Appeal:
The Naked Truth Must Now Be Told

—THE POWER OF TESTIMONY—

When I was a boy, growing up in a classic apostolic-pentecostal church, we used to sing a song that said, "I believe I'll testify, while I have a chance, because I may not have this chance anymore." The testimony service was the witnessing element of worship liturgy, and without it we did not consider the church service complete. The times have changed and models of ministry have changed as well, but one thing has stood the test of time. There is still overwhelming power in an overcoming testimony. They may call them "praise reports" today, but they are testimonies all the same.

My Personal Testimony

My first exposure to anyone or anything homosexual was during my adolescent years. There was a boy in our neighborhood whose mother had six children, and each of them had a different father. None of the fathers was actively involved in any one of their lives. Their mother was the leader and role model in the home. One of the children, Dennis (name changed to respect privacy), was clearly effeminate in his ways. He walked and talked like a girl. Everything about him, from his clothing to his entire appearance and demeanor, was girlish. He never played with the rest of us, and from time to time, I would hear of his having performed oral sex on a number of the boys in the neighborhood. *Personally, I found Dennis to be very nice, but also very disgusting. I did not want him around me, and I never wanted to be seen with him. In retrospect, perhaps I was being wise, but maybe I was just being somewhat homophobic as well.* Regardless, Dennis eventually became overtly gay, and he was the brunt of much ridicule and slander.

This is when I first started hearing the denigrating names associated with homosexuals.

My Personal Experience

I also recall as a child riding in the car with a family member who was driving. We were riding through the streets of Baltimore when we saw a stereotypical-looking gay person standing on the corner. He was wearing a dolled-up hairstyle, makeup, and lip gloss, and was standing as if he was posing, profiling, or trying to be picked up. My family member hollered out, "Look at that punk—that faggot." Of course, we were already looking, because something so outrageous will definitely get your attention. This person was the epitome of disgraceful. I had no gracious words for him either. Though I did not verbalize it, everything about him incensed me. I took his actions and antics quite personal and internalized my disdain and horror at such a ghastly sight. Ironically, years later, that same family member who called the guy standing on the corner a "faggot" had several sons of his own. One of them was sexually molested and consequently struggled with homosexuality, and another became a homosexual—or to use his chosen term of defamation for the gay on the corner, he became a full-fledged faggot.

It is important to note that the Bible says, *"Judge not according to the appearance, but judge righteous judgment"* (Jn. 7:24). It also says, *"With what measure* [judgment] *ye mete, it shall be measured to you again"* (Mt. 7:2b). Isaiah 58 records that the "chosen fast" is one that results in the taking away of the putting forth (pointing) of the finger (see Is. 58:9). Whenever you point the finger at something, there are three more pointing back at you. Whenever you point at something, you literally yoke yourself to it. Curses always recoil upon the head of those who imprecate them. Therefore, prophetically speaking, I believe that when this family member made disparaging remarks about someone else's son, it (the curse) came on his own son. Fortunately, this person's son gave his life to Christ, and today he is truly a changed man.

My Personal Upbringing

As aforementioned, I was raised in a classic apostolic-pentecostal church where there was a very strong emphasis on holy, sanctified, and clean "living." The bishop of our church was the holiest and humblest man I have ever met. However, over the years as I grew older, I discovered that some of the ones in the power positions of our local and national church organization definitely had gay and lesbian issues. As a saved young man in my late teens, this realization was devastating to say the least. I was solicited several times by different brothers for varied sexual encounters. I praise God that I was sustained and unscathed in my response. I made it through this difficult time without falling prey to the deceptive grips of this demonic assault against my soul and sanity.

As I traveled to different church conventions held throughout the country, I began to meet scores of men. Many of them were aged, and did not have a female companion, nor did they want one. They had no interest in being married. Why was this so? Because, simply stated, they were gay. They were tongue-talking, choir-directing, organ-playing, sermon-preaching, in-the-closet, gay men. A number of times when the services were over, I would go to dinner, and of course, many of these individuals would be present. They had cloaked their gayness well, but it has a way of peeking through the eyes like the sun peeks through the blinds on a sunny day.

My Personal Observations

The eyes are the mirror to the soul. *If the eye is single (pure), then the body is full of light; but, if it is double, the body is full of darkness* (see Mt. 6:22). Occasionally, these men would "slip" in their conversation, and I would hear words like "girl" or "miss thing." (These are common expressions in the gay community used to reference men as girls.) Again, I found this unsettling because of who they were and because some of them were my friends. I remember once, upon greeting some of them, one of them hugged me and I halfheartedly hugged him in return. I was as cold as arctic ice and as stiff as an ironing board. I am sure he noticed it. Though this may sound stupid to educated ears now, back then I was afraid it would rub off on me. I learned later that some closet gays would use church conventions as the time for their homosexual rendezvous. As a young Christian, I was so offended that I almost stumbled right out of the church. For the overwhelming part, most of the bishops simply ignored the state of affairs. The spirit of Eli ruled, and they failed to discipline their homosexual sons (see 1 Sam. 2:29).

My Personal Exposure

Years later I found out why. I had been traveling with a bishop on a ministry trip to Detroit, Michigan, and we were in the process of checking into a hotel. The front desk clerk asked if we needed a single or a double room. The leader replied, "A *single* room will be sufficient." I quickly retorted that we needed a *double* room, and so it was. Throughout the week, I was treated very distantly and indifferently, and this person was relatively reclusive as if I had hurt him. It dawned upon me that he was peeved over the fact that his agenda of seduction had not been successful. Still, in my mind, I made allowances for this person because, after all, he was a "man of God." I made *concessions in my consciousness,* although I did not *compromise my character.* As a teenager in the early stage of maturity, I did not want to acknowledge what was blatantly obvious. In time, confirmation would come to attest that this was not an isolated incident. The Bible says that *"in the mouth of two or three witnesses every word may be established"* (Mt. 18:16b). Other young men secretly shared that they had similar experiences with him.

My Personal Parts

I will never forget one particular day prior to graduating from high school, while I was ministering at a church within the organization. I had driven all night without any rest to the location of the services. Between services, the pastor said that if I wanted to rest I could lay down on the sofa bed in his office. So I took him up on his offer. Before long, I dozed off to sleep. I awakened a short time later to the awful realization that he had decided to lay down next to me and get some sleep as well. Of itself, that was not bad, although this was a very small sofa bed. It was the fact that his hand was placed on my private parts. When he recognized that I was awake, he proceeded to act as if he was laying hands on me, in the pretense of praying for me. Though I was riveted and troubled, I never said anything. I just pondered it in my heart. Soon thereafter, my inner pondering became repulsion, when I recognized that this leader had used this ploy with other young men as well. God only knows what else happened with them. As a leader of God's people, his influence was significant and not suspicious, and this is probably how many innocent ones were lured into positions of compromise. The old adage is that you teach what you know, but you reproduce what you really are. The naked truth is this: If it walks like a duck, quacks like duck, and smells like a duck, more often than not, it is a duck. If a person puts his hands on the private parts of another person of the same sex, and that person is not a medical doctor conducting a physical examination, more than likely he is a homosexual or he has some serious tactile, touchy-feely issues going on.

—THE POWER OF ATMOSPHERE—

My Teenage Years

I have learned over the years that atmospheres are powerful conduits of either a holy or a hellish presence. The right environment can breed sexual wholeness and the wrong one can do severe sexual damage to the psyche. Being among many gays during several years of my young Christian life served as a wake-up call and a shock treatment to life in the church. What once shocked and disgusted me was apparently all around me. The church was infested with it. In my teenage years I attended a church of less than one hundred people, and there were at least five brothers and two sisters who were either former homosexuals or practicing ones. There was also another teenager who appeared well on his way to becoming a charter member of the "graduated gay auxiliary." I did not accept it, but I did accommodate it. In other words, I did not ask, and they did not tell. We just kept on hanging around the church and claimed that we were having church. In time, however, the naked truth was told, because the philosopher Carlisle was right, "No lie can live forever." Soon the cover was blown and the light was shone. "I'm okay, you're okay" was no longer the motto, and "che serà, serà—whatever will be, will be" was no longer the word for the day. In the past, mum was the word, dumb was the demeanor, and deaf was the disease. Eventually, the sin came out of incubation and into manifestation.

My Senior Year

In the midst of this period of my life, my precious father asked a very disturbing question. At the time he was not a Christian. I eventually had the privilege to personally baptize him some years later, and today he proudly calls me his pastor. When I was elevated to the office of the Bishopric, he reached and hugged my mother saying, "We got ourselves a bishop...we got ourselves a bishop." He is proud of me and he has always loved me as any good man would love his son, but he once momentarily had genuine concerns about my heterosexuality. When I was in my senior year of high school, he asked me if I was "funny." In those days the term "funny" was a term of derision used to identify gay people. I was very hurt by his blunt question, and I fired back at him as if he had just plucked my last nerve, pulled my last string, and eaten my last potato chip. I sharply answered, "Of course not." I then asked him why he would ask me such a "hurtful" question. He simply answered that he had never seen me with a girlfriend since I had become a Christian three years earlier. The truth is that I did not have a girlfriend because I did not trust myself with one. I was simply too hot to trot, and I was endeavoring to live and lead a life of abstinence. I had done so, effectively, since the Lord Jesus Christ had captured my heart. My father also expressed concern about some of my friends whom he thought were questionable in their sexual identity and orientation. Naturally, I responded by becoming defensive of my peers, although in my heart I knew that there were a few questionable ones, who though they were also living a life of abstinence, in reality, had definite gay issues going on in their past. Perceptive people can always detect anything close to a gay/lesbian transmission or telegram.

Some may wonder why I am bringing up these occurrences of my life nearly 30 years after the fact. *After all, isn't it better just to let sleeping dogs lie?* Perhaps so, but I would argue: Sleeping dogs can sometimes wake up to bite you. Anything that is swept under the carpet may someday serve to trip you up. It is best to deal with the past by putting it into perspective, and then and only then can you embrace the present with power and face the future with faith. In retrospect, I believe that there were several things that were transpiring in the realm of the spirit at that time that were a part of the enemy's modus operandi or assault against my sanctified soul.

—THE POWER OF THE ADVERSARY—

Unrealistic Expectations

First, the adversary used *unrealistic expectations*. As a member of a "holiness church," I had extremely high standards of morality that included taking very seriously the Pauline injunction to *"abstain from all appearance of evil"* (1 Thess. 5:22), and to *"not make provision for the flesh"* (Rom. 13:14). Therefore, I infrequently dated girls, and I regularly spent time with my male friends. To my knowledge, all of them were saved and loved the Lord. Though some of them were not exactly the prototype for "macho men," I was not concerned because the gay issue was theirs to resolve, and not mine. By this time, I had overcome my childhood homophobia, and I no longer viewed them as having a disease that you could catch. In retrospect, I think that in an effort to "keep it real," Christian young men in their teens should not be taught to stay away from girls. Rather they should be taught what situations to avoid with girls. Teenage hormones have a tendency to rage.

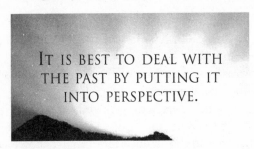

IT IS BEST TO DEAL WITH THE PAST BY PUTTING IT INTO PERSPECTIVE.

Unholy Associations

Second, the adversary used *unholy associations*. I believe that *"evil communications corrupt good manners"* (1 Cor. 15:33), or as the slogan goes, "Birds of a feather flock together." Association will at times produce assimilation. Therefore, it is wise to heed the scriptural admonition to *"walk with wise men"* if you desire to be wise (see Prov. 13:20). Whatever you desire to be, then that is what you should be around. If you do not desire to be like something or someone, then do not be with them. In all interpersonal relationships there is what is known as the "law of exposure." You should never expose yourself to something that you do not wish to be. If you do not wish to be gay, then you will need to get yourself some friends who are straight like you. If you do not wish to be a lesbian, then leave lesbian company and be with those who are otherwise disposed. Fellowship affects faith and faith works by love. The mistake that I made is that I assumed that my "straight" influence could straighten them, but it never did. It did not even faze them, let alone straighten them.

Unrelenting Pressure

Third, the adversary used *unrelenting pressure* in an effort to beguile my soul. I realize that when the tempter targets a soul for the gay lifestyle, he will strategically place people in proximity to that person to wear his resistance down, eventually hoping to wear him out (see Dan. 7:25). During that same time, there was a fellow student in high school, whose father was one of the teachers at our school. In a private moment, as I was sharing the gospel with this teacher, he asked me, "Do you think I can corrupt you?" (see Col. 2:4) To *corrupt* is to ruin, spoil, pollute, and contaminate. My response was one of silence, because I did not know what he meant, even though I did *somewhat* sense it. The naked truth is that I did not want to believe what I had just heard him say. I was in a state of denial for his sake. Therefore, it did not really dawn on me what was going on.

Unexpected Overtures

Fourth, the adversary used *unexpected overtures* of authority figures. In my naiveté, I was clueless to the fact that he was making a not-so vague "homosexual overture" towards me. Later on, it was revealed that this man was gay. His earlier inquiry was in fact a "pass." I am truly grateful that, in my innocence, I did not catch the pass, but kicked the ball out of his hands and never entertained any more dialogue with him concerning the subject. The adversary continued to come at me with this foul presence, but thanks be to God who giveth us the victory, I was being shielded by a faith that would not fail.

There is an old expression that when it rains, it pours, and whenever there is a gathering of black clouds, it is a sure indication that it is going to rain. The black clouds had begun to gather around me, seeking to seduce me from the divine design and cause me to trip the wire that leads to destruction. Something was going on.

—THE POWER OF THE ANOINTING—

And it shall come to pass in that day, that his burden shall be taken away from off thy shoulder, and his yoke from off thy neck, and the yoke shall be destroyed because of the anointing (Isaiah 10:27).

He that committeth sin is of the devil; for the devil sinneth from the beginning. For this purpose the Son of God was manifested, that He might destroy the works of the devil (1 John 3:8).

A Demon Prince Called Lust

The final black cloud gathered on a day that I was scheduled to meet with a visiting representative from a college located in West Virginia. As he and I talked, I had an experience that I had never had before. I experienced firsthand the appeal and approach of the seducing spirit that seeks to send the saints into same-sex attraction. As he and I were talking about college possibilities, I had a vision painted on my mental screen that can only be described as having been *produced, directed, and choreographed by a demon prince spirit named Lust.* I immediately cast down the imagination (see 2 Cor. 10:3-5) or the thought that I was thrust with, as I was so disturbed by it. Prior to that moment, as God is my eternal witness, I had never even remotely felt any attraction for the same sex before. For days, I literally walked around in a dazed stupor. Truthfully, this experience scared me. I thought within myself, perhaps my father was onto something! Perhaps, I further thought, I had homosexual tendencies and I was in denial. As a teenager, I was at a moment of truth. The demon attempted to get me to embrace the lie.

The Demon of Seduction

I prayed for God to open my eyes and show me what was going on with me. Within days, God answered my prayer, and He did indeed show me the *root* behind the fruit and the cause behind the effect. He revealed to me that

DEMON SPIRITS THAT INFLU-ENCE PEOPLE CAN ALTER ENTIRE ATMOSPHERES.

this person (the college representative) had a spirit of seduction operating in his life, and when I came into contact with its power, the enemy attempted to use this to overtake me. Demon spirits that influence people can alter entire atmospheres. Once you enter their abode with your mind unshielded, you can be overcome by the prevailing atmospheric spirit. In this case, it was seduction. First Timothy 4:1 says, *"Now the Spirit speaketh expressly, that in the latter times some shall depart from the faith, giving heed to **seducing** spirits, and doctrines of devils"* (emphasis added). In fact, Second Timothy 3:13 says, *"But evil men and seducers shall wax worse and worse, deceiving, and being deceived"* (emphasis added). The apostle

Peter declared that we are *"kept by the power of God"* (1 Pet. 1:5a). The older saints used to say that God will keep you even during the times you do not want to be kept. In this instance, the adversary was attempting to confuse my young mind, by putting on me what was clearly his spirit of perversion. The major component working with me to keep me was that my human spirit, being filled with the Holy Spirit, was stronger than his human spirit that was possessed by an unholy spirit.

The self-doubt that succeeded this temptation was aided and abetted by a legion of demonic cohorts. This is where all the ensuing, doubtful, shameful, condemning, and evil thoughts came from (see Mk. 7:21-23). As I recall, during that time I even had thoughts that I needed to go out and have sex with girls just to prove that I did not have this same-sex tendency, over-taking preference, or orientation. That demonic strategy eventually failed as well, but my unblemished abstinence record was tested in the process. Thank God I passed the test.

The Demons Were Defeated

Unbeknownst to me at the time, there were a group of prophetic inter-cessors praying for me who lived in Philadelphia. The Holy Spirit had alerted them that the "gay" demon was trying to attach itself to my life. By the use of the term "demon," I am not implying that everyone who is gay is demon pos-sessed; I am implying that this was the name or distinctive characteristic of this spirit that had me in its scope during my late teen years. Within weeks, one of the intercessors, a young man a few years older than me, met with me and shared that the Holy Spirit had revealed to him what the devil was up to. In a private ministry session, he laid hands on me and prayed me through in a fashion that truly liberated my soul and lifted the black clouds that were gathering on my horizon. I immediately took vital steps to put major dis-tance between myself and any of the same-sex suitors or the contaminated environments. I moved to Columbus, Ohio, where I met my lovely wife. I lit-erally knew upon first sight that she was to be my wife. Praise be to God, the demons were defeated.

—THE POWER OF A DELIVERANCE—

O wretched man that I am! who shall deliver me from the body of this death? (Romans 7:24)

The Personal Pursuit

When God brought my wife into my life, we pursued marriage within months of meeting each other. She has been my wife for life, and we have remained steadfast and stalwart for 25 years. Her purity of virginity was a prayer answered and indeed a testimony of her relationship with the Lord. We were both ready and right for each other, and we married within one year. The spirit that tried to seduce me had lost its hold. Jesus loosed me before I could ever get bound, just like he had protected Abraham's wife, Sarah, when she was slated to become the king's wife because of Abraham's momentary lapse of faith. The Lord protected me lest I be lent even for a season to such an experience. Genesis 20:3-7 says, *"But God came to Abimelech in a dream by night, and said to him, Behold, thou art but a dead man, for the woman which thou hast taken; for she is a man's wife....for he is a prophet...."*

The Personal Assault

For well over a quarter of a century I have never had anything even close to that happen again. The personal assault was slaughtered at the prayer altar. I have shared my teenage *exposure* to help those who may be trapped by the secretive situations of their *experience.* When I married my wife for life, I married for all the right reasons. Having never participated in the gay lifestyle, I had no prior baggage to bring into the marriage. In *Craving for Love,* Briar Whitehead wrote:

> A homosexual is not cured by marriage, or by having a girl-friend. He is seeking affirmation, identity, and affection from males, not females. If marriage cured homosexuality, married men would not constitute such a high percentage (anything from 30% to 70%) of practising homosexual men.[5]

The Personal Practice

In the early days of my pastorate, I had a secretary whose husband had been a practicing homosexual. Apparently, he had given up the lifestyle to be married and had become a deacon in the church. Before long, however, his repressed dysfunction began to resurface, and he left her for another man. The devastation that resulted in both their lives was a terrible thing to witness. He was a man on the down low, who married on the down low, and now he is connected to a minister on the down low. The last time I saw him, he was walking in a mall looking as effeminate as a VH-1 diva. The gay spirit carries a gay look. He had married on the down low, and he could no longer live a lie, so he left a bleeding heart behind.

—MARRYING ON THE DOWN LOW—

For without are dogs, and sorcerers, and whoremongers, and murderers, and idolaters, and whosoever loveth and maketh a lie (Revelation 22:15).

Homosexuals who receive Christ need to be ministered to before they ever contemplate marriage. Marriage before ministry is a mistake in the making. I strongly advise that no person enter into marriage with the naive notion that they can change someone's character, alter their behavior, transform their temperament, or reverse their chosen sexual preference or past proclivity. A person who marries on the down low is living, loving, and making a lie.

Many years ago, I knew a young couple who was married. The young lady knew that the fellow was gay, but she thought she could change him. Sadly, she was wrong. They had the most elaborate wedding imaginable. The wedding party was made up of at least 25 people. Not a stone of grandeur was left unturned. In fact, it was quite a beautiful display of elegance and excellence. However, there was just one problem with all of it which resulted in a major mess, a major divorce, and ultimately a major heartbreak. The young man was a Christian who had never properly dealt with his predisposition and practice of the homosexual lifestyle. He had stopped it long enough to get married to this precious sister, but he was in inner turmoil throughout the engagement and brief marriage. Eventually, he left his wife and returned to his former life. Sadly within a few years he died of AIDS. He was only in his mid-40's. The statistics do not tell lies, although many times smiling faces do.

A Supreme Tragedy

It is my belief that somewhere the church and his pastor failed him, by neglecting to minister the word of deliverance and continued therapy to his sexually-scarred soul. He was molested as a child, which had been imprinted in his psyche and violated his being. He thought that marrying a beautiful woman of God would solve his problem and resolve his perversion. It did not happen for him, and very seldom does it happen for anyone else. Deliverance does not happen at the wedding altar; it happens at the

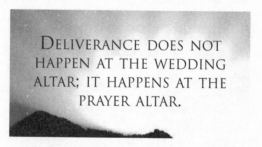

DELIVERANCE DOES NOT HAPPEN AT THE WEDDING ALTAR; IT HAPPENS AT THE PRAYER ALTAR.

prayer altar. It is important to remember that homosexuals are not born; they are made. They are not created; they are caused. They are not cursed; but their sin is. No matter how life deals a person a bad hand, there is help available at the hand of God. The songwriter said, "Let Jesus fix it for you, for He knows just what to do. Whenever you pray, just let Him have His way. He knows just what the problem is, let Jesus fix it for you." Despite the past, despite the predisposition, despite the problems of the practice of the lifestyle, "all things are possible to him that believeth"(Mk. 9:23b).

—MEN ON THE DOWN LOW—

For there are certain men crept in unawares, who were before of old ordained to this condemnation, ungodly men, turning the grace of our God into lasciviousness, and denying the only Lord God, and our Lord Jesus Christ (Jude 1:4).

The term in the African-American community for married closet homosexuals is "on the down low." A recent Oprah Winfrey show highlighted the apparent rise in the trend of men who are married and are secretly engaged in an incognito lifestyle with the same sex. J.L. King recently wrote a book on the same subject entitled, *On the Down Low*. He states:

> Down low means masculine, unreadable, uncloakable. It means I've got a girlfriend or a wife. It means you can't tell I'm having sex with men... If it was okay for DL (down low) men to have both, there would be no such thing as down low....This is a desire that you have no control over. The desire will hit him (down low) out of the clear blue. He may say no a few times, but eventually he will fall. DL men prefer women over men. They will always have a woman in their life. This is not a learned behavior. Who would want to live like this where you're constantly lying, hiding and scared of being busted? This desire makes some men lose all common sense. Look at the many celebrities caught with a prostitute, with a man or in the wrong place. Sex is powerful.[6]

A Supreme Opportunity

Although J.L. King confronts homosexuality in the black church, he continues to believe that the African-American church is an avenue of hope and healing for those in the community.[7] He recognizes that the institution and culture of the church continues to be the place where those in homosexuality as well as all other compulsive behaviors can receive help. King's experience and observations may indeed seem shocking to the average church attendee. Yet, they are in no way exclusive to the so-called black church. He

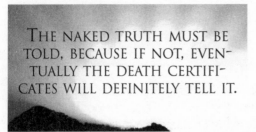

THE NAKED TRUTH MUST BE TOLD, BECAUSE IF NOT, EVENTUALLY THE DEATH CERTIFICATES WILL DEFINITELY TELL IT.

points out that many church conventions and meetings have been fertile places for men living on the down low to find plenty of willing men to have sex with.[8] He finds duplicity in pastors who preach against homosexuality while committing adultery with women in the church or having sex with brothers. According to King, there are frequent occurrences of pastors living on the down low. King points out that the homosexual situation and the accompanying HIV/AIDS issues are an opportunity for the black church to step up and to be leaders in showing empathy and caring compassion while educating the congregants. The possibility of ministry opportunity is supremely plentiful.[9]

—MEN OF GOD ON THE DOWN LOW—

Pastors aren't allowed to admit their vulnerability. It's rare for a pastor to feel comfortable as anything other than a model Christian. Most churches require their pastors to live in denial.[10]

Dr. Larry Crabb, *The Silence of Adam*

Same-Sex Sickness

Many may think that "men on the down low" is reserved for the world and that it is barely existent in the church. I am sorry to inform you of this, but you are wrong…very wrong! Denial is resident and president throughout Christendom. Denial is not a river in Egypt. Denial is de-nigh-el. It will (de)stroy the ability to draw (nigh) to (El) God. It is in the church, and regretfully it is in the ministry. Dietrich Bonhoeffer, the German theologian and author of *Life Together,* once said:

> The more isolated a person is, the more destructive will be the power of sin over him and the more deeply he becomes involved in it, the more disastrous is his isolation. Sin wants to remain unknown. It shuns the light. In the darkness of the unexpressed it poisons the whole being of a person. This can happen even in the midst of a pious community.[11]

Bonhoeffer's words are revealing. Pious communities are not immune to creeping things, crawling critters, and insect creatures that always run whenever you turn on the light. According to his own testimony, at the time that I met him, J. L. King was participating in a life on the down low, and was an avid member of a full-gospel church. I was invited there to speak nearly 20 years ago, and J.L. was in the congregation listening to my sermon. I preached a sermon entitled "Shake the Snake." I have included the amplified version of this message and I have renamed it, "Serving the Gay Serpent an Eviction Notice!" It has been revised to directly address the homosexual

43

subject matter of this book. I applaud J.L's courage in addressing this issue with intensity.

A Sickening Thought

Over the years I have preached in many pulpits and spoken on many campuses throughout the world. Oftentimes, I have been called upon to minister to people in situations such as the one I have declared. Several years ago, I met the late prophet, Keith Grayton, who pastored a thriving church in Salisbury, Maryland. As a young man, according to his own testimony, Keith had been introduced to a lifestyle of homosexuality at the age of six, by a minister who was a guest speaker at his church. It is not essential to know exactly how this happened, but it set him on a course of battling the gay issue all his life. It was a course that included frequenting the gay clubs after the church service to get his groove on and meet his promiscuous encounter for the night. He had gone through a number of repeated deliverance exorcisms throughout his young life, but they were all to no avail. Toward the end of his life, his spiritual covering once shared with me that she and her husband walked with him through many anguishing years of his incessant yielding to this proclivity. Thank God for true pastors such as this great woman of God, who never gave up on this young prophet in the making!

Healing the Sick

In time, her loving compassion paid off, and he was healed of the sin-sickness and set free by the liberty of the Spirit of God. According to Prophet Grayton, he was conducting a revival in a particular city, and when the revival concluded, he requested that the pastor allow him to stay and shut-in before the Lord.

This would prove to be the defining moment and turning point of his life. The patriarch, Noah, and his family were shut in with God aboard the ark. The ark represents a "salvation experience." There was one ark, just as there is one God. There was one door, just as there is only one door to the Father and that is the Son. There was one window, just as there is one Holy Spirit. The window was up high, representing the illuminating power of God's Spirit. The believer should always look up and never down. The Scripture records the complete dimensions of the entire ark, with the exception of

> IN THE CHURCH, THE STINK ON THE INSIDE IS NOT NEARLY AS BAD AS THE STORM OF PROBLEMS AND PERVERSIONS ON THE OUTSIDE.

the door. There were no dimensions given. It is the "whosoever will, let him come" door. No person's sin is too high or wide to keep them from entering in. Jesus is the door (see Jn. 14:6). Noah, whose name means rest or comfort, prefigures the believer who receives and finds rest upon taking the yoke of Jesus (see Mt. 11:30). All believers can receive the same rest today. If you do what he did, you will get what he got. Noah got a new beginning and so did my dear friend. There was stink (animals) on the inside and a storm (atmosphere) on the outside. However, no person ever attempted to leave the yearlong shut-in, because the stink on the inside was not as bad as the storm on the outside. Despite the problems and perversions in the church, the stink on the inside is not nearly as bad as the storm of problems and perversions on the outside. Everyone should run in, before time runs out.

And they that went in, went in male and female of all flesh, as God had commanded him: and the Lord shut him in (Genesis 7:16).

Sick and Tired

Shut-ins are intense periods of seeking God that close out the rest of the world as an individual focuses fully on obtaining a move of the Spirit of God in their life. It is for those who are sick and tired of being sick and tired. It is for those who no longer want the same-old, same-old. It is for those whose questions need answers. It is for those whose problems need real solutions. It is for those who have a yearning for the burning—who have zeal to feel after God. It is for those who have left a place to which they shall never return.

The first day into Prophet Grayton's shut-in, nothing significant happened. The second day, again nothing significant transpired. However, on the third night, sometime in the middle of the night, Prophet Grayton said that he could literally hear the spiritual chains when they fell from his body and hit the floor. *He was instantaneously, miraculously, and marvelously changed by the power of God!*

He was healed, cured, and made whole in one master stroke and shortly thereafter fell in love with a beautiful young psalmist, named Melody, who he eventually married. She honors his legacy to this day. However, in the process of preparing for his new life, he tested positive with the HIV virus. Soon, it progressed to full-blown AIDS.

Sick of Sin

During the years before he passed away from AIDS, Prophet Grayton became sick of sin and led a powerful crusade against closet homosexuality in the church. His ministry was one of the most profound that I ever witnessed. He literally could call people out and tell them that they were HIV positive or that they had been living a homosexual life. He ministered at All Nations Church, and several times he called people forward to pray for them. His private words of prophecy were confirmed time and again. He once said, that he "hated the demon that deceives people into the lifestyle" and that he "could spot it anywhere." Once while ministering for us, he called out a young brother in his 20's and prayed for him, because he discerned that he was HIV positive. When he did this, I was absolutely certain that he had missed it and that he was mistaken. However, I did not say anything, but proceeded to simply pray quietly as my friend spoke the words of the faith over this individual's life.

The Sick Look

I specifically recall that after the meeting, this young man was seemingly "shell-shocked" and had a very troubled look on his face. Some weeks later, through a series of circumstances, he became sick; and upon being taken by ambulance to the hospital, he admitted to the paramedics that he was HIV positive. Upon hearing this, the young lady whom he'd been steadily dating became hysterical and instantly phoned the ministry requesting immediate prayer. She had been sexually involved with him. She was tested, and unfortunately she had also contracted the disease. Unbeknownst to the leadership of the ministry, they were sexually active with each other while quite active in the church. Personally, they were two of the most loving, loyal, and lively people, and it was a joy to pastor them. They attended, they worked, they consistently supported, and were pursuing marriage to each other. God has miraculously sustained them through the ensuing years, and they are faring quite well.

The naked truth must now be told that satan, sin, and sickness are nothing to play with. The devil will push you out on a limb and then cut the branch off. The devil will blow up your balloon one minute and then stick a pin in it the next minute. The devil will knock you down and then kick you for falling. He has not always been the devil, but now that he is, he is full of the devil. He is going to be the devil as long as there is a devil.

Sickness Subdues the Prophet

I met Prophet Grayton in 1995, and in 1997 he went home to be with the Lord. I received the news while traveling from Las Vegas, Nevada, to Denver, Colorado, where I was scheduled to minister. I learned of his death after disembarking from the plane. I was deeply saddened and immediately made plans to attend the funeral services that weekend in a Maryland suburb, just outside of Washington, D.C. Ironically, I was scheduled to speak that same weekend in a very thriving congregation located within minutes of the nation's capital. The young pastor who was hosting me joined me in attending the home-going celebration. Neither of us had any idea that within one year I would be attending his funeral

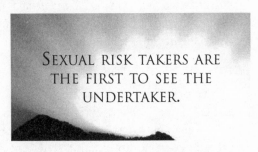

SEXUAL RISK TAKERS ARE THE FIRST TO SEE THE UNDERTAKER.

service as well. He was in his early 30's, and within months his health deteriorated because of AIDS. During his life, I never even knew that he had the disease, and evidently no one other than his immediate family did either. As is often the case, upon his death, his secret could no longer be concealed. Many of the church members were traumatized when they were told the truth. Upon reflection, I believe that my pastoral colleague was inclined to keep his status hidden because HIV/AIDS continues to be a taboo subject in the church. It is seldom compellingly addressed or compassionately approached by the leadership. My friend, as well as many, many others, are able to lead double lives because of the "hush-hush, don't ask, don't tell" cover-up atmosphere that exists throughout the church. This is particularly true within the so-called African-American church. However, since sexual issues are constantly revealed through the intense media coverage of the Catholic church, it is obvious that these issues are in no way endemic of the African-American community. Other branches of Protestantism are also dramatically affected.

My friend's diagnosis of HIV positive had come much earlier than expected. He had evaded its ultimate prognosis for as long as he could, but eventually (as my grandfather would say), "Death issued a warrant for his arrest." The legendary boxer, Joe Louis, used to boast to his opponents that "you can run, but you can't hide." Ali, the self-proclaimed greatest, and the possessor of the gift of gab said it this way, "Your hands can't hit what your eyes cannot see." My friend ran from death, but eventually he got caught, and when he did, he could no longer hide. He got hit with the knockout punch of death. The final bell rang, and he was here no more. The poet said, "...for whom the bell tolls...it tolls for thee." "*It is appointed unto men once to die, but after this the judgment*" (Heb. 9:27). Death is the only appointment that you cannot break. The appointment is inevitable, but the timing is indeterminate. You have a lot to do with it. Sexual risk takers are the first to see the undertaker.

—MINISTRIES ON THE DOWN LOW—

But I keep under my body, and bring it into subjection: lest that by any means, when I have preached to others, I myself should be a castaway (1 Corinthians 9:27).

Ministry Standards

Just prior to his untimely death, this young pastor confessed to me that a Christian leader, with whom he was formerly affiliated, requested that he serve as a personal adjutant on out-of-town trips, so that they could engage in homosexual activity together. The leader was living on the down low and letting the ministry standard down. This perpetrating leader was married and assured the young pastor that his wife would never know. The young pastor resisted his invitation, and as a consequence he was ostracized by this powerful personality. Quite simply, he was disassociated and kicked to the curb by the minister on the down low. Thankfully, the situation was never exposed any further, and the people of God were not negatively affected by it. Whenever the stink hits the fan, it is quite putrid, repulsive, and ugly. The only reason he confided in me was so that I might exercise oversight of his life and ministry at his request.

The Ministry of Blood

When he died, I preached at his church the day after the funeral and encouraged the congregation to go on despite their loss. Today, the congregation is thriving and has more than doubled in size. *Though death is fatal, it is not necessarily final,* because the believer's blood, like Abel's, who though he was dead, cries from the ground (see Heb. 11:4). Both of these young preachers are preaching to the church from the ground. The blood has a ministry that never loses power. The blood of Abel cried because the life of his soul was in his blood.

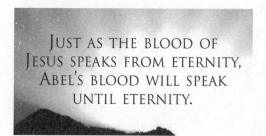

JUST AS THE BLOOD OF JESUS SPEAKS FROM ETERNITY, ABEL'S BLOOD WILL SPEAK UNTIL ETERNITY.

For the life [nephesh/soul] of the flesh is in the blood: and I have given it to you upon the altar to make an atonement for your souls: for it is the blood that maketh an atonement for the soul (Leviticus 17:11, emphasis added).

When Adam inseminated Eve with seed that produced Abel, it was for a divine purpose. Abel's life was to be a meaningful, fully-lived one, but the spirit of *murder* cut it short. In a spiritual sense, Abel's blood had a voice, just as in a criminal investigation, there is what is known as a "trail of blood." The DNA in the blood is equivalent to a life signature. Just as the blood of Jesus speaks *from* eternity, Abel's blood will speak *until* eternity. Abel's blood is saying, "I was not born to die like this." Abel's blood is saying, "Father's impartation was not to end in a pool of blood." Likewise, because of God's redemptive power, I believe that my friends did not live or die in vain. Their blood still speaks to us today, saying, "Do not forget *to pour in the oil and the wine*" to those who are trapped in same-sex attraction that threatens to also leave them in a pool of blood.

The Ministry of Sweat

[Sex] is as religious a subject as a discussion on belief in God.[12]

The priest should wear no garment "that causeth sweat" said the prophet Ezekiel (see Ezek. 44:18). Sweat denotes human effort without holy effect. The sweat of the brow is a part of Adam's curse. The curse of the law was redeemed by Jesus (see Gal. 3:13), thereby allowing the believer to have sweatless victories.

I had the privilege during the mid-90's to minister in Freeport, Bahamas, as the keynote speaker of a weeklong, citywide conference. On the evening that I was to be the keynote speaker, an internationally renowned gospel artist was the featured psalmist. I preached the message that evening that I would soon be called upon to preach all over the world, as well as on major Christian networks such as Trinity Broadcasting Network. The message was entitled, "Sanctified Sexuality." Upon preaching it, I had never seen such a demonstration of the Spirit of God in all my life.

Nearly one hundred percent of the audience responded to the message. In fact, it was so many people that I had to pray for them by dividing them into males and females. This mass deliverance session went on for at least two hours. The sweat poured from the people as they became exasperated in their efforts to seek God. Soon thereafter, the host dismissed the service and the saints proceeded to go home. It was an amazing sight to see so many people who had come in one way but left differently. They came in bound, but left set free. They came in captive, but left as conquerors. When all the people had finally filed out of the building, I noticed that the guest psalmist continued to sing even though his singing was no longer part of the scheduled programming. He was doing so because God had put a song in his soul that he could not help but sing.

The Ministry of Tears

The message, "Sanctified Sexuality," ended with an explanation that sexual sin causes a person to lose his soul, which is split into as many divisions as the amount of sexual partners that he has had. The message also included how to recover one's soul, or how to get your soul back. That night, the young psalmist/minister sang "until the cows came home." Two hours later, he was still singing, "I got my soul back and I will never be the same again." Those were the only lyrics. "I got my soul back and I will never be the same again." Shortly thereafter, he began a personal crusade to help Christians who are struggling with gay and lesbian issues to come out of the closet, out of the corner, and out of the confines of concealed and covert undercover activity. His bold and uncompromising stand is blessing the world.

—THE NAKED TRUTH NOW MUST BE TOLD—

The Truth of Vultures

A few years later, he spoke at the Azusa conference, in Tulsa, Oklahoma, on the Oral Roberts University campus. When he extended an altar call to the Christian audience to come forward if they were involved in or currently struggling with same-sex issues, nearly two thirds of the audience came forward weeping, evidencing the beginning of brokenness. I could not believe my eyes because this was a conference attended by very elite and established Christians from all walks of life and regions of the country. It was as if they were saying, "Finally, a time and a place where we can get some help to bring closure to this reoccurring and undesirable nightmare in our life." In his book, *Eternal Victim/Eternal Victor*, Pastor Donnie McClurkin writes:

> I discovered that there were VULTURES also in the church....I discovered that in the homosexual lifestyle, when you're young, you are the prey to be hunted. But when you get older, and lose youthfulness, you become the predator. Every predatory and scavenging creature seeks out the young, weak and wounded. A vulture can smell the sick, infirmed and dying from miles away. Once spotted, they will circle, swoop and bear down on their prey until they fall and succumb to the constant assault....My world of security (the church) was invaded when other broken

men, in need of healing, made themselves known as predators. Secret lifestyles were revealed and I was introduced to a deceptive underworld in the church....Gospel singers, musicians, ministers, pastors, and bishops were hiding their secret lives and living them out in hidden circles.... UNHEALED ministers, singers, and those in leadership involved those people who looked up to them with respect and regard. Those brothers and sisters were looking for help from these men and women, but found themselves victims of the unhealed leaders....What a damnable cycle!"[13]

The Truth of Victimization

The damnable cycle is *victimization*. During the decade of the 90's, I ministered at the Faith Dome in Los Angeles, California. It was during the West Coast Azusa. The building was completely filled to its ten-thousand seating capacity. The person in charge of my personal security was an LAPD officer who also had been a personal bodyguard to notable celebrities such as Denzel Washington. As we were driving through the streets of the inner city of Los Angeles, he shared a story that I will never forget.

In earlier years he was called to investigate a possible homicide. When he arrived on the scene, there were two young men (late teens) lying dead in the street in a pool of blood. It started to rain, and the water began to mix with their blood and empty into a sewer hole. My friend said he looked up to Heaven and said, "God, I know that these two men were not born to die like this!" He was determined from that moment

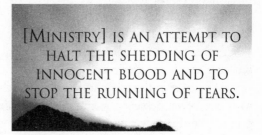

[MINISTRY] IS AN ATTEMPT TO HALT THE SHEDDING OF INNOCENT BLOOD AND TO STOP THE RUNNING OF TEARS.

to do all he could to stop the shedding of innocent blood. God says that He hates the hands that shed innocent blood (see Prov. 6:17). Blood is the life force of the soul. Most fatal diseases are blood diseases. Dr. M.R. De Haan, in his book, *The Chemistry of the Blood*, says that it was not until God blew into men's nostrils the breath of life that his blood began to flow. When the blood flowed, the life began.[14]

> *And the Lord God formed man of the dust of the ground, and breathed into his nostrils the breath of life; and man became a living soul* (Genesis 2:7).

Life does not begin at 40; it begins with the blood. In fact, life is half over by 40. Someone once compared the average lifespan to a 24-hour clock. Based on their scientific calculations, when a person becomes 40, it is equivalent to 4:08 in the evening. Someone might presume that they still have

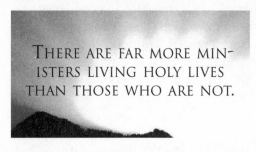

THERE ARE FAR MORE MIN-ISTERS LIVING HOLY LIVES THAN THOSE WHO ARE NOT.

eight more hours because 90 years of age is equivalent to midnight. Most people, however, do not live to 90, but to their mid-70's. At four o'clock, most people are getting off work, not going to work. The life of man is in the blood (see Lev. 17:11). The blood is the life clock. The blood contains a DNA clock. As the Master Teacher knocks, you must remember, in the words of Yitzhak Rabin, the late Prime Minister of Israel (in speaking of the Israeli/Palestinian conflict), "Enough blood and tears. Enough!"[15]

The Truth of Victory

In a sense, ministry to the gay and lesbian populace is similar. It is blood, sweat, and tears on the behalf of another. It is an attempt to halt the shedding of innocent blood and to stop the running of tears. Satan is a murderer, and he specializes in both natural and spiritual abortion. Nearly thirty million babies have died in their mother's womb since the *Roe v. Wade* decision in 1973. What was once the safest place has become the most dangerous place for the baby. Certainly, if anyone qualifies to have innocent blood, it is an embryonic child. Just as satan does not care about killing a baby in the mother's womb, so he does not care about murdering a man or a woman in the prime of their life. This is especially true in the gay community, and the statistics of life expectancy attest to it. However, despite the tragic loss of life, the blood is yet crying from the ground, boldly declaring, "The naked truth must now be told."

Over the years, there have been many occurrences that I am personally aware of; however, I stress that these incidences are the exception. Homosexual ministers are not the rule. It is certainly not the rule that many ministries, proportionately speaking, have a secret life of homosexuality. Same-sex sinning is *definitely present* in the ministry as are other sins, but it is *not desperately prevalent* in the ministry. There are far more ministers living holy lives than those who are not. In light of this, there should be a "zero tolerance policy" enacted against it in church by laws, and anyone who practices the gay lifestyle should be removed from position and placed in a "therapeutic environment" where they can get help for their soul.

The naked truth that must now be told is where there is sin, grace (a gracious word) does much more abound (see Rom. 5:20). The naked truth is that God is a "RE" God. He is a righteous God who acknowledges REpentance; He affects REstoration; He establishes REformation; He will REmove unrighteousness; and REsolve so that there will be proper REplication of the "oil and wine" Church.

—THE NAKED TRUTH OF RESTORATION—

Brethren, if a man be overtaken in a fault, ye which are spiritual, restore such an one in the spirit of meekness; considering thyself, lest thou also be tempted (Galatians 6:1).

Restoring the Fallen

Those who are apprehended while ministering on the down low should be restored *ultimately*, but not *immediately*. They should be restored to ministry only when they have completed the journey to spiritual *recovery* that is evidenced by true *repentance*, which is always accompanied by *renewed humility*. Also, there should be accountability measures put into place and regular monitoring of the situation. This is for his/her good as well as the congregation's. It is bad enough for a minister's sordid sex life to be aired publicly, but it is even worse when there is a repeat performance of moral failure.

Restoring the Faith

When ministers are exposed publicly, it brings humiliation and a loss of faith to the congregation in horrific proportions. It is the same way with heterosexual immorality, but nothing carries a worse stigma in the mind of the majority of congregants and the public like a pastor's homosexual sins coming to light. When you add to this the fact that he may be married and the father of children, it intensifies the shame. If he or she is in sexual sin with someone whom people in the congregation know, it can potentially destroy the church, or do irreparable damage to the church's reputation, thus prohibiting it from ever achieving its true mandate in the community to which it is called to minister. When faith dies, it is impossible for the church to live.

—THE NAKED TRUTH OF RIGHTEOUSNESS—

For He hath made Him to be sin for us, who knew no sin; that we might be made the righteousness of God in Him (2 Corinthians 5:21, emphasis added).

Many have been intimidated from speaking up and speaking out because of secret sexual sin in the leadership of the church today. No person is any more saved than their secrets. It is the discovery of secrets that unearths the deposit of the problem. You know where your problems are when you know what your secrets are. Shamefully, far too many leaders have been led by a sick head or the wrong head.

The naked truth of righteousness is not always received with glad hearts and open arms. Sometimes, it is rejected forthright and immediately. Dr. Frederick K.C. Price in his writing, *Homosexuality: State of Birth or State of Mind,* relates the following story:

> ...Some people get all upset when anyone brings out into the open the truth concerning this issue. Some time ago I said something during one of my Bible studies about this unnaturalness while teaching....There was a young man present who was a homosexual. He wrote me a very lengthy letter, telling me that I was like all other bigoted ministers who were "down on" homosexuals. I have news for that young man. I am not "down on" anybody, except the devil....I do not even have to talk about this issue of homosexuality and incur the wrath of some people, as I did with [this] young man when I first began to speak on this topic. He got up, disrupted the service, and walked out. It is an insult when people walk out on you while you are trying to help them. It is a slap in the face. I do not need to talk about this subject and run the risk of somebody reacting like that. I don't need that kind of grief. I don't appreciate it and I do not have to have it. I could just talk about issues that do not "rock the boat." Then everybody would say, "Praise the Lord."...If you say anything that has any substance to it, you are going to end up hurting somebody's feelings or stepping on somebody's toes. I will rock the boat! Jesus said the truth will make us free and that is all I want to do, set people free by teaching them the Word of Life.[16]

If a minister never deals with the gay subject in his preaching, it is unfortunate and undermining. Avoiding the subject is not showing true compassion. Confronting the subject is the preferred method of ministry. Compassion is confrontive, but denial is synonymous with complicity. If a minister demonstrates compassion for the gay populace to the extreme and embraces them without ever confronting them, he or she in effect has become an advocate for them; he or she is out of balance. The gay community will flock to that particular local church by the droves. It will become a haven for the homogenous kind. Shortly thereafter they will not be seeking deliverance, but only mere acceptance. They will infiltrate every auxiliary and aspect of ministry because many gays are extremely gifted people and activists by temperament; therefore they will not remain idle. In time, they become a valuable part of the fabric of that local expression of the Body of Christ. Their vocational and financial contributions become essential to the church's well-being, and thus many pastors simply turn their heads as if they cannot see what everyone else plainly sees. The word soon gets out into the local community that there is a haven for gays and lesbians at such-and-such a church. Before long, everywhere you look, you will see effeminacy on display every Lord's day.

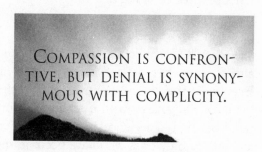

COMPASSION IS CONFRON-
TIVE, BUT DENIAL IS SYNONY-
MOUS WITH COMPLICITY.

Lesbians Loosed in the Church

The same holds true for women. It is more difficult to distinguish women who are lesbian, unless they have the stereotypically masculine "butch" demeanor. They usually go unrecognized and thus not dealt with. Women are known to hug and kiss one another in public settings without garnering much of a second thought. Madonna and Britney Spears' infamous kiss turned a few heads, but I do not recall anyone asking them or implying that they were outright lesbians. On the other hand, when Will Smith once starred in a movie whose popular character was a homosexual, he refused to actually kiss on screen. Consequently, the director had to creatively doctor the angles he was shooting from to give the impression that an actual kiss had taken place. Why did Will Smith refuse? I am certain it is because of the difference in men and women when relating to the same sex. Men, for the most part, are completely grossed out or sickened at the thought of another man's lips pressed against theirs. It causes a nauseous chill to go throughout the male body at the thought of any homo-erogenous, homo-genitalia, or homosexual actions. In the *Fresh Prince of Bel-Air* sitcom, Will's sister's name was Hillary. She was known to often say, "Eee-w." Most men, when they think of the same-sex attraction of man to man, they say, "Eee-w," too! Ironically, today there is an onslaught of girl-on-girl activity, and men are the biggest purveyors and consumers of it. It is flashed on MTV, the movie screen, in magazines, in nightclubs, and now it has made its way into the church.

Lesbian Bible School Graduate

A few years ago, a young lady who had graduated from a Christian Bible school confessed to me that she had been in a lesbian relationship since graduating from school. I asked her how it happened. How did she allow herself to get in that situation. She said that she had been engaged to get married, and when it was broken off by her boyfriend, she became very depressed. She and another sister started going out and talking with each other quite a lot. Eventually, they found themselves in each other's arms and engaged in lesbian sex. She shared with me that as a young teenage girl, she had encountered her first experience, but had not repeated it until now. Male ministers are not the only ones who have been on the *down low*. Ladies have also been living and laying low. Righteousness reels when unrighteous behavior reeks.

—THE NAKED TRUTH OF REALITY—

And they rose up early on the morrow, and offered burnt offerings, and brought peace offerings; and the people sat down to eat and to drink, and rose up to play (Exodus 32:6).

The Church Game

Most people are wise enough, as Dr. Gerald Lloyd says in his book, *Preachers Are People Too*, to recognize that Christians are not perfect—just forgiven. However, at the same time, they are looking for living examples of the power of the cross of Christ and the Holy Spirit in a believer's life to help them overcome their proclivity to sin. This is one of the things that motivates them to attend a local church. The church game is a game that no believer should ever have to learn to play.

The Games Church People Play

Most people figure that if you are going to hell, then you might as well do it in style and not with a seat in the choir stand, a position on the deacon's board, a Sunday school certificate on your wall, or a minister's license behind your desk. If you are on your way to hell, you might as well go while doing your thing, which you cannot do in church (or at least you are not supposed to be able to). It is my contention that people attend church, not to see and experience the same games they see played in the nightclubs or in the hardcore streets. Inevitably, when people are exposed to the "games" that church people (are known to) play, they become disillusioned. It leads to disappointment, which leads to dismay with the Bible way and perhaps even a departure from the Christian faith. When this takes place, seven worse devils may attach themselves to the person's life. The Master Teacher taught:

> *Then goeth he, and taketh with himself seven other spirits more wicked than himself, and they enter in and dwell there: and the last state of that man is worse than the first...* (Matthew 12:45).

Playing Games With the Gay Issue Is Illegal

> While the church remains respectable, many of us will remain hypocrites, people, who look good on the outside but keep our compulsions hidden on the inside....Where a Christian will not own up to himself and God (and preferably someone else), about his private compulsion, he closes Christ out. ...The more we close Christ out, the deeper our darkness grows and the more evil finds a home within us.[17]

> —*Briar Whitehead*

Some things are not lawful, nor are they expedient. It is illegal and criminal to play games with God. It has been my experience that whenever a church accommodates and accepts a loose liturgy and a lewd doctrine of tolerance, it should be named, "The Church of the Loosey Goosey." The people's lives are looser and ultimately licentious because their liberty in Christ gets turned into a license to sin. The problem is that it isn't a valid license. The gaming becomes illegal. Married couples have a license to have a sexual relationship with each other, but many couples do not engage in sex often. This opens the door to the adversary. Heterosexual singles and gay and lesbian singles do not have a license to have sexual relations, and yet they do so quite frequently. This is graciousness gone awry. This is what the Bible calls turning the grace of God into lasciviousness.

> *For there are certain men crept in unawares, who were before of old ordained to this condemnation, ungodly men, turning the **grace of our God into lasciviousness**, and denying the only Lord God, and our Lord Jesus Christ* (Jude 1:4, emphasis added).

Let the Church Games End

In every Olympics, there is the lighting of the Olympic flame. The herald declares, "Let the games begin!" At the conclusion of 16 days of competition, the flame is extinguished. The Church today needs to put out the fire of fleshly lusts that declare, "Let the games end!" Game-playing is a wicked, twisted, and perverted thing. Many ministries endorse *evang-elastic* living, which is an indication that satan has put a *prophe-lying* spirit into the mouth of the so-called prophets while deceiving the so-called saints. The Scripture says that in the last days, even the elect will be deceived if it is possible (see Mk. 13:22). Seduction is well under way, and seducing spirits always bring with them doctrines of demons.

> *Now therefore, behold, the Lord hath put a **lying spirit** in the mouth of all these thy prophets, and the Lord hath spoken evil concerning thee* (1 Kings 22:23, emphasis added).

> *Now the Spirit speaketh expressly, that in the latter times some shall depart from the faith, giving heed to **seducing spirits**, and doctrines of devils* (1 Timothy 4:1, emphasis added).

A lying or seducing spirit is a satanic emissary assigned with the exclusive purpose of perverting and subverting the *truth*, by insinuations and innuendos, by accusations and incrimination of the souls of the sincere seekers of God. When sexual sin is on parade in the local church, it is evidence of the lying seduction of both the people and the preacher or the priest. A highly effective modern-day minister of Solomonic wisdom principles has said that the willingness to confront the reality of your present circumstances, habits, and situations comes before any possibility of changing them. How true that principle is. A ministry cannot help parishioners who, first of all, do not want to be helped and, secondly, react bitterly to being lovingly confronted. Churches that do not confront the counterfeit will soon be filled with "wolves in sheep's clothing," parading with clergy collars. In effect, they collar the consecration of the congregation. Martin Buber, in his classic work, *Good and Evil*, addresses this grave concern. He writes:

> Since the primary motive of evil is disguise, one of the places evil people are most likely to be found is within the church....I do not mean to imply that the religious motives of most people are in any way spurious....only that evil people tend to gravitate towards piety for the disguise and concealment it can offer them.[18]

—THE NAKED TRUTH OF REPRODUCTION—

> *...and God said unto them, Be fruitful, and multiply, and replenish the earth...* (Genesis 1:28).

Ministers teach what they know and reproduce who they are. Occasionally, the opposite is true. The congregation molds the minister after their heart, as opposed to the minister molding the congregation after God's heart. The primary difference between King Saul and King David was that the former was after the people's heart and the latter was after God's heart. During the scandals of the Clinton administration, at least 75 percent of the American public who was surveyed expressed severe disagreement with the handling of the investigation that seemed to focus on the former President's sexual indiscretions. Amazingly, the percentage nearly equaled the Promise Keepers' survey of men which concluded that approximately 70 percent reportedly struggled with sexual temptation on a daily basis. It stands to reason that if the populace at large struggles daily, then they will bring their struggles with them into the church. The minister who is consistently aware of the possibility of reverse transference is safe. The minister who is not aware of it is in danger of having the problem(s) of the people become his own problems, in a literal sense. Reproduction works both ways.

In Hosea 4:12, the Scripture records that *"...for the spirit of whoredoms* [literally, the whore's domain] *hath caused them to err* [commit sin, etc.]*, and they have gone a whoring from under their God."* He further states *"...like people, like priest...."*

> *And there shall be, **like people, like priest:** and I will punish them for their ways, and reward them their doings. For they shall eat, and not have enough: they shall commit **whoredom**, and shall not increase: because they have left off to take heed to the Lord. Whoredom and wine and new wine take away the heart...for the spirit of **whoredoms** hath caused them to err, and they have gone a **whoring** from under their God* (Hosea 4:9-12, emphasis added).

Please notice that the text says, *"like people"* before it says, *"like priest."* Normally, the people (the followers) are the direct result of the priests' (the leaders') impartation. People are definitely influenced by the transference of the leaders' spirit upon them both individually and corporately. However, the prophet Hosea states it otherwise when he says, *"like people,"* first and then, *"like priest,"* second. The prophet's

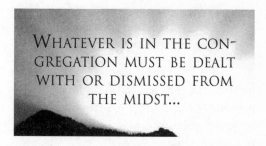

WHATEVER IS IN THE CONGREGATION MUST BE DEALT WITH OR DISMISSED FROM THE MIDST...

words speak definitively to the real nature of the problem. Whatever is in the congregation must be dealt with or dismissed from the midst, or else it could pollute and pervert not only the other people, but also the preacher himself.

—THE NAKED TRUTH OF REFORMATION—

The church should consist of communities of loving defiance. Instead it consists largely of comfortable clubs of conformity. A far-reaching reformation of the church is a prerequisite if it is to commit itself to Jesus' mission of liberating the oppressed.[19]

Ronald J. Sider

When the Sodom-like spirit penetrates the church, it takes on demonic proportions with the accompanying manifestations. Demons travel in groups. They work in close association with each other. In the Bible, Jesus, the Master Teacher, inquired concerning what a particular demon's name was and the demon responded, *"Legion: for we are many"* (Mk. 5:9). A Roman legion was comprised of about five thousand men. It is possible for thousands of demons to work in accordance with each other to corrupt the local church, capture the congregants, and castigate the name of Christ. Sexual sin in the life of the leadership and the laity can shut the ministry down as quickly as it got started. Why is this so? It is because people attend church to get answers for their questions and solutions for their problems. People attend church to be introduced to the presence and power of God. The wineskin of the same-old, same-old must be burst and a new one must be formed if the church is to experience reformation. It has been said that insanity is defined as doing the same thing the same way and yet expecting different results. Reformation is not a 400 year relic of Martin Luther's day or a 40-year reminder of Martin Luther King Jr.'s day, but it is a firm removal of anything that hinders the revealing of God's glory.

—THE NAKED TRUTH OF REMOVAL—

As the Lord commanded Moses His servant, so did Moses command Joshua, and so did Joshua; he left nothing undone of all that the Lord commanded Moses (Joshua 11:15).

Individual and mass deliverances are possible only when we leave nothing undone. For sin to be removed, the surgery must be radical. In St. Paul's first Epistle to the Corinthians, he was literally incensed that they were boasting about their beautiful ministry while there was blatant and nonconfrontational heterosexual sin in the midst (see 1 Cor. 5:1). The people had departed from gross idolatry, which was always connected to sexuality, but there were still remaining practices attempting to hold them. St. Paul adjured them by telling them to purge the wicked person from their midst. He referred to them as leaven, which is a symbol of evil (see 1 Cor. 5:7). He also said that because sexual sin had been found, they must personally flee it and have no fellowship with it (see 1 Cor. 5:9-13). Why was he taking such a hard line against homo-and heterosexual sin? Why did he demand its removal and disallow its access to the administration of the sacrament of communion? It is because he knew the power of influence. He knew that *"evil communications [lifestyles] corrupt good manners"* (1 Cor. 15:33).

Removing Sympathy

The prophet Samuel gave the order to execute the Amalekites and their heathen king Agag (see 1 Sam. 15:18). When Agag came to him *delicately,* Samuel showed him no sympathy. There is no sympathy for unrepentant sin. Sin must be hated if it is to be overcome. King Saul's failure to deal the decisively death blow to Agag cost him his kingdom and resulted in the forfeiture of God's favor. The thing he failed to kill, eventually killed him. God's ways do not change. He is still *"angry [with the* (willfully) *wicked] every day"* (Ps. 7:11emphasis added).

The "oil and wine" Church of the 21st century must wake up and recognize that it needs to take a good spiritual laxative and purge the body of toxic laxity. The removal of waste is as necessary as trash removal. Sanitary standards are a necessity, and they must be regularly maintained. Everyone is free and welcome to attend church gatherings on a regular basis as much as anyone else, including the preacher himself. There are no perfect Christians in the literal sense. *"All have sinned* [and sometimes they still sin], *and come short of the glory of God"* (Rom. 3:23). If the Lord were to mark iniquities, who could stand (see Ps. 130:3)?

Removing Empathy

Sinners are indeed welcome in the church. People should show *empathy* for the sinner, but only *enmity* for the sin. All churches should be full of redeemed sinners but not relaxed ones. Scripture abounds with evidence of sins' eviction. St. Paul says to, *"put away from among yourselves that wicked person"* (1 Cor. 5:13). The prophet Amos declared, *"Woe to them that are at ease in Zion"* (Amos 6:1). There is a difference between a

> THERE IS A DIFFERENCE BETWEEN A MINISTRY THAT BRINGS COMFORT TO SINNERS AND ONE THAT MAKES PEOPLE COMFORTABLE IN THEIR SIN.

ministry that brings comfort to sinners and one that makes people comfortable in their sin. The Bible says that the *"ungodly shall not stand in the judgment, nor sinners in the congregation of the righteous"* (Ps. 1:5). The *"hypocrite shall not come before Him"* (Job 13:16). The liar *"shall not tarry in My sight"* (Ps. 101:7). Empathy with sin is how it gets in.

Removing Apathy

It was the sin of apathy that sent Jesus to the cross. The indifference of the ungrateful nation cut Him off in the prime of His life. His precious back was lacerated until His flesh hung like torn ribbons, exposing His subcutaneous tissue. It was human sin that caused the Father to forsake His own Son as He languished in appalling misery upon the tree. It was because of human sin that the innocent Lamb of God became mercilessly marauded, nastily spit upon, and sentenced to death by His own people. It was all for a crime that He did not commit. It was for our sin that His Father gave permission to the smiters. Was it not the purpose or the passion of the Christ that they smote Him as the price for the penalty for our sins? If sin is what crucified the Christ, how can we act as if it is no big deal if it is in the church? The sinning church is not a sanctified church. Neither is the fornication-filled, pornography-ridden, pedophilia-driven, sensually-sounding den of thieves a set-apart church. It is a synagogue of satan with the blind leading the blind followers into a ditch (see Mt. 15:14). Sometimes, it is led by the half-blind who have lost their sight, the half-dead who have lost their soul, the half-saved who have lost their heart, and the half-delivered who have lost their way. A one-eyed man is always king in the land of the blind. When you are blind, you do not know what you have never seen. You just keep on not seeing whatever there is to be seen. The church is the pillar and ground of the truth. It is not a pillow that is placed upon the ground of truth (see 1 Tim. 3:15). J. L. King writes that:

> The black church must preach the truth and become a place where all men can come and hear the Word without feeling they will be judged or ostracized, regardless of their sexual orientation. It should be a place where sisters can depend on getting sound advice and be counseled to love and protect themselves first.[20]

Churches that endorse same-sex marriage and ordain homosexual preachers border on becoming identified as synagogues of satan (see Rev. 2:9). Rather than taking the route of accommodation, churches should work to help individuals get free of homosexuality while promoting viable singles ministries for men and women who truly desire to wait in purity and holiness for their God-ordained mate. The church must protect the people and the priest from the powerful forces of perversion.

The Removal of Antipathy

Hosea was right. *Like people, like priest,* is a principal way that many ministers fall. Every preacher must be surrounded by those who love him and hold his name before the throne of God in prayer, because many times as the church goes, so goes the preacher. As the preaching goes, so go the strongholds of satan. It is impossible for a minister to deliver somebody from something that he is bound by himself. It is impossible for a believer to lead someone somewhere that he will not go himself.

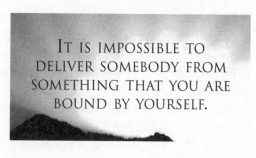

IT IS IMPOSSIBLE TO DELIVER SOMEBODY FROM SOMETHING THAT YOU ARE BOUND BY YOURSELF.

—THE NAKED TRUTH OF RECKONING—

Likewise **reckon** *ye also yourselves to be dead indeed unto sin, but alive unto God through Jesus Christ our Lord* (Romans 6:11, emphasis added).

Whenever there is a significant change in a person's accommodation and acceptance of homosexuality, there is normally something that is privately influencing them. This must be reckoned with. Whenever ministers preach against a particular sin more than others, it is generally an indication of either their personal participation in it or something that is just like it. People always hate the negative things that they see in others, especially when it reflects what they despise about themselves. Parents always are harder on the child who most reminds them of their own rebellious days and ways. Pastors are always legalistic, harsh, and hard on the church when they are hiding or hating something about themselves. On the other hand, there are those who refuse to ever speak out about or against certain sins in the congregation. They are afraid of public exposure. Whenever a minister has a sexual history outside of his marriage or outside of abstinence, *he is held hostage* by it, especially if he has fallen since becoming a pastor. Most ministers know that, generally speaking, people will forgive you for what you have done (to a limited degree), but they will seldom and most likely never forget that you did it. *It is difficult, if not nearly impossible, for a minister to recover his prophetic prestige and apostolic authority once the news of his fall or his duplicitous life is discovered or publicized.*

Dumb Dogs

His watchmen are blind: they are all ignorant, they are all dumb dogs, they cannot bark; sleeping, lying down, loving to slumber (Isaiah 56:10).

The watchmen are compared to watchdogs in the above text. A dog may not always bite, but the least it can do is bark. A dog that *cannot*, or even worse, *will* not bark is a poor specimen of a dog. A minister may not bite, that is, he may not be very effective in the demonstration of the Spirit of God, but at least he can bark. At least he can lift up Christ and His cross. Scripture says that uplifting Christ, who died on the uplifted cross, results in all men being drawn up to Him. "*I, if I be lifted up from the earth, will draw all men unto Me*" (Jn. 12:32). The lyrics of a popular hymn recite:

> How to reach the masses, men of every birth;
>
> for an answer Jesus gave the key;
>
> He said, if I, if I be lifted up from the earth,
>
> I will draw all men unto Me.
>
> Lift Him up, lift Him up for the world to see.
>
> He said, if I, if I be lifted up from the earth,
>
> I'll draw all men unto Me.

Because of their own sinful failures, many ministers become mute and avoid the subject of "sin" altogether. Their messages never meet the mess head-on, but speak only about being blessed from now on. The dumb-dog preacher is more social than spiritual. The first thing to exit stage left is any semblance of the anointing. Judgment is replaced with jokes, songs, newspaper headlines, motivational quips, irrelevant anecdotes, and human interest stories; and the people never see or hear the naked truth. Where there is no knowledge of sin, there can be no deliverance from it. The laws of God always serve as a schoolmaster that lead a person to the ways of Christ, the Son of God. Surely the great evangelists of the Church, such as Jonathan Edwards, George Whitfield, Charles G. Finney, D.L. Moody, C.H. Mason, Billy Sunday, and Kathryn Kuhlman must be leaning out over the banisters of glory shouting, "Hold up the standard, Church. The devil is a liar. No sin shall inherit the Kingdom of God."

Beware of Dogs

Beware of dogs, beware of evil workers, beware of the concision (Philippians 3:2).

The Church must beware of dogs that are in the wolf family. Sleeping dogs of laxity and looseness are waking up to bite the Church. They are infesting the ranks, infiltrating the righteous, and influencing the rest of the Church. If the preacher has private homosexual issues, he will probably refrain from addressing homosexuality in his preaching. Sometimes, he will even placate those who have the problem. After all, if a preacher is not right with God himself, his ministry will become more of an occupation, a job, or a career instead of a calling. This results in a lack of *fiery passion in the pulpit* and a yielding to *fleshly passion in the pews*. The ministry simply becomes a means of making money, which means the preacher becomes a preaching pimp and the people become the tricks which, of course, is a street term that prostitutes use for their customers.

Preaching Dogs

Thou shalt not bring the hire of a whore, or the price of a dog, into the house of the Lord thy God for any vow: for even both these are abomination unto the Lord thy God (Deuteronomy 23:18).

The minister oftentimes takes on the spirit of a whore or a prostitute himself, because he sells his services to the highest paying customer. In such cases, the people will prostitute the ministry of the preacher and will many times pay him as little as they can for his professional services. They treat this type of preacher as if he were a street-walking woman of the night. Prostitutes never get paid much unless they can "trick" the customer or even rob him. Prostitution, simply stated, is sex in exchange for something else, like money or possessions. It is intimacy without covenant. It is the spirit of the whore's domain (whoredom) that causes the people to err. This is why the prophet, Moses, instructed Israel to disallow the dog from contributing anything in the house of God.

Temple Dogs

And he brake down the houses of the sodomites, that were by the house of the Lord, where the women wove hangings for the grove (2 Kings 23:7).

The term *whore* is translated "dog" in the same translation because it was believed that a man who sold himself as a prostitute became dog-like in his sexual demeanor. His constitution necessitated him having sex in the position of a dog. Therefore he was insultingly referred to as a dog. In biblical times, men became temple prostitutes as a means of bringing in revenue for the temples dedicated to heathen deities such as Baal, the god of fertility, or Asherah and Astarte, goddesses of fertility and reproduction. The Mosaic denunciation included the injunction to never bring the proceeds or the hire from this hideous, hedonistic, and hellish practice into the temple. A church with righteous standards understands that money is amoral. That is, it is neither good nor bad of itself. However, whenever a ministry is founded by the fueling of money gained from ill-gotten gangrenous greed, it has a responsibility to refuse it. It is dirty money, and it should not be laundered through the house of God.

Who Let the Dogs In?

*And she said, Truth, Lord: yet the dogs eat of the crumbs which fall from their masters' **table*** (Matthew 15:27, emphasis added).

A famous secular song asks the question, "Who Let the Dogs Out?" A famous sermon tells the story of a dog that escaped the yard, and it concludes with the fiery preacher saying, "Who in the world let the gate open?" The Church today needs to rephrase the question to, "Who in the Church opened the gate and let the dogs in?" Anal intercourse, a common feature of homosexual activity, is done in the same position as a dog. It is not just a matter of sexual position, however. It is the penetrating of the male anal area by a male penis, and involves the mixing of semen with fecal matter, which often results in horrendous disease. That is why it falls into the category of the unclean. Homosexuality is *feminization of the masculine*. For women, it is the very opposite. It is the *masculinization of the feminine*. The Scripture says that "God is not the author of confusion [contrary to fusion]" (1 Cor. 14:33). Anal sex is damaging; it is disease ridden; it is degrading; it is degenerate; and it is often deadly. It is confusion. It is contrary to fusion.

—THE SPIRIT OF JEZEBEL—

Jezebel's Blood and the Dogs

*And of Jezebel also spake the Lord, saying, The **dogs** shall eat Jezebel by the wall of Jezreel* (1 Kings 21:23, emphasis added).

The spirit of Jezebel operates through the "spirit of whoredoms." Second Kings 9:22 says, "*And it came to pass, when Joram saw Jehu, that he said, Is it peace, Jehu? And he answered, What peace, so long as the whoredoms of thy mother Jezebel and her witchcrafts are so many?*" Jezebelians must be dismissed from the midst if they refuse to desist. Otherwise, possible spiritual transference may follow. This is why the apostle John received a strong word concerning the church of Thyatira. The Lord commended them for their good deeds, but confronted them for allowing the *spirit of Jezebel* to permeate the church, resulting in commonplace perversion taking place.

*...because thou sufferest that woman **Jezebel**, which calleth herself a prophetess, to teach and to **seduce my servants to commit fornication**, and to eat things sacrificed unto idols* (Revelation 2:20, emphasis added).

Witchcraft is essentially three things. It is *intimidation*—that is, the subordination of another person's moral ability to resist or restrain themselves. Secondly, it is *manipulation*, which is taking advantage of circumstances and the ordering of events that precipitate the subjugation of someone's will. Thirdly, it is *domination*, which is the actual controlling or "puppeteering" of someone at your particular beck and call.

The spirit of Jezebel operates through the spirit of *emasculation*. It will take the head and make him the tail. This spirit will make a man spend his whole life acting like a dog and chasing after his tail. An elderly bishop once shared with me a story that his father told him. It helped prepare him for adulthood. One day, a dog was on the railroad tracks chasing his tail, when a train came roaring down the tracks. Since the dog was not paying attention, the train cut his head off. The moral of the story is "Jezebel will make you lose your head while you are chasing after some tail."

Everyone should remember the words of the urban poet, who said, "It is the mind and not the behind that determines the bottom line. Heads, you win, but tails you lose." God's children are the head and not the tail. The difference between the two is simple. The head gives the order, and the tail simply wags behind. Every man is advised not to think with the wrong head. Every woman is advised not to be reduced to a piece of tail. It may sound crude, and even lewd, but in exposing the nude, we are keeping it real, Dude!

The Testicles Testify of a Dog's Life

Jezebel is always in a house of eunuchs, or castrated men. They have no testicles; they have no ability to procreate. Without testicles, they will never be able to testify, become a testator, or leave a testament of a godly seed in the form of children. Jezebel emasculates the man and makes him less than a man or no man at all. Jezebel produces effeminacy in a man. The Scripture says that the effeminate will not inherit the Kingdom of God (see 1 Cor. 6:9). Webster's New College Dictionary defines the word *effeminate* as "having qualities or characteristics more often associated with women than men."[21]

No Agreement With Dogs

And what agreement hath the temple of God with idols? for ye are the temple of the living God... (2 Corinthians 6:16).

The "oil and wine" Church must have no agreement with idols. Ancient idolatrous worship turned the young men out and into a lifestyle that identified them with the spirit of a woman. The Church must engage the culture with a clarion voice of "Thus saith the Lord." Twenty-first century apostles must arise, rebuild the walls of salvation and repair the gates of praise, while repairing the breach and restoring the path. The Church must arise with a *gracious word for gay and lesbian America. God loves you just as you are. He loves you too much to let you stay the way you are.* God's gracious power to those in homosexuality is the message of the hour. It should be shouted from the housetops and reverberated into the deepest valleys so that the vices of the victims and victimizers can be eliminated, eradicated, and terminated into the virtues of the victorious.

—ALL DOGS GO TO HELL—

*And desiring to be fed with the crumbs which fell from the rich man's table: moreover the **dogs** came and **licked** his sores* (Luke 16:21, emphasis added).

The movie entitled, *All Dogs Go to Heaven,* is a family favorite. It is viewable and acceptable to all ages. But the truth concerning homosexuality is that, if one engages in this dog-like sin, it will result in both an immediate and ultimate hell. James Baldwin, an African-American writer and self-professed gay, wrote a best-selling book entitled, *The Fire Next Time.* The title was developed from the biblical story of Noah's Ark, where God promised that the earth would never again be destroyed by a flood. According to Genesis 9:13, God hung a glorious rainbow in the eastern sky as a seal and sign of the Noahic covenant. It is ironic that the symbol of the gay and lesbian movement is the rainbow, since in the Bible, the rainbow is a sign of covenant, not casual and promiscuous sex. People may not want to hear it, or heed the warning, but it is still true. The ark included two animals of every kind. It was inclusive and exclusive. The doors shut Noah and his immediate relatives in, while shutting the ultimate rejecters out.

Splitting Hell Open

The naked truth is that the now-church that is endeavoring to reach the now-generation must now tell the truth. The truth is, *not everybody who is talking about Heaven is going there!* Those who crucify Christ afresh are going to be the first ones, in the words of my dear mother, "to split hell wide open."

Unfortunately, the fire-and-brimstone sermon approach does not work for most who are caught up in same-sex attraction. The message has been muddied in the waters of post-modern theology. Many people do not believe in hell's permanency. Therefore they have exhumed ancient teachings of post-mortem conversion. This teaching states that once someone dies, he or she will have a second chance to be saved, having suffered for an indeterminable amount of time in the purging (purgatory), purifying fires of hell. Hades, sheol, or more commonly called hell, has even been interpreted to mean that the earth is hell, and that to live upon it is to live in hell. Although I've never been to hell and I do not intend to make any reservations for a visit, I still believe that there is a Heaven and that there is a hell. The Scripture says that after death there is the judgment (see Heb. 9:27). After judgment, for those who are lost, there is hell.

Hell No, We Won't Go!

During the days of the Vietnam War, protestors were often seen and heard outside the White House defiantly declaring, "Hell no, we won't go!" Of course, they were referring to going to the disease-infested, dangerous jungles of Vietnam. Despite their protests, many did have to eventually go there because of the draft system that was in place at the time. Shouting, "Hell no, we won't go," was not enough. When Uncle Sam called, they had to go. Go they did, and many of them died. When the numbers were counted, over, 55,000 of America's bravest and finest were to have had their names engraved on the Vietnam War Memorial in Washington D.C. as a result of paying the ultimate price—the sacrifice of their lives.

Those who think that there is no penalty to be paid for disobeying God are in a state of *catatonic* shock. They are in a *comatose* condition. They are in a *con-fused* state of neurosis, and they have reserved their one-way tickets to the domain of the damned (see Mk. 16:16).

Hell Is Still Hot

The story is told of a man who dreamed that he died and went to hell. While there, he noticed a man running throughout its searing flames as if he was searching for someone. He kept grabbing individuals, turning them and looking them straight in the eye and then going to others and repeating the procedure. Eventually, the man having the dream went to the frantically frenzied man, detained him, and asked, "What are you doing?" The desperate man replied, "I'm looking for the preachers who didn't tell me the *truth*!"

Sadly, there are a great number of ministers who, may not be living on the down low, yet their meaningless, monotonous meanderings in the pulpit have produced a low and lower, dumb and dumber standard of living among those in the pews. They will give an account to God for the *sin of omission* that has resulted in the *sins of commission*. They will face God, and reface those who have been sentenced to hell because of their silence concerning same-sex sinfulness.

Ministers must recognize the soon-coming of the Lord Jesus Christ and commit themselves, as Jonathan Edwards did, to keeping sinners from falling into the underworld abyss. A momentary glance at the Master Teacher's description of hell should convince any compromising man or woman of the cloth to boldly declare along with St. Paul, "*Woe is unto me, if I preach not the gospel!*" (1 Cor. 9:16b)

A Picture of Hell

> And he cried and said, Father Abraham, have mercy on me, and send Lazarus, that he may dip the tip of his finger in water, and cool my tongue; for I am tormented in this flame. But Abraham said, Son, remember that thou in thy lifetime receivedst thy good things, and likewise Lazarus evil things: but now he is comforted, and thou art tormented. And beside all this, between us and you there is a great gulf fixed: so that they which would pass from hence to you cannot; neither can they pass to us, that would come from thence. Then he said, I pray thee therefore, father, that thou wouldest send him to my father's house: For I have five brethren; that he may testify unto them, lest they also come into this place of torment (Luke 16:24-28).

"What in Hell Do You Want?"

The late Reverend Leo Daniels of Texas preached a message entitled, "What in Hell Do You Want?" In the message he developed an acronym for hell. Hell is *H*-hot, *E*-evil, *L*-low, *and L*-lonely. Throughout the sermon, he kept asking the audience, "What in hell do you want?" Pastor Donnie McClurkin speaks to the issue of hell and unforgiveness in the life of the homosexual.

> Unforgiveness is like a death sentence the victim renders upon himself, committing him to the confines of his own personal hell. Bitterness slows a person down and hinders progress.[22]

The woefully inadequate but usual approach to homosexuality is the occasional sermon preached against it. However, the church has to move beyond this Band-Aid remedy. Unbeknownst to some ministers, the reality is that mere sermons of themselves are not impacting the lives of those living on the down low. They just go lower and lower. Preaching vain repetitions does not get the job done.

When I was a teenager, I attended a great Pentecostal church in Baltimore, Maryland. There was a young man in his teens who attended the same church and had become a committed Christian. In nearly every worship gathering he had the most morbid expression and seemed to be always having the worst day of his life. Eventually, it came out that he was waging an unsuccessful battle in his struggle with homosexuality. It was no wonder that he frequently looked as if he were struggling just to smile. Before long, he left the church and embraced the gay lifestyle. Sometimes, preaching a great message alone does not get the job done. Homosexuals need *living* sermons of fleshed-out messages (see Jn. 1:14). This is what

THE CHURCH CANNOT CONTINUE TO IGNORE THE EXTERNAL AND INFORMAL ASPECTS OF THIS ISSUE.

the apostle Paul meant when he referred to the Corinthian believers as living epistles, *"known and read of all men"* (2 Cor. 3:2). Helping people handle their hopeless, hapless, and helpless conditions should be a wonderfully addictive experience.

Typically, men who have had sex with other men on occasion, do not consider that they are gay and therefore do not consider that the sermons concerning homosexuality speak to them. While the internal perspective to homosexuality is eternal in its relevance, the church cannot continue to ignore the external and informal aspects of this issue. That means that the church must switch from the judgmental, pointing-of-the-finger condemnation to the gracious love-of-God contemplation and acceptation. We must become a thinking church once again.

—THE NAKED TRUTH OF RESOLUTION—

And when the day of Pentecost was fully come, they were all with one accord in one place (Acts 2:1).

The naked truth must now be told and the Church should be in one accord as they were on the day of Pentecost. There must be a replication of another Pentecost. Christian author, Leonard Ravenhill, called for this over 40 years ago, yet we are still waiting 40 years later. If the *"oil and wine"* Church will pay the cost to be satan's boss, there will be another Pentecost—the Lord of the harvest will do it again. He will save again, restore again, reform again, and replicate again. The end of the Church will be even better than its beginning. The Church in accord is found throughout the Book of Acts. Clearly, this is why they experienced an unprecedented growth rate and evangelism of the world. It is no wonder that they turned it rightside up for Jesus. The opposite of *accord* is *discord,* and the *record* of the Acts of the Holy Spirit through the apostles is in *accordance* with the recipe for replication. The times of refreshing and seasons of joy that the prophets spoke of are upon us (see Acts 3:19).

The Confrontive Appeal: In Conclusion
The Naked Truth Must Now Be Told

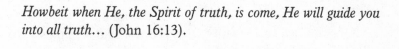

Howbeit when He, the Spirit of truth, is come, He will guide you into all truth... (John 16:13).

The confrontive appeal speaks with one voice and tells the devil, "No to hell." The naked truth must now be told. Let God be true and every post-modern revisionist a liar. Let God arise and let His revisionist enemies be scattered. In the words of the psalmist, *"Thou shalt arise, and have mercy upon Zion: for the time to favour her, yea, the set time, is come"* (Ps. 102:13, emphasis added). Pronounce Thy judgments and let Thy glory be shown until all the earth bows before Thy throne. Arise, oh God...Arise, oh God! It is time for God to arise and save those who are on the down low from themselves. Those who are born from above should never live from so far below. The wisdom from beneath is devilish, but the wisdom from above is delivering. The truth of God must never be turned into a lie. Therefore, let us discern and deal a decapitating deathblow to the perverted lies from beelzebub, the lord of the flies. Let us purge the atmosphere of the putrid, thereby purifying the per-fumed presence of the precious Spirit of Truth. The truth that is known must be shown in this valley of dry bones.

No matter what any sacred or secular societal voice says, the same-sex lifestyle is teeter-totter against the *Truth*. It will lead a person away from a right mind into a reprobate one. It will lead from the eternal purpose into an earthly prison. Unchallenged, it will collar a person into less than change from a dollar. Throughout His earthly tenure, Christ repeatedly said that He came to bear witness of the *Truth* (see Jn. 18:37). He declared Himself as the *Truth* (see Jn. 14:6). He declared the Comforter as the Spirit of *Truth* (see Jn. 14:7). He declared His teaching as the word of Truth. He wrote the *Truth* in the ink of His blood, sweat, and tears and sealed it in His commandment to love one another and to preach the gospel to every creature throughout every kingdom and not just Christendom. The gospel of *Truth* is good news. It is news of salvation and not condemnation. Jesus converts, the Holy Spirit convicts, but the devil condemns. The *Truth* of itself does not make one free, but rather, knowing *Truth* experientially, liberates the emaciated soul.

The Bible is a Holy handbook of *Truth*, the whole *Truth*, and nothing but the *Truth*. Nowhere in Scripture is a so-called "homosexual Christian" recog-

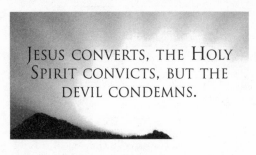

JESUS CONVERTS, THE HOLY SPIRIT CONVICTS, BUT THE DEVIL CONDEMNS.

nized as a leader to God's people. When held to the standard of the infallible Word of God, it is quite evident that such a term is an oxymoron. *"Can two walk together, except they be agreed?"* (Amos 3:3) Homosexuality and all that it represents does not agree with Christ, the mind of Christ, nor does it exhibit a Christ-like nature (in any way whatsoever). The wrath of God is based on the holiness of God, and the mercy of God is founded on the love of God; and they are in full cooperation for the deliverance of a sin-ravaged soul. When the wrath of God is poured out, it brings a person to the holiness of God. When the mercy of God is poured out, it brings a person to the love of God. The naked truth must now be told. This is not a dress rehearsal. It is the closing act. The Church is about to sing. But before we do, we must be all the *Truth*, the whole *Truth*, and nothing but the *naked Truth*. The next chapter, entitled *The Church of the Apostles: Is God's Church a Gay Church*, will continue to speak the truth. Selah.

> Prayer: Arise, O God of Truth, in our midst as a mighty Man of War. Conquer all Your enemies with the two-edged sword of Your Word. Rescue the perishing, restore the fallen, repair the breach, and renew our faith. Deliver us from the shame of our nakedness, for all things are naked before Him with whom we have to do. Let the men, the ministers, and the multitudes rise up from the dust of the down low to the glorious heights of holiness. Clothe our nakedness that our shame not be seen. Cover us with Yourself, that the world might see Thee through us. Purify the priesthood, protect the people, and perish the perversion. In the name of the Perfect One, Rabboni, the Master Teacher, Amen.

ENDNOTES

1. George Grant and Mark Horne, *Unnatural Affections: The Impuritan Ethic of Homosexuality and the Modern Church* (Nashville: Legacy Press, 1991), 70.

2. Edythe Draper, *Draper's Book of Quotations for the Christian World* (Wheaton, IL: Tyndale House Publishers, Inc., 1992), Entry 1105, Bible Illustrator 3.0 for Windows, Parsons Technology, Inc. 1990-1998, Illustrations Copyrighted at Christianity Today, Inc., 1984-1995, Faircom Corp.

3. Brennan Manning, *The Wisdom of Tenderness* (San Francisco, CA: Harper Collins, 2002), 73.

4. Draper, *Draper's Book of Quotations*, Entry 11512.

5. Briar Whitehead, *Craving for Love* (Grand Rapids, MI: Monarch Books, 2003), 114.

6. J.L. King in interview in *Jet Magazine*, May 3, 2004, Vol. 105, Issue 18, p. 32.

7. J.L. King, *On the Down Low* (USA, 2004), 84.

8. Ibid., 82.

9. Ibid., 84.

10. Dr. Larry Crabb as quoted by Briar Whitehead in *Craving for Love*, 304.

11. Dietrich Bonhoeffer, *Life Together*, as quoted by Briar Whitehead in *Craving for Love*, 305.

12. Rabbi Shmuley Boteach, *Kosher Sex: A Recipe for Passion and Intimacy* (New York: Doubleday, 1999), 46.

13. Donnie McClurkin, *Eternal Victim/Eternal Victor* (Lanham, MD: Pneuma Life Publishing, Inc., 2001), 39-40.

14. Dr. M.R. De Haan, *The Chemistry of the Blood* (Grand Rapids, MI: The Radio Bible Class Publication, 1943), 4.

15. "Fallen Heroes Can Inspire Israeli People," *Houston Chronicle* (November 6, 1995), 14.

16. Dr. Frederick K.C. Price, *Homosexuality: State of Birth or State of Mind* (Los Angeles, CA: Faith One Publishers, 1999), 25,43-44.

17. Whitehead, *Craving*, 305.

18. Martin Buber, *Good and Evil*, http://www.godulike.co.uk/phpBB2/viewtopic.php?p=2286.

19. Draper, *Draper's Book of Quotations*, Entry 1437.

20. King, *On the Down Low*, 84.

21. *Webster's II New College Dictionary* (New York: Houghton Mifflin Co., 2001), 359.

22. McClurkin, *Eternal Victim*, 109.

CHAPTER
TWO

The church must be reminded that it is not the master or servant of the state, but rather the conscience of the state.[1]

Dr. Martin Luther King, Jr.

A person does not usually join a cult because he has done an exhaustive analysis of world religions and has decided that a particular cult presents the best theology available. Instead, a person generally joins a cult because he has problems that he is having trouble solving and the cult promises to solve these problems.[2]

Ron Rhodes as quoted by Joe Dallas
in **A Strong Delusion**

In her voyage across the ocean of this world, the church is like a great ship being pounded by the waves of life's different stresses. Our duty is not to abandon ship but to keep her on her course.[3]

Saint Boniface

The church does not lead the world nor echo it; she confronts it. Her note is the supernatural note.[4]

Oswald Chambers

The Church of the Apostles:
Is God's Church a Gay Church?

And I say also unto thee, That thou art Peter, and upon this rock I will build My church; and the gates of hell shall not prevail against it (Matthew 16:18).

The question that requires immediate resolution is simply this: Is God's Church a gay church? To the straight who have already entered the s-t-r-a-i-t gate, this question is obviously a settled one. To those of the gay and lesbian populace, this question must be answered with a clear and concise apostolic apologetic.

The term *church* is from the Greek word, "*Ecclesia*," and it means the "called-out ones." It is the word used in Matthew 16:18. There are several things to note about the text. First, the rock to which Jesus referred is not the rock of a man, namely, Peter. He was a preeminent apostle, commissioned as a *sent one* to represent Christ to the Jewish people, but he was never to be referred to as the rock of the Church. Secondly, the rock that Jesus was alluding to is the *revelation* that Peter confessed, namely that Jesus is the Christ, the Son of the living God (see Mt. 16:16-17). The apostle John wrote that every spirit that confesseth that Jesus is the Christ is only doing so by the Spirit of Truth (see 1 Jn. 2:22). Accordingly, he said that whosoever denies this is of the antichrist and they deny both the Father and the Son. This is a very simple litmus test on the surface; and if one is not careful, he could be deceived into believing that everyone who verbally confesses Christ or simply names the name of Christ is Christian. Therefore, an overly simplistic mistaken premise of faith will result in a misguided proposition that is fake. Jesus, the Master Teacher, said many will say to Him, "*Lord, Lord,*" and He will say, "*I know you not whence ye are; depart from Me, all ye workers of iniquity*" (Lk. 13:27; see also verses 25-26).

> EARLY CHRISTIANS WERE EXHORTED TO LIVE A LIFESTYLE OF SEPARATION FROM SIN PARTLY BECAUSE MANY PROFESSING BELIEVERS DID OTHERWISE.

Jesus further stated that those of this deceived order will even work miracles, which the Scripture calls lying wonders (see 2 Thess. 2:9). They will prophesy and even appear to be casting out devils (see Mt. 7:22). The pertinent key is found when Jesus says they work iniquity (perverse, twisted sin) and that He never knew them. The Greek word for *knew* is *ginosko*, which means "experientially or intimately." To assure that people would not be confused about supposed Christians whose professions are different from their practices, the apostle Paul says, *"Let every one that nameth the name of Christ depart from iniquity"* (2 Tim. 2:19b). Early Christians were exhorted to live a lifestyle of separation from sin partly because there were many professing believers who did otherwise. Their *profession* did not match their *possession. Homosexuality is a sin regardless of the stages of its development. Those who practice it are living in sin.* It is not recorded that Jesus ever directly ministered to anyone with this problem. However, His silence cannot be interpreted as a sanction for same-sex attraction. In fact, He counseled and prayed for His disciples, whom He later named apostles, and also for those who would believe on Him through their word. Therefore, whatsoever the apostles addressed was equivalent to the Master Teacher addressing it, since He had personally commissioned them and personally appeared to and called Apostle Paul.

Neither pray I for these alone, but for them also which shall believe on Me through their word (John 17:20).

Upon His ascension, He laid the foundation of the Church through His apostles, and He went to Heaven to be seated next to the Father as the chief cornerstone and the apostle of His Church.

And are built upon the foundation of the apostles and prophets, Jesus Christ Himself being the chief corner stone (Ephesians 2:20; see also Hebrews 3:1).

The Church that is built upon the foundation of the apostles is known as the apostolic Church, just as the Book of Acts is known as the Acts of the Apostles. Jesus Christ is the chief Apostle of His Church. The early Christians were so connected to the apostles of the Lamb that some of them even identified themselves by the apostles' names.

Now this I say, that every one of you saith, I am of Paul; and I of Apollos; and I of Cephas; and I of Christ (1 Corinthians 1:12).

They were dogged in their determination to follow the apostolic doctrine without compromise or the fear of contradiction. Their tenacity in defending the apostolic truth resulted in martyrdom for many of them.

And they continued stedfastly in the apostles' doctrine and fellowship, and in breaking of bread, and in prayers (Acts 2:42).

But ye shall receive power, after that the Holy Ghost is come upon you: and ye shall be witnesses unto Me both in Jerusalem, and in all Judaea, and in Samaria, and unto the uttermost part of the earth (Acts 1:8). (Note: The Greek word for witnesses is martyr.)

Therefore, to answer the question, "Is God's Church a gay church?," we must categorically concede that the word of the holy apostles is the only acceptable course of the "oil and wine" Church. A dear friend once asked me a profound theological question "Which came first—the Church or the Bible?" Was it the apostles or the Bible that came first? The obvious answer is that the Church and the apostles came before the written Word of the New Testament (as it is recorded) in the Holy Bible. The sacred text says:

> THE CHURCH AND THE APOSTLES CAME BEFORE THE WRITTEN WORD OF THE NEW TESTAMENT (AS IT IS RECORDED) IN THE HOLY BIBLE.

For the prophecy came not in old time by the will of man: but holy men of God spake as they were moved by the Holy Ghost (2 Peter 1:21).

These holy men in the Church dispensation were prophetic apostles. Prior to that time, it was principally the prophets and scribes. Second Timothy 3:16 affirms this:

All scripture is given by inspiration of God, and is profitable for doctrine, for reproof, for correction, for instruction in righteousness.

The word of the apostles formed the basis of Christian faith. Hence, we have the nearly 2,000-year-old Apostle's Doctrine and the Apostolic Church.

—THE APOSTLE'S CREED—

I believe in God the Father, Almighty, Maker of heaven and earth: And in Jesus Christ, His only begotten Son, our Lord: Who was conceived by the Holy Ghost, born of the Virgin Mary: Suffered under Pontius Pilate; was crucified, dead and buried: He descended into hell: The third day He rose again from the dead: He ascended into heaven, and sits at the right hand of God the Father Almighty: From thence He shall come to judge the quick and the dead: I believe in the Holy Ghost: I believe in the holy Catholic church: the communion of saints: The forgiveness of sins: The resurrection of the body: And the life everlasting. Amen.

Catholic: Universal

The Apostolic Church is not the denomination that is a major branch of Pentecostalism. It is the entire Body of Christ. The high priestly prayer of Jesus recorded in John 17 was that the Church might believe on Him through their (apostles') word. Jesus placed unparalleled authority in the original apostles. Their teaching was doctrine of the Church throughout the Church age until His return.

The Post-Modernism Judgment

The term *post-modern* means "the time period after the industrial age." It is inclusive of the information and technology ages as well. The distinguishing characteristic of this age is that the art, architecture, literature, and philosophy, developed during this period, reacts against what was once considered modern. Unlike the ancients, and the moderns, post-modern culture is accommodating in its view of homosexuality. The same-sex controversy is the raging result. It is now penetrating the place of worship. It has come to a crescendo, but it has been in existence since recorded history. For nearly 1,970 years the church's stance was relatively assured. Homosexuality was viewed as unnatural. The changing of the guard in the last three decades in church leadership has resulted in current teachings that are not only sympathetic to the gay cause, but even endorsing of gay marriage and ordination to ministry. The media, with its technological marketing prowess, has caused this generation to view homosexuality differently, and it has infiltrated the pulpit in its attempt to desecrate the "oil and wine" Church of the apostles. Daily, images of homosexuality are often paraded throughout the media, creating an illusion that it is a newly emerging alternative lifestyle that is both acceptable and prevalent. The secular line of reasoning states that the church must stay current with the times. Therefore, if the culture is changing, accordingly Christianity must alter its sacred identity. However, fundamentalism and orthodoxy demand the opposite response. God did not authorize homosexuality in the beginning of history, and He does not approve of it now. Neither the apostles nor the early Church fathers accepted it as a viable alternative, and neither should the "oil and wine" Church. The Master Teacher taught that the devil is a bold-faced liar and has nothing to do with the *naked truth* (see Jn. 8:44).

If the homosexual who expresses belief in Christ is sympathetically sanctioned in his lifestyle, which is legitimized through marriage, by the church, then the church will no longer be distinguished from the larger society. The "oil and wine" Church will have lost its savor or saltiness, and it will be *henceforth good for nothing* (see Mt. 5:13).

If the apologetic of today is different from what the apostles taught, it must be discarded, disbelieved, and denied entrance into the revelatory canon. A historical study of the compilation of the 27 Books of the New Testament reveals that quite a few books were disallowed because they deviated, differentiated, or detoured from the apostolic writings. These books were rejected even though they contained major elements of truth. The recipient of Jesus' commendation in Matthew 16, the apostle Peter, says, "*Knowing this first, that no prophecy of the scripture is of any private interpretation*" (2 Pet. 1:20). Whether you like it, love it, do not like it, or even hate it; if a person adds or takes from the Scripture, he or she can quite possibly be guilty of wresting the Scriptures to their own destructive detriment (see 2 Pet. 3:16). St. John, the beloved, writes:

> *For I testify unto every man that heareth the words of the prophecy of this book, If any man shall add unto these things, God shall add unto him the plagues that are written in this book* (Revelation 22:18).

The problem with revisionist, post-modern teaching is that it rebels against the original ideal. It either subtracts what the original canon says or adds deviant interpretations that were never intended by the original apostles. Therefore, upon discovery, any interpretation or purported revelation that is deviant from the annals of Apostolic Church didaché (teaching) should be seen as a counterfeit gospel being preached by false (though sometimes sincere) angels of light. St. Paul warns the church at Corinth about this, saying, "*For such are false apostles, deceitful workers, transforming themselves into the apostles of Christ. And no marvel; for satan himself is transformed into an angel of light*" (2 Cor. 11:13-14).

The total revelation of God's Word to the Church did not end with the 12 apostles of the Lamb. There is revelation that is yet coming forth. However, no other successive revelation is allowed to contradict the original one. A contradiction is not a revelation, but error, and at times it is *heresy*, which is a departure from *orthodoxy*.

We are of God: he that knoweth God heareth us; he that is not of God heareth not us. Hereby know we the spirit of truth, and the spirit of error (1 John 4:6).

In apostolic discourse, error can lead to apostasy, which is an advanced form of theological lunacy. When error becomes heretical, it threatens the foundation that the apostles have laid and that the subsequent generations have built upon.

For other foundation can no man lay than that is laid, which is Jesus Christ (1 Corinthians 3:11).

The Bema Seat of Judgment

The apostle Paul says to take heed how you build upon the foundation of the gospel of Jesus Christ, because everyone will stand before the Bema or Judgment Seat of Christ. Those who are not saved will stand before the White Throne Judgment to receive the recompense of their deeds. In all the New Testament Scriptures throughout the history of the Apostolic Church, there is not one small allusion to any apostolic sanction of a church catering exclusively to homosexuals. There is no biblical precedent for the ordination of gay ministers or the blessing of a homosexual union throughout two thousand years of Christian history. Churches that participate in ordaining homosexual ministers are in direct violation of apostolic order. Such acceptances are a recent occurrence and should be seen as a revisionist accommodation.

The Gay Church Judgment

God's church is not a gay church, nor could it ever be. The apostle Paul's admonition to the Corinthian Christians in First Corinthians 6:11 included the phrase, *"such were some of you."* The Corinthian church had embraced a new lifestyle in Christ, and a great deal of St. Paul's apostolic assessment was associated with their sexual abstinence or non-indulgence. It is preposterous to assert that the Scriptures would adamantly denounce something and then sanction an entire denomination known as the gay church being built on it. It is impossible for God's Church to be a gay church. It is equally impossible for a so-called gay church to be God's Church. The twain do not meet, and they are in direct opposition to each

> IT IS IMPOSSIBLE FOR GOD'S CHURCH TO BE A GAY CHURCH. IT IS EQUALLY AS IMPOSSIBLE FOR A SO-CALLED GAY CHURCH TO BE GOD'S CHURCH.

other. Just as there is no such thing as a Muslim Christian or a Christian Buddhist, there is no such thing as a true Christian who is a practicing homosexual. A person may persist in his choice of behavior if he so wishes, but he cannot redefine the meaning of a new creature in Christ Jesus. God's Church, by definition, is the *justified* ones, *sanctified* by Christ, *identified* through the waters of baptism, and *deputized* to represent the Kingdom of Heaven as high-ranking ambassadors preaching the word of reconciliation. *The Church of the apostles is known by many denominational names, but "gay and lesbian" is not one of them.*

—THE APOSTOLIC CHURCH FATHERS—

And are built upon the foundation of the apostles and prophets, Jesus Christ Himself being the chief corner stone (Ephesians 2:20).

The early Church fathers were either direct descendants or disciples of the apostles of our Lord Jesus Christ. Therefore, their word was *revered* by the early Christian Church, and it was adhered to. Just as the elders in Joshua's day were committed to setting up stones as a memorial so that the future generations would have a landmark of faith, a moral compass, and a spiritual guide to lighten their path, so the Church today must do the same.

...and take you up every man of you a stone upon his shoulder, according unto the number of the tribes of the children of Israel: that this may be a sign among you, that when your children ask their fathers in time to come, saying, What mean ye by these stones? Then ye shall answer them, That...these stones shall be for a memorial unto the children of Israel for ever (Joshua 4:5-7).

The Church Father Clement of Alexandria said, "...physical relations between males, fruitless sowings, coitus from the rear, and incomplete, androgynous unions all ought to be avoided; and nature herself should, rather be obeyed, who discourages [such things] through an arrangement of the parts which makes the male not for receiving the seed but for sowing it.[5]

Commentary: This is a categorical rejection of the homosexual argument. Clement's appeal to the natural argument is insistent and consistent. In fact, it was the only established opinion that was existent in the apostolic ranks.

The Church Father Tertullian said that the blessing of marriage (man and woman) is glorified in the natural way. Those who practice "all frenzies of lust

exceed the laws of nature...[should] be banished from the church...."
Homosexual acts are "not sins so much as monstrosities."[6]

Commentary: Tertullian was a powerful church father who first coined
the term "trinity," but his policy of banishment from the church of all "gay
members" is a bit extreme. Excommunication is not an acceptable alternative
of administering discipline to someone with a sexual identity crisis, especially, if he is sincerely seeking to be sanctified in his sexuality.

The Church Father Origen (A.D. 185-254) wrote of acts of homosexuality
as sodomy and referred to individuals who participated in them as "lawless."
He said "they disgrace their bodies in uncleanness and abuse...[they] have
despised these virtues and have wallowed in the filth of sodomy, in lawless
lust, 'men working that which is unseemly.' "[7]

The Church Father Cyprian (A.D. 258) said of homosexuality, "...not
restraining itself within the permitted limits, thinks it little satisfaction to
itself, unless even in the bodies of men it seeks, not a new pleasure, but goes
in quest of extraordinary and revolting extravagances, contrary to nature
itself, of men with men."[8] He further considered "men committing shame-
less acts with men" as "an indignity even to see..." and that "a chaste countenance cannot even look at..."[9]

Ambrosiaster 4th Century Commentator said that the tongue should never
be a substitute for the male sex organ and the anal orifice should never be a
substitute for the female organ. He believed that such practices evidenced
contempt for God and a deep disregard for the real meaning of man's sexual
nature.[10]

Commentary: It is obvious that all three church fathers believed that
homosexuality was unclean, unnatural, and ungodly. They unabashedly condemned the practice.

The Church Father John Chrysostom (A.D. 347-407) said, "Real pleasure
is only in accordance with nature....When God has abandoned someone,
everything is inverted...beliefs are satanic...their lives...diabolical...they were
unpardonable...I maintain that not only are you made [by it] into a woman,
but you cease to be a man: yet neither are you changed into that nature, nor
do you retain the one that you had. You become a betrayer of both, and are
worthy of being driven out and stoned by both men and women, since you
brought injury upon both sexes."[11]

Commentary: There are several things that I must note from Chrysostom's vehement berating and carefree condemnation of homosexuals. *First,*

there is a complete absence of the tenor of love in his aggressive appeal. *Second,* he is wrong when he asserts that God has absolutely abandoned them. Only a minuscule fraction of humanity, regardless of their evil deeds, have been forsaken by God. Such situations are handled by God on an individual and not wholesale basis. *Thirdly,* his charge that they have committed the unpardonable sin is horrifically overstated. *Fourthly,* in the Old Testament, a person could be stoned to death for about 50 different abominations including adultery, dishonoring parents, etc. In the New Testament, Jesus never excused sin, but He forgave the woman caught in the act of adultery (see Jn. 8:3-11). There is no scriptural evidence that mentions she even asked for forgiveness. The Master Teacher simply said, *"Go and sin no more"* (Jn. 8:11). Chrysostom's scathing and scintillating rebuke contains correct *perception,* but incorrect *penalty.* It does not represent the heart of the compassionate Christ who is *"not willing that any should perish, but that all should come to repentance"* (2 Pet. 3:9). Though Chrysostom was quite impassioned for the cause of Christ, it is very apparent that he exceeded the scriptural guidelines for judging sin. Though he lived in a much earlier and less educated culture, his message of condemnation confirms an espousal of alienation and not reconciliation. The church of Chrysostom's day followed his lead, and it is a tragic fact that many homosexual people were probably never given a fair chance to get right with God and order their steps uprightly. Sadly, the homophobic tirade continued progressively throughout the Apostolic Church Age. Only God knows how many souls fell through the net that is designed to draw in all manner of fish (see Mt. 4:18-19). The "oil and wine" Church must not repeat this grave mistake.

The Early Church Councils of Elvira (A.D. 305-306) and Acrya (A.D. 314)—The councils basically concluded that those who were guilty of any homosexual act of defilement were to suffer the penalty of "exclusion from sacrament of communion for fifteen years for the unmarried and under twenty years old and for life for married men over fifty years of age."[12]

Commentary: It is an interesting insight that David was 50 years old when he committed adultery with Bathsheba and second-degree murder of her husband in a subsequent cover-up that was greater than Watergate or Monica-gate. Despite this, he never was banished from celebrating the Passover. David came to a place of repentance. Initially, his reaction to his fall bordered on self-justification. However, once he was confronted by the prophet Nathan, he immediately accepted responsibility for his actions. He described this in Psalm 51, saying that God was justified in calling his action sin and judging it accordingly. David's acceptance of God's decree was the fruit of true repentance. If David had been outright banished because of his moral failure at age 50, about half of his accomplishments, including many of the songs, like Psalm 51, would never have been written. Imagine the Bible without this beautiful prayer of penitence.

PSALM 51

Have mercy upon me, O God, according to Thy lovingkindness: according unto the multitude of thy tender mercies blot out my transgressions. Wash me thoroughly from mine iniquity, and cleanse me from my sin. For I acknowledge my transgressions: and my sin is ever before me. Against Thee, Thee only, have I sinned, and done this evil in Thy sight: that Thou mightest be justified when Thou speakest, and be clear when Thou judgest (verses 1-4).

The early council may have been well-intended, but they were ill-advised. A priest, a preacher, or any ordained power cannot forbid your communion for 15 years or more to life because of a sin. St. Peter cursed and swore that he did not know the Christ at the moment of His arrest. Yet, 50 days later, he preached his first sermon, he opened the doors of the Church, and 3,000 were saved. What if Christ had made him wait for 15 years? What if Christ had banished him for life? Then there would have been no patriarchal Pentecostal preacher; there would not be three Epistles; and there would be only 11 foundations in the holy city of New Jerusalem. Eleven is the number of confusion in the Bible. God is not the author of confusion. Chrysostom was on target, but he was also off. The "oil and wine" Church must not have an off-spirit about ministry to the homosexual.

The Church Father Basil (A.D. 329-379) instructed young men to "flee from intimate association with comrades of your own age and run away from them as from fire. The enemy has indeed set many aflame through such means and consigned them down into that loathsome pit...on the pretext of spiritual love."[13] He warns young monks, "when a young man converses with you...make your response with your head bowed lest perchance...the seed of desire be implanted in you by the wicked sower and you reap the sheaves of corruption and ruin."[14] Basil also recommended the same punishment for homosexual offenses as for heterosexual immorality, including exclusion from the sacraments for 15 years. St. Gregory of Nyssa, who died in A.D. 398, agreed with Basil, classifying homosexuality as an unlawful pleasure.[15]

Commentary: Clearly St. Basil must have had something sensual in mind when he specifically warned against "the seed of desire" being planted in someone as a result of their association or contact with a young man. In light of today's thinking, it is hardly realistic that avoidance of personal contact is the remedy for the "seed of desire" being planted within you by a person of the same sex. Certainly, physical proximity is not an issue for *straight* people and probably only directly applies to those individuals with a gay propensity. Perhaps St. Basil was justified in his recommendation considering the setting of his remarks, but it seems that his sensitivities were based primarily on his own personal idiosyncrasy or insecurity. For the most part, men are not attracted to other men, regardless of their age, when they look into their eyes. Overreaction to the presence of the homosexual in the pew borders on homophobia. The "oil and wine" Church must conduct its business better than that.

The Church Father St. Augustine (A.D. 354-430), who served as the Bishop of Hippo in North Africa, wrote that homosexuality was full of "foul offenses, which be against nature...to be everywhere and at all times detested and punished, just as those of the men of Sodom."[16]

Commentary: St. Augustine's words clearly connect the sin of homosexuality as the sin of Sodom. He was one of the most prominent theologians of his day who had enormous influence on the Church of the West. It is reported by Augustinian critics that he was sexually obsessed, because the theme of many of his writings centered on the subject of sex and the Christian's proper response and involvement. As mentioned in "The Naked Truth" chapter, often a person's obsession with something is an indication of a personal struggle in that particular area. This is not to suggest that St. Augustine had a difficult time maintaining his vows of purity, but as a human being, he was constantly aware that he had to gird up the loins of his mind, and hide the Word in his heart, lest he sin against the Lord, or his own body, the temple of the Holy Ghost. Augustine's denunciation of the practice of homosexuality helped steer the Church through trying times of moral laxity and sensual depravity.

The Theodosian Code (A.D. 390) authorized "exquisite punishment" for guilty participants in homosexual acts.[17] In fact, this code also recommended the death penalty of being burned at the stake for anyone found guilty of the "shameful custom of condemning a man's body, acting the part of a woman's."[18] At the time that Theodosian Code was decreed, Rome had become officially Christian. The edict emphatically stated that the City of Rome was not "...any longer to be defiled by the pollution of effeminacy in males...." The vicar of Rome was commended for the "practice of seizing all who have committed the crime of treating their male bodies as though they were females, submitting them to the use becoming the opposite sex, and being in no wise distinguishable from women...." The edict goes on to describe homosexuality as a crime of "monstrosity."[19]

Commentary: It is apparent from the Theodosian Code that the early Church truly believed that the revisionist, post-modern teachings concerning homosexuality are indeed erroneous. However, the punishment of *being burned at the stake* in some way reminds one of the "Salem Witch Trials" several centuries ago in which innocent women and men were killed in similar fashion, by being burned at the stake. History records that they were later proven to have been falsely accused and condemned to death. The legendary Joan of Arc, a self-proclaimed French prophetess, was executed the same way.

History has proven that the prescribed punishment was ill-advised, excessively cruel, and that it was based on people's fears, versus the pertinent facts. The term, "exquisite punishment," probably meant *extremely cruel measures.* Execution was a well-intended effort to keep the land cleansed of the scourge of same-sex attraction. However, the reality is, the action of extermination did not eradicate it, nor is there any New Testament justification for it. Homosexuality is primarily a sin against one's own body, and often has grave mental and gross physical health consequences. Societal standards are necessary and welcome, but unjust penalties for personal sins are not grounds for being literally *charred while tied to a wood post.* This harsh punishment only served to push it underground and undercover. It did not accomplish anything worthwhile. Down-low living must be shunned and up-high forgiving must be done in the "oil and wine" Church. If the Church is merciless, it may result in a massacre.

Emperor Justinian Novella (A.D. 540). He issued two edicts that referred to homosexual acts as punishable by death."[20] It further states that homosexual acts are "diabolical" and that individuals "practice among themselves the most disgraceful lusts, and act contrary to nature...."

Commentary: The influence of the church upon society was evidenced by the enactment of the death penalty by the magistrates of government. This is a shameful episode of church history. The "oil and wine" Church must acknowledge this in sincere repentance to God on behalf of our predecessors.

The Council of Toledo (A.D. 693). This council concluded that the punishment for homosexuality should include exclusion "from all communion with Christians, and in addition have their hair shorn, receive one hundred stripes of the lash, and be banished in perpetual exile."[22]

Commentary: The council certainly did not sugarcoat their opposition to homosexuality and for this, they are commended. However, their penalties were a seeming prefiguration of Nazism's anti-Semitic program in Germany. They were essentially banished to concentration camps; their heads were shaved bald for the purpose of shame and humiliation; and they were executed in Hitler's gas chambers or before his firing squads. To castrate a homosexual is not scriptural and is similar to the insane punishments meted out by tyrannical religious zealots and despots. This has given credence to those who have rejected the church throughout the centuries. The Master Teacher would never approve of castration being done in His name. Yielding to the sexual temptation presented by determined demonic forces and the lusts that war against one's soul should not be met with the amputation of one's sex organ. The church fathers were sincere, but at times were quite severe and did not reflect the heart of a *gracious* God.

Church Father Thomas Aquinas (A.D. 1225-1274) wrote in his *Summa Theologica*, that homosexuality was "the unnatural vices" by which "man transgresses that which has been determined by nature...." He further reflects that sex with the wrong gender is the vice of sodomy and that sodomy is an unnatural transgression that is to be considered a sin that is the "gravest of all."[23]

Commentary: Aquinas considered the sin of homosexuality as second only to murder, in that it subverted natural reason. To call homosexuality the gravest sin of them all is a bit of a stretch. It is not necessary to make any sin worse than what it already is. Sin is bad and is in a class all by itself, and homosexuality is bad in a class by itself. It does not need exaggeration to be viewed correctly. The "oil and wine" Church need not overstate the abomination.

Church Father John Calvin refers to homosexuality as an *unnatural* and *filthy* thing.[24]

TO CALL HOMOSEXUALITY THE GRAVEST SIN OF ALL IS A BIT OF A STRETCH. IT IS NOT NECESSARY TO MAKE ANY SIN WORSE THAN WHAT IT ALREADY IS.

Commentary: The church of the apostolic doctrine, having held steadfast to the singular conviction of the wrongness of gay and lesbian activity throughout two millennia, has come to a critical crossroad in the 21st century. Throughout church history, there has been little deviation from the traditional view of homosexuality despite the many other significant differences in doctrine. There has hardly been any distinction in the various denominational streams or even in the larger Catholic or Protestant context. This is still true today. There is also a myriad of mutant interpretations and teachings as well. The "oil and wine" Church is called to present Christ in this time of crisis of faith.

OFFICIAL POSITIONS TOWARD HOMOSEXUALITY —IN THE 21ST-CENTURY CHURCH—

Catholicism

The Catholic Church believes that "Every human being is called to receive a gift of divine sonship, to become a child of God by grace." However, to receive this gift, we must reject sin, including homosexual behavior—acts intended to arouse or stimulate a sexual response regarding a person of the same sex. The Catholic Church teaches that such acts are always violations of divine and natural law and that there is a "basic, ethical intuition that certain behaviors are wrong because they are unnatural." We perceive intuitively that the natural sex partner of a human is another human, not an animal. The same reasoning applies in the case of homosexual behavior. The natural sex partner for a man is a woman, and the natural sex partner for a woman is a man. Thus, people have the corresponding intuition concerning homosexuality that they do about bestiality—it is wrong because it is unnatural. The Catholic Church teaches that homosexual acts are acts of grave depravity. Tradition has always declared that homosexual acts are intrinsically disordered. They are contrary to the natural law. They close the sexual act to the gift of life. They do not proceed from a genuine affective and sexual complementation. Under no circumstances can they be approved *(Catechism of the Catholic Church 23570).*

"Homosexual persons are called to chastity. By the virtues of self-mastery that teach them inner freedom, at times by the support of disinterested friendship, by prayer and sacramental grace, they can and should gradually and resolutely approach Christian perfection" (CCC 2357-2359).[25]

Scandals in the Priesthood

In her outspoken view of the Catholic priest scandal, nun Karol Jackowski provides a historical overview of the hidden sexual sins, which have permeated the Catholic Church. *The Silence We Keep, A Nun's View of the Catholic Priest Scandal,* offers response to the issue of forced celibacy and resultant homosexuality and immorality within the clergy and laity.

Those who think the abuse was predominately perpetrated on children and teens, should think again. Jackowski cites that on January 5, 2003, Bill

Smith of the *St. Louis Post Dispatch* reported in a national survey completed by Saint Louis University. The 1996 study revealed that a minimum of 34,000 Catholic nuns or about 40 percent of all nuns in the U.S. have suffered some form of sexual trauma, victimized by priests as well as nuns.

Based on the teachings and lifestyle of Jesus and His apostles, the impetus of the early Church was sharing the gospel through community, having *all things in common.* Women as well as men were influential as leaders, benefactors, evangelists, healers, celebrants, and worshipers. The entire Christian community was one holy, apostolic Church. They became to the people, *in persona Christi,* in the person of Christ. In its early beginnings, the Catholic Church was free of the gay influence in its priesthood. However, as corrupt men of privilege assumed leadership, they equated the priesthood with the power of position. From the lowest to the highest ranks in the priesthood, abuse crept in. Celibacy was mandatory and not voluntary for the priests. Therefore, sexual activity went underground and at times emerged as a predatory problem. As it was then, so it is now. Sexual scandals within nunneries and convents were explosive issues. Although lesbianism existed, celibacy and virginity were embraced as the highest forms of living for women, freeing them to love, serve, and worship in its purest sense. For nuns and those who chose to live virginal lives, sex was not seen as something denied or even something to obtain. It was seen as an obstacle to true freedom and serving and loving Christ. It was their perspective that allowed chastity and disallowed hypocrisy.

As early as the fourth and fifth centuries, there existed documented accounts of molestation and even bestiality within the church. Although prohibited, marriage was not uncommon. Popes, bishops, priests, and monks fathered offspring only to later sell their wives and children into slavery, because it was too expensive to support families. Strategically, the church did not plan to share its wealth, and marriage of priests would be expensive for the Catholic Church because the heirs would be in line to receive the property they managed and controlled. This property was intended to pass to the succeeding generation of clergy. It is no small wonder the Catholic Church is *the* materialistically wealthiest church on earth.

In the early Middle Ages, monasteries grew into the singular centers of learning, reading, and writing. As a result, monks and nuns were in exclusive control of the educational system and held the power to impose their beliefs and practices. At times, this resulted in *the depraved and immoral behavior that saturated these institutions of higher thought.* In addition to sex between monks and priests, double monasteries housed nuns and priests. Sex between the two was commonly known as a way of life in European monasteries. *Homosexuality and abuse of children were epidemic, along with theft, forgery, rape, slavery, and murder.* Criminal activity and institutional hypocrisy were the norm. Jackowski further cites that a 12th-century bishop fathered 65 children, and Pope John XII (955-964) was highly recognized for adultery and incest,

> PROFESSING HOMOSEXUALS WHO PROMISE TO LIVE A LIFE OF ABSTINENCE SHOULD NOT BE ORDAINED INTO A POSITION OF MINISTRY.

dying of a heart attack in the bed of a married woman. Pope Innocent VIII (1492) apparently could not live up to his name. He candidly boasted about his offspring of bastards, but was forgiven by his priestly colleagues for being honest about his affairs. Does this sound familiar to anyone? Lawsuits have resulted in millions of dollars being spent because priests have been allowed to continue in ministry, by simply an acknowledgment of the allegation of homosexuality.

The Majority of Catholic Priests

Is the Catholic Church a pro-gay church? Of course not! The majority of Catholic priests have been scandal-free. However, throughout history one cannot deny the practice of homosexuality of priests and nuns within the Catholic Church. Sexual relationships between heterosexual priests and nuns continue to occur today. Many within and outside the church believe the number of homosexual priests and those in heterosexual relationships are much higher than the recent surveys report. The solution to ridding the Catholic priesthood of homosexual behavior rests in whom the church screens, admits, and ordains to serve. If there is no change, but only charges and cover-up, time dictates that the truth will forever speak. If there is no change, sadly, the foundation laid by its architects will continue to be corrupted. The pope is believed to be the "vicar of Christ" to professing Catholics. Surely, the powerful influence of the papal authority, both today and in the future, must reconsider its policy and remove the homosexual presence. Professing homosexuals who promise to live a life of abstinence should not be ordained into ministry. It should not be assumed that they will be able to uphold the vow of celibacy. The nature of the Catholic liturgy and its involvement of young altar boys is an open invitation for sexual predators of homosexual orientation to infiltrate. To keep the church safe from this, it must change its ordination and toleration policy. Wisely, the church is adopting change because of the scandals. This is helpful to the

Protestant church, because all Christian people of faith are viewed as one and the same by the world. In all fairness, it is not just the Catholic priests who are having a problem. Protestant churches are also having a problem with sexual scandal of one kind or the other. How can the church point out the mote in the homosexual's eye when there is a beam in its heterosexual eye (see Mt. 7:3)? The leadership of the church must preach the "gospel of change" to itself while preaching it to the gay and lesbian person. A dose of the gos-pill medicine will resolve the epidemic of ministerial sexual misconduct throughout Christendom. Satan has bishops in his bull's-eye, pastors in his periscope, and those called to be saints in his sights. He seeks to sabotage, subterfuge, and suffocate the sacred solution. Therefore, it behooves those who minister the sacraments to safeguard the sanctity of the solemn session. This is the challenge of the "oil and wine" Church leadership.

—PROTESTANTISM—

The Anglican Church

The Anglican Church Communion is a *communion* of churches worldwide. In the United States, the Anglican Church is known as the Episcopalian Church (see below). In a 1998 conference, gay practices were declared "incompatible with Scripture." In a 526–70 vote with 45 abstentions, the Anglican bishops upheld opposition to gay practices. They also opposed gay ordinations and same-sex blessings.[26] Since then, consecration of an openly gay bishop in New Hampshire in November 2003 has threatened to split the Anglican church, with the 17 million large, African Anglican Church leading the way.[27] In addition, some Episcopalian congregations as well as the Anglican Church of Canada have sanctioned and blessed same-sex unions.

The Assemblies of God

The official position was approved August 6, 2001, by the General Presbytery of the Assemblies of God. They are in complete opposition to homosexuality, noting that it is a "*sin because it is disobedient to scriptural teaching.*"[28] Homosexuality is considered the result of "moral erosion" and should not receive "sympathy as a viable alternative lifestyle."

The American Baptist Church

Though the American Baptist Church declares that there is no scriptural endorsement of homosexual lifestyles as a Christian lifestyle, "two Baptist churches in North Carolina have taken the unprecedented step of solemnizing the union of two gay male couples."[29]

The Baptist Church

Like many other denominations, there are a host of different organizations and sub-denominational ranks among the Baptist Church including Freewill, Southern, Missionary, and Full-Gospel. There is, however, a general consensus among those groups that homosexuality is a sin; it is contrary to nature; and the ordination and marriage of such individuals should not be allowed. Also, the commonly held belief among them is that it is the "responsibility and privilege of the church to minister to homosexuals."

The Church of God

They believe that the Bible teaches that homosexuality is a sin as directed throughout Scripture.[30]

The Church of God in Christ

The official position is fundamentalist. It actively opposes homosexuality and teaches that it is a sin. COGIC opposes ordaining homosexuals as well as marriage for same-sex couples.

The Full Gospel Baptist Church

The FGBC is opposed to the recognition of same-sex marriage and views homosexuality as a sin against God and nature. The presiding Bishop Paul Morton, of New Orleans, Louisiana, has preached a landmark message, telecast nationally. In it, he states, "Homosexuality is unnatural and every homosexual can be delivered and must seek it for themselves."

The Episcopalian Church

The Episcopalians have allowed for the ordination of "qualified persons of either heterosexual or homosexual orientation." The only stipulation is that the church must consider them "wholesome" individuals whose relationships are characterized by fidelity, monogamy, mutual affection and respect, careful, honest communication and the holy love which enables those in such relationship to see in each other the image of God.[31]

The Evangelical Lutheran Church (USA)

The conference of bishops in 1993 concluded that there is no basis in the Scripture nor tradition for the establishment of an official ceremony of the blessing of a homosexual relationship.

The Lutheran Church

This church openly allows admittance to gays and lesbians, but still acknowledges that it is a sin and therefore a deviation from God's original plan and purpose for mankind. The Lutheran Communion on Human Sexuality states that whatever the cause of such a condition may be...homosexual orientation is profoundly: unnatural without implying that such a person's sexual orientation is a matter of conscious deliberate choice...As a sinful human being, the homosexual is accountable to God for homosexual thought, words, and deeds.

The Presbyterian Church

The Presbyterians are officially opposed to the licensing of homosexual ministers. The founder's influence, John Calvin, is still being felt throughout the Presbyterian ranks despite various factions.

The Southern Baptist

This denomination believes that marriage and sexual intimacy is one man and one woman for life. Homosexuality is condemned in the Bible as a sin and is not considered a "valid alternative lifestyle." (See the official website of the Southern Baptist Convention, http://www.sbc.net/aboutus/pssexuality.asp.) They do not believe that homosexuality is an unforgivable sin; they consider homosexuals to be eligible for the same redemption that is available to all sinners. They can become new creations in Christ too.

They oppose the granting of civil rights, normally reserved for immutable characteristics such as race, to a group based on its members' sexual behaviors. They believe that to accept homosexuality as an appropriate, alternative lifestyle would betray the life-changing sacrifice of Christ and leave homosexuals without hope for a new and eternal life.[31]

The Unitarian Universalists

The Universalists have established an open-door policy for gays and lesbians that permits their ministerial ordination, as well as their civil unions and marriage. This same group, however, also believes that all religions have access to Heaven, because whether their faith is in Muhammad, Buddha, Confucius, or Osama Bin Laden, Christ's meditation on Calvary automatically saves all men, even without their repentance and confession of His lordship. Obviously, their beliefs cannot be considered orthodox Christian ones.

The United Methodist Church

The official Methodist position is that homosexuality as a lifestyle is not sanctioned by the Word of God, and therefore, those who practice it should not be accepted as legitimate ministers in the church.

The Metropolitan Community Church
(*otherwise known as the gay church*)

This church was founded by an openly homosexual, former Baptist minister, Troy Perry.[33] According to the church's website, members adhere to the following beliefs:

- The Bible is full of errors that have resulted from being copied, recopied, and translated over and over again.

- Homosexual behavior is not a sin in God's eyes. Instead, the teaching that homosexual behavior is sinful is the result of twisted teaching of "homophobic" men.

- The references to homosexual behavior in the Bible really do not mean what they say.

- Sodom and Gomorrah were destroyed not because of homosexual behavior but because the people ignored the poor and needy.

- Jonathan and David were homosexual lovers.

- Ruth and Naomi were lesbian lovers.

- Christ lived an alternative lifestyle and He loved other men besides John.

- Christ wore a purple robe to the cross as a connotation of His homosexuality.[34]

The spirit of deception lies at the root of the gay and lesbian movement and the so-called gay church of America. One of the chief founders was a married man suppressing a homosexual inclination until he eventually *abandoned* his marriage, threw the closet door wide open, formed an *accepting* church, and began to devise an *accommodating* theology to *accompany* his *alternate* lifestyle. Thousands of deceived individuals frequent these bogus institutions of faith feeling justified in their farce love lifestyle. They call it free love. If it is really free, why does one have to pay such a high price if one chooses to live it? "*Having a form of godliness,* [they have denied] *the power thereof: from such,* [all are advised to] *turn away* (2 Tim. 3:5). The gay church is a play church which will face serious consequences at the judgment.

The Church of the Apostles: In Conclusion
Is God's Church a Gay Church?

At one time it was clear that God's Church was not a gay church. Today, it is not clear at all. The gay church confuses the two. The gay church mocks God's Church by calling itself a church. The "oil and wine" Church is holy and not homosexual. The homosexual church is everything but holy. The so-called gay church says that both the person and the practice are welcome to come as they are and stay as they are. God's Church says, *"Come out from among them and be ye separate."* A perusal of two thousand years of the "oil and wine" Church history reveals several things. The *apostolic* dictates of the church fathers, the *actions* of the church ages, and the *antics* of the old way-churches justified their anti-homosexual actions in the name of the *"Lamb of God, which taketh away the sin of the world"* (Jn. 1:29). The "oil and wine" Church must adopt the method of the Master Teacher, who graciously loved people to life while providing therapy for their troubled soul. God's Church is God's. The gay church is gay and that is sad.

Founded

The Church of the Apostles is *founded* upon the rock of revelation of *who Jesus is.* It is *grounded* in apostolic doctrine. It is *surrounded* by a cloud of apostolic witnesses. Throughout church history, we discover that there was never a time that the Apostolic Church granted the ordination of homosexual ministers or admittance of practicing homosexual members. The apostolic fathers were vehement in their opposition, adamant in their differentiation, and inclement in their vitrolization. Their posture toward homosexuality was hard, harsh, and oftentimes hostile. Their hatred of it bordered homophobia. They were aware of the potentiality of its transference, transmission, translation, and transportation into the church. Therefore, they treated it more severely than any other sexual deviation. There is no precedent for a so-called gay church denomination throughout all two thousand years of Apostolic Church history.

Grounded

The nation of Israel was chosen by God as a foreshadowing of the "oil and wine" Church of the Lord Jesus Christ, which was *grounded* upon the foundation of the apostles and prophets. Judaism, as a religion, is vehemently opposed to same-sex relationships, marriage, or lifestyle. The Church has a Judeo heritage in the moral sense. The Church in America has an apostolic and prophetic call to the nations of the world. Though America comprises only 10 percent of the world's population, our financial support provides for 90 percent of worldwide missions outreach. This is quite significant. It has been said that when America sneezes, the world catches a cold.

WHERE THE CHURCH FATHERS WERE HARSH, HARD, HATEFUL, OR HOMOPHOBIC, WE MUST BECOME LIKE SHEM AND JAPHETH.

One thing is for certain: The voices of the pulpits, conferences, synods, symposiums, etc. of this nation are heard, and the ramifications are felt all throughout Christendom.

Surrounded

Many throughout the entire world have *surrounded* the Church. They are watching and waiting to see what the "oil and wine" Church of the Apostles in America will do concerning the issues that relate to this and all other subsequent generations to come. To stay compassionate is our goal. To remain sensitive is the key. To do so, we have to remember what we used to be.

The issue of homosexuality is much like an aggravating injury that seemingly never gets properly healed. Admittedly, it is in our midst, and it is not going anywhere anytime soon. This is not the time for apathetic inertia, but rather it is the time to raise up the stones (see Josh. 4:7). The stones of memorial serve as a reminder of the faith of the fathers as well as the journey through which God's grace has carried the Church. The voice of the holy fathers should reveal the heart of the heavenly Father. Where the fathers were harsh, hard, hateful, or homophobic, we must become like Shem and Japheth. Unlike their brother Ham who brought shame to Noah's nakedness, they backed up and covered their father's nakedness. The Church must cover the apostolic fathers. Not to do so perpetuates the distancing, the disconnecting, and the degeneracy. The absence of a connection to the church fathers is the first and foremost error of course.

And Noah began to be an husbandman, and he planted a vineyard: and he drank of the wine, and was drunken; and he was uncovered within his tent. And Ham, the father of Canaan, saw the nakedness of his father, and told his two brethren without. And Shem and Japheth took a garment, and laid it upon both their shoulders, and went backward, and covered the nakedness of their father; and their faces were backward, and they saw not their father's nakedness (Genesis 9:20-23).

In order to facilitate the faith of the fathers, the heart of the children must be turned to them. The prophet Elijah's ministry of restoration and reformation serves as the backdrop for such an occurrence.

Behold, I will send you Elijah the prophet before the coming of the great and dreadful day of the Lord: and He shall turn the heart of the fathers to the children, and the heart of the children to their fathers, lest I come and smite the earth with a curse (Malachi 4:5-6).

The "oil and wine" Church of the Apostles must settle the derision concerning the *decision* of gays in the church. We must consider the *concerns* as we *discern* the times. Jesus is indeed the answer, but what are the questions? The question: "Is God's Church a gay church?" The answer: "No." The question: "Is the gay church, God's Church?" The answer: "No, again!" The question: "What then shall we do with the homosexual?" The answer: "We must take the *compassionate approach: prophetic solutions for pathetic situations.*" Selah.

Prayer: God of our Fathers, help us to not remove the ancient landmarks that our fathers have set up. Help us to raise up the stones of remembrance that will enable this generation and all others to come to know what the Lord has done in our midst. We pray for a complete restoration of the foundations of our apostolic faith. Help us to re-dig the wells that were dug deep by those who have preceded us. Grant that the torch that is in our hands may illuminate this iniquitous age in which we live. Turn our hearts to the fathers and keep us from embracing any error that we discover in their ways. Amen and Amen!

ENDNOTES

1. *Leadership,* Vol. 16, No. 1, Bible Illustrator 3.0 for Windows, Parsons Technology, Inc. 1990-1998, Illustrations Copyrighted at Christianity Today, Inc., 1984-1995, Faircom Corp.

2. Ron Rhodes as quoted by Joe Dallas, *A Strong Delusion* (Eugene, OR: Harvest House Publishers, 1996), 21.

3. Edythe Draper, *Draper's Book of Quotations for the Christian World* (Wheaton, IL: Tyndale House Publishers, Inc., 1992), Entry 1398, Bible Illustrator 3.0 for Windows, Parsons Technology, Inc. 1990-1998, Illustrations Copyrighted at Christianity Today, Inc., 1984-1995, Faircom Corp.

4. Draper, *Draper's Book of Quotations*, Entry 1428.

5. John Boswell, *Christianity, Social Tolerance, and Homosexuality* (Chicago, IL: University of Chicago Press, 1980), 357.

6. Tertullian, as quoted by Byrne Fone *Homophobia: A History* (New York: Picador, 2000), 103.

7. Origen, as quoted by James R. White & Jeffrey D. Niell, *The Same Sex Controversy* (Minneapolis, MN: Bethany House, 2002), 171.

8. Cyprian, as quoted by White & Niell, *The Same Sex Controversy*, 171.

9. Ibid., 171.

10. Ambrosiaster, as quoted by Maxie E. Dunnam and H. Newton Malony, *Staying the Course* (Nashville: Abingdon Press, 2003), 92.

11. Chrysostom, as quoted by Fone, *Homophobia,* 104.

12. Henry R. Percival, ed. *The Seven Ecumenical Councils of the Undivided Church: Their Canons and Dogmatic Decrees* (New York: C. Scribner's Sons, 1916), [A Select Library of Nicene and Post-Nicene Fathers of the Christian Church. 2nd Series. Vol. 13.] 70.

13. As quoted by Fone, *Homophobia*, 106.

14. As quoted by Fone, *Homophobia*, 106.

15. Timothy J. Dailey, *Dark Obsession* (Nashville: Broadman & Holman Publishers, 2003), 77.

16. David F. Greenberg, *The Construction of Homosexuality* (Chicago: The University of Chicago Press, 1988), 225.

17. Dailey, *Dark Obsession*, 78.

18. Quoted in Louis Crompton, *Homosexuality & Civilization* (Cambridge, MA: The Belknap Press of Harvard University Press, 2003), 136.

19. Fone, *Homophobia*, 117.

20. Fone, *Homophobia*, 117.

21. Ibid., 115.

22. Fone, *Homophobia*, 120.

23. Quoted by Dailey, *Dark Obsession*, 78.

24. Ibid., 79.

25. Catholic Church website http://www.catholic.com/library/homosexuality.asp.

26. http://www.apologeticsindex.org/a112.html.

27. Sam Eyoboka, *African Anglicans Bishops' Bold Statement on Gay Marriages*, October 31, 2004, http://allafrica.com/stories/200411010468.html.

28. *Homosexuality* (Official Assemblies of God Position Paper), http://ag.org/top/beliefs/position_papers/4181_homosexuality.cfm.

29. American Baptist Church statement quoted in *The Advocate* (April 7, 1992), 20.

30. See www.wcg.org/lit/AboutUs/media/brieflist.htm.

31. Dailey, *Dark Obsession,* 156.

32. *The Advocate,* 98.

33. Alan Sears & Craig Osten, *The Homosexual Agenda* (Nashville: Broadman & Holman Publishers, 2003), 126.

34. Stephen Bennett, "Was Jesus Gay?," *WorldNet Daily,* July 16, 2002.

CHAPTER
THREE

If I had known what trouble you were bearing;

What griefs were in the silence of your face;

I would have been more gentle and more caring,

And tried to give you gladness for a space. [1]

Mary Carolyn Davies

Regardless of how we define Christ's separation from the world, one fact is clear: he did not separate himself from human beings and their needs. Nor did he limit his concern to the spiritual part of man's personality. Christianity demands a level of caring that transcends human inclinations. [2]

Erwin W. Lutzer

Teach me to feel another's woe,

To hide the fault I see;

That mercy I to others show,

That mercy show to me. [3]

Alexander Pope

The mark of a man is how he treats a person who can be of no possible use to him. [4]

Edythe Draper

The Compassionate Approach: Prophetic Solutions for Pathetic Situations

But he, willing to justify himself, said unto Jesus, And who is my neighbour? And Jesus answering said, A certain man went down from Jerusalem to Jericho, and fell among thieves, which stripped him of his raiment, and wounded him, and departed, leaving him half dead. And by chance there came down a certain priest that way: and when he saw him, he passed by on the other side. And likewise a Levite, when he was at the place, came and looked on him, and passed by on the other side. But a certain Samaritan, as he journeyed, came where he was: and when he saw him, he had compassion on him, and went to him, and bound up his wounds, pouring in oil and wine, and set him on his own beast, and brought him to an inn, and took care of him. And on the morrow when he departed, he took out two pence, and gave them to the host, and said unto him, Take care of him; and whatsoever thou spendest more, when I come again, I will repay thee. Which now of these three, thinkest thou, was neighbour unto him that fell among the thieves? And he said, He that showed mercy on him. Then said Jesus unto him, Go, and do thou likewise (Luke 10:29-37).

THE GOOD SAMARITAN
—THE COMPASSIONATE APPROACH—

Compassion Is Always in Fashion

The textual setting of the Good Samaritan story begins with the lawyer coming to the Master Teacher and inquiring about the prerequisites for eternal life. The King James Version says that he was endeavoring to *tempt* Jesus. Jesus' response to him was that he should love God primarily and his neighbor secondarily. The lawyer proceeded with a follow-up question. In true prosecutorial style, he sought to *justify himself*, asking, "*And who is my neighbor?*" Immediately, the Savior launched into the all-encompassing parable of the Good Samaritan. It is a story that vividly shows us the method and the means of meting out the love of God in this new millennium. Our heavenly Father knows the monumental task. The "oil and wine" Church is especially graced to extend grace in the face of the displaced. Compassion will never go out of fashion because it is en vogue eternally. From everlasting to everlasting, He is God (see Ps. 90:2). God is love and Christ is God. He is the God-Man whose compassion is foundational to human function. Man can live 40 days without food, 3 days without water, minutes without air, but not a second without hope and love. The compassion of Christ is to lodge the saved and to locate the lost. The compassion of Christ is the navigation system on the Church's dashboard of destiny. It is the motivating factor in the mobilizing force. The compassion of Christ will cause the altars to be filled and churches to be full. The compassion of Christ is the most impenetrable defense and irresistible offense imaginable. The compassion of Christ is the catalyst that rebukes same-sex marriage; reunites fatherless families; recharges fizzling relationships; redirects our fired upon youth; and restores the hurting homosexual. Christ's compassion activates the spiritual womb, thus making it capable of carrying and caring for the children of the Church of Christ. Christ's compassion is the emotion that confronts the commotion with full locomotion. Without Christ's compassion, the dying cannot live and the sick will not be healed. Without Christ's compassion, the hungry will not be fed, nor the naked clothed. Without Christ's compassion, the gay or lesbian is predestined to a lifelong "gay-la" without the glory of God. Without Christ's compassion, the Church is unable to vocalize the vision or fertilize the overshadowing of the Omnipotent One. The reception of seed is met with a barren response and infertility rules the day. The wombs are empty and the hearts are even emptier.

—A PROPHETIC PICTURE—

The parable of the Good Samaritan accurately depicts, in many instances, what is happening in the church regarding the homosexual. In this parable we see a prophetic picture of the "oil and wine" Church. Two of the three characters depicted in the parable, namely the priest, who represents a church leader, and the Levite, who represents a church member, are uninterested in providing assistance to the damaged soul whom the Bible describes as half dead.

The Lapsed Masses

Having been victimized on the road of life, he was a mere shell of a man. He is a type or shadow of what theologians would call "the lapsed masses." When something is lapsed, it is considered out and overdue. This half-dead man represents the half dead of mankind. The patriarch Jacob's son, Joseph, was sold by his half brothers. Tamar, King David's daughter, was raped by her half-brother Amnon. There are many so-called saints that are half-saved. That is, they are saved from the waist up, but not from the waist down. They are half brothers. They are saved from Monday through Thursday, half the week; but they thank God it's Friday so they can let their hair down and do "their thing." They sing, "Get Down Tonight, Baby," on Saturday, and get up early on Sunday to sing, "Rise, Shine, Give God the Glory." They are half saved. They are half dead. They are hybrids. They are like the mule, that is, half donkey and half horse. They are halfhearted. Nonetheless, they are bleeding and dying on life's Jericho Road. While the others were too busy to minister to the problem, the Samaritan traveler had the compassionate approach. Of the three, only he gave help to the helpless man who fell among thieves.

The Samaritan's role is being fulfilled by many dedicated Christians throughout the world. Franklin Graham, son of Dr. Billy Graham, heads a ministry that is called "Samaritan's Purse." It is a missions organization that majors in evangelism and ministry to the poor, doing good works in a fallen-world.

Neither the priest (the church leader), nor the Levite (the church member) exercised courage, but rather cowardice. Perhaps they should have remembered their credentials. Those who are like them should reexamine the great commission. To go into *"all the world"* includes the highways and byways, the very places where the hedges have been broken.

Ministry to the Masses

Ministry does not begin until you have helped somebody who is at life's dead end. The hordes of humanity and the masses of mankind are messed up. Unfortunately, it is not an unusual practice for church members to be Missing In Action during missionary moments. It is one thing to sing, "Do not pass me by." However, the believers themselves must *not pass people by*! Unfortunately, as is the case for many congregants, those words are much easier to sing than they are to serve. "Well sung" is not the same as "well done"! Many believers spend all their time beating the devil running. They have little or no time to beat the devil out of the beaten of society, who are in misery. When the "oil and wine" Church does its job, the world will sing, "How sweet it is to be loved by God." Those who live the fast and footloose life have lost their way. The Lord of Isaiah's vision still wants to know, *who will go?* (see Is. 6:8) The first two letters of the word *gospel* spell *go*. You cannot spell *God* without first spelling *go*. Many Samaritan saints are unfamiliar with the streets. The unchurched will perceive them as strangers and sometimes alien.

Good Samaritans introduce themselves through their deeds. They do not need to pass out their business cards. Their strangeness is their uniqueness. Their kindness is their signature. This journeyman was a stranger and that was a good thing. Familiarity breeds contempt. To those who are straight, the gay way is indeed strange. The Bible exhorts believers to minister to the *"stranger within the gate"* (Deut. 31:12). We must not leave it up to humanism, existentialism, and hedonism to meet the needs of a world steeped deep in pessimism, skepticism, and cynicism. Far too often we walk past our family members, fellow workers, and our fallen brethren who are bleeding and dying on the Jericho Road of victimization. We do this out of self-imposed ignorance and love of ease. Heterosexuals are not convinced that homosexuals are gay at all. They normally think of them as very sad. All who are sad are not sinners, but all who sin with the same sex are more than likely sad. All sexual sin is sad, because it is sin. There are far too many who pray sad supplications, sing sad songs, and listen to sad sermons; and that is why they are "sad-you-see." There is nothing sorrier than a sad saint.

The Masses in Sin

Those who are strangers to sin must reach the masses that are caught within. Jesus did this very thing on the cross, when He became sin for us. *"The Lord hath laid on Him the iniquity of us all,"* declared the prophet (Is. 53:6b). He became propitiation for our sins. He took our place. The Son of God became a Son of man to make sons of men, sons of God. The divine became human to restore the divine in the human. The heavenly came to earth to take us to Heaven. The rich became poor that we might be rich. The blessed became cursed that we might be blessed. The Savior became a sinner that we might be saved. The late Christian author, Derek Prince, called this, "the great exchange." The exchange rate of Heaven is: If you give Him the old filthy garment, He will give you a robe of pure white. It is without a doubt the deal of the millennium and in the words of St. Paul, *"How shall we escape, if we neglect so great a salvation?"* (Heb. 2:3)

The Masses Are Messed Up

Jesus was the ultimate Good Samaritan, who went about doing good, not just for some, but for the whole world (see Acts 10:38). He was a stranger to this world, for even His own did not know Him and they received Him not (see Jn. 1:11). Despite this, Jesus identified with the masses of messed-up humanity and died *vicariously, violently,* and *victoriously.* We have the same *purpose* (to reconcile the world); the same *potential* (through the love shed abroad in our hearts); and the same *power* (the *exousia*, the right to do, and the *dunamis*, the ability to do) that the Master Teacher had. The salvation of our generation is not the work of soothsayers, social scientists, or prognosticating psychics. It is ours alone. We are the Church, the pillar and ground of the truth. Divine design dictates that the Church meet the needs of dying and half-dead victims (see Lk. 10:30) by *sharing, caring,* and *bearing* the insignia of the love of Jesus. This will fulfill the exhortation to let our light so shine and glorify God with our good works (see Mt. 5:16). Then the Church will truly be a *Christian* one and thus we will have become truly *Christ-like.*

The Saving Station for the Masses

The Church is constructed as a saving station for the masses and not merely a social center to conduct a mass gathering. The Church serves an authentic God and considers ungodliness anathema. If the *"righteous shall scarcely be saved, where shall the sinner and ungodly appear?"* (see 1 Pet. 4:18) The Church is not to be an *anti-homosexual, straight saints-only* conclave of congregants. There is no greater evidence of true love than when a believer lays down his *self* life for others. *Christ-like* compassion produces a Christian Church. *Christ-like* compassion is tough but tender, and it will reach the sexually challenged person who realizes his need for reality and for a taste of a life free from sexual gridlock. Christ-like compassion in gracious action will disarm the militant gay agenda at its core. Christ-like compassion qualifies one to be called a Christian (see Acts 11:26).

> CHRIST-LIKE COMPASSION IN GRACIOUS ACTION WILL DISARM THE MILITANT GAY AGENDA AT ITS CORE.

Those bleeding on life's Jericho Road are the STD victims. STD's are Spirit-Transferred Diseases and Soul-Tie Dis-eases. Their lives are in a state of daily dis-ease. They have been "dissed" by the devil. The *dying* AIDS victims, who have been recipients of Accusation, Intimidation, Deception, and Seduction, are ready to receive the oil of the Spirit of God, and the wine of the joy of the Lord. The 64 million-dollar question does not compare with the millennial millions of years old question: *Is the "oil and wine" Christ-like Church ready to receive the real harvest of Jesus Christ? The Master Teacher showed us in His life as well as in His death that the harvest is truly plenteous, but the labourers (the Good Samaritans) are truly few* (see Mt. 9:36-38).

How to Reach the Masses

"...I stand amazed that you (God) should call me friend."

– Lyrics of "Radical for Christ"

Greater love hath no man than this, that a man lay down his life for his friends (John 15:13).

Jesus reached the masses by being the ultimate Good Samaritan and prototype prophetic Minister. He is the pattern Preacher, as well as the perfect Son. Even as Jesus only did that which He saw the Father do, the Church is to do only as we have seen of Jesus. Jesus sacrificially laid down His *self-life.* He was not *self-seeking, self-willed, self-sufficient,* or a *self-preservationist.* His whole purpose was to live and die for the benefit and betterment of others. In First Corinthians 15:31, Paul says, "*I die daily.*" Usually people do not welcome death before their days are fulfilled, so the law of self-preservation is definitely understandable. However, God perfects His life and love in us as we lay down our *self-life.* The emphasis here is on the word *self.* Self is not stealthy because it can easily be seen, when it is in operation. The apostle John said, "*We know that we have passed from death unto life* [zoe: the God-kind of life]...*we ought to lay down our lives for the brethren* [psuche: the self kind of life]" (1 Jn. 3:14-16 emphasis added).

The goal of Christ-like life is to walk in unselfish love. Love is the fruit of a regenerated spirit. Therefore, authentic Christianity is a lifelong love lesson. Love lessons are life lessons learned in the classroom of the concerned and compassionate. God's classroom is the *world of reality.* When life lessons are learned, they leave a legacy for the lineage. The Church must join the great John Wesley, who once said that the "world" was his "parish." The world is best defined as the unregenerate, the unsaved, and the lost, and thus it is inclusive of the gay and the lesbian person. The world is the *cosmos,* the orderly arrangement of the material and non-material elements. The world is the *aion,* the age or the dispensation of time. The prophetic nature of the Church is demonstrated through its prophetic ministry to the masses who have lost their way on the lonely highway. It is a painful, bloody, dangerous (and the wrong) way.

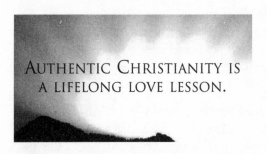

AUTHENTIC CHRISTIANITY IS A LIFELONG LOVE LESSON.

—PROPHETIC MINISTRY—

And by chance there came down a certain priest that way: and when he saw him, he passed by on the other side. And likewise a Levite, when he was at the place, came and looked on him, and passed by on the other side (Luke 10:31-32).

Jesus was Heaven's Prophet, sent to the earth to rescue a runaway planet. His life was an *inclusive* one and not an "us and them" *seclusive* statement of God's love. Jesus paid the ultimate cost to reach the lost. His deeds are recorded in the Bible, a Book of the *lost* and *found*. The church (the priest and Levite) was called in as the lost, before it was called out. The word for *church* in the Greek New Testament is *ecclesia*, which means, "the called out ones." During the New Testament times, they were known as people of "the Way" (see Acts 19:23)! The prophetic ministry of the "oil and wine" Church is to engage those who have lost their way on the lonely highway of life. The bloody way of death is surrounded by thieves along the way.

Those Who Have Lost Their Way

Each of us was counted among the lost until we *found Christ*, or better stated, until He *found us*. After all, He was not lost. He is our example. The Church is a place for the *lost to be found* so that they can become *finders of the lost*. The Father rewards with a very significant finder's fee. The Church is comprised of many who have been *convicted*, and thus they have been converted from the gay and lesbian lifestyle. The Church is not an ecclesiastical intelligentsia of insulated individuals who in their isolation cannot identify with the who, what, where, and whys of life. The Church is a hospital and not a hotel. The Church is a training center and not a penal center. *The Church is a place where whether you are a whore or a homosexual you will not be told no. Whether you come from the ghetto, the get-mo, or whether your name is Flo, Joe, or Bo makes no difference. The Church is to be a discrimination-free institution of higher learning, lifting, loving, and leading the lost into the life of Christ. He will in no wise reject those who come to Him. This is a gracious word for the gay and lesbian community.*

Life's Lonely Highway

The go-spel is still good news. In the words of R.W. Shambach, "The only pill you need is the gos-pill." St. Paul says, "*For I am not ashamed of the gospel of Christ: for it is the power of God unto salvation to every one that believeth; to the Jew first, and also to the Greek*" (Rom. 1:16). Jesus *volitionally* gave His life out of love for the straight, the gay, and the lesbian, as well as those in every category from A to Z. That includes the nympho, the switch hitter, and the no show. That includes the asexual, the bi-sexual, the homosexual, the heterosexual, and the tri- (try anything) sexual. *Upon the cross, Jesus looked beyond the outward appearance and saw the inner appeal. He looked beyond the needy lifestyle and saw the style of a new life. He looked beyond the perverted tendencies and saw potential testimonies. He looked beyond private preferences and saw perfected praise. He looked beyond orientation and saw opportunity. He looked beyond problems in upbringing and saw possibilities that are unlimited. He looked beyond paralyzing predispositions and saw transformed temperaments. He looked beyond the faults and saw the needs.* This is a gracious word for the gay and lesbian community.

The Painful Way

Satan, the original double agent, works hard to convince believers who see the homosexual in his plight, to pass by, far away from the *painful place.* He convinces the Church to write them off as unregenerate degenerates who deserve to be reserved and not conserved. However, the truth is that if those of us who are heterosexual got what we deserved, who then could stand? *"All have sinned, and come short of the glory of God"* (Rom. 3:23). It is because of God's mercy, and only because of it, that His justice does not jolt us with immediate rejection instead of consummate election.

Satan works to convince the Church to pass by the homosexual by convincing them that he is *incorrigible* and *unchangeable.* By accomplishing this, he has undermined the power of the blood of Jesus in the hearts and minds of Christendom. If Jesus' shed blood stops short of transforming a particular person (and it does not), then what else can it not affect? This is the de facto reality of denying its power over homosexuality.

And Jesus answering said, A certain man went down from Jerusalem to Jericho, and fell among thieves, which stripped him of his raiment, and wounded him, and departed, leaving him half dead (Luke 10:30).

The Bloody Way

The road to Jericho was known as the "bloody way." It was crime-ridden and thief-infested. It was equivalent to the most dangerous streets in the drug-ridden inner cities. It represents the way of sin today, which is a way of blood. Ironically, the Jericho Road was often used by Jews who wanted to avoid contact with Samaritans as they traveled to Jerusalem. The Samaritans were half-breed Jews whose history and heritage traced back to the days of Jewish captivity. Many of the captives engaged in mixed marriages that resulted in producing miscegenational offspring. To the orthodox Jews, they represented the days of deracination. Therefore, Samaritans were treated like second-class citizens, much like the minority cultures in America in earlier decades. They were viewed as dogs, and treated as mutts (the common name for non-thoroughbred dogs). The Good Samaritan crossed the tracks to minister a prophetic solution for a pathetic situation.

The Wrong Way

Several years ago, I was privileged to minister at a church in the Northeast. I was in my early 20's, and the pastor was one of the greatest preachers, singers, and musicians whom I have ever met. For a number of years, he invited me to come and minister to his people. He was such a blessing to me that it pains me to relate the rest of the story. While conducting a revival service at the church, I saw an open vision of him on a train. All of a sudden, the train *switched tracks*, and the vision ended before there was a crash. I made the unintentional mistake of prophesying this publicly, and it obviously caused him some chagrin. He was actually quite livid at my insensitive audacity. The truth is, I did not understand at that time that the spirit of the prophet is subject to the prophet and that for every true prophesy, timing is also critical. Consequently, he never invited me back to preach there again.

Within three years, this precious brother was dead. Though he was married, the father of several children, the pastor of a successful church, a gospel singer par excellence, and a gifted preacher, there was just one chink in his armor. He was also a closet homosexual. He had come out of it, but unbeknownst to me at the time that I saw the open vision of the train switching tracks, he was living his life as a "switch-hitter." His code name in the gay world of his double life was David. This became known because there were other church attendees who were also living the double life, and upon his demise, they revealed it. In his last days, this former "Davidic worshiper" had sunk down to a gay David, dying in a hospital bed of a blood disease. Soon thereafter, AIDS was touted as a public pestilence, and everybody knew that this brother was quite possibly stricken by it. What a supreme tragedy. He was the joy of his family and one of the brightest stars to light the Christian sky. The open vision did not end in a crash because there did not have to be one. He did not die of AIDS; he died of disobedience to the prophetic solution for his pathetic situation. There are many Davids like him who line the church pews, sing in the church choirs, preach in the pulpits, and yes, they even pastor churches. Sometimes, even your daddy can be a "David" and your mother can be a "Davina."

The Deadly Way

In the text of the Good Samaritan, "a certain man" represents the sinner. He was assaulted, and an ordinary everyday journey became a jostling match with death. All sinners are not homosexual, but all practicing homosexuals are sinners. This also applies to immoral heterosexuals. The homosexual population is an estimated two to five percent of the population at large. The Church can no longer avoid the gay and lesbian person. It is estimated that in every church of at least two hundred members, five-to-ten men and two-to-five women have either participated in or are currently practicing the lifestyle of same-sex attraction. As with all statistical studies, these numbers vary with each particular local church and decrease or increase accordingly. The infamous Kinsey Report, which was published several decades ago, purports that ten percent of the population are either gay or lesbian. All other reputable studies consider this a humongous exaggeration. Anyone who has been victimized in life is the "certain man." He "fell among thieves." The thief's motto is, "What's yours is mine." Satan is known as a thief and murderer (see Jn. 8:44). He steals innocence and integrity. He violates virginity and confiscates victory.

Thieves Along the Way

Jesus was crucified between two thieves. One was converted, while the other complained. One was saved, the other was sentenced. One believed, the other was belligerent. One was promised paradise, the other was simply pronounced dead. One was translated from death to life in his dying moments. The other went from life to death, when his moments ran out. One was befriended by the Savior, and the other was beset by his sin. Jesus knew how to kill an enemy by making him a friend. It is the thesis of this writing that people are not created homosexual, but rather they are caused to be and sometimes they choose to be that way. Life brings many thieves. Pre-natal, post-natal, parental, and personal ordeals seek to steal one's sanity, sensitivity, and sexual identity.

Where was this man going? Was he on his way to Jerusalem to worship? Was he on his way to the inn? If he was, we can say that the Samaritan loved him to the end, to his final destination. Was he returning from Jerusalem, on his way to Jericho? If so, he would have been in need of even further follow-up ministry. Ministry encounters people coming and going.

Touching the Dead on the Way

According to the Mosaic Law, a priest would become unclean if he touched a dead body (see Lev. 21:1-4). The priest's *religious laws* kept him from *reaching out* in compassion. When nobody reaches, nobody gets touched. The Levite looked on the man, saw his condition close up, and then made the decision not to help him. Both the priest and the Levite could have helped, but they were unwilling to share what they had. Their motto was, "What I have is mine." Dr. Martin Luther King Jr., in his last speech, "I've Been to the Mountaintop," interpreted this text by saying that the priest and the Levite both asked the question, *"If I stop to help this man, what will happen to me?"* The Good Samaritan, said Dr. King, asked a different question: *"If I do not stop to help this man, what will happen to him?"* The people erupted in applause because he was referring to the garbage collectors of Memphis, Tennessee, whom he was endeavoring to assist to receive higher wages and benefits. The next day he was killed by an assassin's bullet.

On another occasion, Dr. King told the story of driving alone in his car one night and seeing a male hitchhiker. He confessed that he had kept driving and passed the man by, because he was very concerned for his safety. That truthful confession prompted a different audience response of laughter. The truth is, human nature is very self-preserving; it is quite understandable and should not be viewed as regrettable. After all, if you do not take care of and save yourself first, who else can you depend on to do it for you? In fact, every time you board an airliner, the airline staff will always tell you that in the unlikely event of a loss of cabin air pressure, you are to put your mask on yourself first and then on your child if you're traveling with one. Self-preservation is a basic instinct, and it should not be penalized by prejudiced opinion. However, *gracious* ministry requires the gratuitous giving of relief to those touched by the thieves of *life*.

> PEOPLE ARE NOT CREATED HOMOSEXUAL, BUT RATHER THEY ARE CAUSED TO BE AND SOMETIMES CHOOSE TO BE THAT WAY.

—POST-MODERN RELIGION—

For ye may all prophesy one by one, that all may learn, and all may be comforted (1 Corinthians 14:31, emphasis added).

St. Paul says that *"all may prophesy."* All believers should be prophetic and not just religious. The priest and the Levite represent *religion* in the post-modern age. *Post-modern* refers to the time period after the industrial age. It is inclusive of the information age and the technology age. Religion during this age is composed of three things.

The first element is *ritualism*, which is doing things the same way all the time. Rituals *bind* people and can often *blind* people. Religious ritualism will keep you from thinking outside the box.

117

The second element is *ceremonialism*. That is, adhering to specific customs, traditions, pomp, and circumstance. Religion always requires a liturgy. However, a move of God simply requires a relationship. Submission and subjection to the will of God is the "trump card" of the day. All other programs are subject to change by order of the Holy Spirit. Religion will resist change like a dog resists the dog catcher. It will resist change like a mouse resists a trap, while attempting to steal the cheese. It will resist change like a fish resisting the hook, while nibbling the worm. Religion is an unholy Houdini that will not submit, and will not quit, even though it is ill-legit.

The third element is *legalism*—that is, rules and regulations, laws and bylaws. Legalism deals in externals. Love deals in internals. Legalism cleans the outside of the cup; love cleans the dirty inside. Legalism makes you look good. Love makes you live good. Legalism is Pharisaical. Love is practical.

Woe unto you, scribes and Pharisees, hypocrites! for ye are like unto whited sepulchres, which indeed appear beautiful outward, but are within full of dead men's bones, and of all uncleanness. Even so ye also outwardly appear righteous unto men, but within ye are full of hypocrisy and iniquity (Matthew 23:27-28).

Fishing Poles Versus Nets

The priest represents church leaders, and the Levite represents church members. Their style of leadership is easily seen in their attitude towards sexually sinful people. They fish with poles versus nets. The Kingdom of Heaven is likened to a *man casting a net that draws all manner of fish*. The Kingdom of Heaven is not a fishing pole with bait for specific fish. Many churches function this way. They fish with hooks and bait, rather than with wide-open nets which are equivalent to outstretched arms. When God the Father was asked the question, "How much do You love the world?" He replied, "*So much that I'll give My only begotten Son*." John 3:16 could have said that He loved us *much*, but instead it says that He "*so*" loved. The little word "*so*" makes so much difference in the meaning. They asked Christ how much He loved the world. He shut His mouth, became silent, and submitted. In closing His mouth, He was opening His magnanimous heart. He stretched His arms wide, and while they were stretched wide, they hung Him high. Three days later, He came out of the grave with arms that were still wide-open saying, "*All power is given unto Me in heaven and in earth. Go ye therefore, and teach all nations...*" (Mt. 28:18b-19). Max Lucado says that Jesus stretched open His arms and said, "Tah-dah!"

Present Versus Ultimate Reality

The post-modern Church needs to be a reality Church, not just a religious one. To effectively engage homosexuality, church leaders (priests) and church members (Levites) need training in *homo-reality*. *Anyone embracing a virulent, vitriolic, and even venomous anti-homosexual attitude does not represent the Lord. The Church opposes the sin of homosexuality but not the homosexuals themselves.* The Samaritans (half-Jews) were despised by the Jews because they represented something in Jews' own past that they did not want to remember. All of us have things in our past that we conveniently choose to forget. Anything under the blood should not be dug up for display. In order to reach *ultimate purpose, a person must master his present reality by dealing with the "dead Egyptians" that are buried under the sand.* This is an analogous reference to Moses, who killed an Egyptian and then

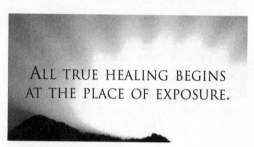

ALL TRUE HEALING BEGINS AT THE PLACE OF EXPOSURE.

buried him under the sand upon fleeing Egypt (see Ex. 2:12). To fulfill his ultimate purpose and become the present *Israelite* leader, he had to deal with his *Egyptian* past. The Church of today must be prepared to become the Church of tomorrow. In the process, we must deal with the dead Egyptians of homophobia buried under the sand. We must dig up the bones buried under the sand. The Bone Collector ministry must bring to the surface what has been submerged in the ground.

> At that time, saith the Lord, they shall bring out the bones [exposure] of the kings of Judah, and the bones of his princes, and the bones of the priests, and the bones of the prophets, and the bones of the inhabitants of Jerusalem, out of their graves: and they shall spread them before the sun [disclosure], and the moon, and all the host of heaven, whom they have loved, and whom they have served, and after whom they have walked, and whom they have sought, and whom they have worshipped: they shall not be gathered, nor be buried; they shall be for dung [closure] upon the face of the earth (Jeremiah 8:1-2).

Exposure of the past brings healing. All true healing begins at the place of *exposure*. *Exposure* brings full *disclosure* and then all involved can experience true *closure*. Without *exposure*, there is no *disclosure*. Without disclosure there is no closure, but rather a doomed repetition of the same-old, same-old. Those who forget the past are doomed to repeat it.

—PATHETIC SITUATIONS—

People Are Dying

First, the certain *man was left half dead.* He was literally on his way out of here. Without help, it was only a matter time. He was halfway to hell, halfway to judgment, and halfway to complete loss of his created purpose and inherent potential. Help was needed desperately. Pathetic situations require prophetic solutions.

People Are Stripped

Secondly, this certain man was *stripped.* Have you ever been stripped of something in your life? Wholeness has been stripped from those who struggle with their sexuality. The garment of praise has also been removed. Those who have been depleted and drained by homosexuality have been stripped of their clothing and their covering. The shame of nakedness is the result. They have endured an assault on their dignity. Their issues of privacy are engaged publicly with a spirit of piracy.

People Are Wounded

Thirdly, this certain man was *wounded.* Many gays today are wounded by their families and by the unchallenged sin that is in the house of God. They may not show it on the surface, but there are hurts deep within. Many grow bitter instead of better. A gay person seeking deliverance needs to exercise definitive forgiveness. He must first offer forgiveness to the offender(s), in order to receive forgiveness from the offerer, who is God Himself. Psalmist Donnie McClurkin gives a vivid testimony of this in his life story, *Eternal Victim/Eternal Victor.* He writes,

> You have to let go and stop lamenting about the things in your past. You have to find a way, through faith or counseling, to forgive the ones that did you evil. You have to forgive the abusers and misusers. You have to get over the victim mentality before it causes you any more damage. You have to get over the "licking of your wounds."[5]

People Are Alone

Fourthly, this certain man was *left alone.* The word *alone* means "all one." The Word of God states that it is not good to be alone, or all one (see Gen. 2:18). The late Dean Martin sang a song in the 50's, "Everybody Loves Somebody Sometime." I do not know about that, but I do know that there are times when everybody *needs* somebody. The songwriter says, "I need you,

you need me, that's the way that it is supposed to be." This is a truth in simplistic expression. Another songwriter declared, "I need you, you need me. We're all a part of God's body…I pray for you, you pray me. I need you to survive….It is His will that every need be supplied. You are important to me, I need you to survive." The first death that an AIDS victim dies is a social one. They are left alone by a systematic walkout of friends, associates, and sometimes even their family members.

Dr. King once said that all of humanity is "caught in an inescapable network of mutuality, tied in a single garment of destiny. Whatever affects one directly, affects all indirectly."[6] The half-dead man was stripped, wounded, and alone. Perhaps he was too weak to cry out for help, or perhaps he thought it was useless to do so. Maybe he cried out with all his remaining strength, and the religious community (represented by the priest and the Levite) turned deaf ears to him. The same thing is happening today. The great English missionary to China, India, and Africa, C.T. Studd, once said, "Some want to live within the sound of church or chapel bell; I want to run a rescue shop within a yard of hell."[7] The Church is where and through whom God shows His gracious love.

—PROPHETIC FEELINGS—

That they should seek the Lord, if haply they might feel after Him, and find Him, though He be not far from every one of us (Acts 17:27).

Ours is a generation of feeling where emotions reign supreme. If you touch someone's feelings, you will move their emotions. If you do not, then they will not move and nothing else will either. Empathy is the way to move the multitudes for the move of God. The "oil and wine" Church must "feel" them in their pathetic situations in order to fill them with prophetic solution. Twenty-first century issues of life are making a demand on God's chosen deliverers to pour out "oil and wine" that will eradicate toxic worldly beliefs, assumptions, habits, addictions, aberrant lifestyles, maligned reactions, and poisoned mind-sets—"oil and wine" that will cause a paradigm shift to open prison doors, set the captives free, cause the lame to walk, and the blind to see, so that they can be catapulted into precision prophetic position for their destiny. The revelation of preparation must be preeminent in the hearts of God's true deliverers. An active demonstration of faith in God's Word will reveal who carries the "oil and wine" for the 21st century. The relevant Church that will make a difference will demonstrate the assignment of the Great Commission to work in the world and bring in the harvest. The true carriers of the "oil and wine" will not be wooed by the wiles of the enemy, nor will they be afraid to compassionately approach those whose souls are afflicted by same-sex sin. They will know that they have what it takes to get the job done and administer the gracious word. The parable of the Good Samaritan brings forth the order for deliverance that the Church must embrace in order to bring complete deliverance to the captives. It is a typology of the "oil and wine" Apostolic Church that boldly goes forth into her commission. The Good Samaritan actively flowed through ten moves of faith to bring healing and deliverance to the fallen man. The number ten is prophetically significant in that it indicates the end of a cycle of captivity to a sinner. These ten initiatives provide a blueprint for the brethren who desire to pour in the *oil* and the *wine*. The following list is what the 21st-century Church can do as we continue the ministry of reconciliation of the world unto God, as the ambassadors of Christ (see Eph. 6:20).

—COMPASSIONATE APPROACH—

But a certain Samaritan, as he journeyed, came where he was: and when he saw him, he had compassion on him (Luke 10:33).

The first prophetic solution for the pathetic situation was that *he put passion into action and went to him.* By going *to him* he initiated the flow and course of ministry. This marks the beginning of a new life for the fallen man. By faith, the Good Samaritan took that first step forward and left his place of comfort, seeking to save that which was lost. The priest, the Levite, and the Good Samaritan each saw the same man. However, the Good Samaritan drew near the man and did not let the outward manifestation of deeply rooted infestation repulse him into judgment of a half-dead soul. He went to him without reservation. He had a prophetic perspective. He saw him not simply as he was, but as he could become. (In Chapter Twelve, the issue of perspective is addressed at length.)

His bowels of compassion yearned for this man's deliverance, and brotherly love took charge, shifting him to approach a soul in need of deliverance and healing. The priest and the Levite saw the man from a pathetic perspective. They were both operating from the spirit of rejection as they passed by this person who was in need. Rejection projected more negatives, binding the man tighter in darkness. The order in which the Good Samaritan moved reveals that he was a man knowing what his purpose was as he utilized what his hand had found to do. The "oil and wine" Church must take their preparation for ministry seriously; otherwise, souls will slip into hell because the Church is not ready for the engagement of prophetic ministry.

The "oil and wine" Church will not be a church that ordains ministers without a thorough searching, fearless moral inventory of their life, and a working out of their salvation. It is the normal course of preparation to go to basic training before going to the front line of battle. It is not practical to fight a battle without allowing yourself to expel out of your being that which the enemy can use to hinder your prophetic flow. Twenty-first century "oil and wine" carriers are true deliverers. They will not only have the biblical academia, but also will have made personal paradigm shifts into high levels of discernment by dealing with every issue of their own personal journey with God. Prophetic ministry is not an academic exercise, but it is an awesome demonstration of the anointing. There can be no deliverance by the hands of the undelivered. A purpose without preparation leads to ineffectual ministry. Anyone can pour out what is in them, but the key is the ability to pour it in. Prophetic ministry is when the "oil and wine" leaves you and enters those in need of it. To minister deliverance, one must be willing to give all for the sake of the call. Ministers must be monitored by elders with experience.

> PROPHETIC MINISTRY IS NOT AN ACADEMIC EXERCISE, BUT IT IS AN AWESOME DEMONSTRATION OF THE ANOINTING OF THE OIL AND THE WINE.

This will facilitate "working out of their salvation" by addressing issues that have hindered them from maximizing their full ministry potential. Personal issues left to fester into putrefying wounds place the Church in a disadvantaged state with open doors to spirits of gross neglect, dereliction of duty, depression, and many more demonic schemes of darkness that silence the prophetic voice in the Church. Wounded people continue to wound others if the imbalances are not discovered.

Issues of life hide in numerous crevices, ultimately manifesting symptoms of stages of codependency, such as repetitive imbalances in emotions, dysfunctional relationships, poor financial stewardship, eating disorders, sexually aberrant lifestyles, activity shifts, unstable spiritual beliefs and practices, employment instabilities, incarcerations, addictions, physical illness, mental health disturbances, and educational setbacks, to name a few. Eventually this shifts people out of stability and into passive/aggressive stances, ultimately skewing their prophetic vision.

The fivefold ministry gifts must connect for a collective effort. Their strength as a team will acknowledge and annihilate unstable issues that have killed some of the greatest warriors of all time. Together, with a *nouthetic* approach of confrontation, a genuine concern for the standards of the Word of God, and a desire to provoke change, the application of Scripture will shift fallen individuals back to proper stance for clarity of vision.

The apostle Paul used the term *nouthesia* in Romans 15:14 as he encouraged the Church to engage in informal, mutual counseling. He wrote, *"And I myself also am persuaded of you, my brethren, that ye also are full of goodness, filled with all knowledge, able also to admonish one another."* In addition, St. Paul instructs that all Scripture is breathed out by God and useful for teaching in righteousness in order to fully equip ministers for every good task. God's fivefold ministers are responsible for lovingly confronting with Scripture and not their own ideas, trusting that the breathed Word of God will cause transformation in every area of an individual's life. *Noutheteo*— that is admonishing, correcting, and instructing with the Word of God— gives counseling the warmth of a family helping one another to become more like Christ.

Any approach less than this will paralyze the Church from moving in the direction of those who are lost along the way. In particular, the gay and the lesbian require much more than superficial ministry. They require specialized ministry of gracious love. The Good Samaritan went to him. The "oil and wine" Church must engage the homosexual culture in our effort to emancipate it. While saving their soul we will soon discern that we are actually saving our own.

—HE BOUND UP THE EXTERNAL WOUND—

And went to him, and bound up his wounds... (Luke 10:34).

The second prophetic solution for the pathetic situation was that the Good Samaritan *bound up the external wound.* He was not only prepared to go to the fallen man, but he also noticed the traumas of his life that required immediate attention. When God gives you prophetic sight to see another's wounds that have hindered them from their destiny, He also stirs compassion in your spirit that He desires that none should perish. The Good Samaritan interceded for this man by intervening on his behalf, reinforcing that *"two are better than one"* (Eccl. 4:9). Two is representative of divinity and humanity. God shows up divinely to work through human vessels to bring His power and strength. We are colaborers with Him. Prayer is a conversation with Deity, and ministry is contact with Deity.

True warriors of the "oil and wine" Church will know how to bring forth intercession and tie down the enemy from striking repetitive battle blows so that intervention can begin. The prophet Isaiah spoke of *"wounds, and bruises, and putrifying sores: they have not been closed, neither bound up, neither mollified with ointment"* (Is. 1:6). Wounds are often deep and unseen. A bruise is on the surface and is easily seen. In an effort to conceal past hurts, sometimes people cover their bruises. Though undetected, the bruises remain. A putrifying sore is seen, sensitive, and has a signature. *It stinks.* Infected souls ooze uncleanness.

The "oil and wine" Church that offers prophetic ministry cannot avoid specifically tailoring programs to train its people for 21st-century ministry. It is practical to learn of the besetments of life before engaging in ministry. It is not practical to attempt to minister to some-

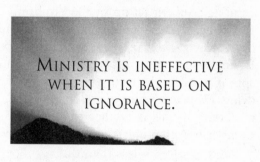

MINISTRY IS INEFFECTIVE WHEN IT IS BASED ON IGNORANCE.

thing you know nothing about. Ministry is ineffective when it is based on ignorance. It is no wonder that many gay and lesbian individuals have been wounded in the house of friends. Unskilled and insensitive doctors generally do not have many returning patients.

It is important to note that the pouring of the oil and the applying of the wine did not begin until the wounds were bound. Too often, the Church has poured out oil (anointing) without accurate intercessory engagement, resulting in prophetic words falling to the ground, as well as people not being changed. Faith comes by hearing the Word of God. Many sit on the pews with spiritual hearing deficits that are caused by demonic interference as they hold inside traumatic life attacks and suffer in silence. An implosion can be just as damaging as an explosion. Those who are *preyed* upon need someone who has *prayed* for them.

The Samaritan was not a physician, but he was prophetic. If there were any internal wounds, he could do nothing about them, but that did not stop him from doing what he could. *Everyone should do what they can, while they can, for as long as they can. An act of kindness is great, but a life of benevolence is greater.* Resolve to *be all* and *do all* that you can to help another soul, including the gay and lesbian one. As you sow mercy, you shall also receive it when needed. Prayers never roll on the wheels of inevitability. They are answered as the result of persistent efforts to work with God. The prophetic solution of binding up the external wounds helped the man deal with the pathetic situation. The "oil and wine" Church must master the ministry of binding and loosing. Unless we do this, the bleeding will continue, and result in death.

—HE POURED IN THE OIL—

And went to him, and bound up his wounds, pouring in oil... (Luke 10:34).

The third prophetic solution for the pathetic situation was that the Good Samaritan *poured in the oil, which represents anointed ministry.* This was a defining moment set up by God to bring the healing balm so that recovery could begin. Jesus rose on the third day. The "oil and wine" Church is a third-day Church. *Three* represents Divine perfection, Divine manifestation, and Divine resurrection. Good Samaritan Christians are reinforcements, who appear to bring the resurrecting power of anointed ministry to the lost and dying. *The pouring out of the oil* brings light and life to supercede all the effects of darkness. This is further expounded in the next chapter entitled, "The Composite Anointing: Ministry in the New Millennium."

—HE APPLIED THE WINE—

*And went to him, and bound up his wounds, pouring in **oil and wine**...*
(Luke 10:34, emphasis added).

The fourth prophetic solution for the pathetic situation was that the Good Samaritan *graciously applied the wine.* The number *four* prophetically speaks of earthly completeness, universality, and creativity. When the love of God and the Word of God is applied to human weakness, the result is a *processing for earthly completeness.* The applying of the wine was done after the pouring of the oil because love (wine) is what makes anointing (oil) work. Fermented wine is aged and processed. Deliverance ministry is not something that happens overnight. It is practical to allow a processing of the Word in the spirit of warriors and worshipers. It builds strength and depth of character. It is not practical to pour *unprocessed wine* on people in need of help. When the *fermented* wine of love is applied into the spirit of a truly awakened soul, then the result is change from glory to glory. Too many saints have had God's Spirit and love applied to their slumbering spirits, yet they remain in stupors, needy, petrified, and stupefied. The candle of their spirit was lit at salvation, but the flame has been limited and flickering. Anointed prophetic deliverers will have the sight to see firmly rooted toxicities that have made their way into the hearts of men. They will carry the understanding of how to *take the axe to the bitter root that springs up trouble, defiling many* (see Heb.

12:15). The Good Samaritan knew when to *apply the wine* to bring the desired effects of deliverance. So should the end-time "oil and wine" Church. The anointed Word without practical application will only result in more confusion in the person's life. It is equivalent to getting excited about a picture of a destination, but not being furnished with a road map. To get happy without receiving help is only hype. The end result is that the sheep is skinned. You can fleece a sheep many times, but you can skin them only once. God's refined teachers in the Church must come forth to minister to those who need to know how to enact Scripture into an active force in their lives.

The *compassionate approach* requires the application of the wine, which is representative of love. Cults are successful, not because of gracious love, but because they indoctrinate their victims with specifics of how to live the standards that match their doctrines. They provide a support net in case they fail to successfully keep the rules. The true army of God must be skillfully ready with their spiritual radar attuned to readily assist any breaks in application of the anointed Word. When you join an army, you must maintain a code of ethics and honor. You are taught the high standards and you learn to live by them. Anything short of that could possibly have grave consequences. The "oil and wine" Church must press beyond our own carnality, lay down our own agendas, and seize divine moments to bring mobility and life to all, including God's gay and lesbian children. The prophetic solution of pouring in the wine is not mere rhetoric, but it is righteousness revealed in demonstration.

—HE TOOK PERSONAL RESPONSIBILITY—

...and set him on his own beast... (Luke 10:34).

The fifth prophetic solution for the pathetic situation was that the Good Samaritan *took personal responsibility for the wounded soul.* He picked the man up in his dirty, bloody condition and set him on his own beast. In order to do this, he had to pick the man up with hands of healing and lift him in arms of agape. It probably meant that he had to walk for a short season rather than ride his own beast. If he also sat on his beast, his beast was double-burdened. Either way, he modeled the sacrifice associated with prophetic ministry. Personal commitment is never easy, nor is it necessarily difficult. Knowing the purpose he was prepared for, the Good Samaritan pressed beyond the tendency toward selfishness. Personal ministry offered a propelling motion by mounting the man on his own beast. This injured man had been paralyzed in the natural from reaching his purpose in the spiritual. God predestinated a person to be in the right place at the right time to assist this fallen soul so that he could reemerge into purposeful living.

The practical lesson for the Church is one of humility of giving what we have to those who need it. We must link arms with those who have fallen and be their legs for them, giving them the strength of our walk until they can stand on their own. Deliverers will stick with the souls brought in the harvest, until they can walk by faith, operating from sound minds. They may kick and scream like a little child until the deliverance is complete, but they will say thank you in the end. To set the homosexual on our beast is to set them upon our burden and to pray for them as if it were our own son or daughter. Taking personal responsibility is an effective way of eliminating the excuses for non-involvement and it is the *compassionate approach*.

—HE ARRANGED RESIDENT RECOVERY—

...and brought him to an inn... (Luke 10:34).

The sixth prophetic solution for the pathetic situation was that the Good Samaritan *arranged resident recovery. Six* is the number of man in his incompleteness. It is one number short of seven, the perfect number. The inn is a wonderful place, but it cannot replace the perfection of the secret place. The Good Samaritan brought him under cover to refuge, a place of protection from the enemy. The inn is representative of the church. It is a place of residential recovery where the Holy Spirit (oil) is resident and president. Ministry will offer safety inside the gates.

Shame continues to follow a person even when they have exited the mean streets and have come into the Lord's house. The "oil and wine" Church is responsible for gently leading lost souls out of the violence of shame that molests the human spirit. People who have suffered shame keenly sense when it is reappearing in sermon topics or insensitive saints. The lack of compassion is obvious and quite offensive. They will recoil into hesitancy if they hear it coming from preachers with legalistic overtones masqueraded in haranguing words that are hard and harsh. It will not be long before they will be gone.

Just as a hotel has front desk workers, receptionists, and concierges who courteously care for the concerns of customers, the "oil and wine" Church must be ready to court the gay and lesbian community who come needing holistic help. Deliverance ministers must fine-tune their approach to assure that all avenues of ministry to the wounded spirit offer a protection of confidences and that all individuals are free from reprisal that stems from personal opinions and private prejudices. The approach of *"what you see here, what you hear here, when you leave here, will stay here"* must be enforced. Those who pick up someone's (gay or lesbian) secret that has been laid at the altar and take it to others in the form of gossip detonate an internal implosion in the betrayal of trust of their brother or their sister. The greatest fear of a hurting heart is that they will hear their business preached over the pulpit or whispered at the after-church time of fellowship. When the "oil and wine" Church fails to keep a secret, it has failed to keep the faith. When God cannot trust you to be discreet about people's secrets, He will never trust you with any of His own. Just as a hospital operates with confidentiality of its patients, so should the church (the inn). When people feel the safety net of protection, they will keep coming back for more. When they feel like they are the topic of discussion and the object of dissection, to

> DELIVERANCE MINISTERS MUST FINE-TUNE THEIR APPROACH TO ASSURE THAT THEY OFFER A PROTECTION OF CONFIDENCES.

be sliced and diced, they will disappear into the dark hole of shame again. When people come to the *inn* with their *sin*, we should let them *in*, help them to get well *again*, and pray fervently that the man will be the man and the woman will be the woman that each was naturally created to be. The perverting of their nature will have been dealt a decisive death blow and *wholeness* will be the new song that they sing. The "oil and wine" Church is the inn and the prophetic solution is ministry that goes out and brings them in, just as Jesus came out of Heaven to one day take us to Heaven. In the interim, He has brought us to the place of residential recovery. It is His favorite place to stay.

—HE ARRANGED FOR SUPPORT MINISTRY—

...and took care of him... (Luke 10:34).

The seventh prophetic solution for a pathetic situation was that *continuing supportive ministry* followed, bringing this man into the house of God. An unconditional support system offering radical recovery must be presented to every seeking soul coming into the house of God. The Good Samaritan took care of him; he did not just take him to an inn and leave him. This represents a *continuing ministry*, and it speaks of the supportive follow-up ministries of the church. Every fish must be scaled, once it is caught. The church has too often made the assumption that only people with active obvious addictions are the ones who need support, while others sit in the church for years who are oppressed, depressed, suppressed, obsessed, and even *possessed*. The seventh act of the Good Samaritan is an act of spiritual surgery. *Seven* is the number of spiritual perfection. Nouthetic counseling, with the Word of God as the scalpel, cuts through all issues, including the hidden ones. As the Word is *"sharper than any twoedged sword, piercing even to the dividing asunder of soul and spirit"* (Heb. 4:12), it reveals bitter roots and maladjustments. That is why it must be anointed with fresh oil.

It is practical to offer therapeutic support to new converts, as well as to every saint. It is not practical to assume that everyone is automatically prophetically aligned for destiny the day they receive salvation and new birth. A person is not secured always, just because they are saved. There are qualifications of continuation. A person must continue in the Word to be a disciple indeed (see Jn. 8:31). Periodic assessments of beliefs and lifestyles will assist in keeping precision in prophetic balance. Deliverance ministers as accountability partners to newly freed captives can divert the plans of the adversary, keeping footholds from becoming strongholds. No person ever graduates from the need for a support system. This includes the highest levels of authority. Human beings do not always see their own situations the way another person outside of those situations see them. Submission to wise counsel is the safety plan of God at all levels. The "oil and wine" Church must never fail to follow up and finish. Nobody bakes a cake and serves it half done. Nobody pays tuition and then never attempts to show up for class. The next time someone says to you, "Take care," reply, "Thanks, but no thanks, because Jesus told me to *cast* all my *care* upon Him (see 1 Pet. 5:7). Therefore, I do not *take care*; I *cast* it." The only *care* the believer is to take is when he *takes care* of another soul. In prophetic ministry, always be careful to be prayerful, because it blesses the seeking soul to be carefree. Years ago, the Greyhound bus company used a slogan that the "oil and wine" Church would do well to heed. They invited the passenger to "Leave the driving to us." No person who enters a bus, an ambulance, or a taxi has to drive for themselves. Likewise, no gay or lesbian person who is drawn by the Holy Spirit should be told to simply take care of himself and stay free of same-sex sin. As we become helpers of one another, it qualifies us to become colaborers with God.

—HE WATCHED AND PRAYED—

And on the morrow when he departed (Luke 10:35a).

The eighth prophetic solution for the pathetic situation was that he stayed until the next day. This speaks of *watching* and *praying,* or overnight ministry. Such ministry shows *real* concern. Remember the words of Jesus: *"Could ye not watch with Me one hour?"* (Mt. 26:40b) *Eight* is the number of new beginnings, the number of a new order of things, the dawning of a new day, and the new beginning that is associated with resurrection and regeneration. The Good Samaritan watched and prayed overnight for this new soul. This spoke of the importance of maintaining the deliverance by being a watchman and a prayer warrior. A new convert or a returning backslider may not necessarily know how to prevent the circumstances from reoccurring that had taken them into the grips of the enemy. Spiritual intensive care until a "regeneration" takes place is crucial; or the enemy will come to steal, kill, and destroy. The practical ministry application of ongoing prayer keeps spiritual sensitivity keen, knocking out sneaky demonic plans. The watchman prayer warrior must make himself available to God to pray at a moment's notice, as it could mean life or death to a soul. True deliverers must move out in boldness to take back what the devil has stolen and take dominion. The "oil and wine" Church must engage in a vigil of prayer if it is to fulfill its prophetic ministry demands.

—HE PAID THE EXPENSE—

...he took out two pence, and gave them to the host... (Luke 10:35).

The ninth prophetic solution for the pathetic situation was that he *paid the expense.* The Good Samaritan covered the cost of the man's lodging for the next two days. Matthew 20:2 indicates that laborers were hired to do a day's work for one penny. Two pence was worth two days' wages to the Samaritan. The average person today makes about $15 an hour, or about $120 a day. Two pence equates to giving the innkeeper approximately $250 for the care of the wounded man. He placed value on the man by giving two days' wages for his lodging. The Good Samaritan saw that this was a son of the double portion who was worthy of the double sacrifice. Proverbially speaking, he did not just go one mile with him, but he went two (see Mt. 5:41). Placing value on someone who has been devalued is the practical lesson in this parable. The "oil and wine" Church must not operate as the "old-way" church. It must not draw in all manner of fish and then discard the ones it does not want for whatever reason. There was hardly a single effort, let alone a double one. The Church must *e-valu-*ate its assessment of another person's soul. To do this, one must see things as God sees them. The very one who is callously rejected by the priest and the Levite is the very one that Heaven concentrates on reaching. That is why all of Heaven rejoices at the repentance of even one sinner (see Lk. 15:7). It is reported that the late Sam Walton built the multibillion dollar Wal-Mart business teaching his associates that "customers still walk through the door one at a time." The "oil and wine" Church must practice applying this principal in the Father's business of the redemption of renegade and rebellious gay and lesbian humanity. Homosexuals are human beings, and they deserve to be treated with human dignity. Even animals are afforded the protection of the humane society. Shame on the church that operates like the infamous National Lampoon's Animal House! Ministry to others should be devoid of devaluation and deprecation. The person who is appreciated will never be depreciated. The prophetic solution will yield enormous dividends amongst those who were formerly deprived during the state of their depravity. *"All have sinned and come short of the glory of God"* (Rom. 3:23). Jesus has paid it all. All to Him we owe. The believer who picks up the tab for others is in reality making an interest payment on a debt of gratitude to Jesus Himself.

The gay and lesbian community needs more anointed Good Samaritans. His actions of pouring in the oil and applying the wine were done freely and from the heart. There was no tab left for the man to pay. Although the Samaritans were looked down upon, this minister of the Lord's justice did not allow the low blows of low self-esteem and the stigma of racial ostracism to dissuade him. He did not allow bitterness to block the blessed flow of oil. Instead, he provided much more than a *"Band-Aid"* for the bleeding and dying one. He provided the *"belief"* that life would be better. His benevolence bestowed bountiful beneficence.

—HE APPOINTED A PASTOR—

Take care of him; and whatsoever thou spendest more, when I come again, I will repay thee (Luke 10:35b).

The tenth prophetic solution for a pathetic situation was to *appoint a pastor*. In other words, the innkeeper served in the role as an appointed under-shepherd, or someone to watch for his soul. When God is in the matter, He will never leave you alone. The appointment of someone to watch over this man's soul completed the task at hand. The lesson here is that God does not lead a person out of the gay club to lose them to that life again. He brings them into the house of God to sit them at the feet of a shepherd. The appointed pastor, who is apt to teach, possesses time-tested truth to keep them from returning to their former tendency (see 1 Tim. 3:2). Practical ministry offers the opportunity for one to sit under a pastor after God's heart who will teach the person to love God with all of their heart. Without a pastor, the person will relapse, and the cycle will restart. The latter state will be worse than the beginning. Every gay or lesbian person who comes to Christ must get a pastor with all their getting. *Ten* is the number of the end of a cycle, the end of wandering without spiritual direction, the end of submitting to sexual sabotage, the end of listening to the triggering toxic echoes, the end of being without protection, the end of feeling alone without help, the end of immobility, and the end of being without a Father. At ten, the gay or lesbian can announce, "I'm through with the sin of being sexually intimate with men, or of being a lesbian."

He told the innkeeper that if the care cost more, he would pay it when he returned. What a limitless love! When a pastor walks in love, the sermons make a lot more sense. Even when people do not understand the sermon, they will still sense God speaking to them through it. We often *talk too much and do too little*. Dr. David Yonggi Cho pastors a great church in South Korea where the membership has exceeded 750,000. One of the secrets to this accelerated church growth is found in Dr. Cho's teaching to the body of believers. He instructs that they are not to witness to any person about Christ until they have done at least three good deeds for them first. This is the embodiment of the statement that actions speak louder than words. When people see the *"Word made flesh,"* they will be able to then see God's glory, which is full of grace and truth (see Jn. 1:14,18).

As the "oil and wine" Church embraces this ten-step process, it will never see a barren altar. Demons will have to let go, and major shifts of conscience will happen. Each delivered soul will then be equipped to deliver someone else from same-sex sin. The gay church will empty and God's Church will be filled with those escaping sin's false-comforting clutches. The plan for the gay and lesbian's deliverance is God-given. Now, we must use it. The "oil and wine" Church must have prophetic pastoral coverings for those whose preference presumes upon grace. The Master Teacher said, *"Heal the sick, cleanse the lepers, raise the dead, cast out devils: freely ye have received, freely give"* (Mt. 10:8, emphasis added). St. Paul declared, *"Now we have received, not the spirit of the world, but the spirit which is of God; that we might know the things that are freely given to us of God* (1 Cor. 2:12, emphasis added).

The Compassionate Approach:
In Conclusion—
Prophetic Solutions for Pathetic Situations

The compassionate approach to the gay or lesbian person is the only acceptable course of action. It is not a compassionate conservatism as much as it is a radical realism. The "oil and wine" Church has been given a prophetic mantle that will equip us to speak God's precepts and pronounce God's judgments into every perverse predicament. *To be prophetic means to speak beforehand and to also speak into whatever is at hand. Same-sex sin is an irritating itch in our world, and believers must know where to scratch with the Word.* The challenge today is to avoid being apathetic in addressing what is inappropriately called an "alternative lifestyle." According to the Word of God, it is more aptly termed an abhorrent and aberrant one.

The Church that is prophetic will never be pathetic. The prophet Ezekiel prophesied to the dry bones (souls) and to the wind (spirit). In like manner, the Church must lift its voice declaring the lines of demarcation between clean and unclean, and saved and unsaved. Allowance for everyone's salvation has been made. Acceptance by everyone is the condition. Salvation must be believed for, if it is to be received. It is not any more automatic than drinking fountain water. The water may be there, but the person must open their mouth wide to drink it.

> SAME-SEX SIN IS AN IRRITATING ITCH IN OUR WORLD, AND BELIEVERS MUST KNOW WHERE TO SCRATCH WITH THE WORD.

A prophetic Church provides God's perspective in our respective place. A great apologist, C. Eric Lincoln, has said that the church remains, "...the mother of our culture, the champion of our freedom, the hallmark of our civilization. "[8] Dr. King said, "There was a time when the church was very powerful. It was during that period when the early Christians rejoiced when they were deemed worthy to suffer for what they believed. In those days the church was not merely a thermometer that recorded the ideas and principles of popular opinion; it was a thermostat that transformed the mores of society. "[9] The church should be the one place you can go to be *confronted* while being *comforted*, but never *coerced* or *coaxed* in sin. The church should be where you can get the *oil* and the *wine* of the Spirit and love of God applied in the open wounds of wayward existence. The Good Samaritan was prophetic in that he exercised advanced care while approaching in compassion. He was a prophetic person prepared to minister to pathetic predicaments.

New Millennium Ministers

Prophetic people will roar and soar, and walk through the open doors.

Prophetic people PUSH.

They praise, persevere, and Preach Until Something Happens.

They give the devil his walking papers. They fast (from food) so they can last (the fight). They pray so they can stay. They take it so they can make it.

They seek and find, so they will never lag behind.

They do not sit and then try to get.

They have the upward look of holiness; the inward look of their own sinful hellishness; and the outward look of the world's hopelessness without Christ.

They have faces like the seraphim.
They have flaming swords like the cherubim.

Prophetic people are people of transformation, impartation, manifestation, and demonstration. They touch the untouchable, see the invisible, and hear the inaudible.

They know the unknowable, see the invisible, accomplish the impossible,

and they experience the incredible power of God.

They are New Millennium Ministers.

Prophetic people are absolutely awesome, and they are auspiciously appointed

for the

devastation, obliteration, denigration, degradation, extermination and dilapidation

of the devil.

They take the devil's best shot.

They have everything thrown at them but the kitchen sink.

They take a licking and they still keep ticking.

They are risktakers instead of caretakers.

They look for the uppertaker, and never the undertaker.

They step out of the boat when there is nothing to step on except their faith.

They know, go, and show the way.

They are New Millennium Ministers.

Prophetic people set up the upset and upset the set up.

They can't go under for going over.

They can't go backward for going forward.

They are aggressive and never passive.

They expire, but they do not retire.

They are inspired and refired.

*They challenge, charge, and change the conscience of the crowd,
while they are in passionate pursuit of the cloud.*

*They stand up, and they speak out and into the moral conscience of the society.
When something is right, they affirm it to be so.*

When something is wrong they declare it a no go.

They are not afraid of anything but God, and they hate nothing but sin.

They are prophetic people. They are powerful people.

*They are Esthers who say, "If I perish, let me perish,
but I have favor with the king."*

They are Christ's ambassadorial administers of the compassionate approach.

Prophetic solutions for pathetic situations are par for the course for those who take the Kingdom by force. The new breed is the nu-look Levites and no-nonsense Priests of the Great High Priest. They answer the question, "Where does the Church go from here?" It goes to the Composite Anointing: Ministry in the New Millennium.

Prayer: Gracious and compassionate Father, help us to heal the hurting who are half dead on life's Jericho Road. Grant us the grace of the Good Samaritan as we go about our Father's business. Strengthen our hands as we lift the fallen and strengthen our hearts as we endure the misunderstanding of our efforts. Cause us to have an open eye toward the pathetic situations as we apply the prophetic solution. Cause us to have a closed ear to the cynical chants and the self-righteous rants that are raised in opposition to our outreach. Most of all, in whatever we endeavor to do, let men and women alike declare that they have seen the compassion of the Master Teacher working through us. In Jesus' loving name, we pray. Amen and Amen!

ENDNOTES

1. Edythe Draper, *Draper's Book of Quotations for the Christian World*, (Wheaton, IL: Tyndale House Publishers, Inc., 1992), Entry 1545, Bible Illustrator 3.0 for Windows, Parsons Technology, Inc. 1990-1998, Illustrations Copyrighted at Christianity Today, Inc., 1984-1995, Faircom Corp.

2. Draper, *Draper's Book of Quotations for the Christian World*, (Wheaton: Tyndale House Publishers, Inc., 1992), Entry 1551.

3. Draper, *Draper's Book of Quotations,* Entry 1552.

4. Draper, *Draper's Book of Quotations,* Entry 573.

5. Donnie McClurkin, *Eternal Victim/Eternal Victor* (Lanham, MD: Pneuma Life, 2001), 80.

6. Dr. Martin Luther King, Jr., "Letter From Birmingham Jail," written April 16, 1963.

7. C.T. Studd, retrieved from http://www.wholesomewords.org/echoes/studd.html.

8. C. Eric Lincoln, *The Black Experience in Religion* (Garden City, NY: Anchor Press, 1974), 5.

9. Dr. Martin Luther King, Jr., "Letter From Birmingham Jail," April 16, 1963.

CHAPTER
FOUR

The anointing is also like the dew of Hermon. The Psalmist uses the name of Hermon…because it is a high mountain. Hermon is not just a little hill. Here the water does not come up out of the earth as dew normally covers the fields. The morning dew comes up, but the dew of Hermon descends. Similarly, the anointing must come upon us at the highest point of our experience. The anointing first touches what we raise the highest to God in our life.[1]

Dr. Mark Hanby

The office and function of the "apothecary" appears ten times in the Old Testament. It was the art of the apothecary to "compound" the holy anointing oil for the anointing of priests, utensils, and furniture; and to "temper together" the incense that was offered exclusively to Jehovah before the apothecary was to "rub to pieces or pulverize" the elements of the anointing oil and the incense or perfume. Both were a masterful blend, a divine concoction.[2]

Dr. Kelly Varner

We need to come to terms with what may suddenly become yesterday's anointing. It will do us no good to pretend that what happened yesterday is happening today if it isn't. Dr. Lloyd-Jones told me this story. In his former church in Wales a man stood up to read the Scriptures in a Monday evening prayer meeting. The Spirit came on him in an extraordinary manner. It seemed as if the meeting would go on and on into the night, it was so wonderful. But Dr. Lloyd-Jones eventually closed the meeting (he told me he worried for years that he shouldn't have). The following Monday night the same man tried it again. Dr. Lloyd-Jones said, "I knew he'd try to do it again, and I knew what would happen." It didn't happen. You cannot make yesterday's anointing today's anointing if the Spirit isn't willing.[3]

R. T. Kendall

The Composite Anointing: Ministry in the New Millennium

Then shall the kingdom of heaven be likened unto ten virgins, which took their lamps, and went forth to meet the bridegroom. And five of them were wise, and five were foolish. They that were foolish took their lamps, and took no oil with them: but the wise took oil in their vessels with their lamps....And the foolish said unto the wise, Give us of your oil; for our lamps are gone out. But the wise answered, saying, Not so; lest there be not enough for us and you: but go ye rather to them that sell, and buy for yourselves (Matthew 25:1-4,8-9).

The term *composite* means the complete or sum total of the range of a thing. In ancient Israel, the "Holy Anointing Oil" was made after the art of the apothecary (see Exodus 30:25). The oil of the Holy Spirit is exhilarating, bringing life and breakthrough every hindrance. It is the re-presentation of Christ that resurrects a dying soul, giving hope for an expected end. It is the bringing forth of the ministry placed in the womb of the Church, a ministry of reconciliation, restoration, rehabilitation, and recovery. The light shone forth from the Good Samaritan and caused the fallen man to see that he needed God in his life. Those who have been successful at bringing closure to toxic issues of life must begin to offer brotherly love to those in need of adjustment, namely *the homosexual* among us. The "oil and wine" Church must open their doors for instructional classes, mentoring groups, and support groups that are safe havens for open confession of sins and hurtful wounds. These efforts should be combined with spiritual counseling sessions and intercessory prayer groups that work interdependently with one another to lift the wounded. *Together, the various streams of cooperative ministry can navigate the unchartered waters of holistic ministry and activate life in gay and lesbian persons. This will successfully guarantee that we all can make it to Mt. Hermon and Mt. Calvary together as one body.*

Churches that are indifferent to open exposure, which brings closure, breed sickness and disease at all levels. *You will always discover where your problems are when you discover where your secrets are.* Some churches hide behind lame excuses for inaction hoping that no one will notice. However, when a ministry is lethargic, anemic, or toxic, everyone knows. The atmosphere is polluted, the congregation is contaminated, the leadership is corrupted, and the power of God is disrupted. In other words, God is not there. This kind of church should be renamed *Jehovah-Non Shammah*, meaning, "The Lord is not present." The "oil and wine" Church must lay aside all fear and pride and be the safe nonjudgmental sanctuary where sinners can come to tell that hidden thing that they would not go anywhere else to tell. When they come to the church hospital, we must have enough *oil to pour* out that they do not have to go anywhere else. No longer can the church refer to worldly resources and government agencies, as they are tainted with mixture and humanism that will only trap the victim more. Nor can the church adopt any method that is not 100 percent founded in God's Word. We must disseminate the *oil of gladness* if we are to distribute to the bleeding and contribute to the dying soul on life's Jericho

THE OIL MUST BE POURED INDIVIDUALLY.

Road. True deliverance ministers, who are flames of fire, must pour the oil of the anointing into the annoying. It must be poured into areas of worldly idolatries, toxic intimacies, counterfeit idiosyncrasies, sensuous illuminations, perverted inclinations, addictive interactions, demonic interpenetrations, infirm intergenerations, and the soulish injuries of the afflicted. This will be done in an effort to awaken their slumbering spirits from stuporous states enabling them to break out of the shackles that have ensnared them. For prophetic solutions to be effective, they must thoroughly engage pathetic situations. This is *ministry in the new millennium's* insignia.

Oil for the Individual

The oil must be poured individually. There is no mass deliverance of the homosexual person(s). Each situation is unique and it requires individualized and specialized ministry. The Church must help each person who enters its doors to completely awaken to the healing Spirit of God. Partial awakening will result in backsliding at times of crucial crossroads.

Support group leaders who have been trained by God to be sharp-shooters in the Spirit and bold in the natural can be instrumental in *discerning the differences* between behaviors influenced by agents of darkness, and those that are acquired behaviors of the human spirit. Actions of godly alignment are needed. The support group format should consist of: (1) Intensive Intercession Training; (2) Warfare Strategy Discussion; (3) Memory Training of the Word; and (4) Lifestyle Training by the Church. These things will help a struggling person reconcile towards a corrected lifestyle faster.

Active participation shifts from mere casual response to major change—from fear to *"I can do all things through Christ which strengtheneth me"* (Phil. 4:13). The result is the new thing God does, while depth of character takes root. The compassionate approach is the key, because *people do not care how much you know until they know how much you care. No matter how much you care, if your oil well is bare, ministry goes nowhere.* The *Composite Anointing* is the way, because no matter how much you care, without "oil," ministry is ineffectual. The goal of ministry is to personally help others to see from a new perspective and act from a higher perception. Military boot camps require every soldier to get up and be active in their preparation for war. The Church should require its soldiers to fulfill specific requirements before standing in any pulpit to preach, or before being given a position to lead or the power to influence others.

Fresh Oil

The "oil and wine" Church must get a fresh supply of oil because it is in high demand, and it must be poured out on a daily basis. A couple of years ago, I had a supernatural experience that I shall never forget. An angel of the Lord visibly appeared to me somewhere around four o'clock in the morning. I believe that it was an actual dream, although it might have been in person. The visitation was very vivid and real. In the dream, the angel descended out of Heaven on some type of fiery vehicle, though it was not necessarily a chariot. The shape and form of the vehicle were obscured by the brilliance of the effervescent light emanating from it. The angel descended to a height of about 15 feet, slightly higher than the average ceiling height. As he began speaking to me, I shielded my eyes by placing my forearm in front of them, lest I would be blinded by the scintillating radiance. I stood in silent awe as he related specific words from the Father God for my life and ministry. Even until this day, I have never shared with anyone the things that he told me. I now know why. St. Paul says that he *"(whether in the body, I cannot tell; or whether out of the body, I cannot tell: God knoweth;) such an one caught up to the third heaven....How that he was caught up into paradise, and heard unspeakable words, which it is not lawful for a man to utter"* (2 Cor. 12:2,4, emphasis added). He was not released to share the specifics of what he heard while in heavenly discourse, neither have I been released to reveal what I heard. Every visitation of supernatural origin is not necessarily for the multitudes. Sometimes, it is as simple as God sharing a secret with a friend or a prophet that He has raised up for his personal edification. Interestingly, when God got ready to judge Sodom and Gomorrah, He conferred, through angelic visitation and theophanic presentation with Abraham, His friend (see Gen. 18:17).

As the songwriter has eloquently said, "We are the friends of God." The Master Teacher Himself said it (see Jn. 15:15). Friends do not keep deep secrets from their dear friends. The certification of true friendship is in its transparent nature. The degree of friendship is determined by the sharing of the deepest of secrets.

As the dream came to an end and the angel was just about to leave me, I spoke up and asked the heavenly messenger, "Is there anything else that God wants me know and to do? Is there a new commission for me or is there a new message for me to preach?" The angel momentarily paused, and then he gently lowered his hand as if he was beaming in for a heavenly communiqué transmission. Suddenly, he looked up and focused directly at me and said these words: *"God Almighty says, whatever you preach, He will bless!"* Upon releasing those words, he instantaneously departed. It happened quicker than the blinking of an eye. I immediately awakened and came to consciousness, realizing that I had just heard from the throne room of Heaven.

Although it was around four o'clock in the early morning hours, I sensed that this encounter was significant enough to warrant waking my wife. I recounted the specifics of the divine dealing and added this insightful comment: *"God is not saying that I can just preach anything and that He will bless it. He is saying that He trusts my ability to hear from Him and my willingness and boldness to say exactly what He says. He trusts my integrity in ministry."* Since that time, everywhere that I have preached throughout the world, He has blessed it, just like He said He would, even with miracles, signs, and wonders following His word. This is indeed a new season of *ministry in the new millennium.*

Therefore, when the Lord provided me with the inspiration to write this book, I knew that even though I would have personally preferred to write my initial work on another subject, the promise of the Father was, *"Whatever you preach, I will bless."* I believe that this promise includes *writing* as well. Amen!

The Oil Was Poured on Me

The Scripture says that the *"tongue is the pen of a ready writer"* (Ps. 45:1). Much of what is written today is first released as the spoken word, before it becomes the packaged product of an actual book. Such was the case with *Ministering Graciously to the Gay and Lesbian Community: Pouring in the Oil and the Wine.* I studied extensively for several weeks, and I spoke on the subject during a Sunday morning service. The message was riveting, and several parishioners answered the altar appeal for prayer concerning this matter. It dawned upon me that if 2 to 5 percent of the American people consider themselves predisposed to a homo-sexual orientation, then that means out of every 100 attendees, there are 2 to 5 people present who will fall into this category. For a church with 1,000 in attendance, this would mean an average of 20 to 50 people present have this inclination. This actuality can no longer be ignored. It will not go away, and it will not be changed without an intentional effort to minister to it.

When the Oil Was Poured on All Nations Church

A good shepherd is concerned about even one lost soul and will leave the 99 in proper watch care to go after the one who has been wounded and therefore cannot keep up. He will be concerned about the one who has strayed from the path or has been stolen by the preying wolves disguised in sheep's clothing. The Sunday morning that I preached on this subject, I watched as several young people, who have been in All Nations Church all their lives, poured their hearts out to God seeking His divine deliverance. Instead of people looking judgmentally, they were engaged in wholehearted intercession. I was truly delighted to see the response of the spiritual family as they cried out to God along with their young brethren. When I left the pulpit that morning, I was quite satisfied, for I knew that the people were edified; the Lord was glorified; the name of the Lord was magnified; the devil was terrified; and those struggling with same-sex attraction were no longer stigmatized or petrified to seek *"Prophetic Solutions for Pathetic Situations."* Shortly thereafter, the message was transcribed. Then, the transcript became a manuscript. Today, it has become the book that you are now reading. Sometimes, the cloud is no bigger than a man's hand, but it contains an *abundance of rain* (see 1 Kings 18:41).

The "Oiliest" Sermon on the Gay Life

The greatest sermon I have ever heard preached on the subject of ministering to the homosexual was preached by Prophet Keith Grayton. He posed difficult questions in a message entitled, "Oil for the 21st Century." When he was through preaching, we knew we had heard the heartbeat of

God for homosexuals. Nearly a decade later, his words still ring true today with clarion conciseness and indisputable impact. A few of those prophetic words have been preserved in this writing for your earnest consideration. For the 21st-century Church to minister to the hardened souls who live hard lives, it will take the oil to anoint the cold and callous carelessness of complacent Christians.

The Master Teacher did not leave His Bride without oil. The "oil and wine" Church must use this oil for ourselves and secondarily for others. The prodigal son was received back into his father's house with a party, because his dad had *"enough and to spare."* As we minister our oil and obtain more, there will always be enough in the Father's house. The oil of gladness will minister to the madness that will give credence to the gospel, which is, by definition, good news. It is always good news to know that the store is open and that supplies to meet your needs are for sale. Many churches have gone out of business, but have forgotten to take the sign down. They have closed up shop and they do not even have a "We will return shortly" sign on the door. The Good Samaritan represents the Church at its best, preaching the gospel and applying the oil and the wine. In an earlier chapter, "The Confrontive Appeal: The Naked Truth Must Now Be Told," you were introduced to the late Prophet Keith Grayton. In the "Composite Anointing," we will consider his words. He was barely three decades old, yet he spoke with the prophetic wisdom of the ages. His dying breath was used to challenge the Church to have "Oil for the 21st Century." The following transcript of his words is an exposition of the Matthew 25:1-13 text of "The Ten Virgins." Five of them were considered wise; the other five were considered foolish.

Subject: Oil for the 21st Century
Preached: All Nations Church
Columbus, Ohio, January 1995
Text: Matthew 25:1-13

(In progress) ...All ten of them had lamps. Only five of them had oil in their lamps. The oil is a symbol of the Holy Spirit. The distinction between the ten was in the oil. The virgins represent two endtime churches. There are the wise who have oil and the foolish who do not. The Church must have oil for itself and extra oil for the harvest. ...Do we (the Church) have oil for the young brother that is coming in 6'4", 280 lbs? He is coming in with a dress on. Do we have any oil for that? What are you going to do with him? What bathroom does he use? ...I have a friend who is a transsexual. He has no male organs. Is the church ready for that crop? What do you do when he walks in all dolled up and made

up? I'm not asking if he is prepared. I am asking, are we prepared? What do we tell him? Keep your dress on, or put your suit on? This brother is setting in church with breasts....

Young Girls and Lesbian Lovers

...You can say what you want to say. When you turn on Geraldo and Ricky Lake and Jerry Springer, I interpret that as prophetic. Every time I sit there and I watch the way people are living, I hear the Holy Ghost saying that is the harvest. Are you ready for that? The transvestite and the transsexual are the harvest of God. Some of them are prophets. Some of them are pastors. Some of them are evangelists. **You have to have oil for them before they get here.** You cannot wait until they get here, because when they get here, they have already been so devastated in the world, they do not have another six months to live like that.

What are you going to do with the young girl that comes in with her lesbian lover? Are we ready for that? What are you going to do when they set up a meeting with the elders and the pastors and say we want to be married? Women's fellowships, are you ready for that? Women's fellowship is more than shopping trips. It is more than hanging out and ordering pizza. There are some women struggling with lesbianism. Their lives are torn up. They have been hurting. Some of them are sitting in here tonight. They have never told anybody. But the spirit of prophecy is falling on the house. Everybody is walking around like they do not see what is going on. You know that girl is messed up in her flesh. You know she still likes women. What do we do? We avoid them. We say, "I do not want to sit by her. I do not want that stuff to rub off on me." That is, because you do not have any oil. Sit me beside the lesbian. I am already oiled down for it. Sit me beside the homosexual. Tell the homosexual to come on over here. We have some oil. We have oil in the storehouse. We did not know we were going to need it this quick. But we've already been oiled down....

Demons Are Not Impressed

*...Folks with demons are not impressed with buildings. Folks in the harvest do not care anything about a sound system and carpet. They just want to **know if you have oil over here**. Can I get rid of my devil over here? Can I get set free? I have lived like this all my life. Is there a church that has oil?*

Many in the church say that they can't minister to them, because they do not know anything about that. I remind you that Paul was never married, but every time we talk about marriage, we reference him. The famous marriage chapter—who wrote it? Paul. What do you mean? **Paul had oil that he did not need. Some of us are struggling trying to work with our oil.** Everything we get from God, we need it so bad. But God is bringing us into a position where **He gives us this extra oil, where you have more oil than you need. The visitation that you are in is to give you extra oil.** The prophetic eye sees a harvest. I see a generation of people who have been violated. I see a generation of people coming into the house of God whose lives are torn up. I see people coming into our churches who have no concept of God. I see people who will sell their baby to get high. I see people coming in that do not have any suits on. They do not even own a suit. They do not even like suits. They do not even like buttoning the top button on a shirt. I see people coming into the house of God, packing. I see this harvest coming in with their Uzi on them....

Ministering in the Shadow of Death

...One of our female ministers was out ministering on the streets one day. She walked up on a gang of men. One of the brothers pulled out a gun and she said, "Oh brother, you got to come better than that. Is that supposed to scare me?" She kept on ministering. After she finished, he said, "Girl, you're crazy." Are we ready for that? Are we ready for this generation that does not even respect their own mother? If they curse their own mother, you know they will curse the pastor. Are you ready for that generation? Are you ready for a generation who knows nothing about order? There is no need for us to stand up and give them Greek and Hebrew. They cannot even speak English. Are we ready for that harvest? All their life they have been sheep without a shepherd. Are we ready for what the devil has done to this generation? They are filled with murder. They are angry. They are mad. They are hurting. They do not even know who their fathers are. They do not even know their grandfather's name. Their grandmother is just 45 and she is still getting high....

Grandmothers Getting High

...I had a 17 year old in my church who got high every day with his grandmother. Do you know what that must have done to his psyche? They are not coming in speaking in tongues. They are not coming in smelling the best. This generation has seen the worst of the worst. Before you say anything to them about the length of their dress, you have to cast the devil out. **That is our job to pour in the oil and the wine.**

You want to know something about the Good Samaritan. He is on his journey. The Levite comes and sees the man, but goes on the other side. The priest comes and sees him and just keeps walking. The Samaritan comes and sees him and goes to him. **He poured in the oil and the wine. What is amazing is that he did not have to go get the oil.** He had no idea who he was going to run into that day. **He just had some extra oil. Do you have oil for situations that you know nothing about…?**

Swinging Church Members

…What do you do with a couple in the church that is swinging? That means they invite other couples in to have sexual relations. Before we say that is nasty, that is a shame, we ought to put them out…remember, the only reason we have to put them out is that we do not have oil for them.

God is giving you, in this house, oil for the 21st century. At the turn of every century, there has always been a release and a restoration of the next deposit for the restoration of the Church.

Prophetic Churches

…A prophetic church never has church like everybody else is having church. They are always the forerunner. They are always trendsetters. They are always a people who flow outside of the norm. They are always people of great reproach because there is a spirit of Jezebel that is trying to kill the prophetic. You have to know when you have come in contact with the spirit of Jezebel. That Jezebel spirit is a low-down dog. The Jezebel spirit makes the prophet wish he was dead until the prophet prophesies back on her. A prophetic church has the ability to affect other churches. That is why you are prophetic. That is why you are a people of pace and of trendsetting and of breaking out of the norm so that the church can really be filled with the glory….

Set Up for the Harvest

…Whenever God visits a church like He is visiting this church, He is setting you up for the harvest. You do not know how much God loves His harvest. He is not going to set them in anybody's church where they are going to be violated. They have been violated and beat up enough. They have been hurt enough. There are some gate houses and sheep pens where He has shut the door. He will only release the harvest to those whom He knows will take care of the harvest. **In order to give this generation what they need, you have to have oil.**

A prophetic house is **a house that has oil for her enemies.** There are some people that come up against the house. **Do you have oil for them, or do we still want to fight them?** What do you mean? First Samuel 19 (nineteen) says it like this: Saul is trying to kill David. David runs to Ramah where the prophets are. He stays at Ramah. Samuel takes him to Naioth. When he gets down there, Saul finds out where he is. Saul sends his armies to get him. But when they get to the prophetic house, the spirit of prophecy is on the house. When they walk in, they start prophesying. Saul hears what happened and sends another group of people. When they walk in, they start prophesying, knowing that they have come to tear it up. But the atmosphere was so right. The third time he does it, the third group starts prophesying. Saul decides to go for himself. When he gets there, he starts prophesying. All over Israel, they start asking the question, "Is Saul among the prophets?"...

The Word of the Lord

...And the Spirit of the Lord would say unto this house, for you have received the oil. Your season to pour the oil has come. It is your turn to pour it and not just receive it. There are some brothers and sisters who are in the Nation of Islam who belong in the house of God. What is happening? Churches do not have oil for them. This generation wants more than a bump and a dance. They do not know anything about midnight musicals. This generation has questions that need answers. They need a demonstration of God's glory....

Prophet Grayton's message speaks to the "oil and wine" Church today. The revelation of men on the down low, priests with low lifestyles, and the low blow of the homosexual agenda against the long accepted vantage points of marriage, family, and theology have made his message more relevant than ever before. The Master Teacher once gathered 12 baskets of fragments after feeding a multitude. *Twelve* is the number of government throughout the Scriptures. Ministry in the new millennium requires an understanding and application of the 12 acts of the *drama of deliverance*. The *Acts of the Apostles* to the gay community will only take place as the *Acts of the Holy Spirit Oil* are applied.

—ACT I: THE PRESENCE OF THE OIL—

Throughout the Bible, oil typifies the Holy Spirit's anointing. It was used to sanctify, to satisfy, and to certify for service. Consider these passages:

> *Thou preparest a table before me in the presence of mine enemies: Thou anointest my head with oil; my cup runneth over* (Psalm 23:5).

> *My head with oil thou didst not anoint: but this woman hath anointed My feet with ointment* (Luke 7:46).

> *Let thy garments be always white; and let thy head lack no ointment* (Ecclesiastes 9:8).

Moses, the master builder, who did everything according to divine commandment, anointed the temporary structure of worship that was known as the tabernacle (dwelling place). This signified that all ministry must be "oiled" to be on! Without oil it is off.

> *And Moses took the anointing oil, and anointed the tabernacle and all that was therein, and sanctified them. And he sprinkled thereof upon the altar seven times, and anointed the altar and all his vessels, both the laver and his foot, to sanctify them. And he poured of the anointing oil upon Aaron's head, and anointed him, to sanctify him* (Leviticus 8:10-12).

The apostle John refers to the "oil" in First John 2:20 stating, *"But ye have an unction from the Holy One...."* When something was properly dedicated to God, it became known as holy or set apart, because by itself nothing has an inherent or resident sanctifying uniqueness. Holiness is always associated with God's sanction. For the anointing to be holy, it had to follow the divine prescription for its attainment, composition, and application. It was utilized for: Divine Purpose (to sanctify), Divine Presence (to satisfy), and Divine Power (for service). There was a procedure for its attainment. The principal ingredient was derived from the olive tree, known as the king of all trees (see Judg. 9:9). The olive tree is distinctive in several regards.

- First, it grows relatively slowly. (Oil in a believer's life requires great patience and longsuffering.)

- Secondly, it must be cultivated carefully. (Oil does not come by osmosis, but by attention to detail.)

- Thirdly, it must be pruned periodically. (Oil is the result of divine dealings of intense cutting.)

- Fourthly, it survives for decades/centuries. (Oil is the result of endurance of climate/weather and circumstances.)

—ACT II: THE PARTICULAR USE OF THE OIL—

In biblical times, the particular uses of the oil were multifold. The prophetic application relates to the Church today. When the attainment has taken place, the oil is ready to be a part of the composition of the apothecary.

*Oil was used for the **preparation** of meals.* *"And she said, As the Lord thy God liveth, I have not a cake, but an handful of meal in a barrel, and a little oil in a cruse"* (1 Kings 17:12a). It is very unfulfilling to hear a message that is not prepared with oil. Just as oil and vinegar do not mix, neither does teaching and preaching without oil. In the BKW Young Preachers' Institute, the ministers are taught that some audiences and environments may be hard to minister in, but even as Jacob anointed the rock (the hard place) at Bethel (the house of God), so they must learn to anoint the atmosphere by red-hot prayer, radical praise, and revolutionary-prophetic worship. *"And Jacob rose up early in the morning, and took the stone that he had put for his pillows, and set it up for a pillar, and poured oil upon the top of it"* (Gen. 28:18). The rock became his pillow, and it became a pillar upon holy ground. This is called environmental control. Atmospheric pressure results in the oil raining down upon the believer.

*Oil was used for **fuel** for the lamps* of the ten virgins. Fuel is an indispensable commodity. It is essential that the "oil and wine" Church be fueled up. Fuel is costly. The cost of it is rising daily. It is not a luxury; it is a necessity. It is obtained through purchase. To have oil for fuel you must dedicate your energy to the Lord. Crude oil has topped $50 a barrel. It is expensive. The anointing oil is not obtained at bargain basement prices. The late Kathryn Kuhlman said the price of the anointing was *"everything."* She often entreated audiences not to do anything that would cause the Holy Spirit to be grieved and leave. She often said, "He's all I've got!" She paid the price for the oil to heal, and multitudes experienced it without price in her ministry. Oil to deal with the gay, the lesbian, and the

> OIL IS PAID FOR IN THE BLOOD, SWEAT, AND TEARS OF INTERCESSION, SUPPLICATION, AND TRAVAIL.

bi-sexual is paid for in the blood, sweat, and tears of intercession, supplication, and travail. You will never reach a soul that you do not pray for.

Oil was used as a cosmetic ointment. The Scripture says a man's wisdom will cause his face to shine (see Eccl. 8:1). It further states, *"Praise is comely for the upright"* (Ps. 33:1b). The oil of gladness is the greatest witness that motivates the unregenerate to seek to have the "oil" for themselves. The "oil" of Olay does not compare with the "oil" of the Way!

Oil was used in medicine. Isaiah 1:6 says, *"...they have not been closed, neither bound up, neither mollified with ointment."* The healing properties of oil are needed on a daily basis, just as daily bread. *"...Sufficient unto the day is the evil thereof"* (Mt. 6:34). The Psalmist asserts, *"Thou anointest my head with oil..."* (Ps. 23:5b). This is a direct analogy understood by all shepherds of his day. It was customary to anoint the sheep with oil, because they had a tendency to stick their nose into things as they walked in the pasture. Obviously, this behavior could endanger them because of snakes, insects, and parasites that they would encounter. The oil had a twofold effect. It had a pleasant smell and an attractive quality to the sheep and a repugnant, putrefying odor to the enemies of the sheep. It is necessary for believers to be "oiled" up if they are going to remain uncontaminated and undefiled as they reach the unreachable and touch the untouchable.

—ACT III: THE PRECONDITIONS OF THE OIL—

The holy anointing oil was not to be poured upon strangers. The penalty for violation of this ordinance was death. Foreigners who were not a part of the Commonwealth of Israel were not recipients of the anointing due to their alien status. When something is alienated, it is not rightly related to another. In order to be "oiled," the believer must stay in right relationship with God. Loose living and stingy giving will cause the "oil to lack." The believer's head is to lack no oil, but in many instances the church-goer loses all that he has gained within 24 hours of his going out of the church doors.

The story is told of a great evangelist who used to conduct yearly revivals at a local church. Each year one of the members would always go up to the altar to receive personal ministry. His prayer request was to be filled with the Holy Spirit. After the prayer was concluded, he would kindly thank the minister and promptly return to his seat. This same thing went on for several years. Finally, one particular year, the brother again repeated his prayer request to be "filled with the Spirit." This time, however, the evangelist asked him if he minded if he'd pray a different prayer. The man replied, "Of course not, do as you please." The preacher began praying, but this time he said, "Lord, our friend wants to be filled with the Holy Spirit again. I ask that You would do that, but also, Lord, please plug him up, because he's got leaks!" The truth is, when the believer walks with God consistently through daily devotions, he will not live by his emotions and leak the oil that has been freely given to him.

Secondly, the oil was not to be imitated. Counterfeit oil always produces hypocritical lifestyles. Cheap worship soon follows. The real deal is in the real formula. Oil is produced through myrrh (bitterness), cassia (crushing that produces fragrance), and cinnamon (opening and extraction). In the spirit realm, imitation is not a high form of flattery; it is a low form of perjury. The anointing is free, but it is not fake.

Recently, I was in Mexico vacationing and shopping. A man in a jewelry store was selling what appeared to be Rolex watches. I have owned my own Rolex for nearly a decade, and I can readily spot the real from the fake. I quickly remarked that the watch(es) were imitations. Instead of expressing contrition and shame, he simply said, "Yes, but it is the best fake you'll ever see!" I quickly left his store, but I shall never forget the experience. Encountering the "oil of God" is not simply a one-time event; it is to be a life-changing experience. Emulation is a work of the flesh (see Gal. 5:20), and it will never affect those gay and lesbian persons who are engaged with "strange flesh."

Thirdly, the oil was not to be poured upon flesh. At first glance, this would appear to be an impossible precondition. After all, a man's body is merely flesh and bones. However, the term "flesh" has to do with someone who is "in the flesh" or unfit for holy service. A person whose heart is not right with God—who is not living in sanctification, consecration, and dedication—is not endeavoring to honor God. The Scripture says, *"So then they that are in the flesh cannot please God"* (Rom. 8:8). A fleshly person is carnal or sense ruled. They serve God based on their feelings. If they feel like it, they do God's will. If they do not…then they will not. The carnal mind is at enmity (hostile opposition) to God and is not subject to God, nor indeed can it be. Therefore, those who view the pulpit as a place to get their "fleshly groove on" are as off as two left shoes. Carnality kills spirituality.

For to be carnally minded is death; but to be spiritually minded is life and peace. Because the carnal mind is enmity against God: for it is not subject to the law of God, neither indeed can be (Romans 8:6-7).

Walking in the Spirit will annihilate perverted processions and flesh parades. This means that ministers must walk with a made-up mind. Their mind must be made up. *As they hold their head up, up, with their mind made up, they will be on their way up, as they go on with the King.* Their mind must be focused and firmly fixed with fortitude. The oil is applied when the flesh is denied. Oil for the 21st century awaits those who bring their flesh under subjection to a life of discipline to the cause of Christ and to devotion to the cross of Christ. Pastor Benny Hinn teaches that the "presence of God carries *His* voice, and the power of God carries *yours* [the believer's] voice."[4] For the oil to be unassailable, it must become tangible and visible. There were three different anointings.

1. In the Old Testament, the *Cleansed Leper* was anointed with oil, thus representing the believers' salvation, which is obtained by ACCEPTING JESUS. (see Lev. 14:17-18).

2. The *Consecrated Priest* was anointed with oil, thus symbolizing the believers' service, which is the result of COMMUNING WITH JESUS (through the Spirit) (see Exod. 40:13).

3. The *Chosen King* was anointed with oil, thus typifying the sovereignty of God, which is the evidence of OBEYING JESUS (see 1 Sam. 16:13).

Oil is needed for accepting, communing with, and obeying the Master Teacher.

To sustain "Oil for the 21st Century," the believer must recognize that oil has to be *regularly changed* if its potency is to be maintained. Old oil loses its sufficiency, just as yesterday's manna loses its vitality. By the next day, the uncollected manna or the stored manna will have worms (see Ex. 16:20). So it is with the things of the Spirit. The Church of the 21st century must have regular "oil changes." Today's oil cannot meet tomorrow's challenges. R.T. Kendall writes:

> We need to come to terms with what may suddenly become yesterday's anointing. It will do us no good to pretend that what happened yesterday is happening today if it isn't. Dr. Lloyd-Jones told me this story. In his former church in Wales a man stood up to read the Scriptures in a Monday evening prayer meeting. The Spirit came on him in an extraordinary manner. It seemed as if the meeting would go on and on into the night, it was so wonderful. But Dr. Lloyd-Jones eventually closed the meeting (he told me he worried for years that he shouldn't have). The following Monday night the same man tried it again. Dr. Lloyd-Jones said, "I knew he'd try to do it again, and I knew what would happen." It didn't happen. You cannot make yesterday's anointing today's anointing if the Spirit isn't willing.[5]

—ACT IV: THE PROCESS OF THE OIL—

One of the chief components of producing the *composite anointing* is extracting oil from the olive tree. The extraction contained five steps that are prophetic of the oiling process in the believer's life. The process always precedes the product. The product exceeds the process. The power supercedes both the process and the product. God can get it *to* you; but can He get it *through* you?

- First, to produce oil, the limb is shaken severely until the fruit is loosened. (To be "oiled," expect a "whole lot of shakin' to be goin' on.")

- Secondly, the berry is broken harshly. (Chastisement, divine instruction, and suffering are used to release "oil.")

- Thirdly, the berry is subjected to crushing. (It is necessary to have one's feelings crushed, their opinions dashed, and self-will stomped until it is stamped out.)

- Fourthly, the berry is beaten repeatedly. (Even lessons learned must sometimes be repeated in the process of becoming an "oily" believer.)

- Fifthly, the oil is stored until it is poured. (Many times God will take the sum total of His dealings and not utilize them right away until He can get the maximum potency out of them.)

The Psalmist David declared, *"I shall be anointed with fresh oil"* (Ps. 92:10b). When a believer is shaken, beaten, crushed, beaten again, turned over, and pressed, it is then that he is ready to be applied as "Oil for the 21st Century!"

—ACT V: THE PRESSING OF THE OIL—

The oil is pressed from the olive, the berry, or the ground depending on the type. The believer must press into God through reading, researching, and repeating the Word of God. The oil must be poured out, smeared on, and rubbed in. "Oil for the 21st Century" requires believers to press into God for the higher levels. The Psalmist David received three anointings, and they typify what is needed for ministry in the new millennium.

*The first anointing was **poured out***[6] (see 1 Sam. 16:13). After receiving this anointing, David effectively defeated the bear and the lion (see 1 Sam. 17:34-36). Both of these animals typify the wild, unruly, beastly nature of the flesh.

To the degree that the believer's flesh is pulled is the degree that the oil will flow. Flesh will fight the flow.

*The second anointing was **smeared on**[7]* (see 2 Sam. 2:4). Upon receiving it, David promptly became king of Judah, which means "praise now." When the oil is smeared on, it is a higher density, a weightier viscosity, and a thicker composition than what was poured out. The oil causes praise to break forth now. You have oil for now and for later. The oil flows without hindrance in an atmosphere of anointed praise. The believer who attends a church that starts at 10 o'clock sharp and ends at 12 o'clock dull will never receive the smeared-on oil. The garment of praise is the cruse for the oil. The believer who

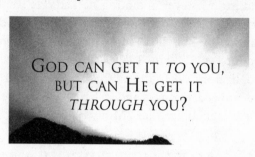

GOD CAN GET IT *TO* YOU, BUT CAN HE GET IT *THROUGH* YOU?

arrives too late for the praise service will only get a "dab'll-do-ya," and not the "saturation of the soaking." Without praise, the oil is spilled, wasted, and absorbed in the dirt of do-nothing to be trodden under the foot of men. Anointed feet must be planted in the perfected praise of smeared-on oil.

*The third anointing of David was **rubbed in**[8]* (see 2 Sam. 5:3). Shortly thereafter, he became the king over the other tribes that were known as Israel. Those who go beyond the little "dab'll-do-ya" levels, and become oiled to the fullness will operate as princes (Israels) of God in this earth. Ministry to the bleeding and dying on the Jericho Road requires the oil to be poured out, smeared on, and rubbed in. It requires an oil change that occurs through application of the Shepherd's instructions. The Word of God is the single most important factor in ministering "Oil for the 21st Century."

(*PRESS-SCRIPTION FOR OIL CHANGE*) —FRESH OIL—

- First, read the Word daily (devotions, studies).

- Second, research the Word diligently (Scriptures that you have learned).

- Third, repeat the Word dauntingly (relisten to taped sermons).

- Fourth, read the Word in books dutifully (edifying, expanding material).

The minister must learn from the example of those who had the oil but lost it. Learn from Samson, who was anointed with oil, until he put his head in Delilah's lap, got his hair cut in the devil's barber shop, and lost it. Learn from Solomon, who was anointed with wisdom, but he put his head in a thousand laps and lost his oil. Learn from Saul, who was anointed with a kingdom (see 1 Sam. 10:1), but he could not complete his lap and became lackadaisical, losing whatever anointing he had. He went into battle without an anointed shield, having nothing to defeat the fiery darts of the wicked one. Unfortunately for him, he thought he could fight without it, and it cost him the kingdom (see 2 Sam. 1:21). "Oil for the 21st Century" is not optional; it is obligatory. When the oil that has been poured out, smeared on, and rubbed in is utilized, the gays and lesbians will see a new Church with a new anointing that is mobilized for "Ministry in the New Millennium."

—ACT VI: THE PROBLEMS WITH THE OIL—

Oil that is used in motor vehicles must be changed because it evaporates. If it is not replenished regularly, eventually it will be all gone. This will result in the destruction of the engine. Spiritually, it equates with burnout. Many of those who are involved in ministry are indeed evidencing that they have gone the last mile of the way with their present oil. They need an oil change. Even the prophet Elisha was bade to arise and eat, so that he might have strength for the journey. The Scripture says that he *"went in the strength of that meat forty days and forty nights"* (1 Kings 19:8). *The sustenance provided by the angel was good for only 40 days and not 41 days. In ministry, it is possible to go too far, stay too long, and come back too late. It is possible to run out of oil or to have reduced mileage because of old oil.* It is possible to break your engine down because of the breakup of spontaneity. Oftentimes, there is weariness with the work. There can be misery with ministry. There can be boredom with the Bible. There can be perseverance problems with performance. There can be an irritating and agitating edginess. The excitement sometimes goes and so does the oil. But...when the oil is changed, it results in fire in the eye, pep in the step, glide in the stride, hop in the bop, and leap in the limp. When oil is changed, it results in starch in the clergy collar and power for the whole hour. When the oil is changed, you can still get up and go when others have gotten up and gone! When the oil is changed, you can take a licking and keep on ticking. When the oil is changed, you take the devil's best shot, look him square in the eye and say," Is that all that you have got?" You can run the race, keep the pace, outlast the storms, and overcome the flesh. In all of your getting, the believer must get his oil changed!

Besides evaporation, another problem with the oil is in the actual weight of it. The proper weight must be understood before utilizing it. Oil has varying densities, such as 30 weight, 40 weight, etc. Believers also have various capacities, such as 30, 60, and 100-fold. The weight of the oil has to do with its thickness or its viscosity. The lower the thickness, the lesser the ability to protect in adversarial atmospheres. The problem with many believers is that they often settle for ministries that lack "viscosity." It has been wisely stated that *ministry increase without anointing increase is deadly.* As a believer matures in the Lord, his weight of glory proportionately increases to his sufferings. Persecution, tribulation, afflictions, and hardships increase the *"far more exceeding and eternal weight of glory"* (2 Cor. 4:17). In some cases, you must seek out a filling station (local church) that carries your grade of oil or else your ministry will stagnate and you could suffocate. Some worship settings have been polluted with the containment of toxicity towards persons whose gay and lesbian conditions do not meet their specifications for approval. Heavyweights in the Spirit can handle the heavy traffic of the coming rush hour as all lanes will be filled with same-sex sinners seeking those who have oil for the 21st century.

—ACT VII: THE PATTERN OF THE OIL—

The oil was used as a pattern for the anointing of kings, prophets, and priests. The king ruled in the name of God. The prophet spoke to the people on behalf of God. The priest served as a bridge from the people to God. The Latin word for priest is *Pontifex.* The term *pontiff* is derived from it. It is an ascription used to identify the pope, the papa, or a father. It is essential to recognize that the priest was anointed with oil in three places. The anointing of the head, the hand, and the foot speaks volumes to the believer today. The leper was also anointed with oil in the same three places. Both sinner and saint require fresh oil. Leviticus 14:17 says:

> *And of the rest of the oil that is in his hand shall the priest put upon the tip of the right ear of him that is to be cleansed, and upon the thumb of his right hand, and upon the great toe of his right foot, upon the blood of the trespass offering.*

> *First, the oil was applied to the right of the head (ear).*

All who minister on behalf of God to others must have *an ear to "hear what the Spirit saith unto the churches"* (Rev. 2:7). Without an oiled ear, the believer will become *"dull of hearing"* (Heb. 5:11b).

A little girl was once asked what it means to be a Christian. She replied, "It is just to do what Jesus would do." An anointed ear hears and heeds. When a missionary was translating the Holy Scriptures into the language of the remote tribal people, he became stymied by the word *obedient*. He couldn't find a suitable expression in the native lesson to adequately address the concept. While pondering the impasse, he beheld a man interacting with his trained hunting dog. Whatever the man commanded is exactly what the dog did. The man remarked to the missionary that his dog was "all ears." Oil on the ear will cause a believer to be "all ears." Without the oil, the ear cannot hear all the Father has commanded. With the oil, ministry becomes what Dr. Robert Schuller calls "a cinch, inch by inch."

Second, the oil was applied to the right hand (thumb). The work of God must be anointed, or else it is annoying. A classic Pentecostal preacher once said that there are too many dead preachers laying their dead hands on dead heads. Oiled hands are living, life-giving hands. The hand that rocks the cradle indeed rules the world. The hand that holds the rod transforms it to the rod of God (see Ex. 4:20). The hand that is raised on the mountain brings victory in the valley (see Ex. 17). Without oil, the hand is simply four fingers and a thumb. With oil, it is the "cloud like a man's hand" that contains the sound of the abundance of rain (see 1 Kings 18:44). God asked Moses, *"What's in your hand?"* Today, God asks the 21st-century Church, "What's *on* your hand?" Selah!

Third, the oil was applied to the right foot (toe). The ability to colabor with Christ is contingent upon walking in the newness of life (see Rom. 6:4). Years ago, the church sang a song, "I want Jesus to walk with me. While I'm on this pilgrim journey I want Jesus to walk with me." Another popular song of years gone by was, "Just a closer walk with Thee, grant it Jesus if You please. I'll be satisfied as long as I walk, let me walk close to Thee." The next verse says, "I am weak but Thou art strong, Jesus, keep me from all wrong. I'll be satisfied as long as I walk close to Thee." The anointed walk is the result of oil on the foot. Oiled feet are beautiful feet. They are feet that do not walk in the counsel of the ungodly (see Ps. 1:1), and they do not walk into temptation (see Mt. 6:13). They walk out of the way to retrieve the wayward and restore them in the way that they should go (see Prov. 22:6). Oil for the 21st century is upon those who are like Asher (happy). They have dipped their foot in the oil of gladness (see Deut. 33:24). As the believer is anointed on the ear, the hand, and the feet, he will function with unction to the gay and the lesbian who desperately need God.

—ACT VIII: THE PLACES OF THE OIL—

And the barrel of meal wasted not, neither did the cruse of oil fail, according to the word of the Lord, which he spake by Elijah (1 Kings 17:16).

First, there was "oil in the cruse." Without oil in the container, there is no sustenance in the Church. The new cruse of Elisha, once emptied of its salt contents, brought healing to an entire region. It was cast into the sea, which is representative of the throngs of humanity. Afterward, the wombs were no longer barren, nor was the land unfruitful anymore (see 2 Kings 2:21). The new cruse represents the new wineskin, structure, outreach, approach, philosophy of ministry, and administrative government of the local church. Fresh oil for the 21st century requires new models of ministry to reach this technological information age. Resurrection is the result of a continuous supply of oil in the cruse. Every church worker, lay minister, and ordained preacher need a new cruse with fresh oil. To obtain this requires prophetic connection. Ministries must link up with the specialists. The general practitioner will always recommend the specialists when the patient requires advanced medical care. People who come out of dysfunction, deviance, and diversion require "oiled experts" to assist them in the recovery of their soul. George MacDonald once said, "If I can put one touch of a rosey sunset into the life of any man or woman, I shall feel that I have worked with God."[9] Amen!

Second, there was "oil in the pot." Second Kings 4:2b says, *"Thine handmaid hath not any thing in the house, save a pot of oil."* In this text, the woman paid her expenditures by exchanging the oil. Because of the wise use of her oil, her sons were saved; her credit was perfectly restored; and her seed met the need for both now and later. Like this woman who was destined for a miracle, every believer has been given oil for their pot. Each has the pot of the measure of faith and the availability of grace through faith (see Eph. 2:8). Each has been given several abilities and talents (see Mt. 25:15). Each has been given "a treasure in their field" (see Mt. 13:44). Those who possess the "Oil for the 21st Century" will always possess more than enough for now and later. As a child, my favorite candy was cherry "Now and Later's." I always thought it was simply because of the taste, but now I know it was because you could have some *now* and you could save some for *later*. The pot speaks of the spirit of a man. Oil in the pot is oil in your spirit. When your spirit is oiled, you are lubricated for love expressions and largeness of heart. Oil in the pot will never be spoiled or spilled. The secret is, as long as you pour, there will always be more. Selah.

Third, there was "oil on the face." Psalm 104:15 says, *"And wine that maketh glad the heart of man, and oil to make his face to shine, and bread which strengtheneth man's heart."* F. E. Marsh once said, "A shining face is indication of inward grace. A shining face is a smiling face." The believer must live his life by the adage, "When you see someone without a smile, then you should give them yours." Many of God's people do not smile enough. A smile is not a smirk. It is never seen on those who are hung up, and hung over with quirks. Jesus was hung-up for the world's hang-ups. It behooves the believer to hang-up on being hung-up. There is liberty in Christ, and if you have the joy of the Lord, you should never forget to notify your face. No Christian should ever look like he has fallen out of the uuugly tree and hit every branch on the way down. Ministry to the gay and lesbian does not start in the cemetery, or the seminary, but in the luminary of the cosmic laboratory. Smiles light up a person's life and they bring sunshine into an otherwise gloomy day. It takes twice the muscles to frown as it does to smile. It is no wonder that many believers are so tired. When oil on the face is running low, the red light of conviction will always flash.

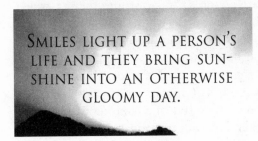

SMILES LIGHT UP A PERSON'S LIFE AND THEY BRING SUNSHINE INTO AN OTHERWISE GLOOMY DAY.

This whimsical story makes the point. Many years ago, a father took his young son to a Sunday morning service at the local church. Upon leaving, they passed a farm and on the property they saw some mules. The little boy inquired of his father, "Do those mules attend the same church that we just left?" The father replied, "Of course not, Son. They're just animals." The little boy replied, 'I know, but they look just like the people we just left." Those who cannot say, "Amen," should say, "Oh my…!"

No child of God should resemble a long-faced mule. The joy of the Lord is your strength (see Neh. 8:10). In other words, it is your *strongest point.* Oil on the face makes it shine. The best place to obtain oil on the face is to get up in His face and then down on your face. *"And it came to pass…when he came down from the mount, that Moses wist not that the skin of his face shone while he talked with him"* (Ex. 34:29). Moses went up the mountain to talk to God (as a priest) on behalf of the people. He came down from the face of God (as a prophet) to speak on behalf of God to the people. Such is the pattern of ministry. Oil for the 21st century is in abundant supply in the holy place of God's face. It is obtained whenever a believer falls on his face and worships under the glory spout, until the oil is poured out. Believers, take heed! *Sin will make you look old and ugly, but glory will make you look gloriously youthful.* The oil beautifies *"the meek with salvation"* (Ps. 149:4b).

Once, there were two boys who were playing in the public park. Suddenly, one of them noticed his teacher, who happened to be walking by. He exclaimed to his playmate, "Hey, it is my teacher. She is the most beautiful woman in the world." The teacher smiled and continued to walk on. Upon her passing out of range, the other little boy replied, "I do not see how you could say that. She is old, and her face is full of wrinkles." His friend quickly responded, "Well, you do not see what I see. She comes to our house and speaks to my whole family about her Savior Jesus, and when she does it, her face shines with beauty, love, and tenderness. It is so beautiful." "Oil for the 21st Century" on the face will bring the believer into the miracle zone. The pitiful, the perishing, and yes, even the perverted will personally experience the glorious grace of our God. Selah.

Fourth, there was oil on the tabernacle and its furnishings. Everything in the tabernacle had to be anointed, if it was to be appointed. The Church cannot successfully function without unction. In all of our getting of understanding, we must not forget to get unction. All the tabernacle furnishings had to be "oiled," if they were to be allowed. A universal oil test should be given to ministers and members. Without the local church tabernacle oil, praise will never boil and lives will be soiled.

—ACT IX: THE PURPOSE OF THE OIL—

For this purpose the Son of God was manifested, that He might destroy the works of the devil (1 John 3:8).

Purpose is the strongest word in all of life. Rick Warren refers to successful living as, "The Purpose Driven Life." Dr. Myles Munroe calls it, "The Power of Purpose." Experiencing a *purposeful* life and ministry is the most efficient, effective, and excellent existence upon the planet. The *purpose* of the holy anointing oil upon the head, hand, foot, and face of the believer is paramount in pursuit of purpose. *Oil* in the cruse, the pot, and the tabernacle typify the totality of ministry that is tried and true.

There are 12 barrels of *oil* for the 21st century necessary for 12 specific reasons. *Twelve* is one of God's favorite numbers, and it represents God's government. There were 12 tribes of Israel and 12 apostles of the Lamb. There are 12 foundations in the New Jerusalem, the city that comes down from God. There are 12 yoke of oxen that the Elisha company must set in order before there can be oil without measure. This is the more excellent ministry that the Psalmist speaks of as *"excellent oil"* (Ps. 141:5). *Excellence means the superlative degree, to exceed the norm, to go beyond and above the standard, the status quo. Oil for the 21st century is excellence of ministry in ignominy and depravity. It is the only remedy for the maladies of the heterosexual, the homosexual, the bi-sexual, and the asexual. It is the only cure for homo-genitality, homo-reality, homo-ology, homo-actuality, and homo-eroticism.* Believers are like the Mercedes S600. They have 12 cylinders in their spiritual engines that must be filled with oil, changed regularly to circumvent leaks, evaporation, or the mundane meandering of weightlessness. The fragments of exposition, once gathered, will eliminate waste and fill 12 baskets of exegesis (see Jn. 6:12-13). The baskets full become barrels full as the Master Teacher takes it, blesses it, breaks it, and gives it. Once received, the believer will be able to say, *"Such as I have give I thee"* (Acts 3:6).

—TWELVE BARRELS OF OIL—

These 12 barrels of oil will enable *ministry in the new millennium*. Multi-faceted ministry is needed if the Word is to be heeded. Applications of the oil are assured to work in the wooing of a person's heart to God.

Barrel One: Oil for Ministry
(To Those in Same-Sex Attraction)

> *...for the anointing oil of the Lord is upon you. And they did according to the word of Moses* (Leviticus 10:7, emphasis added).

As a ministering priest, the believer must be a bridge and not a barricade. A block prevents passage. Priestly ministry begins in the outer court of sin. First, the blood and then the water is used. After the washing, there is worship. After the worship, the believer is ready to go to work. As ministry demands increase, so must the anointing. Otherwise, you will run on fumes and soon be on the side of the road, thumbing a ride for yourself. True ministry starts with ministry to the sinner, proceeds to the ministry to the saints, and graduates with ministry to the Savior. The Outer Court, the Holy Place, and the Holy of Holies are the progressive flow. The process is repeated daily. Ministry increase without anointing increase is problematic and potentially fatal. New levels bring new devils. Higher dimensions require higher degrees. Greater titles demand greater intensity. Heavier weights never deal with feather weights.

Barrel Two: Oil for Vision
(To Discern the Gay Look)

> *...and anoint thine eyes with eyesalve, that thou mayest see* (Revelation 3:18, emphasis added).

As a ministering priest, you must see clearly to minister dearly. Nearly is not good enough. To see is to be perceptive, to be receptive, to be selective, and ultimately effective. The eyesalve is the ointment to meet the appointment despite disappointment. The eyesalve is ointment of clarity of belief, correct biblicism, and concise theology. Seeing is a sense that cannot be done without the oil. Just because a man talks soft and a woman walks hard does not denote that they have gone through a hard day's night and that they've been living like a dog. Judging by the cover will lead to wasted expenditures. Unanointed seeing will lead to faulty vision. Seeing clearly is best done with sensitivity.

Barrel Three: Oil for Knowledge (To Pray for the Homosexual)

> *But ye have an **unction** from the Holy One, and ye know all things* (1 John 2:20, emphasis added).

As a ministering priest, you must know that you know, that you know, that you know, that you know. As the late Dr. Fuchsia Pickett once said to me, upon laying hands and prophesying over my life, "You must know the Holy Spirit as your teacher. When you do, you will know things in your knower." In 30 years of ministry, I have learned that prophetic minds need to know! When you do not know what and how to pray for the homosexual, the Spirit Himself will quicken your spirit with an awareness that makes you acute and accurate in your intercession. For prayer to be accurate, you need the assistance of the Advocate (see Rom. 8:26-27). *When you know that you know, you will know that:* Oil for the 21st century makes you knowledgeable in your prayer ministry.

You will know you have passed from death to life (see 1 Jn. 3:14).

You will know He abideth in you (see 1 Jn. 3:24).

You will know He hears you (see 1 Jn. 5:14).

You will know that you are begotten of Him (see 1 Jn. 5:18).

You will know that you shall be like Him (see 1 Jn. 3:2).

You will know that you have oil for the 21st century (see 1 Jn. 2:3).

Barrel Four: Oil for Good Deeds (To Not Act Out of Homophobia)

> *How God **anointed** Jesus of Nazareth with the Holy Ghost and with power: who went about doing good, and healing all that were oppressed of the devil; for God was with Him* (Acts 10:38, emphasis added).

As a ministering priest, you must live and lead the good life. Goodness is a fruit of the Spirit. Good deeds are the fruit of a good life. God is a good God, who is full of goodness and who sent His Son to do good works. Satanic power is overcome with Spirit power. Giving gracious words and doing gracious works are the **"oil and wine"** in operation. The Good Samaritan did good, and he has gone down in history. History makers, Kingdom shakers, and world changers are all do-gooders! Oil for the 21st century makes your ministry work while you work the ministry.

Barrel Five: Oil for Establishment
(To Deal With the Soul-Tie Diseased)

*Now He which stablisheth us with you in Christ, and hath **anointed us**,*
is God (2 Corinthians 1:21, emphasis added).

As a ministering priest, you are enabled and ennobled. The shaky past is fortified with an ability to stand. The songwriter answered the question, "What do you do when you have done all you can, and nothing seems enough?" with, "You just stand. When there's nothing else to do, you just stand and let the Lord see you through. After you have done all you can, you just stand." The late Ethel Waters once said, albeit in poor English, "God don't make no junk and God don't sponsor no flops." Oil for the 21st century establishes a staunch stance for the standards of God.

Barrel Six: Oil for Domination
(To Break the Demonic Hold)

So all the elders of Israel came to the king to Hebron; and king David
*made a league with them in Hebron before the Lord: and they **anointed***
David king over Israel (2 Samuel 5:3, emphasis added).

As a ministering priest, you are anointed to exercise dominion. You are authorized and deputized as a reigning king, directly answerable to the King of kings' command. You have authority to occupy the office and the ability to answer the demands of the office. As a king in Christ, you are divinely mandated (see Rev. 1:6), a hater of evil (see Prov. 16:12), righteous in life (see Prov. 16:17-18), awesome in action (see Prov. 20:2), trustworthy (see Prov. 20:28), friendly to the friendless (see Prov. 22:11), and sensitive to the poor (see Prov. 29:14). Wherever you go, the anointing will dominate as you learn to anoint the atmosphere with *shouts* of grace unto it (see Zech. 4:7). Oil for the 21st century allows you to dominate as you legislate the divine dictates.

Barrel Seven: Oil for Receiving
(To Bring Them Into the Kingdom)

And the Lord spake unto Aaron, Behold, I also have given thee the
charge of Mine heave offerings of all the hallowed things of the children
of Israel; unto thee have I given them by reason of the anointing, and to
thy sons, by an ordinance for ever (Numbers 18:8).

As a true Levite, you are *joined.* You are anointed to receive the best, just as the Levitical priests were (see Num. 28:9). Scripture says, *"For he that hath, to him shall be given"* (Mk. 4:25a). Givers always receive more than non-givers (see Acts 20:35). In my travels, I have noticed that "Word of Faith" churches have the anointing to receive. They receive millions for their ministries, and they are reaching millions. Receiving requires an anointing, just as giving does. Oil for the 21st century must be something that you believe God for, if it is to be received in force. If you respect an anointing, you will attract that anointing to you. If you sow into an anointing, you have a right to partake of it. The anointing is the receiver that transmits revelation for the revolutions in your life. You must receive oil first to release it later. Receive, in Jesus' name! Oil for the 21st century is available to those who realize that they are anointed to receive it. Selah.

Barrel Eight: Oil for Delivering (From Deviant Dysfunction)

> *Tomorrow about this time I will send thee a man out of the land of Benjamin, and thou shalt **anoint** him to be captain over My people Israel, that he may save My people out of the hand of the Philistines: for I have looked upon My people, because their cry is come unto Me* (1 Samuel 9:16, emphasis added).

As a true Levite, you are oiled to seek and save that which is lost (see Lk. 19:10). The fall of man lowered all of mankind into an abyss of same-sex attraction, sinful shackles, ignorant ideology, and corrupted worship. The believer has been moved upon, to move mountains. The move of the Spirit always moves on the mind of men, through the minds of others. You are saved to be a savior. To save means to salvage. It means to place appreciation on what has been depreciated —to bring to refuge what has been refused, including the recluse. To save is to preserve for a purpose. Many of God's sons and

JESUS OILED THE DISCIPLES TO HEAL THE HURTING HEARTS OF THE HOPELESS AND THE HOMELESS.

daughters have been kept, for a special purpose, despite their past sinister, sordid, sexual bondage. Salvation came to Zacchaeus' house when his faith climbed a tree and knocked on the door of Jesus' Spirit. Salvation comes to your neighbor's door when you knock on it. Simon Peter, upon sinking, cried, "Lord, save me!" Without any hesitancy, Jesus lifted him. The lesson did not begin until he was saved from the jaws of a watery death. To save is to snatch out of water, and to snatch out of fire (see Jude 1:23). The prophet Obadiah declared, *"And saviours shall come up on mount Zion..."* (Obad. 1:21). The "oil and wine" Church has one Lord and Savior and many little saviors and resident deliverers. The anointing is not for simply feeling or filling, but it is for fulfilling the invitation of salvation. Oil for the 21st century fulfills you while you fulfill God's will for your full life. You are saved to save. Selah.

Barrel Nine: Oil for Healing
(The Oppression of Same-Sex Attraction)

*Is any sick among you? let him call for the elders of the church; and let them pray over him, **anointing** him with oil in the name of the Lord: and the prayer of faith shall save the sick...* (James 5:14-15, emphasis added).

As a true Levite, you are joined to a healing Jesus. The songwriter said it this way: "He heals, praise the Lord. I was bound by the power of the devil but He delivers. Praise the Lord." Jesus oiled the disciples to heal the hurting hearts of the hopeless and the homeless, as well as the homosexual and the heterosexual. In the course of a lifetime, many who are caught up in same-sex attraction will cross your ministry path. A smile and a word of welcome can warm the heart while thrilling the soul. A frown will chill the soul. A frown puts a person down. It says, "Stay down." A smile says, "Hey, it is okay! Jesus is the way." He is the way in for those who are out—the way out for those who are in. A smile heals, but even a healing smile can also hurt. It sometimes hurts to hear the truth, even if it is spoken in love. Faithful are the wounds of a friend, because they are to your face and not behind your back. Oiled believers are wounded healers. Their wounds qualify their work.

The oil for ministry comes from your wounds. It is difficult to be used greatly until you have suffered enormously. The glory of infirmities that are born in the works of humility produce the oil and grace. The wounds that you feel turn into words that heal. Oil for the 21st century is contained where the blood has stained. Fresh wounds result in fresh oil. Do not worry about them, but learn to welcome them. Selah.

Barrel Ten: Oil for Yoke Destroying
(Spirit-Transfer Diseases)

And it shall come to pass in that day, that his burden shall be taken away from off thy shoulder, and his yoke from off thy neck, and the yoke shall be destroyed because of the anointing (Isaiah 10:27).

The true Levite is yoked with Christ. You suffer with Him; you reign with Him; you colabor with Him, as those who labor and are heavy-laden come to Him. These are those who become laborers *for* Him. The Isaiah 27:10 passage was spoken to Judah as a promise of God's intervention against the oppression of the Assyrians. People need to hear this word today. Those who are oppressed in the homosexual bondage need anointed yoke destroyers whose oil level indicator light is not flashing, signifying down-low levels. To become fat in the anointing, you must be Faithful, Available, and

Teachable. Oil for the 21st century is available, accessible, and assailable. It makes the minister able, capable, usable, applicable, responsible, and demonstrable in the demolition of darkness. Yokes become jokes and burdens become blessing when the oil is in operation. *The oil does for a believer what spinach did for Popeye; what a cape did for Batman; what the telephone booth did for Superman; what the ring did for Hercules; what the antennas did for*

THOSE WHO ARE OPPRESSED IN THE HOMOSEXUAL BONDAGE NEED ANOINTED YOKE DESTROYERS.

My Favorite Martian; what anger did for the Incredible Hulk; what the sword did for the Last Samurai; what the web did for Spiderman; what hair did for Samson, a mantle did for Elisha, and a song did for David. Selah.

Barrel Eleven: Oil for Wounds (Things Too Deep to See)

The true Levite operates as both the Good Samaritan and the five wise virgins did. Each had oil on their person. They did not have to go get it. Without oil, the end is near. Oil-less churches are never missed when they break down, sit down, and shut down. *The oil that the Good Samaritan applied to the bleeding and dying man had first been applied to himself.* F.E. Marsh says that the Good Samaritan had legs of compassion (he came to where he was). He had eyes of consideration (for he saw him). He had a heart of benevolence (he felt for him). He had hands of healing (for he bound up his wounds). He had a backbone of boldness (he put him on his beast). He had shoulders of support (he brought him to the inn). He had magnanimous concern (for he took care of him). He had liberality of spirit (he provided for his tomorrows). He had an anointed ministry of seeing, knowing, doing good, establishing, dominating, receiving, saving, healing, preaching, yoke destroying, and preaching because he poured in the oil and applied the wine to the wounds! The chosen generation will reach the wicked and adulterous generation, when the oil for the 21st century is applied to the hidden part of the heart. Selah.

Barrel Twelve: Oil for Preaching (Out of Their Homosexual Sin)

*The Spirit of the Lord is upon Me, because He hath **anointed Me** to preach the gospel to the poor; He hath sent Me to heal the brokenhearted, to preach deliverance to the captives, and recovering of sight to the blind, to set at liberty them that are bruised* (Luke 4:18, emphasis added).

The true Levite preacher is completely oiled from head to toe. The preached Word can change anyone. An anointed sermon literally stabs, thrusts, and cuts open the hardest hearts. It can cause anyone to change, even the deranged. The message of God's love is based on the ministration of His justice. The pain Jesus felt was the gain that makes hearts melt. Though the issue of homosexuality is deeply programmed, God can go even deeper and reprogram. The deepness of God calls to the deep propensity and predisposition of the homosexual. The message is that God loves the homosexual, but not homosexuality. God loves the earth, but not its pollution. God loves the Church, but not its corruption. God loves the sinner, but not their sin. The preaching of the cross is foolishness to some, but it is faith-producing to others. Christ denied Himself, and then died to Himself before He raised Himself, declaring, *"All power is given unto Me in heaven and in earth"* (Mt. 28:18b). The message of the death of Christ is soul-tied to the cross of Christ. The oil is upon the message and the messenger. Just as a driver's license needs to be renewed, so does a preaching license. Preaching without a renewed license that is validated by Heaven should result in having one's license suspended. Preaching under the influence of "another spirit" should result in being pulled to the side of life's Jericho Road and taken to the "powers that be" for an arraignment. Times are too serious for preachers to be high as a kite, drunk as a skunk, and cracked up and cracked out.

Many ministers today are preaching, but they are not reaching. They are talking, but they are not teaching. They are proclaiming platitudes that will not move the multitudes, heighten their altitude, expand their aptitude, or change their attitude. Rather, their words leave them in a state of lethargic lassitude, moral turpitude, and vulnerable vicissitude. In the words of James Brown, they are just "talking loud, but they ain't saying nothing."

As a true Levite, you are called to face straight-on what appalls you enough to turn your back on. Preaching is proclamation. Teaching is explanation. Healing is demonstration. These were the three elements of the evangelistic ministry of the Lord Jesus (see Mt. 9:36-38). *To preach is to reach each.* St. Paul charged his son Timothy, "Preach the Word" (2 Tim. 4:2a). Preaching the anointed Word is equivalent to pouring out the oil. It is simply relating the regal richness of God's grace. It is the unveiling of the gracious gospel that leaves a breathtaking view of the wondrous cross. It is the writing of the musical score upon the chart of uncharted areas of exploration, producing a symphonic sound of settlement. It is the painting of an undeniable portrait upon the canvas of the most God-chasing impressionable mind. Preaching isn't foolishness, but God uses the foolishness of preaching to make wise the fool. It is so simple that a fool need not err therein. Eloquence will get the minister praise, but the "oil" is the prize for great ministry. Brennan Manning, in *The Wisdom of Tenderness*, writes,

> The minister or priest, may not be gifted with eloquence, a wide vocabulary, or a charismatic personality, but the quiet fire in his or her belly is unmistakable, and the preaching comes from the heart. Words without poetry, lack passion; words without passion lack persuasion; words without persuasion lack power. When the language of "should"...predominates, both the preached and written word, are a barren wasteland, void of passion, persuasion, and power. At the close of too many sermons, the exhortation "Now let us..." carries neither conviction nor clout. Without the sharing of personal experience, prophetic preaching is impossible. The Word of God must become incarnate in the life of the preacher.[10]

Preachers who have oil preach with torched tongues, honest hearts, eagle eyes, holy hands, and lips lit with live coals. There is no lisp nor lameness in the living creatures. They are known in Heaven and in hell, long before they are known by mortals. Notable pulpits do not make noteworthy preachers. Reaching down to those in the pits comes before standing tall in the pulpit.

Standing on the street corner precedes standing in earshot of the amen corner. It has been said that *you will never be a postmaster before you can master being a postman.*[11] Fellowship, worship, discipleship, and stewardship are not a cruise ship, but rather a battleship. Oiled preaching is O-outstanding; I-intense; L-living; E-excellent; D-dynamic. It is aimed at the main artery of man's heart. When you aim for nothing, you are certain to hit the dead center of nothing every time. Cold preaching from cold hearts makes for a frigid atmosphere devoid of any anointing. Icy sermonettes make Christianettes out of sinner men and wanton women. Deep-freeze revelation will never develop depth of degree in damaged, dysfunctional deviants.

Manning further tells the story of a 19th-century preacher named Zacharias Werner who ministered in the city of Vienna, Austria. He gained a very notable reputation for his fiery messages that denounced carnality among Christians and sinfulness among the saints. Reportedly, he preached a message entitled, "That Tiny Piece of Flesh: The Most Dangerous Appurtenance of a Man's Body."

> Both the men and women in attendance were mortified and became uncomfortable as he continued his exposition of the rancid results of its improper use. His laser-like eyes transfixed

the congregation, with intensity as he spoke graphically of this tiny piece of flesh. At the conclusion of his discourse, Rev. Werner, leaned over the pulpit and screamed at his listeners, "Shall I name you that tiny piece of flesh?" There was a literal holy hush. It is said that smelling salts were extracted from ladies' handbags. He leaned out farther, and his voice rose to a hoarse shout: Shall I show that tiny piece of flesh?" Horrified silence! Not a whisper or a rustle of a prayer book could be heard. Werner's voice dropped, and a smile slid over his face. "Ladies and gentlemen, behold the source of our sins!" And he stuck out his tongue.[12]

The "oil and wine" Church needs preachers to stick out their godly tongue and preach the uncompromised proclamation. This kind of preaching will have oil on it. Believers must lift up Christ and His cross for all the world to see.

Prophet Keith Grayton was an oiled preacher without an ulterior motive or hidden agenda. Oiled preaching is an impartation of grace and not simply the exhibition of a gift. Preaching is acquainting an audience with Jesus and repeating what He has said. The "oil and wine" Church must recognize that it is not personality, persuasion, or profoundness that brings conviction, conversion, and conclusion. It is oiled preaching that electrifies and electrocutes. The Church can survive without buildings, bus ministry, budgets, or better parking; but it cannot survive without oil-soaked preaching![13] Legend has it that the devil one day preached a sermon. A minister discovered that it was lucifer himself, and he immediately came against him. The devil looked at him and remarked, "You need not fear my preaching. It will do no good for there was no oil upon it, in it, or with it." Oil for the 21st century must be on the preacher in the pulpit or it will never be on the parishioner in the pew. Prophets must preach the powerful Word of God, or "Pharaoh," the biggest pimp and purveyor of bondage, will never let God's people go. Without a *vision*, the people perish (see Prov. 29:18). Without the *prophet*, there will be no vision. The prophets must speak by two or three (see 1 Cor. 14:29). The uplifted Christ, who died on the uplifted cross, results in all men being drawn up to Him. The lyrics of a popular hymn recite:

How to reach the masses, men of every birth;

For an answer Jesus gave the key;

He said, and I, if I be lifted up from the earth,

I will draw all men unto me.

Lift Him up, lift Him up for the world to see.

He said, and I, if I be lifted up from the earth,

I'll draw all men unto me.

Preaching will make plain that problems are not permanent and failure is not final. *The healing DNA (Dynamic New Anointing) of divinity is in our voice. The TNT of Telling Necessary Truth is on our lips. The righteous remedy of ABC (Anointing Blessing Cure) is in our hearts.* The Church must break the silence to break the stronghold of dysfunction. The preachers must tell it like it is—no sugarcoating or placating, just advocating against the adversary. No flower, no fiction, and no fables; just faith, fact, and with feeling. Oiled preaching does not just present the successful sides of people. It records their *falls, falters,* and *failures.* When David was confronted, the prophet told him a story about a man who had a little sheep and another man who had many sheep but killed the man's one sheep. The story touched David's heart causing him to say that the man with many sheep should restore fourfold. Then the prophet said, *"Thou art the man"* (2 Sam. 12:7a). The prophet told a story that caused David to see himself. *The problem with much preaching is that we hear it and leave it without recognizing ourselves in it.* We see everyone else, but we seldom see ourselves. Preaching that poetically paints the picture is pretty, but self-portraits that result in self-examination are more practical. Good preaching shows us the *humanity* of persons in the Bible; great preaching shows us the *possibilities* within ourselves; and masterful preaching shows us the *reality* of the power of God. Oil for the 21st century will make preaching easier and will make listening a sweet delight. Selah.

—ACT X: THE POWER OF THE OIL—

How God anointed Jesus of Nazareth with the Holy Ghost and with power: who went about doing good, and healing all that were oppressed of the devil; for God was with Him (Acts 10:38).

Oil for the 21st century is needed if ministry in the new millennium is indeed not to be neutered. Without oil there are no spoils. Religion, ritualism, rules, and regulations will not reach the rebel crowd in the same-sex lifestyle. The Church must exercise its *dunamis* (dynamic) power. The oil that is kept fresh will always flow. There is no power shortage in the oiled sheepfold. When the oil runs out, the Church will eventually blow its engine.

Some time ago, a pastor was exposed as having had a three-year gay affair with a teenage member of his congregation. The child was brought to him for spiritual counseling when it was first discovered that he was fighting gay compulsion. Supposedly, and under the guise of ministry, they spent many hours together and even traveled occasionally to various cities in ministry engagements. The parents thought that their child was getting the help he needed. Nobody knew that the pastor was helping himself with the boy, using him as a sex toy. Criminal charges were filed and the case became a public scandal. This happened, in part, because of the power shortage in the local church, in the parents, and the lack of anointed eyesalve in the leadership. Power is in the oil. Applying it to the gay and lesbian is as simple as getting so much for yourself that you have enough and to spare. Selah.

The Composite Anointing: In Conclusion
Ministry in the New Millennium

Progression

The lesson of the tabernacle is in the progression—*first the order, then the oil*. It is also the lesson of the gospels. Blood first, the oil second. Salvation first, service second (see Ex. 29:7; Lev. 14:14). Consecration first, calling second. The order of the blood and the oil is the pattern of the Master Teacher, the Christ. At the Mount of Transfiguration, He spoke of His death before He spoke of the Holy Spirit coming (see Lk. 9:31; 24:49).

Before the day of grace... there is the day of wrath.

Before Pentecost fire... there is Passover blood.

Before the upper room... there is no room at the inn.

Before the Spirit is descending... there is Christ descending.

Before the Spirit uses us... the Spirit bruises us.

Before the waters of life flow freely... the rock is smitten.

Before the glory is poured... the Savior is pierced.

Before the meat offering (mixed with oil)...there is the burnt offering.

Before the promised land... there is the wilderness.

Those who have the blood applied are ready for the oil to be allocated. Being blood-washed is good, but being oil-soaked is great. The saturation upon this generation must exceed the previous one. The former is the landmark, the present is the trademark; the new breed must press for the mark. Oil for the 21st century is given to those who *"press toward the mark for the prize of the high calling of God in Christ Jesus"* (Phil. 3:14). Gethsemane, the place of the "oil press," or more literally the "squeezing of the seed," is where Christ died *to Himself*. Golgotha is where He actually died Himself. Though they sound similar, the two are not the same. To die to one's self is to squeeze self out of you. *To die yourself* is to squeeze God out of self. Christ gave up His will in Gethsemane; He gave up His breath on

Golgotha. It was in Gethsemane that the shemen, or semen (literally, the seed), was planted into the womb of mother earth before His body was planted in the tomb of Joseph of Arimathaea (see Mk. 15:43-46). The tears of sadness preceded the oil of gladness. The misrepresentation of the Lamb awaits those who represent the Lamb. "Lambs headed to the slaughter" is more than an expression. It is the essence of Christian existence. The world loves God; but strangely, it hates Jesus. He was not slain at Calvary. He was slain before the foundation of the earth. Before time had begun to begin, Jesus was the beginning of the ending and He is the end of the beginning. He was Alpha and He is Omega at the same time (see Rev. 1:8,11). Calvary simply manifested what had always been. Jesus is crucified afresh today by unbelieving believers and sinners who are not godly sorrowful. Most of the carnal crowd is not convinced that Jesus is God manifest in the flesh (see 1 Tim. 3:16). They are unconcerned about glorifying God in their body of flesh. The Scripture says in Galatians 3:29, *"And if ye be Christ's, then are ye Abraham's seed, and heirs according to the promise."* "If ye be Christ's" means, "if you are anointed ones," who have had oil poured out upon, smeared on, and rubbed in. As He is in the world, so are we. The "oil and wine" Church can *do* what He did, if we choose to *do* what He did! The same things done will yield the same results. He decided to die in order that all may live. The blood shed on Calvary preceded the oil poured on Pentecost. Three words characterize the progression of the oil. They are *power, perspective,* and *personification.*

Power

The gay or lesbian person, as well as all others, needs to believe in the power of God. God is love! Tina Turner asked the question, "What's love got to do with it?" The answer is: Everything—absolutely everything. The singer Cher asked, "Do you believe in love?" The answer is: Yes, absolutely yes. André Crouch sang, "Tell them [the lost] for me. Tell them that I love them and that I came to let them know...." The Bible says, *"Greater love hath no man than this, that a man lay down his life for his friends"* (Jn. 15:13). The "oil and wine" Church of the 21st century must do the same. Ministry in the new millennium requires thick and weighty oil that is fit for the Master's use.

> THE GAY OR LESBIAN PERSON, AS WELL AS ALL OTHERS, NEEDS TO BELIEVE IN THE POWER OF GOD.

176

Perspective

When we see those who have fallen prey to same-sex sin in a crisis condition, we should take a prophetic look beyond the faults, endeavoring to feel their pain and focus on their need of God. The seed of worship will meet the need of the wounded. We must look beyond our religious do's and don'ts, beyond legalism, ceremonialism, and ritualism. We must peer beyond our pompous pride, beyond our reputation and relegation. We must look beyond our own private problems or personal convenience. Ministry in the new millennium requires a perspective beyond condemnation into exoneration through the blood of the Lamb. (See Chapter Twelve.)

Personification

*And the King shall answer and say unto them, Verily I say unto you, Inasmuch as ye have done it **unto one of the least of these** My brethren, ye have done it unto **Me*** (Matthew 25:40, emphasis added).

The Master Teacher personifies victory and identifies with the victimized. He is the prime example of prophetic personification. Whatever is done for the gay and lesbian is done unto Him. In this sense, we can then look upon the man who fell among thieves as representing the Lord Jesus Christ Himself. It may be inconceivable to perceive of Jesus as the homosexual person who is in need of a way of escape. However, we must remember that He was *"numbered with the transgressors"* and that the *"Lord hath laid on Him the iniquity of us all"* (see Is. 53:6). Furthermore, He literally became *"sin for us"* and *"the propitiation* [penalty-payer] *for our sins"* (see 2 Cor. 5:21; 1 Jn. 2:2). When Jesus died, He did not simply die *for* sin, rather He died *as* sin itself. He *"bare our sins in His own body on the tree"* (1 Pet. 2:24a) and nailed our trespasses to the cross. This is known as identificational intercession. It is the highest realm of prayer available to the "oil and wine" Church. Our prayers should not simply be directed at "those gay or lesbian people," but they should be prayed as if they were us. A woman came to Jesus saying, *"Have mercy on me…my daughter is grievously vexed with a devil"* (Mt. 15:22). Even though it was her daughter's problem and not hers, she took ownership of it in her prayers. She said, *"Have mercy on me!"* Jesus commended her for her faith, and her daughter was delivered from being demonized that same day.

The day has come when the righteous Daniels of God must confess the sins of others, as if they were their own (confessing). Homosexuals need someone to cry out to God on their behalf. The oil must lubricate our intercession, or else the gay and lesbian world has no hope. The reader is advised to take a good look and picture the real pain of a person participating in perverse pleasure. Look beyond their pretentious outward appearance and see the potential of their heart. Pray for them as if it were you. Internalize the image of their sin as you lift their soul up to God. This kind of praying yields immediate and miraculous results. It will culminate in a greater influx of former gay and lesbian persons into the house of God than the Church has ever seen in its two millennia history. Jesus died for all the world, and He was killed by a small part of what would soon be His Church. Religious people have always resisted change, but world-changers resist the spirit of religion.

The Bible says that *"whatsoever you do, do it heartily, as to the Lord"*(Col. 3:23). We must speak to all men as if we are speaking to Jesus. This means that our speech will be oiled with gladness and not madness. May our attitude and our actions be right towards all men at all times.

In the first four chapters, we have addressed only a fraction of the equation of the homosexuals' reclamation. In *The Christological Apologetic: Homoology—Setting the Gay Record Straight,* we shall seal the deal with certainty and clarity.

> Prayer: Lord of the Harvest. Christ of Compassion who came down from Heaven to earth to show us the way. You went from the cross to the grave and from the earth to the sky. Lord, help us through deeds of compassionate approach to lift Your name on high. Grant us the anointing to be ministers of the new millennium. Let the oil and the wine be poured and applied into our hearts as we pour it into the hurts of others. Let the church be purged in its priestly and prophetic ministry that the bleeding and the dying may once again become the blessed and delivered. Let us possess the 12 barrels of oil for the oil-less generation. In the name of Jesus, the Anointed One. Amen and Amen.

ENDNOTES

1. Dr. Mark Hanby, *Anointing the Unsanctified* (Shippensburg, PA: Destiny Image, 2000), 17.

2. Dr. Kelly Varner, *Corporate Anointing* (Shippensburg, PA: Destiny Image Publishers, 1998), 55.

3. R.T. Kendall, *The Anointing: Yesterday, Today, Tomorrow* (Nashville, TN: Thomas Nelson Publishers, 1999), 41.

4. Benny Hinn, *The Anointing* (Nashville, TN: Thomas Nelson, Inc., 1992), 76.

5. Kendall, *The Anointing,* 41.

6. Varner, *Corporate Anointing,* 22.

7. Ibid., p 23.

8. Ibid., p 24.

9. George MacDonald quote (Source Unknown).

10. Brennan Manning, *The Wisdom of Tenderness: What Happens When God's Fierce Mercy Transforms Our Lives* (New York: HarperSanFrancisco, 2004).

11. Raymond W. Barber, *Profile of a Preacher* (Murfreesboro, TN: Sword of the Lord, 2000), 29.

12. As stated by Brennan Manning, *Wisdom*, 71-73.

13. Barber, *Profile of a Preacher*, 36.

CHAPTER
FIVE

The claim of Biblical support for a homosexual lifestyle is surprising to many. After all, is not the Bible clear in its prohibition of homosexuality? Historically, has not the church consistently rejected homosexuality since it is out of accord with biblical morality? What about all of the passages that...well...so clearly condemn homosexuality? What about these? Have they been misunderstood and misinterpreted and misapplied for all these years?[1]

James R. White and Jeffrey D. Neill

A real book is not one that we read, but one that reads us.[2]

W. H. Auden

Centuries of experience have tested the Bible. It has passed through critical fires no other volume has suffered, and its spiritual truth has endured the flames and come out without so much as the smell of burning.[3]

W. E. Sangster

Its critics, who claimed it to be filled with forgery, fiction, and unfulfilled promises, are finding that the difficulties lie with themselves, and not the Bible. Greater and more careful scholarship has shown that apparent contradictions were caused by incorrect translations rather than divine inconsistencies. It was man and not the Bible that needed correcting. It is the blueprint of the Master Architect.[4]

Billy Graham

The empire of Caesar is gone; the legions of Rome are smouldering in the dust; the avalanches that Napoleon hurled upon Europe have melted away; the prince of the Pharaohs is fallen; the pyramids they raised to be their tombs are sinking every day in the desert sands; Tyre is a rock for bleaching fisherman's nets; Sidon has scarcely left a wreck behind; but the Word of God still survives. All things that threatened to extinguish it have only aided it; and it proves every day how transient is the noblest monument that men can build, how enduring is the least word that God has spoken.[5]

Albert Baird Cummins

The Christological Apologetic:
Homo-ology—Setting the Gay Record Straight

Crisis at the Crossroads

The word *crisis* means "The point in a story or drama at which hostile forces are in the tensest state of opposition." The Chinese symbol for *crisis* is the same symbol that is used for *opportunity*. A *crossroad* is "a juncture where roads converge and alternative avenues avail themselves." The crisis of the Christian community has come to the crossroads of the gay and lesbian community. The opposition is an opportunity for the truth that has been crushed to the ground, to rise again. The Christological Apologetic concedes no ground in this contest for the soul of the Church. *Homo-ology* is a sorry, impoverished substitute for the *theology* that leads to soul prosperity (see 3 Jn. 1:2). The suffix "ology" means the *study* of something. The word *hermeneutic* describes the *analytical process* that brings an interpreter to a conclusion. *Homo-ological Hermeneutics* is the conclusive consensus of the study of homosexual behavior.

The primary passages concerning homosexuality in the Old Testament are found in Genesis 19:4-26; Leviticus 18:22; 20:13; and Ezekiel 16:49-50. The primary passages in the New Testament are the Synoptic Gospels, the Pauline Epistles of Romans 1:18-29; First Corinthians 6:9-10; Colossians 2:16-22; First Timothy 1:10; and the Second Petrine Epistle 2:6-7. We will end with Jude 7. Throughout this chapter, we will engage them in a three-fold manner. We will explicate the confusion with the *Homo-ological Hermeneutic*. We will disseminate the conclusion with the *Christological Apologetic*.[6] We will confront the confusion by setting the gay and lesbian record straight. The opposing view will be referred to as the *"Confusionists"* view, because it is *"contrary to fusion."* The arguments do not come together. Since God is not the author of confusion, any revision and new doctrine must be viewed as not authored by someone under divine inspiration.

Straight Is the Road

The Holy Bible provides a *straight* road to Heaven. It reveals the heart of God. God's thoughts are contained therein. God's ways and thoughts are synonymous. There is no duplicitous schizophrenia within the sovereign God. God's Word and will are inseparable. They say the same thing. They are revealed in the *Holy Bible,* which is the Book of all books. It is the textbook for one's entire lifetime. Its testimonies are true and its tenets are tested. Its exposition is easy. Error results from seeking to evade and erase its efficacy. Its precepts are plain and ministers who preach them that way are never misunderstood by the foolish debaters who engender strife (see 2 Tim. 2:23).

A common debating technique used to disqualify the position of an opponent is to *devalue the message* and to *discredit the messenger.* This is precisely the strategy of the pro-gay activists as they venture into the arena of theology. They refute thousands of years of conclusive scholarly work and factual history in an effort to convert others to their non-scholarly convictions. Unfortunately, many sincere and well-intentioned gays and lesbians, who profess Christ as their Savior, attend churches where the senior minister lacks conviction and preaches with compromise. They cannot get any help to get straight from crooked preachers. The seminary and public libraries, as well as secular and Christian bookstores, abound with a proliferation of material written by sympathizers who suggest that same-sex union is not sinful. Their goal is to provoke a revolution in Christendom; a conflagration in mainline churches; a transplantation of critical thought; and a penetration of the institutions of ministry training. They incite riots between the religious right and the liberal left. Simply stated, they are insidiously bent on dividing and conquering. The Master Teacher said, *"If a house be divided against itself, that house cannot stand"* (Mk. 3:25). The prophet Amos said, *"Can two walk together, except they be agreed?"* (Amos 3:3) These are the days when it is possible that even the elect shall be deceived (see Mt. 24:24). *For this reason, "The Christological Apologetic" is the most essential chapter of the 12 chapters of this book.* The Word of God must be the basis of your beliefs and not rhetoric or "churcheneese" (church language). Without the Word, a person's faith will stand in the wisdom of men and not in the power of God (see 1 Cor. 2:5).

Confusion Making Inroads

The confusionists have made inroads into major denominations, causing them to become shifted from the foundations that their fathers have laid. Now, their foundations are sandy and their house is shaky. They are struggling to make it and scheming how to fake it. They are on spiritual life support. They cannot breathe on their own because what they have identified and certified as normal is abnormal. The breath of God that makes a person or body a living soul is no longer flowing through their lungs.

On the other hand, there are many denominations that refuse to be refuted or have their doctrine diluted. Their adamancy is as assured today as it always was. Covert homosexuals have become uncomfortable peeping and hiding and sinning and grinning in church closets. This has caused some closet homosexuals to leave the ranks of the straight churches. Their unabashed stance toward the gay and lesbian lifestyle is considered intolerable.

One of the most notable of these homosexuals is a former, ordained evangelical minister and periodic ghostwriter for Pat Robertson, Jerry Falwell, and Billy Graham. Needless to say, once his sexual preference and practice became known, his services were no longer employed by any of these notable men of God. He is a self-professed gay author, Rev. Mel White, an active advocate of the gay church. He writes, "Misusing biblical texts out of context to condemn, to silence, and to control is not something invented by the religious right; but in our time, the religious right, Catholic and Protestant alike, is falling back upon that ancient practice once again."[7] He is indirectly referencing the Christological apologists. The truth is, this is exactly what the confusionists themselves do. On one hand, they state that the Bible is unrealistic and has been tampered with. Therefore, it cannot be regarded as reliable. Yet they quote it, when it is convenient to do so. In *The Same-Sex Controversy*, the homo-ological hermeneutic is denounced with a full head of steam.

> More and more the Bible is seen to somehow fall in line with modern "science" and modern impulses. Wherever the Bible opposes homosexuality, these passages are reinterpreted and re-presented so that the modern reader can now "understand" the original context, which was apparently hidden, lost, or buried under a load of cultural bias. The net effect of this revisionist approach is a novel and destructive twisting of Scripture: each passage is considered and, lo and behold, we find that same-sex intimacy is not even being considered, or that the passage addresses an abuse of the supposedly proper place of same-sex intimacy.[8]

The *Christological Apologetic*, simply stated, is the *defense of the Christian faith*. A brief perusal of the Scripture beginning with the Genesis account of Sodom and Gomorrah and concluding with the apocalyptic account in Revelation, reveals a concurring consensus. The Book of Jude declares, *"Earnestly contend for the faith which was once delivered unto the saints"* (Jude 1:3). The "faith" is the sum total of the *rightly divided truth*.

185

While it is quite true that the Bible has been used by people to support the most unscrupulous of motives and to justify everything from the *subjugation* of various ethnicities, the *degradation* of women, the *perpetration* of evil despotism, and yes, even homosexuality, it remains in its purest form, the infallible, inerrant Word of God. When the confusionists approach the sacred text, they do so with an eye to evade the *obvious*, avoid the *apparent*, and interpret as if they are *oblivious* to the original insights. Their translation, interpretation, or explanation is an appalling attempt at *Christological* character assassination. They batter the Book of all books into obfuscation. However, they are lightning-quick to quote the Bible when it comes within a thousand miles of their largesse leap of ludicrousness. They will conjecture till kingdom come, attempting to connect their corruption to incorruption. They disavow the decrees of God when they definitively deny their doctrine of defamation. To put it bluntly, they lie on God. Pray tell me, why would anyone be willing to die for a lie?

Three Kinds of Lies

The life of truth is one of simplicity. To lie to one's self is duplicity. To lie to others is hypocrisy. To attempt to make God a liar is apostasy. Deliverance is the children's bread. Manna is the angel's bread. Delusion is the devil's bread. The prince of darkness, a.k.a. "the devil," tried to take over God's celestial church. His appointed position as the anointed guardian cherub proved not enough. He coveted the high priesthood. He craved the senior pastorate of the universe. Thousands of years later, his modus operandi is the same. As an ungodly usurper, he conspires to turn the Church of Christ against the gospel of Christ. Supposed Christians are now among the leading antagonists opposing the landmarks of antiquity. They are part and parcel of the perverse membership that the "lord of the flies" would permit permanence and preeminence in the Church, if he had his luciferian way. Consecrated Christian leaders dismiss this covert, co-opting concision, because they concur that the devil is a constant liar!

> TO LIE TO ONE'S SELF IS DUPLICITY. TO LIE TO OTHERS IS HYPOCRISY. TO ATTEMPT TO MAKE GOD A LIAR IS APOSTASY.

Two Kinds of Looks

There are two ways to exegete or look at a passage of Scripture. First, there is the subjective way; and secondly, there is the objective way. There is an entire world of difference between *subjectivity* and *objectivity*. According to Webster's New Collegiate Dictionary, the word *subjective* means that which is "produced from an individual's mind or state of mind." The word *objective* is defined as "uninfluenced by emotion, surmise, or personal opinion." Personal opinions are like the exit polls in the 2004 U.S. Presidential election. In the beginning, the polls showed one candidate winning; however, in the end, the other candidate won by a relatively large margin. The exit polls were grossly wrong. *Subjective* opinions will always lead to gross error. *Objective* conclusions are the only ones that can be trusted.

The Almighty God does not have an opinion. He has omniscience. He has the full circle of 360 degrees of knowledge. He knows everything there is to know. He knows the beginning from the end. Jesus, the Son, is the tree of life. Satan, the serpent, offers the tree of the knowledge of good and evil. Its fruit is savored by same-sex advocates and it is seasoned with cyanide. Apostate academia challenges the authenticity of apostolic authority. This is done time and again by *subjective* imaginings of devoutly disguised lies. Anointed academia confronts the asininity of controversy. It does this quite confidently. The Psalmist, in a moment of jealousy for God's glory, unflinchingly declared:

> *Why do the heathen rage, and the people imagine a vain thing? The kings of the earth set themselves, and the rulers take counsel together, against the Lord, and against His anointed, saying, Let us break their bands asunder, and cast away their cords from us. He that sitteth in the heavens shall laugh: the Lord shall have them in derision. Then shall He speak unto them in His wrath, and vex them in His sore displeasure* (Psalm 2:1-5).

Subjective imaginings by heathen heads are the products of unholy hearts. The ranting and the raging of the kings of elitist intellectualism have conspired against the council of the Eternal Godhead. They seek to demolish the declarations of divinity. Their damnable derision seeks to *cast off the constraints of the Christological Apologetic*. The Psalmist asserted that the sitting Savior will have the last laugh from His celestial sanctum. Satan's sinister seduction through same-sex abduction will not survive the insurmountable siege of his sordid system of sinfulness.

One Kind of Wrong Look

Wrong will never be right, and right will never be wrong. It does not matter how many ways a person is wrong. If they are wrong in just one way, they might as well be altogether wrong. There is only one kind of wrong look, and that is the look to oneself as the absolute authority. It is awfully stupid to play God. Playing God is a profession that there is no training for. It is not a course offered in any college, and there are no degrees in "Playing-God-ology." It is possible to play God, albeit unsuccessfully, but it is impossible to know God without a revelation of God. He is revealed by faith.

In Romans 1:17, St. Paul says, *"For therein is the righteousness of God revealed from faith to faith: as it is written, The just shall live by faith."* He is quoting from Habakkuk 2:4, which says, *"Behold, his soul which is lifted up is not upright in him: but the just shall live by his faith."* Objective understandings are revealed by faith, and not by mere human experience or revisionist ransacking. A personal experience should never be taught as doctrine. The Scripture should never be revised simply because personal sexual practice has a problem lining up with it. When the Bible's position is the polar opposite of what a person wishes it to say, he or she is not at liberty to turn it on its head or upside down. This is the inevitable path that perversion leads to. *Perversion* means "obstinately persisting in an error or fault, to be wrongly self-willed."

A perverse perspective is the result of your soul being lifted up in a non-upright position. Those persons who ascribe to the heist of apologetic accuracy are unduly influenced to lose faith and live fleshly. They become spiritually anorexic, and their appearance will reflect their *"leanness of soul"* (see Ps. 106:15). They become bulimic in that they regurgitate righteousness while they impersonate innocence. Their spirit becomes

THEIR SPIRIT BECOMES DISEASED; THEIR SOUL BECOMES DEVOID; AND THEIR BODY BECOMES DEBASED.

diseased; their soul becomes devoid; and their body becomes debased. By downgrading the *Word*, they upgrade the *world*, and they degrade their worship. Woe be unto those who insist on persisting in theological treason. Woe be unto those who persecute those who preach the plain truth. Woe be unto those who think that they are representing God, when in fact, they do not even know God. The Master Teacher said:

> They shall put you out of the synagogues: yea, the time cometh, that whosoever killeth you will **think that he doeth God service**. And these things will they do unto you, because they have not known the Father, nor Me. But these things have I told you, that when the time shall come, ye may remember that I told you of them. And these things I said not

unto you at the beginning, because I was with you (John 16:2-4, emphasis added).

Jesus, the prophet greater than Moses, prophesied that His people would suffer crushing blows at the hands of those whose beliefs stand in diametric opposition to theirs. From the conception of Christ, to the inception of His cause, and the reception of His cross, He suffered a relentless campaign of cruelty. His election by the God of Israel led to His rejection by the people of Israel. Though we are two millennia removed from the Savior's earthly day, we must remember that the students of the Teacher and the servants of the Master will receive the same treatment when they stand for the same things. When an automobile is in proper alignment, there is only one set of tracks. The rear tires match the front ones. As endtime ambassadors, we make up the rear. The apostles of the Lamb make up the front. There must be one set of tracks. Otherwise, it indicates that the "oil and wine" Church is out of alignment and must be taken into the service department to be realigned for its eternal purpose.

—SETTING THE GAY RECORD STRAIGHT— HOMO-OLOGY IN GENESIS 19

*But before they lay down, the men of the city, even the men of Sodom, compassed the house round, both old and young, all the people from every quarter: and they called unto Lot, and said unto him, Where are the men which came in to thee this night? Bring them out unto us, that we may **know** them. And Lot went out at the door unto them, and shut the door after him, and said, I pray you, brethren, do not so **wickedly**. Behold now, I have **two daughters** which have **not known man**; let me, I pray you, bring them out unto you, and do ye to them as is good in your eyes: only unto these men do nothing; for therefore came they under the shadow of my roof. And they said, Stand back. And they said again, This one fellow came in to sojourn, and he will needs be a judge: now will we deal worse with thee, than with them. And they pressed sore upon the man, even Lot, and came near to break the door. But the men put forth their hand, and pulled Lot into the house to them, and shut to the door. And they **smote the men** that were at the door of the house with blindness, both small and great: so that they wearied themselves to find the door. And the men said unto Lot, Hast thou here any besides? son in law, and thy sons, and thy daughters, and whatsoever thou hast in the city, bring them out of this place: for we will destroy this place, because the cry of them is waxen great before the face of the Lord; and the Lord* *hath sent us to destroy it. And Lot went out, and **spake unto his sons in law,** which married his daughters, and said, Up, get you out of this place; for the Lord will destroy this city. **But he seemed as one that mocked unto his sons in law.** And when the morning arose, then the angels hastened Lot, saying, Arise, take thy wife, and thy two daughters, which are here; lest thou be consumed in the iniquity of the city. And while he lingered, the men laid hold upon his hand, and upon the hand of his wife, and upon the hand of his two daughters; the Lord being merciful unto him: and they brought him forth, and set him without the city. And it came to pass, when they had brought them forth abroad, that he said, **Escape for thy life;** look not behind thee, neither stay thou in all the plain; escape to the mountain, lest thou be consumed. And Lot said unto them, Oh, not so, my Lord.... Then **the Lord rained** upon Sodom and upon Gomorrah **brimstone and fire from the Lord** out of heaven; and he overthrew those cities, and all the plain, and all the inhabitants of the cities, and that which grew upon the ground. But his wife looked back from behind him, and she became a pillar of salt* (Genesis 19:4-18,24-26, emphasis added).

The Word is a Bible that utilizes over 26 Bible translations and brings them together to help the reader understand any biblical text. It translates the Genesis 19 passage in an amplified fashion. Here's how the *Word Bible* translates the Genesis 19 passage. ***Know:*** be intimate with them, rape them, abuse them, have intercourse with them, bring them out to minister to our lusts. ***Wickedly:*** do not commit such a wrong. ***Never knew a man:*** never had intercourse with a man. ***Blindness:*** they struck with blinding light, so that they were helpless to fill the entrance. ***Cry is waxen great:*** The stench of the place has reached to Heaven and God has sent us to destroy it.[9]

Homo-ological Hermeneutic: The confusionists say that the men of Sodom simply wanted to determine the purpose of the angels' visit. According to the revisionist interpretation, the Hebrew word, *yada,* means to merely make one's acquaintance. They point out that this word is used over nine hundred times in the Old Testament and in only a small fraction of verses does it mean to know sexually.[10] Another reason given for the destruction of Sodom has been inhospitality towards Lot's angelic visitors. Still another view is that Sodom and Gomorrah were destroyed because the men of the city desired to rape the angelic visitors as a penalty for their lack of respect for the tradition of identifying themselves to the city elders.

Christological Apologetic: Without question, the male citizens of Sodom and Gomorrah were guilty of inhospitality. They were quite unfriendly or unreceptive towards Lot's company. Inhospitality is either perpetrated by actions or by inaction towards someone. Either you fail to do something to make your guest feel welcome or you do something that causes them to feel unwelcome. The inhospitality of the Sodomites was not because of inaction. They were quite busy that fateful night. Both old and young men "compassed" Lot's house. They "called out to Lot." They inquired, "Where are the men?" They told Lot to "stand back" so that they could get at the visitors. They threatened Lot saying, "Now we will deal worse with thee than with them." They "pressed sore" upon Lot. After the men were blinded, they "wearied themselves to find the door." We see that inhospitality by *inaction* was not the case with these Sodomites. Clearly they wanted closer contact and to interact with the angelic visitors in Lot's house. The question then becomes: What would the nature of that interaction have been?

The other aspect of inhospitality is to act in a way that does not make guests feel welcome, comfortable, or safe. Since the Sodomites were not inhospitable by inaction, then it stands to reason that the Sodomites intended to *act* or *do something* that was inhospitable. Their intention, as we know, was never consummated. But let's examine their *inhospitable actions*.

The men of Sodom said to Lot, "... *Where are the men which came in to thee this night? bring them out unto us, that we may know* [yada] *them*." The intended action was to "know" the angels. On the surface, it does appear that these men simply wanted to get to know the "angels unaware" and that they wanted to understand the purpose of their visit. Through the 20th century cultural context of Derrick Sherwin Bailey, who first proposed the acquaintance interpretation in the 1960's, it would seem that the Sodomites only desired to make the angels' acquaintance.[11] However, proper biblical interpretation involves knowing the context of the text, because any text without context leaves one only with a pretext.

Let us digress a bit and apply the revisionists' line of thinking to the story of David and Jonathan. Using a present-day perspective only, someone could possibly think that David and Jonathan were homosexual, because they kissed and embraced when David was fleeing the wrath of Saul. In Western society, we rarely see this behavior among men. A handshake or a very light and brief, almost sideways hug are what men usually extend to one another. However, in Middle Eastern culture, which is the setting of the biblical writers, kissing and embracing among men was, and even is today, quite common and is not thought of as homoerotic affection. If the biblical writers were alive, they would be quite puzzled that their writings have been twisted by the influence of ignorance of revisionist interpreters.

It is easy to see how one who does not employ a holistic hermeneutic of the Bible could confuse the biblical concept of sexual intercourse with our modern-day concept of coming to know or to know about someone, simply because the English word used is *know*. Although the primary biblical use of this word is for ideas other than sexual contact, the context of this passage shows a definite sexual denotation. Within the same passage, Lot offered his daughters who *"have not known* [yada] *man,"* to the Sodomites. It is quite evident that Lot deduced from their behavior (past and present) that the Sodomites desired sexual contact with the angels. Lot did not offer them money or some other bribe, for he knew that only something on a similar level could have possibly pacified them. Thus, he offered his daughters while giving a summary of their sexual history in a futile effort of appeasement. Therefore, if *yada* means sexual contact in Genesis 19:8, it has a sexual meaning also, only three verses earlier in Genesis 19:5 when the men of the city demanded that the two visiting men be brought out, that they may *"know"(yada)* them. Genesis 4:1 says, *"Adam knew* [yada] *Eve."* As a result, Cain was conceived. Adam's knowing of Eve was definitely more than asking her name or phone number, so to speak. His *knowing* of Eve was an expression of intimacy. She conceived Seth after Adam *knew (yada)* her again (see Gen. 4:25). The Bible describes Rebekah, Isaac's future wife, as a virgin and *neither had any man known* (yada) *her...* (Gen. 24:16). *Yada* is obviously a reference to sexual intimacy in all of these texts.

Rape Issues

The context of Genesis 19 clearly shows us the intentions of the men of Sodom. They wanted to have sexual relations with the celestial beings. In fact, they wanted to rape them. Considering the torrid details of homosexual actions during sex, it is one of the saddest pictures in the entire Bible. This alone should convince anyone of the depravity of the demonic spirit associated with same-sex sin. The angels

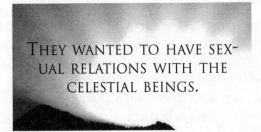

THEY WANTED TO HAVE SEXUAL RELATIONS WITH THE CELESTIAL BEINGS.

were the visitors, and the only hospitality that the men of the city wanted to show them was to gang-rape them. This was (to say the least) the inhospitable intent, and it was homosexual in its overtones.

Lot said to the Sodomites, "*I pray you, brethren, do not so wickedly*." Lot was referring to something far worse than inhospitality. Inhospitality is not an exercise in gross wickedness. It is certainly not a pleasant thing to experience, but seldom does it evoke being referenced as wickedness. The text says that they were "*exceedingly wicked*." The word *wicked* is derived from the word *wicker*, and it refers to that which is twisted. These men were twisted in their sexual desires. The word *exceeding* implies that there was much more to it than inhospitality. *The twisted desire of lawlessness was to violate the two angels sexually with anal penetration.* To them, the celestial beings were simply more new and strange flesh to do the "humpty-hump" with. The Sodomites were moral degenerates who were demon-crazed. Wickedness was the primary reason for Sodom's overthrow and not inhospitality. The Master Teacher experienced far more inhospitality, and yet He never called for fiery, sulfuric rock to be rained down on the Christ rejecters.

Serious Issues

An example of this is found in Luke 7:44-50. Jesus seriously upbraided his host, Simon, the Pharisee, for his inhospitality towards Him. The Master Teacher, the Son of the living God, the Messiah, was not extended basic courtesies that Middle Eastern households extended their guest. The proper reception for Jesus should have included the removal of His sandals for washing His feet. This prevented tracking into the house, dirt picked up on the dusty roads along His way. Next, someone should have poured water over them, rubbed them with their hands, and dried them with a towel (see Gen. 18:4;19:2; 24:32; 1 Sam. 25:41; Jn. 13:3-5; 1 Tim 5:10). Then, His head should have been anointed with spice-scented olive oil. David made reference to this in Psalm 23:5. Simon neglected to extend all of these hospitable courtesies to Jesus when He arrived for the banquet (see Lk. 7:44-46).[12]

How much more grievous is it to be inhospitable to the Prince of Peace, the Bright and Morning Star, than to His angelic emissaries in Genesis. Yet Jesus did not call fire and brimstone down on the house of the Pharisee. Instead, He sat and dined with them. Inhospitality did not precipitate the judgment of a just and holy God in Genesis 19. Something graver was ongoing in Sodom.

> *And the Lord said, Because the cry of Sodom and Gomorrah is great, and because their sin is very grievous; I will go down now, and see whether they have done altogether according to the cry of it, which is come unto me; and if not, I will know* (Genesis 18:20-21).

Destructive Issues

Even before the riot at Lot's front door, the raucous and rancid reveling of the twin cities rang in God's righteous ears. Abraham pleaded, "...*Wilt Thou destroy the righteous with the wicked?*" The wheels of the Almighty's judgment were already rolling before His angelic messengers ever reached the city. Their sin was so great that God came down in the form of a rarely occurring theophany. A theophany is a *"physical manifestation of God in another form."* Inhospitality was hardly the catalyst for the calamity rained upon these condemned cities, but rather their iniquity was. The inhumanity of their attempted gang rape exceeded their inhospitality. *Yes, the Sodomites were definitely guilty of inhospitality, but they were destroyed for gross iniquity.* They were destroyed for the iniquity of a deep disregard for the laws of nature. This began well before the angels passed through the city gates. To suggest otherwise is to take a huge hermeneutical leap that does not have the support of the volume of Scripture. They were guilty of inhospitality on that particular night, but they were destroyed for their deep disregard for the laws of nature. This began well before the angels passed through the city gates.

> SODOM WAS GUILTY OF INHOSPITALITY, BUT THEY WERE DESTROYED FOR INIQUITY.

Real Issues

The real issue of Sodom and Gomorrah was the ongoing practice of male-to-male genital contact. The real issue was the pride of the Sodomites in refusing to repent of their *wicked ways.* The real issue was participating in a sexual order that brings disorder to God's divine order. Even the desire to violate the angelic messengers in the most vile and despicable way was not the reason for these cities' destruction. It was the continued, hard-hearted, unrepented, haughty, prideful practice of sin on the basest level imaginable that brought down these great cities.

Historical commentary concurs that Sodom and Gomorrah were destroyed in major part because of the wickedness of their homosexual practices. "...The men became accustomed to being treated like women," was the commentary of Philo of Alexandria who represents the first-century view of sexuality.[13] Today, the term *sodomy* is a distinct reference to anal intercourse, and derives its etymology from its biblical birthplace.

When God created male and female, He separated the *reproductive* area of the body from the *refuse* area of the body. Any mixing of the two is a sinful abomination to God, a stench in His nostrils, and a screeching in His ears. The occurrence of perverse sexual practice resulted in divine judgment. Today, archaeological discoveries have proven the accuracy of the biblical record in the excavation of the ancient cities of Sodom and Gomorrah whose ruins have been discovered southeast of the Dead Sea at the site of the modern cities of Bab edh-Dhra and Numeira.[14]

—SETTING THE GAY RECORD STRAIGHT—
HOMO-OLOGY IN LEVITICUS 18:22

*Thou shalt not lie with mankind, as with womankind: it is **abomination*** (Leviticus 18:22, emphasis added).

*If a man also lie with mankind, as he lieth with a woman, both of them have committed an **abomination**: they shall surely be put to death; their blood shall be upon them* (Leviticus 20:13, emphasis added).

The passage in Leviticus was written directly to the Israelites who were the original recipients of the moral law given by God. Their interpretation of that law is within the parameters of the oral law, known as the *Talmud*. The written law is known as the *Torah*. Modern Rabbinic interpretations of the law include a certain element of graciousness for the sinner, while still maintaining the original tenets of the law.

Rabbinic discussions of homosexuality begin with the fact of its sinfulness and moral unacceptability but quickly make two important points. First, as in all matters pertaining to human failings, a strict distinction must be maintained between the sin and the person. Although homosexual behavior is to be condemned, homosexual persons are as beloved of God as everyone else; they are to be treated with no less dignity than we want for ourselves. This is, of course, no different than what the Christian position is, ideally—hating the sin but loving the sinner.[15]

Dr. Jeffrey Satinover

The degree of revulsion associated with the homosexual act is suggested by the specific attachment of the word *abomination* to it. It means "an abhorrent thing or something detestable, loathsome, utterly repugnant, disgusting, imitating a particularly revolting and conspicuous violation of boundaries established by God against the defiling characteristics of other people."[16]

Leviticus 18:22 and 20:13 are two of the more troubling passages for the gay advocates. Yet, there are numerous counter theories to explain away the evident truth contained therein. Both heterosexuality and homosexuality are addressed in the Book of Leviticus. It is a Book which lays down the law.

Homo-ological Hermeneutic: The confusionist view is threefold. *First,* the homosexual argument is that these Scriptures are under old covenant and do not apply to believers today. *Secondly,* it is taught that the New Testament Church does not hold to all the practices mentioned throughout Leviticus such as dietary requirements, neither should believers today hold to the ones that speak about homosexuality. *Thirdly,* it is concluded that in Leviticus, the Holiness Code was specified in a Mosaic Law context only. The conclusion of this view is that the forbidding of homosexuality in Leviticus has more to do with the historical connections of homosexuality with idolatry and does not speak to homosexuality that is identified as an orientation.

Christological Apologetic: Let us examine each of these claims. The laws of the Old Testament are divided into the ceremonial law, the dietary law, and the moral law. The Book of Leviticus contains many of the laws that governed the behavior of the people of God. The admonition against same-gender relations appears in a distinct section of the Book known as the Holiness Code. They were written several hundred years after the story of Sodom recorded in Genesis 19. Leviticus 19 addresses sexual offenses, and in chapter 20 the repercussions of violating those standards are addressed. The *ceremonial law* pertained to functions that were associated with the priesthood mediatorial function. The ceremonialism was fulfilled in Jesus Christ who is our High Priest. The dietary law was superceded by Jesus in Mark 7:18-19. The *moral law*, however, is fulfilled in the New Testament passages that restate the same thing. An example of this is in the moral law of not bearing false witness. Though it is stated in the Old Testament, it is repeated in Pauline adjuration (see Eph. 4:25).

The first response is that forbidding of same-sex relationship is clearly in the realm of the moral law. The second and third chapters of Colossians are particularly pertinent to the question of the dietary and moral law described in Leviticus.

Let no man therefore judge you in meat, or in drink, or in respect of an holyday, or of the new moon, or of the sabbath days: which are a shadow of things to come; but the body is of Christ.... Wherefore if ye be dead with Christ from the rudiments of the world, why, as though living in the world, are ye subject to ordinances, (touch not; taste not; handle not; which all are to perish with the using; after the commandments and doctrines of men? (Colossians 2:16-17,20-22)

St. Paul announced that no person should be judged in light of his observance of the dietary law. Today, the dietary law is more like an *elective* and not a *directive*. The dietary law is repealed in chapter 2, while the moral law is restated in chapter 3. St. Paul teaches that there is no prohibition against any particular food and then proceeds to say that there is a price to be paid for sexual sin. It is a violation of moral law.

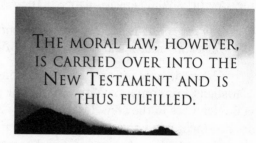

THE MORAL LAW, HOWEVER, IS CARRIED OVER INTO THE NEW TESTAMENT AND IS THUS FULFILLED.

Though homosexuality is not mentioned, it is indirectly implied. The terms *uncleanness* and *fornication* suggest that sex outside of divine sanction is sin. This leaves no wiggle room for wobbly interpretation.

> *Mortify therefore your members which are upon the earth; fornication, uncleanness, **inordinate affection**, evil concupiscence, and covetousness, which is idolatry: for which things' sake the wrath of God cometh on the children of disobedience: in the which ye also walked some time, when ye lived in them* (Colossians 3:5-7, emphasis added).

The term *inordinate affection* means "vile and depraved." Whatever ambiguity the confusionists ascribe to the Leviticus passages, they cannot hold up to the teachings and writings of the Master Teacher and St. Paul in the New Testament. The Scripture does not contradict itself. God does not double-speak. Christ is indeed the end of the law (see Rom. 10:4), but He is the conservation of the moral law which teaches the high standard of character-centered living.

The second response is that the forbidding of same-sex relationships in Leviticus extended beyond Israel. The Canaanite people were dispelled from the land for the abominable sins that Israel was warned against. God referred to their perverted sin as a *"full cup of iniquity"* (see Gen. 15:16). Even though the Amorites were not under the Mosaic Law, they were still held accountable for the *"violation of the law of conscience!"* One may visit another country and not know all the laws, but that does not excuse him from obeying them. Even in America, *ignorance of the law is never an acceptable excuse.* If anything, a person's ignorance may simply modify the degree of conviction and penalty handed down by the powers that be. God forbade same-sex relations in Israel, and the moral prohibition is reinterated in the New Covenant. All nations must receive the gospel. There are no exception clauses given to those who are not Israelites.

The third response is that the Book of Leviticus is first and foremost a book about the *holiness of God* and the required holy standards of God's people. Leviticus 20:26 encapsulates its theses.

> *You shall be holy unto Me: for I the Lord am holy, and have severed you*
> *from other people, that you should be Mine* (Leviticus 20:26).

Granted, there were other admonitions in Leviticus that do not apply to Christians, but homosexuality was not one of them. This is confirmed in several references in the New Testament. The other "abominations" of Leviticus are not mentioned again. They were specific to Israel, and they were ended along with the law, at the advent and ascension of Christ. *The command to be holy in sexual areas is an eternal one.* It is never *recommended;* it is always *required.* Holiness is an essential and moral attribute of God. Therefore, in discussing the ceremonial, the dietary, or the moral law and their relevance today, be assured that the holiness standard will never be compromised by the Holy One. *Holiness is the lifestyle that identifies with God's revealed declaration concerning right and wrong.* To live a holy life is to live sanctified, set apart for God's purposes. Leviticus is the Book of Holiness, and it clearly says that committing homosexual acts is a loathsome, despicable, and sinful abomination. Heaven will pass away and every blatant act of defiant and deviant behavior on earth will too, before God's Word will ever pass away (see Mt. 24:35). As it was said of old, it must be said again, *"Who is on the Lord's side?"* Those who did not step forward were immediately victimized and vaporized by the consequence of selecting wrongly.

> *Then Moses stood in the gate of the camp, and said, Who is on the Lord's*
> *side? let him come unto me. And all the sons of Levi gathered themselves*
> *together unto him* (Exodus 32:26).

> *And the earth opened her mouth, and swallowed them up, and their*
> *houses, and all the men that appertained unto Korah, and all their goods*
> (Numbers 16:32).

Today, the Levitical laws' denunciation of homosexual acts still stands, just as *"Thou shalt not take the name of the Lord thy God in vain"* still stands; just as *"Thou shalt not commit adultery"* still stands; just as *"Thou shalt not bear false witness"* still stands. Though the abomination of homosexuality is not listed in the Ten Commandments, it is commanded as forthrightly in every dispensation from innocence, to conscience, to law, to the church age, and even the final age.

—SETTING THE GAY RECORD STRAIGHT—
HOMO-OLOGY IN EZEKIEL 16:49-50

*Behold, this was the iniquity of thy sister Sodom, pride, fullness of bread, and abundance of idleness was in her and in her daughters, neither did she strengthen the hand of the poor and needy. And they were haughty, and committed **abomination** before Me: therefore I took them away as I saw good* (Ezekiel 16:49-50, emphasis added).

And whosoever shall not receive you, nor hear your words, when ye depart out of that house or city, shake off the dust of your feet. Verily I say unto you, It shall be more tolerable for the land of Sodom and Gomorrah in the day of judgment, than for that city (Matthew 10:14-15).

Homo-ological Hermeneutic: The confusionists implicate the prophet Ezekiel in their attack on the story of Sodom and Gomorrah and the long-held interpretations of it. It is taught that instead of homosexuality, the judgmental sin of Sodom was pride, fullness of bread, and abundance of idleness. To make their argument seem more plausible, they also say that Jesus mentioned Sodom and Gomorrah in the context of inhospitality in Matthew 10:14-15. In other words, the people whose hearts were hardened to the gospel, refusing to receive it, were showing inhospitality to Christ, and in the process were guilty of the same sin as the Sodomites. Since Christ does not mention Sodom and Gomorrah in the context of homosexuality, it is assumed that it was not the preeminent issue involved.

Christological Apologetic: This interpretation is incorrect because of the clear contextual evidence to the contrary. There are five reasons why this homo-ological hermeneutic should be rejected as an errant one. *Five* is the number of grace and the following explanation is a gracious one.

First, the homosexual sin of Sodom and Gomorrah was not the theme of these verses. The rejection of the gospel by the cities that the Master Teacher and His apostles visited was the matter at hand. The people of the twin cities were classified as *"being in a state of grievous sin"* prior to the visit of the angels. This is much more than mere inhospitality.

And the Lord said, Because the cry of Sodom and Gomorrah is great, and because their sin is very grievous (Genesis 18:20).

Secondly, when Abraham pleaded with God to spare the city, he referred to the city and its inhabitants as wicked in three separate instances.

199

1. Genesis 13:13: *"But the men of Sodom were **wicked** and sinners before the Lord exceedingly"* (emphasis added).

2. Genesis 18:23: *"And Abraham drew near, and said, Wilt Thou also destroy the righteous with the **wicked**?"* (emphasis added)

3. Genesis 18:25: *"That be far from Thee to do after this manner, to slay the righteous with the **wicked**: and that the righteous should be as the **wicked**, that be far from Thee: Shall not the Judge of all the earth do right?"* (emphasis added)

This thrice-repeated reference to wickedness is a reference to active deeds and not a passive posture of pride, or pacification and pomposity, because of plenty of bread.

Thirdly, Abraham's intercession to God began with him asking God that if 50 righteous people could be found in the entire twin city complex that it would be spared of the impending judgment. God Almighty, in His *gracious love,* long-suffered on his behalf. Eventually, the minimal number of 50 was reduced to the minuscule number of 10. Abraham offered the same conditions. God gave the same response. There were not even 10 people who were living in right standing with God in the entire region. It is because of His covenant with Abraham that God remembered Lot and spared his life. It was Lot's right standing with God that spared his family (see 2 Pet. 2:7-8). God is a covenant-revealing, a covenant-making, and a covenant-keeping God. Covenant honors God and God honors covenant.

Fourthly, the decision to destroy the place was prior to the so-called inhospitable treatment of the Sodomites (see Gen. 18:28-32). The decision had already been advocated by the heavenly council. It was soon to be adjudicated by the heavenly host, and actuated by the heavenly elements of fire and sulfuric stone. All of this took place before any inhospitality was shown. The decision had been made and the details of Lot and his family's deliverance had to be taken care of before the city was actually destroyed. Therefore, if the men of the city had shown the most gracious hospitality and offered each angel a hot, cooked meal, a cold cruse of water, a warm, comfortable bed to sleep in, and all the other amenities of five-star accommodation, nothing would have averted judgment. It would not have thwarted the foreboding clouds that were on the horizon. Nothing would have spared the city, short of return to righteousness and repentance.

Fifthly, the sin of pride, fullness of bread, and abundance of idleness were clearly the root of, or the foundation to, the conjectured abomination committed there. Pride is the root of all sin, because before there was sin, there was pride. Lucifer was lifted up in pride and fell. He fell down to the garden and utilized the pride of life to entice Eve to be deceived and Adam to transgress. The serpent utilized the pride of life to spin his web of deceit. When a person is caught up in his clutches, they are full of *pride*, of which the middle letter is "I." It is also true of all *sin* and every *lie*. When people are proud, they are unrestrained and they do whatever they want to do. This was the case with the Sodomites. Scripturally, *Sodom* is used as a metaphor of judgment. The words of Leonard Ravenhill illustrate the substance of this, in his classic writing, *Sodom Had No Bible*.

> Sodom had no churches. We have thousands. Sodom had no Bible, we have millions. Sodom had no preachers, we have ten thousand plus thousands. Sodom had no Bible Schools. We have at least two hundred and fifty. Sodom had no prayer meetings. We have thousands. Sodom had no gospel broadcasts. As a nation we are richly blessed with Christian broadcasts. Sodom had no histories of God's judgment to warn it of danger. We have volumes of them. Sodom perished in spite of all these disadvantages. America today is living only by the mercy of God...What obligations has God to a people like us whose aggregate sin as a nation in one day is more than the sin of Sodom and her sister city, Gomorrah, in one year?[17]

Though these words were written over 25 years ago, they were never more true than they are today. Evangelist Dr. Billy Graham once said, *"If God does not judge America, He will have to apologize to Sodom and Gomorrah."*[18]

HOMO-OLOGY
AND THE MASTER TEACHER

Homo-ological Hermeneutic: One of their major pro-homosexuality positions states that the Master Teacher never addressed the subject directly, and that He never categorically denounced homosexuality. Therefore, if Jesus did not consider it important enough to directly address, then why should the Church do so today?

Christological Apologetic: There is no biblical record that Jesus directly addressed homosexuality; however, He *also never directly addressed incest, bestiality, domestic abuse, or alcohol and drug abuse either*. Obviously, the rest of the Bible addresses those issues. His silence on those sins cannot be viewed as a sanction. No person can correctly accuse Christ of condoning this belligerent behavior and conduct because He did not directly speak to it. The Bible does not record that Jesus ever encountered a homosexual in His ministry. There was no need to address it. A minister must always be relevant. Why should a minister talk about Thanksgiving turkey when it is Independence Day? Fireworks would be a more appropriate choice of topics. The cardinal rule of ministry is to *know your audience*. Even the Pharisees did not waste time preaching about issues that were not at hand. *The best way not to make an issue out of something is to not make it an issue.* That sounds redundant, but it is true nonetheless. A perusal of Scripture reveals that the standard concerning these issues is upheld throughout the whole of the Bible. Simply because the four gospels do not speak to this explicitly does not negate the Lord's perspective concerning it. Sound Christian doctrine is based on the entire Bible and not the four gospels only, which individually did not record all that Jesus said and did.

> *And there are also many other things which Jesus did, the which, if they should be written every one, I suppose that even the world itself could not contain the books that should be written. Amen* (John 21:25).

The Bible is properly read and interpreted as one complete book and not as a compilation of many different unrelated books of incongruous thoughts. Scripture must be interpreted according to the patterns of thought woven throughout it. Generally, the first time something is mentioned in the Bible, the same meaning is carried throughout. This is known as the law of first mention. It establishes the meaning through precedence and preponderance.

It is quite true that Jesus never directly addressed homosexuality, but He absolutely held up the holiness and marital standard in sexual relationships. Suggesting that Jesus condoned homosexuality as a practice or lifestyle while extrapolating that He and the apostle John were homosexual lovers is the *epitome of blasphemy against the Son!* It can be forgiven, but it is a forged signature on the document of endearment. The leaning of John's head upon Jesus' breast was not an act of sexual intimacy. It was an act of the deepest endearment and devotion. The apostle John put his head upon Jesus' chest much like a son would do his father. Upon doing this, John could clearly hear the heartbeat of Jesus. It is no wonder that John was known as the apostle of love. He was afforded the greatest unveiling of truth in the vision of the Apocalypse. John was among the last at the cross and among the first at the tomb. Jesus even committed His mother to his care. The counterfeit interpretation will not stand the scrutiny of dissection. Consider these two things.

First, although Jesus did not directly address it, He did hold it up to the light. He did give a picture of what God intended and ordained. In Mark 10:6-9, Jesus teaches:

> *But from the beginning of the creation God made them male and female. For this cause shall a man leave his father and mother, and cleave to his wife; and they twain shall be one flesh: so then they are no more twain, but one flesh. What therefore God hath joined together, let not man put asunder.*

This foundational Scripture teaches the reason for the distinction between genders. As we hold all other sexual activity to the light of this Word, we can clearly see God's divine design and original intention and purpose. What God has ordained from the beginning of creation, serves as the eternal will of God for everyone.

Secondly, the question is, why would Jesus decree again what He had already established? In Genesis 1:26-27, God said, *"Let Us make man in Our image....male and female created He them."* God was speaking to the eternal counsel of the Godhead, because He *"worketh all things after the counsel of His own will"* (Eph. 1:11b). The apostle John wrote, *"In the beginning was the Word, and the Word was with God, and the Word was God....And the Word was made flesh...* (Jn. 1:1-14). Therefore Christ, the Word made flesh—or the logos, the thought, plan, and purpose of God—was there in the beginning of creation. In fact, as Commander in Chief, He (Christ) is the *"beginning of the creation of God"* (Rev. 3:14b). Christ was there when man and woman were created, and He was there when they were commanded to be fruitful and to multiply (see Gen. 1:28). The Scripture says, *"...male and female, created He them."* God ordained distinction between the sexes and definition in their various roles (see Deut. 22:5). In the beginning, it was *Adam and Eve* and not *Madam and Eve,* or *Adam and Cleve.* This was so elementary, so basic, so understood in Jesus' day that He didn't need to address it. Things that are understood do not need to be explained. It was not necessary to reiterate foundational information. The various gospel writers had different targeted audiences, and there is a variety of events recorded and the emphasis is different in each one. St. Matthew was written to show Jesus as the Messiah, the King of Israel. St. Mark was written to show the Servant ministry of Jesus. St. Luke was written to present Christ as the Son of man and Savior of the world. St. John was written to prove conclusively that Jesus is the Son of God, and that all who believe in Him will have eternal life. *None of the gospel writers were concerned with recording and chronicling a subject that was definitely understood from Old Testament Scripture to be an abomination to God.*

—SETTING THE GAY RECORD STRAIGHT— HOMO-OLOGY IN THE PAULINE EPISTLES

The Book of Romans

The theme of the Epistle of Romans is "God's order in the everyday life of the believer." Homosexuality is addressed in the first chapter because it was obviously a stronghold in Roman civilization and culture. There are many pro-homosexual arguments given by confusionists as counterinterpretations of St. Paul's chapter-long denunciation of homosexuality in his Epistle to the Roman Christians. Each is resolutely refuted by sound biblical interpretation. Pro-gay homoliticians often convolute many interpretations for one passage. This approach is in contrast to the majority of biblical scholars, who do not succumb to a *multiple-choice* mentality. They will generally agree on a Scripture's singular meaning. James White and Jeffrey Niell in their book, *The Same-Sex Controversy*, call this the Ph.D. (Piled Higher and Deeper) method.[19] It is a deliberate attempt to cast doubt on authentic interpretation by piling higher and deeper a number of "plausible" meanings of the text.

This method of exegesis (to breathe out) is more of an eisegesis (to breathe in), in that, instead of *reading out* of the text what it actually says, the teacher *reads into* the text ideas that it never did say, or what they wish it to say. This is the foundation of false doctrine. Furthermore, it is often a violation of St. Peter's admonition against *private interpretations of Scripture* (see 2 Pet. 1:20). Systematic exposition of the sacred text should never be seen through the foggy lenses of subjective subjugation. Just as dirty glasses affect vision, an unclean spirit effects vice. Variation in the dissertation is the raucous and raunchy result. Hence, one Scripture becomes a multiheaded monster that breathes threatenings against the Spirit of holiness. A holy profession should never be short-circuited by unholy practice. "*Be ye holy*" is not a debatable suggestion. "*Be ye holy*" is demonstrably and divisibly different than "Be ye homosexual." Sin's deceitfulness keeps a person from deciphering and discerning doctrine. Sin will *take* you, *trap* you, and if you try to escape, it will *trip* you.

The truth of any scriptural text rises above any ignominious and irrational thought. *The Ph.D. method is similar to a tactic used by unscrupulous attorneys who deceivingly raise their voices while making their weakest point.* Their volume serves as a diversion from the shallow and hollow presentation of faulty legal interpretation. When someone possesses the correct case, they can present it quietly and it will still speak loudly. Correct theology beggars no apology. It will stand on its own merit and is consolidated in the preponderance of the evidence. We shall explore each of the revisionist homo-ological arguments against the Pauline perspective in a succinct manner. This will categorically establish the absolute consensus of apostolic canon concerning the subject matter.

—MAKING GOD HOT—
ROMANS 1:18-19

*For the **wrath of God** is revealed from heaven against all ungodliness and unrighteousness of men, who hold the truth in unrighteousness; because that which may be known of God is manifest in them; for God hath shown it unto them* (emphasis added).

Christological Apologetic: In a general sense, the Father is quite longsuffering and slow to anger. By definition, the wrath of God is: *intensified anger or righteous indignation that results in divinely punitive actions that are suffered for redemptive purposes.* St. Paul says, "*...the **wrath** of God is revealed from heaven...*" (emphasis added). The Pentateuch records "*...the Lord rained upon Sodom and upon Gomorrah brimstone and fire...out of heaven*" (Gen. 19:24). The text says, "*The Lord.*" God did it. It was the sovereign God, in full charge and control. This extreme measure was taken because of the extremity of the depravity. There are only a few things in recorded history that have provoked the wrath of God on this level. *An apathetic attitude toward homosexual sin* is one of them. In ancient times, the wrath of God was revealed against the homosexual-laden culture of the twin cities of the plain. Their unrighteousness made them subjects of wrath. Their rebellion against God, their refusal to honor Him and esteem His words to be right, categorized them as unrighteous. Similarly, those today *who hold the truth in unrighteousness* break God's law and precipitate wrath upon themselves. God's law supersedes the litany of man's laws that lend sanction to ungodly antics and edicts.

God's laws are revealed in three principle ways. They are revealed through the *preaching* of the gospel, the *revelation* in nature, and the law of *conscience.* These three things are a *threefold cord that shall not quickly be broken* (see Eccl. 4:12). Those who know God's laws and obey them not, to them it is a sin. Those who know the truth, but distort and contort it, are deceived to think that God turns a blind eye or a deaf ear. He does not. There are some things that make God sick (see Rev. 3), and there are some things that *make God hot!* Self-deception syncs with sin and bars the truth from men's minds. In their self-deception, they become the recipients of God's wrath. Their sin must be repented of, renounced, and removed; otherwise, it will probably hasten the wrath of God.

—NO EXCUSE FOR EXCUSES—
ROMANS 1:20-21

*For the invisible things of Him from the creation of the world are clearly seen, being understood by the things that are made, even His eternal power and Godhead; so that **they are without excuse**: because that, when they knew God, they glorified Him not as God, neither were thankful; but became vain in their imaginations, and their foolish heart was darkened* (emphasis added).

Christological Apologetic: In all of creation, the created things reflect the order of the Creator. Procreation or reproduction is the result. Without procreation, the world ceases to be. Reproduction makes the world go round. This pattern is seen clearly throughout the entire universe of beings. Throughout creation, the male-female pattern is repeated. The rare exception is the mating pattern of certain species. In at least one known species in the created order, reproduction takes place within the same being. In this instance, the process does not include either male or female sexual identification. The species simply "is." Just as God simply is (see Heb. 11:6). However, in nearly one hundred percent of the created order, life requires the merging of the male and female counterparts. Some years ago, there was a movie entitled, *Three Men and a Baby.* Wisely, the movie never suggested that either two or all three of them produced a baby together. There is a stark difference between babysitting a child and birthing one. The developing of a life from microscopic cells to a majestic newborn is a creative mystery and speaks of the eternal power of the Godhead. The pattern of life that is so *"clearly seen, leaves man without excuse."*

St. Paul moves from created things to that which concerns man's relationship with the Creator. He details how individuals and whole societies fall. He shows that the digression of sin leads into the regression of the loss of God-consciousness. *It is equivalent to falling down three flights of moral stairs which contain ten steps to becoming a man on the down low or a sister laying low.*

The First Step to Down Low

Initially, they possess the attitude of ingratitude (no longer thankful).

Those who forget where God has brought them from, will become ungrateful. This will tear down the walls of resistance and open them to renegade rascality. They will shortly thereafter be overtaken in their faults, and major moral failure most assuredly follows.

The Second Step Down

Eventually, they embody the vanity of profanity (vain imaginations). The word *vain* implies something hollow and empty, devoid of substance. Vanity is inexorably connected to vexation and frustration of one's spirit. Unrestrained imaginations will become inventive, and profanity is no longer preventive. The person loses regard for spiritual things.

The Third Step Down

Ultimately, they lose their light as the darkened night (heart darkened).

The subjects of his analogy knew God, but they lost that knowledge when they refused to glorify God. Refusing to acknowledge God's order and ordinance opened them up to inordinate behavior and offensive actions. When light is absent, then darkness is present. When the world was created, light came in when God moved upon the face of the deep. When God removes Himself from man's heart, darkness dominates the depth of his being. Jesus said, *"Men loved darkness rather than light, because their deeds were evil"* (Jn. 3:19b).

—EDUCATED FOOLS— ROMANS 1:22-25

*Professing themselves to be **wise, they became fools**, and changed the glory of the uncorruptible God into an image made like to corruptible man, and to birds, and fourfooted beasts, and creeping things. Wherefore God also gave them up to uncleanness through the lusts of their own hearts, to dishonour their own bodies between themselves: who changed the truth of God into a lie, and worshipped and served the creature more than the Creator, who is blessed for ever. Amen* (emphasis added).

Christological Apologetic: In the second flight of moral stairs, St. Paul provides an analysis of those who fall into same-sex sin and embrace it as the normal course of things. Every believer needs to watch his step. These are steep ones and they could break someone who falls.

The Fourth Step Down

Consequently, they become educated fools. The God-shaped vacuum of their mind is filled with faulty speculations and vain imaginations. In Noah's day, *the imaginations of the people's hearts were evil continually* (see Gen. 6:5). The Hebrew word for "imagination" is *yester*, and it means, "concepts, thoughts, and desires." When the laws of God are moved *out*, sin moves *in*.

The Fifth Step Down

Shamefully, their foolish wisdom led to idol worship. This is the perversion of the creature's purpose. As the Westminster Catechism states, "Man's chief end is to glorify God." St. Paul says, "...*glorify God in your body, and in your spirit, which are God's*" (1 Cor. 6:20). Also, he states that every person is "*to know how to possess his vessel in sanctification and honour*" (1 Thess. 4:4b). Idol worship has a myriad of forms, but today it is generally known as secular humanism, from which springs a whole collage of contaminated contentions. This verse is not so much a description of particular pagan practices, but a vivid illustration of the indulgence of same-sex inclination in biblical times. Contemporary idolatry takes a different form.[20] It is primarily done in the worship of music, media, and movie idols, which provide the stimuli for same-sex sanction. The creature thinks himself wiser than the Creator. This is not God's profession about man, but man's profession about himself. This is what results in the doctrines of devils, such as "situational ethics," and homo-ology justification.

The Sixth Step Down

Unfortunately, they are given over to uncleanness. To "give over" is *to hand over, to deliver, to give up, to turn over, and to abandon.* It is not that God personally delivers man over to evil. That would be against His nature. He is good, and all good things come from Him. Rather, since the apostates rejected His lordship, He honored their request and withdrew His presence. He has done this time and again, including in the wilderness wandering of the Israelites. St. Paul says that they were given up to uncleanness (filthy, dirty, depraved, grimy, smutty, sexual practices) (see 1 Thess. 4:7).

—LESBIAN LOVERS—
ROMANS 1:26-27

*For this cause [because of this, on account of this, for this reason, that is why] God gave them up unto vile dishonorable **affections** [passions]: for even their women [females] did change the **natural** [as it relates to intercourse with males] use into that which is **against nature** [natural design]: And likewise also the men, leaving [having left behind] the natural use of the woman, **burned** [were inflamed] in their lust [with their yearning] one toward another; men with men working [committing] that which is **unseemly**, [indecency] and receiving in themselves that recompense [the paycheck, wages, requital] of their error [straying] which was meet (emphasis added).*

Christological Apologetic: Essentially, in this segment of St. Paul's treatise, he proceeds to the third flight of *moral stairs*. Once an individual falls down these steps, it is quite possible that the devastating and disastrous nature of their sin will prohibit them from ever shaking loose of it and climbing back up.

The Seventh Step Down

Uncontrolled Affections: He states that they are given over to *uncontrolled vile affections (pathe atimias)*. This expression speaks of *shameful, infamous, loose, wild, and completely ungoverned* passions.

The Eighth Step Down

Unnatural Sex: This is the only passage in the entire Scriptures that specifically addresses lesbianism. In the book, *Is It a Choice?*, Eric Marcus gives the etymology of the term *lesbian*. He states, "A lesbian is a homosexual woman. The word derives from the name of a Greek island, Lesbos, where Sappho, a teacher known for her poetry celebrating love between women, established a school for young women in the sixth century B.C. Over time, the word, 'lesbian,' which once simply meant someone who lived on Lesbos, came to mean a woman who, like Sappho and her followers, loved other women."[21] When the women or mothers of civilization are participants in unnatural sex, the entire society is threatened. When the men or fathers are caught up in it, all hope that society will be saved is lost. History and cultural studies of primitive and medieval societies bear this out.

The Ninth Step Down

Untempered Lust: St. Paul refers to living a life of internal lust as burning, raging fire. To burn is to have a temperature that is heated to fiery proportions. Lust is *intense desire*. When one's genitalia dictates to one's desires, sin is conceived. *When sin is finished, it brings forth death* (see Jas. 1:15). Tim Alan Gardner, author of *Sacred Sex*, quotes H. Robinson's analogy of sex and fire.

> Under control, fire serves us by cooking our food and heating our homes. But if you let fire burn out of control, it will destroy everything in its path. It is the nature of this powerful force to do one of two things: create or to destroy...Used well, sex will promote intimacy. Used wrongly, sex will cause division and lead to isolation.[22]

The Tenth Step Down

Unseemly Sin: When the foolish heart is darkened, the lie is accepted, the light goes out, the deception comes in, and the downward spiral accelerates unseemly or removed altogether. Sin's trap has captured the soul as its prey. At this stage, it is no longer philosophical discussion and theological debate where men pontificate in pompously sounding rhetoric, proposing arguments of biology, sociology, and psychology. *It is now the uncontrolled, the unnatural, the untempered, and the unseemly that gains precedence until death propels one over the precipice.* Like gravity that pulls a falling fruit to the ground, one is pulled by the force of sin that is beyond the power of the human will to break. A fruitful relationship with the Father, along with its seeds of innumerable possibilities, is dashed to pieces. Quite clearly, all the devil's apples have worms, and once one has indulged in sexual sin, the spirit, soul, and body become infested with hellish parasites that have succeeded in stealing the person's soul. They will not desist in their parasitic behavior until and unless the believer resists them and casts them out.

—THE REPROBATE MIND— ROMANS 1:28 & 32

> *And even as they did not like to retain God in their knowledge, God gave them over to a* **reprobate mind***, to do those things which are not convenient.... Who knowing the judgment of God, that they which commit such things are worthy of death, not only do the same, but have pleasure in them that do them* (emphasis added).

Christological Apologetic: Continuation in outright rebellion and being unopen to righteousness can result in a *"reprobate [odikimon] mind."* This means *"a mind that is rejected, disapproved, degraded, depraved; a mind that cannot stand the test of judgment."*[23] It is a mind that will believe a lie before it believes the truth. It is the mind-set that is about as far gone as a person can go. In this state, a person is deluded into believing that he or she is right and that everyone who opposes them is wrong. This reprobate state will make them militant, mean-spirited, and sometimes even monstrous in deeds. Isaiah, the eagle-eyed prophet, said, *"They declare their sin as Sodom, they hide it not..."* (Is. 3:9b). In this final segment, St. Paul gives a detailed description of the debauchery contained in degeneration. He provides a short list to illustrate his point. It is by no means exhaustive. Homosexuality is one of many sins described. The other sins listed in Romans 1:29-31 are *unrighteousness, fornication, wickedness, covetousness, maliciousness, full of envy, murder, debate (strife), deceit, malignity (evil-mindedness), whisperers, backbiters, haters of God, despiteful (unforgiving), proud, boasters, inventors of evil things, disobedient to parents, without understanding, covenantbreakers, without natural affection,*[25] *implacable, and unmerciful.*

Homosexuality is not more or less sineful in an *eternal* sense than any other sin. It is more in the *temporal* sense because of all of its spiritual, emotional, and physical ramifications. Throughout these examples, St. Paul never takes responsibility from the individuals themselves. It is the women who exchanged natural affections; it is the men who burned in their lust toward one another. It is a choice made by the person. He has established the path, process, predicament, pain, peril, and perversion of purpose. Now, like a boxer who has an opponent bleeding, staggering, depleted, and exhausted, he goes for the knockout punch. His intention is to be unsparing of satan, while remaining caring of those who are called to be saints. St. Paul's final round contains four power-packed punches against perversion. He hails four blows in successive statements that pulverizes and summarizes sexual idolatry.

First Blow

They did not retain God in their knowledge (experiencing rejection).

Second Blow

They did things that were inconvenient (wholly unrighteous).

Third Blow

They were deceitfully proud boasters (filled with themselves).

Fourth Blow

They were covenant-breaking fornicators (worthy of death).

He boldly asserts that those who persist in unrepentant, idolatrous, sexual sin of any preference are in danger of hellfire and rejection. He does not vacillate, make excuses for victims, or classify vices in rankings. He nails all of it. He is the apostle who wrote two-thirds of the New Testament. If his word is not viewed as valid, then nobody's is!

—IS HOMOSEXUALITY NATURAL?—

Homo-ological Hermeneutic: Many confusionists suggest that what St. Paul is describing in Romans chapter 1 is *unnatural* homosexuality. The inference is that natural homosexuality is when you are born that way. According to gay theorists, unnatural homosexuality is when one acquires the taste for it and adopts the lifestyle of practicing it, even though he was not born so disposed. Thus, they teach that there are two kinds of homosexuals and that St. Paul's condemnation addressed only the unnatural ones or those who choose to engage in the fornication of the homo (same-sex) kind.

Christological Apologetic: To say that he is referring to *unnatural* homosexuality is to desperately grasp at straws. Because of other straws of contention, it is the straw that breaks the camel's back. Adding it is to take out the basic meaning of the text. This argument is closely linked to the idea that homosexuality is biological and assumes that individuals never have any choice in the matter. There is no basis for this in scientific research. As we will state in Chapter Six, "The Causation Argument: Homosexuality and the Unholy Gay Trinity," there are several environmental factors that contribute to the making of a homosexual. None of which are hereditary. Teaching that there are two types of homosexuals is a two-faced lie. It is defeated with the two-edged sword. There is nothing *natural* about men desiring other men. Neither is there anything *natural* about women preferring women over a lawfully wedded husband. Despite its origin in a person's life, the orientation to homosexuality is equivalent to heading on a highway south with a desired destination of the North Pole. It is the wrong direction. All homosexuality is *unnatural,* even if it feels *natural.* There is no precedent for the premise. The proposition is based entirely on supposition. It is misdirected sex.

Neither the Lord Jesus nor any of the prophets ever made an assertion that there are *natural* or *unnatural* homosexuals. In fact, there was no concept of a *natural* or *unnatural* homosexual throughout all of human history. This is a recent theoretical concoction. It falls into the category of those who profess themselves to be wise, becoming fools. It is foolish to think that one is wiser than God. Contextually, St. Paul was addressing *"the unrighteous behavior"* of homosexuality and *"the unfortunate besetting"* of it. He expounds upon *unnatural* sex at length, whereas the other sins in this passage are simply listed. He teaches that same-sex sin among such civilizations as Sodom and Gomorrah was the result of people falling down proverbial flights of moral stairs. The apostle does not teach the concept of "sexual orientation," either here or anywhere else. A rocket scientist intelligence quotient is not required to figure out that this is a relatively recent term. It has gained oft usage because it is an effective deflection for same-sex advocates. Truthfully, it is an aberrant alibi for autonomously governed carnal minds who wish to engage in homosexual hedonism. To accept this line of reasoning, one would have to say that all who do *unrighteousness, fornication, wickedness,* or commit *murders* (verse 29) do so either *naturally* or *unnaturally.* There is no breakdown for the others, and neither is there a distinction for homosexuality. Just as there is no *natural* murderer, fornicator, thief, and so on, there is no natural homosexual either. If homosexuality was condemned as unnatural to the Romans, it is wrong to Americans and everyone else too. Individual nations may have different laws, customs, traditions, and ordinances, but citizens of Heaven have only one standard. It is righteousness!

—HOMO-OLOGY IN FIRST CORINTHIANS—
AND FIRST TIMOTHY

Know ye not that the unrighteous shall not inherit the kingdom of God?
Be not deceived: neither fornicators, nor idolaters, nor adulterers, nor
effeminate [malakos], *nor abusers of themselves with mankind*
[arsenokoites], *nor thieves, nor covetous, nor drunkards, nor revilers, nor*
extortioners, shall inherit the kingdom of God (1 Corinthians 6:9-10).

For whoremongers, for them that defile themselves with mankind
[arsenokoites], *for menstealers, for liars, for perjured persons, and if there*
be any other thing that is contrary to sound doctrine (1 Timothy 1:10).

Homo-ological Hermeneutic: The confusionists narrowly interpret the
word "effeminate" as a reference to male prostitutes (*arsenokoites*), meaning
that this refers only to men selling themselves for money. They also say that
Paul was referring to abusive homosexuality and not the orientation toward
it. They concede that male prostitution is immoral, but they object to calling
male-on-male contact immoral.

Christological Apologetic: Obviously, Paul used this word "*arsenkoites*" for
a specific reason. The context of the apostle's letter to the church in Corinth
was that there were problems and pressures facing them in the midst of a
pagan society. Homosexuality was ingrained in the culture. The ancient
Greeks viewed it favorably, especially as it related to pederasty. Man-boy love
was sanctioned in the name of older-younger male relationship. St. Paul's
Epistles make it obvious that he was exposed to the gay and lesbian supple-
mentation of their sex life. In his missionary journeys, he personally confronted it and addressed it in his Epistles to the Church. His awareness of a
gamut of same-sex arrangements in Corinth is apparent.[25] Yet, he chose not
to distinguish the abusive homosexual acts from those done in longer relationships. In that day, the fictional concept of "natural-vs-unnatural" homosexuality was not even fathomed. For him there were no degrees of
acceptability or any permissible forms of it. All forms were grouped together.
It was a sin, *period*. He also clearly distinguished homosexual immorality
(effeminate, abusers of themselves with mankind) from heterosexual
immorality (fornicators). Neither group can say that they were excluded in
his apostolic address.

Any sex outside of covenant is a detriment and an impediment to intimate fellowship with God. He gives explicit guidance for husbands (men)
and wives (women) as they live in the covenant of holy matrimony. Nowhere
does the apostle offer such guidance to homosexuals. In fact, he instructed all

213

the Corinthian Christians to cease their lustful practices. He cautioned them about the deception which says that wanton sexual indulgence in fulfilling your needs is excusable. All of his entreaties held the exclusive standard of sexual intercourse in the marriage union. Further, First Corinthians 6:9-10, as well as other passages, should always be interpreted in light of the standard of *Scripture interpreting other Scriptures.*

Perhaps the apostle's contemporaries were arguing as confusionists argue today that the *law* of the Old Testament was not applicable to the Corinthian church. To be emphatic and explicit in his guidance, St. Paul was quite precise in his word choices. He could have possibly used other words such as *porneia* to group together homosexuality and other sexual sin. However, by the time of his writing, this term, as well as others, had come to mean general *sexual immorality.*[26] To dispel any ambiguity concerning homosexuality, he coined a completely different word by gleaning directly from Leviticus chapters 18 and 20, using the Septuagint, the Greek translation of the Old Testament. These two passages directly forbid homosexuality. The Greek translation is as follows:

> *meta **arsenos** [male] ou koimethese **koiten** [koiten—have sexual intercourse] gynaikeian* (Leviticus 18:22, emphasis added).

> *hos an koimethe meta **arsenos** koiten gynaikos* (Leviticus 20:13, emphasis added).

Though most Christians are not Greek scholars, it is obvious that there are similarities in the words of the Levitical passages and the above Corinthian text. There are two words that are found in both Leviticus and First Corinthians. They are *arsane* and *koite.* In the New Testament, without exception, arsane refers to a male. Koite appears twice, and it is used only in a sexual connotation. It refers to a "bed" or "couch" (see Rom. 13:13; Heb. 13:4). The text combines *arsenos (male)* and *koiten (bed)* to form the word *arsenokoites,* which literally means *male who lies on a couch with a male.* Nothing in the component parts of this word, nor in the context of its use, refers to homosexual abuse or to male prostitution. The passage speaks directly against the homosexuality of his day using the specific words that speak to it.

The word *effeminate* is translated from *malakos,* which means, "soft to the touch." It is the third Greek word that confusionists have sought to alter. They claim that *malakos* simply refers to moral weakness. However, other references show that *malakos* was used to refer to passive males in homosexual acts. Jesus used *malakos* in reference to soft clothing (see Mt. 11:8; Lk. 7:25). It is used only once in reference to persons. This is the way that St. Paul uses it in First Corinthians. In addition to its use here, *malakos* is used in ancient Greek literature to describe men who were the passive participants in homosexuality. In no way is it used to describe male prostitution as revisionist writer, John Boswell, claims.[27]

The Corinthian Conundrum

First Corinthians 6:9 begins with *"Know ye not that."* In essence, St. Paul is saying that it is understood that homosexuality along with the other sinful practices are against God's law of holiness. If homosexuality was okay, then why is it mentioned along with adultery and fornication as unacceptable conduct? Quite simply, because it is not okay. This is one place that, "I'm okay, you're okay," doesn't work.

Males on Couches

The apostle Paul implicitly states that there were current members of the church at Corinth who were *once males that laid on couches with other males,* but had received salvation and become changed individuals. They had been marvelously made new by the mercy of God. They were sanctified in their sexuality and set apart unto the Lord. They were justified, just as if they had never sinned. He taught that the new birth in Christ will make a person become a *transformed, reformed,* and *conformed* child of God (see 2 Cor. 5:17), no longer committing sin, but fulfilling the calling of the will of God.

What was true yesterday is still true today. The expression, "Such were some of you," is a direct reference to this. The Corinthian conundrum was that they were born again, but in some instances they were acting out of their old nature and yielding to their past profession. All of this was going on in the midst of a mighty move of God. Their past likes and dislikes were washed away in the sea of forgetfulness by the blood of Jesus, but their flesh was seeking to hold on to it. They needed to be reminded that satan uses sex to strip the saints. St. Paul taught them that as a person is conformed to Christ, he is transformed by the renewing of his mind. As a person's thinking changes, so does the person himself. Romans 12:2 says, *"And be not **conformed** to this world: but be ye **transformed** by the renewing of your mind, that ye may prove what is that good, and acceptable, and perfect, will of God"* (emphasis added). Through baptism, the believer is identified with the death of Christ, and thus they are no longer identified with their former lifestyles. Romans 6:1-2 states, *"What shall we say then? Shall we continue in sin, that grace may abound? **God forbid.** How shall we, that are dead to sin, live any longer therein?"* (emphasis added)

The mentioning of the "effeminate" and "abusers of themselves with mankind" in First Corinthians 6:9-11 is a categorical condemnation. The Amplified Version of the Scripture renders these expressions as *"those who participate in homosexuality"* (1 Cor. 6:9). It does not mention male prostitution, but it clearly says *homosexuality*. The phrase *"such were some of you"* states that to a born-again believer, this behavior is to be *past* and not *present*. God loves the homosexual, but He hates the perversion of His eternal purpose for a man or a woman. Adopting the gay and lesbian way, as well as unsanctified sex, does just that. Homosexuality was considered wrong by the Israelites, the early Christians, and the saints of God throughout the Church's two thousand years of history. Time changes many things, but it does not change wrong into right, especially as it relates to the moral laws of God. The more things change, the more some things stay the same. The Scriptures teach, *"Jesus Christ the same yesterday, and today, and for ever"* (Heb. 13:8, emphasis added; see also Mal. 3:6, Jas. 1:17).

—SETTING THE GAY RECORD STRAIGHT—
HOMO-OLOGY IN SECOND PETER AND JUDE

Second Peter 2:6-7 and Jude 7 corroborate the other passages found throughout the canon of Scripture. These passages reveal the sexual nature of the sins of Sodom and Gomorrah.

> *And he condemned to ruin and extinction the cities of* **Sodom and Gomorrah,** *reducing them to ashes [and thus] set them forth as an example to those who would be ungodly* (2 Peter 2:6 AMP, emphasis added).

> *Even as Sodom and Gomorrah, and the cities about them in like manner, giving themselves over to fornication, and going after* **strange flesh,** *are set forth for an example, suffering the vengeance of eternal fire* (Jude 7, emphasis added).

Christological Apologetic: The law of hermeneutics declares that *Scripture interprets Scripture.* When textual ambiguity exists, one need only look at the totality of what the holy writ says. This is what is meant by *"...rightly dividing the word of truth"* (2 Tim. 2:15). In light of the Genesis account and the subsequent Scriptures, we can unequivocally say that it was principally, though not totally, because of the *abominable practice of homosexuality* that God destroyed Sodom and Gomorrah. Homosexuality is like Hurricanes Frances, Ivan, Charlie, and Jeannie of 2004 all rolled into one. It leaves behind abundant evidence of its all-destructive presence. Just as a hurricane is not an act of God, but a perversion of nature, neither is homosexuality an act of God, but a perversion of the perfect will of God, as revealed in human nature. *The scriptural conclusion is this: It is counterfeit copulation. It models the mystery of iniquity. Its chief propagator is satan himself. His nature is the antithesis of procreation. He deals in death in his damnable drive to steal, kill, and to destroy* (see Jn. 10:10). Diablos, the devil, is the conspirator of this attempted coup of created covenantal order. He comes to annihilate its

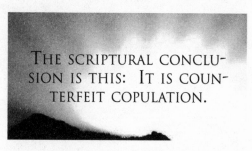

THE SCRIPTURAL CONCLU-SION IS THIS: IT IS COUN-TERFEIT COPULATION.

adherents. It is so captivating that the angels urged Lot and his family to *make haste and escape for their lives* (see Gen. 19:17-22).

Both passages list Sodom and Gomorrah with other groups that were destroyed by God. The Egyptian army was destroyed for unbelief, the angels in Heaven were cast out for their rebellion, and the people of Lot and Noah's day were obliterated for their lascivious and lewd liaisons. All of these were grave offenses that garnered judgment. It would be incongruous for God's justice to rain down fire and brimstone on Sodom and Gomorrah for inhospitality. If that were the case, the disciples would never have been told that whenever they preached the gospel in a city and were not received (shown hospitality), to wipe the dust off their feet (see Mt. 10:14). They would have been instructed to pray that God rain down fire and brimstone upon the Christ rejecters as He did upon the twin cities of the plain. On one occasion, James and John suggested this, and Jesus rebuked them saying, "*Ye know not what manner of spirit ye are of...*" (Lk. 9:55b; see verse 54 also). The smell of the same-sex sin threatened to export itself over the entire earth, and God came down. Enough was enough, and He rained on the flesh parade. The cup of wrath is always poured out when the cup of iniquity is full.

The Christological Apologetic: In Conclusion
Homo-ology—Setting the Gay Record Straight

Today it is something of a colossal understatement to say that we live in a world that doesn't respond to authority very well...If you doubt it, ask the police. Is it any wonder then that people question the authority of the Bible?[28]   *John MacAuthor, Jr.*

—25 GAY-STRAIGHTENING REASONS—

Every valley shall be exalted, and every mountain and hill shall be made low: and the crooked shall be made straight, and the rough places plain (Isaiah 40:4).

Setting the gay record straight is no easy task. Many traditionalists summarily dismiss every single aspect of homo-ology as nonsense. However, many confusionists are making a formidable, though failed, attempt to exegete the Scriptures and formulate an alternative faith. From the origination of the sons of man in Genesis, to the consummation of the Son of God in Revelation, there is a single thread that repeatedly and resoundingly remonstrates that *God is not gay*. His Church is not gay, and His people are not gay either. There are at least 25 scriptural reasons that set the gay and lesbian record straight accordingly. After a life of vanity, a wise preacher said, *"Let us hear the conclusion of the whole matter: Fear God, and keep His commandments: for this is the whole duty of man"* (Eccl. 12:13). The Master Teacher exhorted: *"Search the scriptures; for in them ye think ye have eternal life: and they are they which testify of Me"* (Jn. 5:39).

1. It is founded, grounded, and surrounded in idolatry.

   *And changed the glory of the uncorruptible **God into an image** made like to corruptible man, and to birds, and fourfooted beasts, and creeping things...who changed the truth of **God into a lie**, and worshipped and served the **creature more than the Creator**, who is blessed for ever. Amen* (Romans 1:23-25, emphasis added).

2. It is lustful, lewd, and *lascivious* behavior.

   *Who being past feeling have given themselves over unto **lasciviousness**, to work all uncleanness with greediness* (Ephesians 4:19, emphasis added).

3. It *dishonors and devalues* the body through uncleanness.

   *Wherefore God also gave them up to **uncleanness** through the lusts of their own hearts, to **dishonour** their own bodies between themselves* (Romans 1:24, emphasis added).

4. It causes domestic wars between the male and female genders.

   *For this cause shall a man leave his **father** and **mother**, and cleave to his wife* (Mark 10:7, emphasis added).

5. It uncovers and smothers the children.

   *What mean ye, that ye use this proverb concerning the land of Israel, saying, The fathers have eaten **sour grapes**, and the **children's teeth are set on edge**?* (Ezekiel 18:2, emphasis added)

6. It promises pleasure, but it produces perversion.

   *Choosing rather to suffer affliction with the people of God, than to enjoy the **pleasures of sin for a season*** (Hebrews 11:25, emphasis added).

7. There is no peace, purpose, promise, or power with it.

   *There is **no peace**, saith my God, **to the wicked*** (Isaiah 57:21, emphasis added).

8. It is a voluntary act of the will and not a mandatory one.

   *But every man is **tempted**, when he is **drawn away** of his **own lust**, and enticed* (James 1:14, emphasis added).

9. It is a personal choice and not a providential one.

   *And if it seem evil unto you to **serve** the Lord, **choose** you this day whom ye will **serve**...but as for me and my house, we will **serve** the Lord* (Joshua 24:15, emphasis added).

10. It confuses, diffuses, and abuses one's identity.

    *For God is not the **author** of **confusion**, but of peace...* (1 Corinthians 14:33, emphasis added).

11. It rearranges creation, but it cannot change procreation.

*...Be **fruitful**, and **multiply**, and **replenish** the earth, and subdue it: and have **dominion**...* (Genesis 1:28, emphasis added).

12. It undermines scriptural authority and validity.

*All **scripture** is given by **inspiration** of God, and is profitable for doctrine, for reproof, for correction, for instruction in righteousness* (2 Timothy 3:16, emphasis added).

13. It is *unnatural, unseemly,* unrighteous, and unhealthy.

*And likewise also the men, leaving the **natural** use of the woman, burned in their lust one toward another; men with men working that which is **unseemly**, and receiving in themselves that recompense of their error which was meet* (Romans 1:27, emphasis added).

14. The *law of sin* controls it and not the law of life.

*For the **law of the Spirit of life** in Christ Jesus hath made me free from the **law of sin and death*** (Romans 8:2, emphasis added).

15. It is *unacceptable,* unpleasing, and unworthy of God's image.

*I beseech you therefore, brethren, by the mercies of God, that ye present your bodies a living sacrifice, **holy**, **acceptable unto God**, which is your reasonable service* (Romans 12:1, emphasis added).

16. One cannot practice unmarried sex and be saved.

*What shall we say then? Shall we continue in sin, that **grace may abound**? God forbid. **How shall we**, that are dead to sin, **live any longer therein?*** (Romans 6:1-2, emphasis added)

17. There were no homosexual apostles of the Lamb of God.

*And the wall of the city had twelve foundations, and in them the names of the twelve **apostles of the Lamb*** (Revelation 21:14, emphasis added).

18. The Church fathers treated it as cursed behavior.

*And he shall turn the **heart of the fathers** to the children, and the **heart of the children** to their fathers, lest I come and smite the earth with a curse* (Malachi 4:6, emphasis added).

19. There are no same-sex marriages in the Holy Bible.

*For this cause shall a **man** leave his father and mother, and shall be joined unto his **wife**, and **they two** shall be **one flesh*** (Ephesians 5:31, emphasis added).

20. All of creation defies and denies the pattern of same-sex.

*And of **every living thing** of all flesh, **two of every sort** shalt thou bring into the ark, to keep them alive with thee; they shall be **male and female*** (Genesis 6:19, emphasis added).

21. It is not good for you.

*For I know that in me (that is, in my flesh,) dwelleth **no good thing**...* (Romans 7:18, emphasis added).

22. It opens the door for demonic control.

*Neither give **place** to the **devil*** (Ephesians 4:27, emphasis added).

23. It has *always* been wrong.

24. It is still wrong.

25. It will *always* be wrong.

*Thou **shalt not lie with mankind**, as with **womankind**: it is **abomination*** (Leviticus 18:22, emphasis added).

*Likewise also as **it was in the days of Lot**; they did eat, they drank, they bought, they sold, they planted, they builded...Lot went **out of Sodom** it rained fire and brimstone from heaven, and destroyed them all. Even **thus shall it be in the day** when the **Son of man** is **revealed*** (Luke 17:28-30, emphasis added).

*For without are dogs, and sorcerers, and whoremongers, and murderers, and idolaters, **and whosoever loveth and maketh a lie*** (Revelation 22:15, emphasis added).

These 25 reasons defiantly look eyeball-to-eyeball into the heart and soul of homo-ology. The above listed Scriptures require little or no explanation because they *clearly* say what they mean and *certainly* mean what they say. There is nothing more precious than the Word of God. To twist and turn the Scripture, spinning it on its head, is a sinister, iniquitous notion. It is sin to make crooked what God has made straight, and it is sterling to make straight what the enemy has made crooked. The *strait gate* awaits the *straight* who will not allow it to be said too *late*.

Normally speaking, it is never too late to do what is right. In the case of Noah and Lot, there was a divinely set date that precluded anyone from being late. Knocks upon the door do not get answered after midnight. Everyone must run in before they run out. This Christological Apologetic sets the gay record straight. This is a gracious Word indeed.

David Chilton, as quoted by James R. White in *The Same Sex Controversy*, speaks to this:

> Calling homosexuality a sin would seem to be a cruel, insensitive attitude, a homophobic response of condemnation rather than concern. But the truth is that it is the beginning of true freedom and joy for the homosexual. For if homosexuality were either an inescapable human condition (like height and skin color) or an incurable disease, there would be no hope. The homosexual would be locked in his lusts forever, with no possibility of escape. Once we see clearly that homosexuality is a sin, we can also see the way of deliverance....That homosexuality is a sin means that it is only a sin—nothing more. It is not some mystical force within the person, some genetic or psychological programming that cannot be overcome. It is a transgression of God's law, a form of self-love that expresses itself in a particular heinous attack on God's image.[29]

—FOR YOUR INFORMATION—

Given Over to Three Things

The lifestyle of sexual idolatry, both hetero and homo, may disguise itself as erotic, but in reality it is rebellion against revealed righteousness. It results in being "*given over.*" When God gives someone over, it is over; and they will be overtaken, overcome, and overwhelmed. They will not be over easy. The way of the transgressor is hard, but the yoke of Christ is easy (see Prov. 13:15; Mt. 11:30). In Romans, God gave them over three times to three different things, and there was a threefold exchange as listed in Romans chapter 1. Please note the progression. At her current rate, America is on pace to be given over, just as the once mighty Roman Empire was. The "oil and wine" Church must pray for America's soul.

First He *gave them* to *uncleanness* of *passions* that dishonor the body (see Rom. 1:24).

Second, He *gave them* over to *dishonorable* affection of same-sex attraction (homo-erotica) (see Rom. 1:26).

Third, He *gave them* over to a *reprobate*, unfit, rejected state of mind (see Rom. 1:28).

Threefold Exchange

First, they *exchanged* the *glory* of God for *idols* (see Rom. 1:23).

Second, they *exchanged* the *truth* of God for a *lie* (see Rom. 1:25).

Third, they *exchanged* the *natural* sex function with the opposite sex for the *unnatural* sex (see Rom. 1:26).

Three Different Hills

The words of the Master Teacher were, "*What shall a man give in exchange for his soul?*" (Mk. 8:37) There is not an erotic thrill on "Blueberry's Sugar Hill" that should make a person forget about the hill far away, where there stood an old rugged cross. The songwriter called it, "the emblem of suffering and shame... where the dearest and best, for a world of lost sinners was slain." It is a hill called Mt. Calvary. It stands in close proximity to a third hill. It is called Mt. Zion. Every believer is bound for Mt. Zion. The tabernacle is there. The glory is there. The Shammah is there. The Lord is there. There is no sin there. There is no *hetero* sex there. There is no *homo* sex there. The angels do not marry, and in the kingdom to come, neither will the saints. The Lamb shall be married to His Bride, the Church. She is a holy and spotless Bride, made perfect by the blood. She *exchanged* the old for the new. She *exchanged* the idols for the glory. She *exchanged* the lies for the truth. She *exchanged* the unnatural for the supernatural. She is the Church, the army, terrible with banners, fair as the full moon. Oh what a day, what a day that will be! When we all get to Heaven and see Jesus, we will sing and shout the victory. *The Christological Apologetic sets the gay record straight* and mandates that *The Causation Argument and the Unholy Gay Trinity* will be cast down forever and ever.

Prayer: Lord of Creation, Thy Word is a lamp unto our feet and a light unto our path. Help us to always hide it in our heart that we might walk worthy of the path to which our feet are called. Your ways are right and Your judgments are true altogether. We bless Your veracious name. Even as You judged Sodom, we know that You will judge all sexual sin. Help us to run in before we run out. Help us to make the crooked path straight. Amen.

ENDNOTES

1. James R. White and Jeffrey D. Neill, *The Same-Sex Controversy* (Minneapolis, MN: Bethany House Publishers, 2002), 16.

2. Edythe Draper, *Draper's Book of Quotations for the Christian World,* (Wheaton, IL: Tyndale House Publishers, Inc., 1992), Entry 638, Bible Illustrator 3.0 for Windows, Parsons Technology, Inc. 1990-1998, Illustrations Copyrighted at Christianity Today, Inc., 1984-1995, Faircom Corp.

3. Draper, *Draper's Book of Quotations,* Entry 646.

4. Draper, *Draper's Book of Quotations,* Entry 679.

5. Draper, *Draper's Book of Quotations,* Entry 730.

6. For greater exposition of all relevant texts, the reader is advised to read Robert A.J. Gagnon, *The Bible and Homosexual Practice* (Nashville, TN: Abingdon Press, 2001). Our stated purpose is to present a gracious word to the gay and lesbian community and not necessarily to render an in-depth analysis of the above referenced passages.

7. Mel White, *Stranger at the Gate* (New York: Penguin Books, 1994), 17.

8. White and Neill, *The Same-Sex Controversy,* 17.

9. *The Word: The Bible from 26 Translations* (Moss Point, MS: Mathis Publishers, 1985).

10. D. Sherwin Bailey, *Homosexuality and the Western Christian Tradition* (Hamden, CT: Show String Press/Archon Books, 1955), 3.

11. Ibid.

12. R. Gower, & F. Wright, *The New Manners and Customs of Bible Times* (Chicago, IL: Moody Press, 1997). Updated and rewritten version of *Manners and Customs of Bible Lands,* by Fred Wright; Includes indexes.

13. John Jefferson Davis, *Evangelical Ethics: Issues Facing the Church Today* (Phillipsburg, NJ: Presbyterian and Reformed, 1985), 116.

14. Bryant Wood, Associates for Biblical Research, 2001, accessed at http://www.christiananswers.net/q-abr/abr-a007.html.

15. Jeffrey Satinover, *Homosexuality and the Politics of Truth* (Grand Rapids, MI: Baker Books, 1996), 218.

16. Gagnon, *The Bible and Homosexual Practice,* 113.

17. Leonard Ravenhill, *Sodom Had No Bible* (Minneapolis, MN: Bethany Fellowship, Inc., 1979), 27-28.

18. Draper, *Draper's Book of Quotations,* Entry 679.

19. Niell and White, *The Same-Sex Controversy,* 124.

20. Confusionists argue that St. Paul is actually referring to idolatrous homosexuality. This was practiced in the heathen religions of paganism. Accordingly, they teach that he is not denouncing the homosexuality of Christians. Supposedly, believers are not implicated in this passage because they do not worship idols. If that statement were true, then why would the

apostle John tell the Church to *keep themselves from idols* (see 1 Jn. 5:21)? Idolatry is one of the many manifestations of rebellion. This rebellion manifests in pagan practices, including sexual perversion. All idolaters are not homosexuals and all homosexuals are not actual idol worshipers. St. Paul connects the two because it was true of those in his analogy. He does not distinguish homosexual groups. This is another confusionist attempt to obscure the clear meaning of the passage.

21. Eric Marcus, *Is It a Choice?* (New York: Harper/Collins, 1999), 3.

22. Tim Alan Gardner, *Sacred Sex* (Colorado Springs, CO: Waterbrook Press, 2002), 172-173.

23. *The Preacher's Outline and Sermon Bible* (King, NC: Christian Publishers and Ministries, 1991), 30.

24. Ibid., *Without natural affection* (astorgos): abnormal affection and love, heartless, without human emotion or love, a lack of feeling for others, abuse of normal affection and love. Others become little more than pawns for a man's own use and benefit, pleasure and purposes, excitement and stimulation. Abnormal affection, sex, and perversion prevail.

25. Willard M. Swartley, *Homosexuality: Biblical Interpretation and Moral Discernment* (Scottdale, PA: Herald Press, 2003), 70.

26. Donald J. Wold, *Out of Order: Homosexuality in the Bible and the Ancient Near East* (Grand Rapids, MI: Baker Books, 1998), 196.

27. John Boswell, *Christianity, Social Tolerance, and Homosexuality* (Chicago, IL: University of Chicago Press, 1980), 341.

28. John MacArthur, Jr., *How to get the Most from God's Word,* (Dallas, TX: Word Publishing, 1997), 57.

29. David Chilton as quoted by James R. White in *The Same-Sex Controversy,* 200.

CHAPTER
SIX

O God, may we so value our bodies and minds that we never mar them. May we not be tricked into bad habits by publicity and advertisements that deliberately mislead, or by the desire for easy applause, or by the fear of being thought narrow. But may we be sturdy and upright in our thinking and our behavior, and treat our bodies as the temple of thy Spirit.[1]

Sid G. Hodges

We have a bodily machine which we must regulate. God does not regulate it for us. Until we learn to bring the bodily machine into harmony with God's will, there will be friction, and the friction is a warning that part of the machine is not in working order.[2]

Oswald Chambers

Self-acceptance is basically a spiritual issue. What it boils down to is this: are we able to thank the Creator for the way he made us? If not, we are casting doubt on his wisdom. If we can thank him, we display our belief that he knows what is best for us. And that will help us accept ourselves—limitations, failures, and all.[3]

Erwin W. Lutzer

The homosexual's real enemy is his ignorance of the possibility that he can be helped.[4]

Dr. Edmund Bergler

The homosexual has gender needs that he is trying to meet erotically, that is the problem.[5]

Briar Whitehead

"Do you believe homosexuality is a choice?" (Bob Shieffer, CBS News)

"I just don't know" (President George W. Bush, Incumbent)

"I think if you talked to anybody, it's not a choice"(Senator John Kerry, Challenger)[6]

2004 Presidential Debate
Tempe, Arizona

The Causation Argument:
Homosexuality and the Unholy Gay Trinity

I will praise Thee; for I am fearfully and wonderfully made: marvellous are Thy works; and that my soul knoweth right well (Psalm 139:14).

```
                    ┌─────────────────────────┐
                    │      HOMOSEXUALITY      │
                    └─────────────────────────┘
         ┌───────────────┐ ┌───────────────┐ ┌───────────────┐
         │    BIOLOGY    │ │   PSYCHOLOGY  │ │    SOCIOLOGY  │
         └───────────────┘ └───────────────┘ └───────────────┘
```

In theology, the concept of the triune nature of God is clearly established. God is Father in creation, Son in redemption, and Holy Spirit in regeneration. In homosexuality, the unholy gay trinity seeks to become established thought and exalted as truth. This chapter will explore this end-time occurrence.

Activists in the gay and lesbian community are convinced that the predisposition possibilities that are presented in this treatise are ludicrous nonsense, and they reject their validity. Many homosexuals do not consider themselves as victims of anything and resent the suggestion that their so-called preference and orientation are associated with trauma as the result of victimization or prenatal influence. Those who disagree will not readily acknowledge nor will they completely deny the obvious truth that there are certain environmental factors involved in influencing someone into homosexuality. In most cases, their *inconclusive conclusion* has nothing to do with research and facts, but everything to do with politics.[7] The homosexual hypothesis is the antithesis of available research data, and provides no synthesis of the collective college of documentation. Their thesis is not a thoughtful conclusion, but rather it is based on wrongful thinking. Dr. Edmund Bergler offers this insight saying, "The homosexual's real enemy is his ignorance of the possibility that he can be helped'"[8] The truth is, many do not want help because they do not think that they need any.

Unfortunately, activists for homosexuality seem to be having some success in gaining acceptance of their view. It is estimated that about one-third of homosexuals believe that they are born that way.[9] More startling is that nine out of ten churches that are pastored by seminary graduates do not believe that homosexuals can change, or they are unaware of how to assist in the change.[10] The assertion that homosexuals cannot change is incorrect and must be challenged by the facts and the testimonies of those who have escaped its unrelenting clutches. This apathetic assumption must be debunked by the truth. There are three arguments of the unholy gay trinity that form the thesis of the errant supposition. They are described in the oft-used terms of *biology, psychology*, and *sociology*. In this case, three is surely a crowd.

—THE BIOLOGY ARGUMENT—

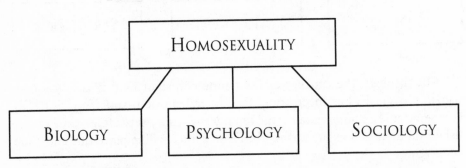

...careful scientific observation will harmonize with the biblical position. *Interpretations* of that research may differ from the biblical perspective, but the observations themselves, assuming they are reliable, will not. And this is indeed the case: the findings of science support rather than challenge this biblical view...biology is not destiny. Human sexual response is too complex to be reduced to a neuron deficit in the brain...biology can't make us sin. At most, biology is analogous to a friend who tempts us to sin. Such a friend could be bothersome, but he can be rebuked and resisted...Our sinful hearts express themselves in behavior via hundreds of factors, biology being one...The ultimate cause of sin is always the sinful heart....[11]

Edward T. Welsh,
Blame It on the Brain

The Gay Gene Myth

Many homosexuals are convinced that they were born as such, thereby being biologically predisposed to this lifestyle. They delight in saying, "Just as I am...I come to thee." The Scripture does indeed say *to come as you are*, but it does not say to *stay the way you are* because God *made you to be the way you are*. Many have accepted the view that, because of biology or birth, their same-sex attraction is innate and therefore they are not straight. They are naturally homosexual and not heterosexual. The biblical position rebuts this argument as a myth. The American Heritage Dictionary defines myth as "a notion based on tradition or convenience rather than on fact; a received idea." There are no facts substantiating the widely circulated claim of a biological basis for sexual orientation. It is not substantiated by empirical scientific methods employed by those who have studied homosexuality from every angle and on numerous occasions.[12] Consistently, such bogus claims are refuted by credible scientists and their community of works. In the words of the old, broken-English speaking preacher, "You *is*, what you *is*, because you *is* determined to be that way."

More importantly, studies that conclude that there is a genetic cause for homosexuality have yet to be replicated by other scientists. No one has been able to produce the same results and come to the same conclusion. To simplify this concept, think of the proven fact that plants need light to grow properly. Anyone can reach the same conclusion by performing a simple experiment that many grade-school students all over the world do every year. Place one plant (the control) in the light and place another one in the dark (the variable) for the same length of time. Give both plants the same amount of water and nutrients and document the results. Invariably, the data gathered supports the purported fact of the necessity of light. Therefore, the same conclusion is made.

On many occasions scientists have tried unsuccessfully to replicate the results of studies that claim to have found a biological basis for homosexuality. Not only have such efforts proven to be futile, but when some replication is possible, the conclusions reached lend themselves to contradictory interpretation.[13] When other scientists are not able to reproduce the results of an initial study, then *nothing at all has been proven*.[14] Since no two studies of a biological cause of homosexuality have had the same results, there is no evidence, but only mere theory behind the presumption of the biological basis. The information that is available as general data has been stretched out of proportion into specific exceptions. This, of course, is a violation of ethics. It is tantamount to promoting perverted propaganda.

The Gay Gene Theory

At one time, it was widely reported in the media that a gay gene was discovered, even though the information was clearly speculative and unsubstantiated by scientific confirmation. In the book, *Science, Scripture and Homosexuality*, authors Alice Bellis and Terry L. Hufford point out that there are no actual research findings that support an existence of a gay gene.[15]

The Human Genome Project, commissioned in 1986 by the United States Government and concluded in 2003, yielded a trove of information about the genetic makeup of humans. The number of possible genetic combinations a person can receive from two parents is mind-blowing.[16] Geneticist, Dr. Dave Unander, in his book, *Shattering the Myth of Race*, describes it this way:

> Each human sperm or egg cell contains one out of more than eight million new genetic combinations of the person it came from. Since each conception is the result of two parents, each new individual is one combination out of a minimum of some eight million times eight million possibilities just for that particular mother and father. In addition, each new person then grows up with all the influences of his or her native language and culture, the personalities of the people around him or her, and the impact of any nutritional deficiencies or diseases. Attributing a simple genetic cause to predict any complex behavior or lifestyle is absurd.[17]

When addressing the biological myth for homosexuality, it is important to understand the difference between *heritable* and *inherited*. Few complex human behaviors such as homosexuality or even criminality are inherited as one's height and eye color are. *Inherited* means "to receive genetically from an ancestor."[18] It means that there is no way to alter or prevent the trait, and there is no way to modify it. By contrast, *heritable* does not mean *unmodifiable* and is closely linked to one's environment.

ONE'S TASTE BUDS ARE THE SOLE REASON FOR INDIVIDUAL LIKES AND DISLIKES. THE SAME HOLDS TRUE FOR THE GAY AND LESBIAN LIFESTYLE.

To suggest that same-sex attraction is attributed to a gay gene is equivalent to saying the reason some people love broccoli and other people loathe it is because they were preprogrammed by the Creator with this propensity.

One's taste buds are the sole reason for individual likes and dislikes. The same holds true for the gay and lesbian lifestyle. In a lot of instances, people who are so disposed and identify themselves as homosexual do so because it is palatable to their sexual and sensual tastes, which have been programmed into them by a variety of environmental factors. This is why the Bible says that *they love it so.*

> The prophets prophesy falsely, and the priests bear rule by their means;
> *and My people love to have it so*: and what will ye do in the end
> thereof? (Jeremiah 5:31, emphasis added)

Male/Female Genesis

Those who are lovers of pleasures more than lovers of God often go beyond being mere homosexuals to being addicted to homo-erotic pleasures. The forbidden fruit, once eaten, may provide a pleasurable sensation that serves as a stimulus for greater indulgences. *A person who heads up an AIDS victims ministry shared with me that when he was young, he was molested by a relative. As he grew older, he felt a perverse attraction for other boys. When he became a man, he was aroused by the very thought of a man-boy encounter. Despite having a wife, this inner craving was constant. In the process of varied encounters with other men, he became HIV positive. Amazingly, the power of God came into his life and in subsequent years, he received healing and now is an ordained minister of the gospel, living a life of sanctified sexuality.* He was delivered from it because he acknowledged to God that he truly liked it and that it was indeed a sin. He recognized that the imprints for sin and a taste for it had been woven into his spirit and that he had developed a propensity for it. His honesty with God was equivalent to what the Bible teaches as "true confession." The word *confessions* is from the Greek term *homologeo* and it means to speak the same thing. By not blaming it on his birth or justifying its rightness, he received the escape from it. It is impossible to deliver someone who continues to like and love the things they do. Therefore, it is disingenuous for gay activists to play the blame game on the Creator for those poor souls who go through life undelivered. It is not God's fault.

The *divine design* does indeed provide for both X and Y chromosomes for both male and female. The *divine design* does indeed include estrogen in men and testosterone in women in a limited portion, but it does not tip the scale so that one is justified in referring to themselves as "gay by gene." The *divine design* does not drop the he-she disorder on anybody; therefore it is a gross misrepresentation of the grace of God to state otherwise. *There is no such thing as a "homosexual" gene nor does the homosexual male have more female hormones than normal.*[19] Every person has both male and female hormones in their body; however, this cross-hormonal situation does not produce a homosexual, any more than cross-pollination causes a tulip to become a rose. There is no such thing as a tu-rose or a ro-tulip.

Shakespeare declared rightly, "A rose is a rose, no matter what name you call it." For a man to act as a woman is evidence of delusion in a limited sense. For a woman to act like a man is indication of abnormality. Delusion is a mental state that is best described as "beyond reason or reasonable rationale." Granted, there are indeed some men who are *effeminate* in their ways and some women who are *masculine* in their mannerisms, but that does not make them gay nor does it make them lesbian. I have known men who could sing notes so high that they could nearly crack glass, but there was absolutely nothing "girlish" about them. I have known women who were stronger than me, but there was nothing "butch" about them.

Dr. Jeffrey Satinover states, "There is absolutely no evidence whatsoever that the behavior of homosexuality is directly inherited."[20] A study was done by Australian researcher Michael Bailey and a team of scientists involving a group of adoptive brothers and twins. They found that 9 percent of brothers, 11 percent of adoptive brothers, 22 percent of the fraternal twins, and 52 percent of the identical twins were homosexual.[21] While gay activists tout such studies as proof of the inheritability of homosexuality, the studies themselves actually paint a very different picture. The incidence of homosexuality between identical twins should be 100 percent since identical twins share identical genes. Rather than corroborate the claim of a gay gene, the results of this study clearly and evidently refute such a presumptuous conclusion and make a strong case for environmental factors.[22] Incidentally, the researchers recruited their subjects through homosexual publications that have a target audience of homosexuals. This is significant because Bailey, himself a homosexual, did not examine a random selection of twins.

Effeminate and Masculine

William Byne and Bruce Parson write in *Homosexual Orientation: The Biologic Theories Reappraised* that "Recent studies postulate biologic factors as the primary basis for sexual orientation. However, there is no evidence at present to substantiate a biologic theory, just as there is no evidence of any psychosocial explanation."[23]

A woman with broad shoulders and big hands is still a woman. A man may have long fingernails and a high-pitched voice, but he is still a man. A woman may have hair on her lip, and a Melvin Franklin (former singer for the Temptations) bass in her voice, but she is still a woman. In each instance, their sexual identity is in their "apparatus" not in their "attributes." Homosexual activists have even argued that homosexual males are born with more female hormones than normal. Again, this is pure speculation, resulting in the propagation of a myth. It is simply not true. Studies have shown that males (homosexual and heterosexual) have entirely "normal" hormone levels.[24] Everyone's DNA is different, so are their estrogen and testosterone levels. It is clear that those who sanction the legitimacy of homosexuality are guilty of obscuring the facts.

A team of researchers at the National Cancer Institute attempted to show that homosexuality is transmitted maternally through the X chromosome. They were prompted by an observation of higher rates of maternally related homosexuality. Led by Dr. Dean Hamer, these scientists specifically investigated 22 regions of the X chromosome of 40 pairs of volunteers who were homosexual brothers. Thirty-three of the 40 pairs were found to share the same genetic markers in five regions or "loci" of the q28 region of the X chromosome. They concluded that a gene or genes in this loci influenced the manifestation of homosexuality in at least 64 percent of the brothers tested.[25]

Like other studies, this one proved nothing. One major flaw is that the researchers failed to do a control experiment that checked the heterosexual brothers of the gay men for the same chromosomal markers.[26] The result has been resolutely rejected by the scientific community.

Roger Montgomery, a former homosexual prostitute who became a born-again believer, prior to his untimely death, wrote in his classic testimonial entitled, "My Life in Homosexuality," that,

According to the neurophysiological theory, because the brain is irreversibly "sexed" before birth, post-birth experiences cannot preprogram the brain in an alternate sexual direction. This theory is especially dear to homosexuals, because it allegedly offers a "scientific, medical support" to the homosexual lifestyle. Thus, they claim that post-birth experiences (such as the sexual molestation of a young boy by an older man) do not influence or alter sexual development in any way...The homosexual community wants us to believe that they were born gay in hopes that this would absolve them of personal responsibility, including the responsibility for recruiting children through molestation. Thus, a lack of responsibility for who one is, automatically carries with it the lack of responsibility to change their orientation and behavior.[27]

As unscientifically reliable as the medical data is, at least one-third of the gay and lesbian populous use it to justify their same-sex orientation. If a practicing homosexual accepts the conclusion that he is predetermined to be that way, he will automatically link the events of his life and will cite only those experiences that seemingly match his convenient conviction. This is the spirit of delusion operating through deception.

There are many post-birth activities that affect brain development, such as the use of pornography and alcohol. A person with either of these behaviors could never suggest that he is preprogrammed to it and therefore he should never resist the compulsion to give into the desire. The mistruth of the biological claim is injurious to a person teetering on the line clearly drawn between homosexuality and heterosexuality. This lie may push him into it because he may feel that he is created to be that way. Straddling the fence of sexuality is a most uncomfortable feeling.

A person's biological state is not a choice, and an individual's blessing status is not by chance. Homosexuality is a choice. It brings a burden that leaves no cause to rejoice. To believe that one is born a homosexual sets up the "idiosyncrasy of inevitability." It produces an "I cannot help myself" mentality. It is sinister, seductive, and conscience searing.

Brain Study

Researcher Simon LeVay did a postmortem study on the brains of 41 men and women who were reported to be homosexual. (LeVay is homosexual and his lover died of AIDS). Nineteen were alleged to be homosexual and 16 were assumed to be heterosexual men. He reported that in a particular area of the brain of heterosexual men, the cells were twice the size as that of homosexual men.[28] LeVay surmised that if homosexual men had smaller brain cells in this area, then they were responsible for homosexuality and that larger neurons in heterosexual men caused their heterosexuality. His biased goal was to prove a biological reason for homosexuality by showing that 100 percent of the time, there is a size difference in these neurons between homosexual and heterosexual men.[29]

While the homosexual activist agenda rallied support for their cause through his study, LeVay at most cautioned, "...it's important to stress what I didn't find. I did not prove that homosexuality is genetic, or find a genetic cause for being gay."[30] Several disturbing aspects of LeVay's study should be noted.

Living Lies and Dead Truth

First, since the subjects were deceased, their sexual orientation could not be completely verified. Three of the heterosexual men actually had smaller nuclei than their homosexual counterparts. When confronted about this by Dr. John Ankerberg during an interview, Dr. LeVay had to admit that he did not know for certain the sexual orientation of his subjects since they were not alive.[31] Quite possibly, Dr. LeVay could have had more homosexual subjects than he thought. Dead men do not lie or tell the truth.

As with all these studies, no one has been able to replicate LeVay's results. In *The Myth of Safe Sex*, John Ankerberg summarized the comments of Dr. Joseph Nicolosi, a renowned specialist in working with homosexual males. He astutely points out that sexuality is just one function of the area of the brain that Dr. LeVay studied. It also controls emotions. No one really knows what the exact function of that area of the brain is.[32] Psychiatrist, Dr. Charles Socarides, formerly of the Albert Einstein College of Medicine in New York, observes that LeVay's study does not solve the question of cause and effect.[33] Could it be that the homosexual behavior itself and other environmental factors cause the difference in size of these neurons in the brain?[34] It has been proven that the brain can be altered by behavior. As long as questions like these linger with no answers from Dr. LeVay himself or from other replicating studies, the discerning public will have to say that the study proved nothing.

Unfortunately, the public has been misled by the premature conjecture of the media. Troy Duster, an African-American geneticist, documented the coverage of LeVay's study in the media. Although LeVay himself advised caution in the interpretation of his results, the media flaunted the discovery of a "gay gene" in the headlines. Duster pointed out that within a few weeks the debate began about the gay gene as if such a thing was indeed factually established.[35] While scientists generally acknowledge the limitations of their findings to their fellow colleagues, the media readily runs with information without understanding the true conclusions that the researchers have reached.[36]

> THE FIRST EXAMPLE OF TWO MEN PRODUCING A BABY BY ANAL AND ORAL SEX HAS YET TO BE DISCOVERED.

Many times a lie will sound like the truth when it is repeated enough. The Scripture says in Second Thessalonians 2:11, "*And for this cause God shall send them strong delusion, that they should believe a lie."* God's Word is truth and in clarion terms it says, *"Male and female created He them"* (Gen. 1:27), and further states, *"Be fruitful, and multiply"* (Gen. 1:28). The first example of two men producing a baby by anal and oral sex has yet to be discovered. It is safe to say that a man and another man copulating will never produce children. A woman having a same-sex experience cannot become impregnated either. The divine design is a perfect one, and the Creator has a purpose for every man, woman, boy, and girl. That purpose is not discovered and uncovered in same-sex relationship. Just as you would not take a Lear jet to a Volkswagen dealer and ask him to repair the engine, you do not take a human being to the secular humanist and the liberal sexologist and ask them to define the design of someone. Only the Creator of all mankind can do that. The original blueprint sits on His architectural desk. The deception of the biological argument is aimed at getting people to view homosexuality initially in a more tolerable way and ultimately in a more favorable way.

The Biology Myth Does Not Touch First Base

There is no basis to the "biology myth." To use a baseball analogy, it does not come close to touching first base. However, in baseball, even if you strike out and the catcher drops the ball, you may still run to first base. The biology myth has struck out, but the Church has dropped the ball. The proponents of these perpetrations are not just running to first base, but they are trying to round the bases. The Umpire, the Mediator, the Advocate, the Judge of all men, the God of all flesh is saying loudly and clearly, *You're O-U-T!* The biology argument must return to the dugout. Better yet, it should take a cold shower, pack its bags, empty its locker, take its name off the door, and go home and stay forever. Since we know who the father of lies is, and we know where his home is, I strongly suggest that anyone aligning themselves with this damnable heresy is making reservations of their own accord to join him in his eternal place of destination. Selah.

> THE BIOLOGY ARGUMENT IS A BLATANT FABRICATION, AN ERRONEOUS EXEGESIS, AND AN EXERCISE IN NONSCIENTIFIC IMAGINATION.

If the "biology myth" has been the basis of your thinking, you are advised to rethink it, because thoughts are silent words and they are the things that ultimately manifest into reality. Everything starts with thought. Therefore, when you change your thoughts, you will change your life. Proverbs 23:7 says, *"For as he thinketh in his heart, so is he...."* You are what you think about all day long. Destiny's footprints are on the map of your mind.

The biology argument is a blatant fabrication, an erroneous exegesis, and an exercise in nonscientific imagination; and thus it is dismissed and should be thrown out of the court of public opinion. Let God be true! Let God arise! Let go of it and let God fix it. He can. He will. He is able.

—THE PSYCHOLOGY ARGUMENT—

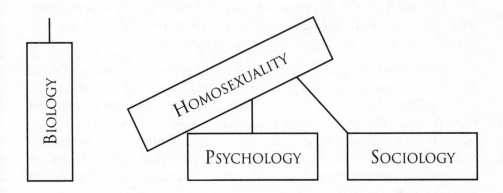

Current Scientific Observation

Without a biological cause of homosexuality, the gay activists are left with only two legs of their argument. The next argument is one of *psychology*. The acceptance of the biological argument means that since the homosexual was born that way, they cannot or should not seek to change. The refusal to believe that change is possible or even needed hardens the heart and forms what is best described as a pathological condition. Otherwise stated, the denial of an existent tendency is what causes abnormality in one's psychology. This means that a person psychologically, affectionately, and emotionally is homosexual; and therefore, a pathway of thinking results in them that carries the accompanying feelings and preferences. They are programmed for same-sex preference by their acceptance of the biological basis, thereby opening themselves up to the pervading influence and accompanying mental baggage of acceptance. This produces an array of emotions causing a person to be attracted to the same sex believing that it is their psychological, emotional preference, and that it is irreversible and incontrovertible. Michael Bailey (twins study) says this about the pathological nature of homosexuality:

> Homosexuality represents a deviation from normal development and is associated with other such deviations that may lead to mental illness or, another possibility, that increased psychopathology

239

among homosexual people is a consequence of lifestyle differences associated with sexual orientation.[37]

The psychology argument states that to be gay and lesbian is not so much a matter of personal preference as much as it is pre-wiring, predestination, and preprogramming. The heart is tuned to the frequency of the same-sex dial, and there is no static heard or felt because their antenna is powerful and quite capable of distinguishing and deciphering the transmission of the mixed signals that they are prone to receive. It is quite simply, what they like, *what they want,* and *what they intend to get.* They are bent on it and lean toward it like a limb blowing in the direction of the wind.

If the root is holy, how can the fruit be otherwise? Having the mind of Christ is the cure-all and the panacea for psychological indoctrination. The mind of Christ delivers one from the lewd, lascivious, and loose lifestyle that seeks to divert the pure in heart from seeking God. The mind of Christ is what Dr. Tim LaHaye calls a "Transformed Temperament." The psychology argument is without merit, and therefore like its predecessor, the biology argument, it should not be allowed admittance as evidence into the court of public opinion.

Concurrent Realistic Evaluation

...God condemns it [homosexuality] and heaven's testimony denounces it. Homosexuality is physiologically unnatural, unsafe and harmful. Death is usually the result.[38]

The Reformer Publication

The deadly danger of the psychology argument is that it assumes that because you like the gay lifestyle and it feels good to your flesh, you should do it until you are satisfied. If this is the case, morality is an archaic relic of ancient antiquity that deserves to be thrown on the ash heap of history. Society might as well hang a sign that says, "ALL WHO WOULD LIKE TO GET AIDS, DIE IN YOUR FORTIES, OR CONTRACT STD's, PLEASE SIGN UP FOR YOUR RIGHT TO KILL YOURSELF." The psychology argument leads to situational ethics where there are no absolutes or resolutes. Scripture teaches that "absolute resolution" is never *obsolete* despite how men may attempt to *obfuscate* it. Christ is our example, who, for sin, suffered in the flesh and condemned sin in the flesh that all men might be saved (see Rom. 8:1-3). He died of a broken heart while weeping over a people whose will to live godly, righteously, and blessedly had been broken by sinful choices. His psychological state at the time of His life was predisposed to do God's will and not to fulfill the dictates of His genitalia. He is the embodiment of holiness. That is why we worship Him today in the beauty of holiness. Follow His example. There is a legacy in your loins and a lineage in your lifestyle.

The homosexual life is a one-stop shop, a one-way, dead-end street that leads to "psychological" problems—some of which may never be resolved in his lifetime. It is simply fleshly gratification. Surely, life does not consist only of the thrill of sexual release or of promiscuous partner increase until you eventually decease. Life is arrived at in dimensions, and it is lived out in moments and seasons. The seasoning of life is not in sexual

THE HOMOSEXUAL LIFE IS A ONE-STOP SHOP, A ONE-WAY, DEAD-END STREET THAT LEADS TO "PSYCHOLOGICAL" PROBLEMS.

variety or notoriety, but it is in sexual propriety. The psychology argument *fails, falls,* and *falters* at the *foot* of the old rugged cross, where indeed all trophies will finally be laid down.

—THE SOCIOLOGICAL ARGUMENT—

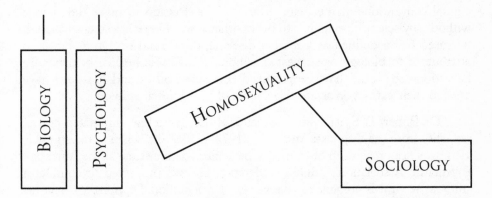

The third basis is the *sociological argument*. Simply stated, it means that the homosexual population should be granted minority status and afforded civil rights protection and full admittance to all professions on all levels. This includes all positions in religious faith, including those of the clergy. Every single day, the evening news abounds with stories of gay marriage, gay ordination, homophobia, or the so-called hideous hate crimes perpetrated against a gay person. This relentless campaign of coverage is aimed at establishing a normalized assessment of homosexuality. Ironically, there are published openly gay and lesbian writers and intellectuals who beg to differ. Lesbian social activist, Camille Paglia, is one such person. She states:

> Homosexuality is not "normal." On the contrary it is a challenge to the norm...Nature exists whether academics like it or not. And in nature, procreation is the single relentless rule. That is the norm. Our sexual bodies were designed for reproduction...No one is born gay. The idea is ridiculous...homosexuality is an adaptation, not an inborn trait....[39]

Generally, one would not quote a lesbian in making a point concerning the abnormality of homosexuality. However, it could not be stated better. This is precisely the biblical stance. In Acts 17:28, St. Paul addresses the Athenian idol worshipers. He states, "...*some of your own poets have said....*" He quoted from the secularists because their insights sometimes contain spiritual truth. For a lesbian to acknowledge the abnormality is grounds enough for the public to say, "*Case Dismissed!*"

When Did Homosexuality Start Being Gay?

In 1973, the American Psychiatric Association stopped calling homosexuality a "mental disorder" after being successfully lobbied and influenced by gay activists. According to reports, they were virtually held hostage in their annual conventions in the years prior to their decision to make the change without any scientific evidence to prove otherwise.[40] Nonetheless, even though it ceased being defined as a mental disorder, they could not go as far as to attribute it to biology or suggest that homosexuality is normal behavior. To have done so would have jeopardized their credibility, and it would have assured their extinction as a viable source of professional opinion.

Dr. Robert L. Spitzer was the leader of the group that eliminated homosexuality from the diagnostic manual in 1973. In 1999 he began to question his view after seeing a group of former homosexuals demonstrate at the American Psychiatric Association's annual conference. He was prompted to conduct a study to see if it is possible to change sexual orientation. Dr. Spitzer began his research expecting to affirm his belief that homosexuality is unchangeable. To his surprise, he found that 67 percent of the men studied actually were now heterosexual with more masculine (the men) and more feminine (the women) feelings.[41] Most of the participants in this study relied on their religious faith to help them come back to heterosexuality. The first two years into the process of changing did not seem to render significant results. However, with persistence and motivation, change was possible for a majority of them. Dr. Spitzer noted: "...some highly motivated individuals, using a variety of change efforts, can make substantial change in multiple indicators of sexual orientation, and achieve good heterosexual functioning." He also said:

I'm convinced from the people I have interviewed, that for many of them, they have made substantial changes toward becoming heterosexual...I think that's news...I came to this study skeptical. I now claim that these changes can be sustained.[42]

Although he conceded that it is possible for homosexuals to change, it continues to be a sad commentary on the many lives destroyed because of the A.P.A.'s prideful refusal to submit to scientific enquiry prior to making such a drastic decision in 1973 to reclassify the behavior of homosexuality.

The Untouchables

Homosexuals are not untouchables. Society should accept the homosexual as it does anyone else and should not discriminate their entrance into the normal flow of life. Homosexuality is not a disease that can be contagiously passed on. A homosexual should not be quarantined as were the carriers of leprosy in ancient times. Gay people are not bubonic-plague, germ-carrying rats. In fact, many of them are more loving and considerate than their heterosexual counterparts. After all, gays have always been here, and they are not going anywhere. The mistreatment of anyone should be opposed. However, just because they are accepted into the mainstream flow does not mean that society should change its laws to accommodate the behavior. The gay lifestyle is more an aberrant lifestyle than it is an alternative one. Biblically speaking, it is better described as abhorrent, and should be avoided. Each individual institution must govern itself according to its own value system. Churches and institutions geared to children (such as the boy scouts) must not drop the ball while playing loosely with the Word of the Almighty God and the lives of little ones. Admittedly, the homosexual argument of sociology is a difficult one to diffuse

> THE GAY LIFESTYLE IS MORE AN ABERRANT LIFESTYLE THAN IT IS AN ALTERNATIVE ONE.

and engenders great sympathy because normal people do not like to see someone discriminated against, especially if they have been a victim of it themselves. Despite this, no institution of faith should be expected to be an equal opportunity employer of others whose lifestyle(s) contradicts their moral convictions.

Touched by Angels

Be not forgetful to entertain strangers: for thereby some have entertained angels unawares (Hebrews 13:2).

I have had many associates and acquaintances over the years who either were previously gay or to some degree currently living the lifestyle. Many of them touched my life for the good in one way or the other. In most instances, I did not know they were gay; nonetheless, when it was discovered, it did not diminish the genuineness of their friendship. Jesus Himself was known as a friend of sinners. He even dined at their homes, but never was He with them for mere social reasons. It was always for ministry reasons. In my view, this is the key to the Christian response to the *social argument*. As a strong believer who is sexually adjusted, you should avail yourself to others, whose strength may not match yours. If the person happens to be a homosexual, the platonic friendship can often prove quite positive and life-changing for the other person. There have been members of All Nations Church who have had relapses into the homosexual lifestyle. In each reported instance, we have attempted to minister a gracious word by calling upon them to repent and then submit to the process of restoration. This is the preferred course of action, as opposed to expulsion, disfellowship, and excommunication.

If No One Reaches, No One Gets Touched

The Scripture says, *"Let not then your good be evil spoken of"* (Rom. 14:16). Be careful that your *good intentions are not misunderstood and misapplied.* Being in a social setting with a homosexual person does not transfer anything upon you; however, if you are susceptible to lust in any form yourself, it could possibly influence and affect you. First Corinthians 15:33 says, *"Be not deceived: evil communications corrupt good manners."* At the very least, it could give the impression that your association with the person is equivalent to your agreement with their chosen lifestyle. At all times, the believer is admonished to walk in wisdom to those who are without the knowledge of Christ. *"Walk in wisdom toward them that are without, redeeming the time"* (Col. 4:5).

—THE NERVE TO CALL GOD GAY!—

		BIOLOGY	PSYCHOLOGY	SOCIOLOGY

HOMOSEXUAL

Every valley shall be exalted, and every mountain and hill shall be made low: and the crooked shall be made straight, and the rough places plain (Isaiah 40:4).

Now that you are aware of the facts of the "unholy gay trinity," you can plainly see that it does not have a leg to stand on. The truth of God's Word eliminates the foundation of this errant perspective. The Church, the salt of the earth and the light of the world, cannot change its definition to mean "the called-out ones who never came out." Time and again, the Scripture exhorts the believer to come out, be separate, and to not partake in their sins (see 2 Cor. 6:17).

The "ecclesia," the Church, the called-out ones must recognize that the gay priesthood and marriage controversy is an assault on the holiness of God. *For homosexuals to say that God made them that way in a certain sense says that God Almighty is homosexual Himself.* Though that statement is a shocking one, it accurately describes the biology argument. All people are created in His image, and God is not confused about Himself. God is the pattern; we are the garment. God, our Father, is the potter; we are the clay. He is able to mold and make everyone after His will and way. He is the God of glory, and He is able to overcome the vain imaginations and arguments of men's hearts by the righteous standards of His Word and the executive power of His godhead. The God of glory can take a diseased leper's skin and make it like an infant baby's skin. He can take an African leopard and remove its spots. He can take an Ethiopian and make him a different hue. If God desires, He can paint an elephant with pink skin and give it wings to fly, thereby defying the laws of gravity and aerodynamics combined. He is God! He can do as it pleases Him. He can take the

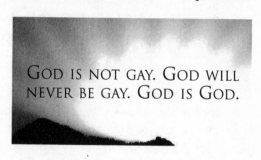

GOD IS NOT GAY. GOD WILL NEVER BE GAY. GOD IS GOD.

worst-case scenario and work it together for good (see Rom. 8:28). He is God yesterday, today, and forever. He is God and He changes not. He will not lie nor alter the Word that comes from His mouth. Has He not spoken it; shall He not do it? Has He not declared it; shall it not come to pass? The I AM that I AM is everything that He desires to be. But there is one thing that He will never be. God is not gay. God will never be gay. God is God. Woe unto him who has the nerve, the mitigated gall, the brazen audacity to call the Almighty God gay!

The reality of God's Word and scientific data serve to cast down the imaginations of the biological, psychological, and sociological arguments, and declare in the loudest voice possible, *"Let God be true, but every man a liar"* (Rom. 3:4a)! Heaven and earth bear witness that whenever the heathen rage and take *counsel* against the Lord and against His anointed, God arises in their midst *as a mighty man of war.* The counsel of *"the ungodly shall not stand..."* (Ps. 1:5); and *"He that sitteth in the heavens shall laugh"* (Ps. 2:4a). He that laughs last shall last and last. Solomon declared in Proverbs 1:26, *"I also will laugh at your calamity; I will mock when your fear cometh."*

God's Word is no joke, and His will is no laughing matter. Isaiah declared *that every high place shall be brought down* (see Is. 40:4). Thus, the biology, psychology, and sociology arguments fall, leaving no leg to stand on. They cannot hold water because they are full of leaks. They are vain imaginations (see Gen. 6:5).

The worst part about the biology argument is that it gives headway to the other ones. Once defeated, the toppling of the other two is an easily accomplished fact. Once people realize that they were not born *with a predestination to homosexuality*, they will either have to accept God's Word or reject it, but they can no longer be indifferent to it. God sets two options before everyone on the planet. Those options are life or death. Therefore, it is highly recommended that everyone chooses life (see Deut. 30:19).

—THE MAKING OF A HOMOSEXUAL— TENDENCIES, ORIENTATION, AND PREFERENCE

While scripture teaches that we are born with fallen natures that incline us toward any number of vices, it does not permit us to excuse any particular inclination as inevitable or uncontrollable. Many gays reject morality while offering any one of a variety of rational and emotional reasons for doing so. The thought is, as ideologies go, personal immorality is...nobody else's business. The mortal enemy of that convenience is the value judgment.[43]

An interviewer once asked Boy George, an entertainer of world renown in the 1980's, if he was a homosexual. His short response was in the form of a question. Evasively, he asked if that means that he has *sex at home.* Obviously, his elusive answer was meant to make light of a very serious inquiry into his personal sexual preference.

In reality, *homosexuality has nothing to do with a place, yet it has everything to do with the practice.* Technically, a homosexual is a man or woman who has a sexual experience or ongoing relationship with individuals of the *same sex or gender.* A theological definition of a homosexual is a person who has chosen to live in a contrary fashion to the lifestyle of male-female covenantal relationship. If a person engages in sex on any level with the same gender without seeking *to change,* then they are clearly a homosexual. Briar White-head describes lesbianism as "an absorbing relationship between women that is eroticized...a preferential and erotic attraction to other women over a significant period of time."[44] Tendencies toward homosexuality are described as those impulses or impressions that seem to incline one sexually to the same gender as one's self. *Orientation* implies the acceptance of the apparent reality that one is born and thus predisposed toward the same sex; and therefore, one's attraction and attempt at a "love relationship" is automatically accommodating to one's physical, emotional, and natural inclination toward the same sex.

Created Purpose Versus Chosen Preference

Contrary to popular beliefs concerning sexual orientation and proclivities, I was not born with these sexual tendencies. It had nothing to do with some false theory of genetic make-up. It wasn't chromosomal, and had—nor has it in today's society, either—nothing to do with my DNA. These tendencies that I had and displayed came about because someone touched a little boy.[45]

Pastor Donnie McClurkin

Having pastored for 20 years and having counseled many practicing homosexuals, the answers to this *created purpose or chosen lifestyle* question are quite diverse because some testify that they have had same-sex tendencies all their lives. As far back as they can remember, their attraction has been toward the same gender. They have concluded that they must have been born genetically preprogrammed to be homosexual. They are adamantly insistent that there is nothing that they can do to wrest their lives, their sanity, and their very being from the vice grip hold of homosexuality, nor do they want to do so. In fact, after a period of trying unsuccessfully to change their ways, many have given up on the likely occurrence of change and therefore accept that the homosexual inclination is their "created purpose" as opposed to their "chosen preference." It is easy to understand this compliant attitude in light of the intense struggle. The making of a homosexual differs depending on the individual. There are many factors that make up the predisposition toward becoming a gay or lesbian person.

The following eleven reasons are not meant to set forth excuses, but rather explanations, of this behavior or lifestyle. Dr. Tim LaHaye's book, *What Everyone Should Know About Homosexuality,* served as the primary reference for the development of this information.

—LEARNING TO RELATE AND UNDERSTAND—

Predisposition to Homosexuality

Dr. Charles Wahl, a researcher in the area of homosexuality, has disagreed with the conclusion that homosexuals are born and not made. He writes, "The vast preponderance of evidence clearly indicates that homosexuality is a learned disorder and is not genetically inherited."[46] In other words, homosexuals are not oriented as such, but circumstanced events in life lead them to be that way. Dr. Robert Kronemeyer, a clinical psychologist, agrees. He writes,

> I firmly believe that homosexuality is a learned response to early painful experiences and that it can be unlearned....[47]

This is the preeminent issue of contention and cannot be summarily dismissed with patronizing answers to either perspective. How does a person born like any other human being accept, adopt, and acquiesce to this practice? The answer to that is both complex and revealing. No one final factor or mitigating circumstance causes a person to develop into a homosexual. *The causes are varied, but the effect is always the same.* Each person's experience is unique to him or her, but there are very common elements found throughout a perusal of the underlying conditions. There are eleven principle causations. The number *eleven* is one short of the number *twelve,* which represents God's government throughout Scripture. *Eleven* is six (the number of man) plus five (the number of grace). Six plus five equals eleven and represents man's sin and coming short of the glory of God. Homosexuality is the embodiment of eleven.

Reason One: Inherent Sin Nature

> *Behold, I was shapen in iniquity; and in sin did my mother conceive me* (Psalm 51:5).

Sin is the product of the fall of man, and its effect was passed down to all others. Apart from Christ, sin is as natural as breathing is to the Adamic creation. Some people become homosexuals because they prefer the same gender. They have not been molested, traumatized, coerced, or "turned out." They just like the way that it makes them feel. There are men who like men and women who love women. There are homosexual body-builders, exotic dancers, and models, as well as blue-collar and white-collar ones. They are in love with the body that looks like theirs. This results in same-sex attraction. In a certain sense, it is a form of narcissism or self-love. Dr. Robert Kronemeyer says,

> Living under the dominion of a sinful nature establishes habits which eventually form a lifestyle. Deep ruts are dug into the person's life. He becomes comfortable responding to his inner longings. By the time he becomes a believer, the passions of the flesh have already ruled his life for many years. These deeply entrenched habits have been constantly reinforced and strengthened by the old nature which has become accustomed to having its own way. When the desire for sexual behavior wells up within him, he gives into the craving without a second thought. Again, the foundational purpose for life, even for the most decent non-believer, revolves around pleasure, gratification, and self-preservation.[48]

Reason Two: The Child's Temperament

Train up a child in the way he should go: and when he is old, he will not depart from it (Proverbs 22:6).

One of the most significant links to the person's predisposition is their temperament. There are four basic personality types. They are choleric, sanguine, phlegmatic, and melancholic. The latter is found in an overwhelming majority of homosexuals. These categories date back thousands of years and yet are still relevant and widely utilized today. Studies indicate that those of a melancholic personality are somehow more prone to succumb to the root causes of homosexuality. Unlike the choleric who is the strong-willed leader, the melancholic is quite sensitive, artistic, and gifted. The sanguine is the lively super-extrovert; the melancholic is the introverted perfectionist. The peaceful phlegmatic is generally easygoing in contrast to the melancholic who is the superintrovert-perfectionist.

Twenty-five percent of Americans are considered melancholic, but of course, only a minuscule percentage are considered homosexual. It is critical to note that all humans possess some characteristics of all the personality types. Through anecdotal observation from those who work with and counsel homosexuals, the melancholic temperament seems to be the leading one among gays and lesbians. To a great degree, the melancholic are predominate in areas such as fashion, hair design, creative arts, music, dance, ballet, acting, journalism, writing, etc. In many churches, they are preeminent in the music ministry and sometimes in the spoken word ministry itself. The gifts and callings of God are given by God and not necessarily only to those whose lifestyle is in alignment with the revealed righteousness of God. St. Paul says in Romans 11:29, *"For the gifts and calling of God are without repentance."* This means that God does not change His mind once He gives them and also that the recipient of God's gifts does not necessarily deserve them, because it is not based on their repentance. They may not be right with God and still be gifted. God uses them not because of them, but in spite of them. God can use anything. He can use the ass to prophecy or even the jawbone of the ass to destroy the enemy (see Num. 22:28-30; Judg. 15:15). God programs the person's temperament. The devil and life itself programs the perversion of it.

The temperament of a person often has to do with whether or not he is open or closed to a particular suggestion, attitude, or behavior pattern. However, the temperament itself does not cause a person to develop into a homosexual. Gay and lesbian persons are represented in all four personality types. However, the melancholic disposition generally sets up a person to be more vulnerable to certain culpable factors that contribute to a person developing into a homosexual.[49] Human personality is directly linked to personal abilities, inabilities, and disabilities. When Jesus declared to His disciples, *"Ye know not what manner of spirit ye are"* (Lk. 9:55b), this was indeed a veiled reference to their temperament or disposition at the time of their action. Every credible teacher of human social behavior, as well as every serious student of human personality, will readily testify that the "knowledge of self" is a key building block of a successful life and social interaction and adjustment to others. The spirit of a person is the sum total of the attributes that constitute who they are in their unseen or internal dimension. The spirit of a person embodies their temperament and is the significant factor in the forming of their personality and personal choices. An individual's temperament *is the core of their individual being.* It is the primary root cause of human behavior.

Reason Three: Misunderstanding and Rejection

> *He is **despised** and **rejected** of men; a man of sorrows, and acquainted with grief: and we hid as it were our faces from him; he was **despised**, and we esteemed him not* (Isaiah 53:3, emphasis added).

Oftentimes children are misunderstood due to their parents' inability to properly distinguish the child's personality type and accompanying characteristics. The child's parents have a presumptuous idea of what disposition their child should have been or a prejudicial viewpoint concerning the child as he is. When misunderstanding is present, it often leads to unfair or harsh criticism, accompanied by unfair comparisons with siblings and peers that cause a complex. Even worse, it can cause an identity crisis. The result of this toxic parent-child relationship oftentimes is sexual identity frustration, a propensity toward promiscuity, a development of dysfunction, or deviation from the norm. *The gay lifestyle is the fruit of the problem, but the rejection from the parent is often the root of the practice.* Parental misunderstanding and misguided actions often serve to imprint the mind of a child,

THE GAY LIFESTYLE IS THE FRUIT OF THE PROBLEM, BUT THE REJECTION FROM THE PARENT IS OFTEN THE ROOT OF THE PRACTICE.

thereby alienating them and sometimes pushing them in the direction to succumb to the seductive force of homosexuality. In addition, any misunderstandings or misguided actions are exacerbated by misspoken words towards the child.

Reason Four: Spoken Word Curses

As the bird by wandering, as the swallow by flying, so the curse causeless shall not come (Proverbs 26:2).

To be blessed is to be smiled upon. To be cursed is equivalent to being frowned upon. Every blessing has a basis. Every curse has a cause. Characteristics that manifest in the child's personality are generally evident within days, weeks, months, and the early formative years of their life. Sometimes, beginning behavior and tendencies seen in the infant or toddler will gradually germinate and come to full manifestation at any time within the first two or three decades of the person's life. For example, babies who are quiet are also soft-spoken when they grow older. Babies who are kickers and screamers are still that way many years later in adulthood. Often, parents may not understand their child and they become frustrated and solidify, through their verbal confession, the child's inclination.[50] Spoken words have a force that is either constructive or destructive. Unfortunately, many have been *considered, called, and caused to be homosexual* by ill-advised parents, siblings, peers, or others who continue to reinforce the image with the invocation of negativism. *The tongue, though it is a little member, kindles a great fire. Often it is set on fire of hell* (see Jas. 3:6). Solomon said, "*Death and life are in the power of the tongue*" (Prov. 18:21a). When a parent speaks repulsively over a child, it has the effect or the "self-fulfilling" prophecy or the invocation of a curse. The curse will cast a dark shadow over the child all the days of his life. After all, "If Daddy or Mommy says it, then it must be true." *The remedy for curse reversal is in the acknowledgment of it, the renunciation of it, the revoking of it, and the reinforcing of the exact opposite results by speaking words of affirmation and comfort.* People should be very careful what they invoke over another person's life. Many have been made homosexual by spoken word curses, reinforced by demonic forces.

Reason Five: Detachment From the Father

Children's children are the crown of old men; and the glory of children are their fathers (Proverbs 17:6).

The masculinity in a boy and the femininity in a girl must be affirmed by their parents or other authority figures throughout their childhood years. A boy or girl alienated from the father through various circumstances (death, absenteeism, emotional distance, divorce, etc.) misses the important opportunity to identify and receive love from the primary male figure in his or her life.[51] Consequently, in the case of a male, he will often unconsciously seek for the affirmation of his father through the misguided arms of another male figure. In the case of a woman, it may have a reverse effect and cause her to shun other males, because of the lack of bonding of the "primary male," which is her father. The father is the daughter's first line of defense. He is the

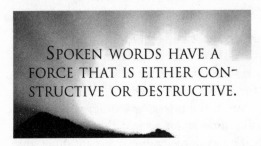

SPOKEN WORDS HAVE A FORCE THAT IS EITHER CON⁻STRUCTIVE OR DESTRUCTIVE.

first man of her life, and if the relationship is strained or non-existent, it could grossly affect her in subsequent relationships with other men. She may be unconsciously drawn to a man who is similar to her father, which would be unhealthy for her if he is not a loving and con-siderate man. In some instances, she will reject men altogether and consistently be attracted to and compelled to seek out same-sex relationships that may be an indication of the relationship she experienced with her mother.

Dr. Tim LaHaye tells the story of a boy who was working with his father one day in the garage fixing a car. His father asked him for a crescent wrench. The little boy did not know what it was, and the father became indignant concerning his apparent ignorance. The father came out from under the car and very definitively called him a "sissy," telling him to go in the house with his mother to do girls' work. That experience traumatized him and dramatically hurt his feelings. He grew up with that incident always in his subconscious.[52] He was wounded as a child and carried the scars as an adult. Children evolve into the image that the adults in their lives paint of them. Children hold adult comments as the truth and are greatly influenced by them. This reality repeats itself throughout time immemorial. The root of *dysfunction* will result in the fruit of *distortion*. This can even sometimes manifest in an inordinate affection of boys and their mothers. Briar Whitehead, in *Craving for Love*, wrote, "To be attached to one's mother is, in itself, entirely normal. But what is normal in the presence of a healthy father attachment is abnormal in isolation from it."[53]

Inordinate and abnormal relationships with the mother or the father make impressions upon the mind of the child, which culminate in dysfunctional relationships. In the case of a passive, absent, or abusive father, the boy is often made to be the "man" of the house. Because of his assumed role, he may be the one whom the mother vents on emotionally or depends on for support. He identifies with his father's masculinity, but his father is not there to mirror that masculinity to him and to affirm him. He has a void that only a man can fill. His mother as the leader of the house is the image of masculinity that he sees. This may produce effeminacy or inordinate affection toward his mother. There is obviously something wrong with this picture. There may be an obscuring of the separate and dissimilar concepts of masculinity and femininity. This is what Leanna Payne describes as a "crisis in masculinity." The confusion may develop into an effeminate man or the stereotypical "sissy." The bent wrist, the high-pitched voice, the sensual walk, and the mannerisms will soon line up with the mind-set, and the making of a homosexual is well under way. Also, the inordinate or inappropriate affection of the boy and his mother may manifest in self-loathing or in rejection of the female gender as a subconscious form of resentment, due to the suppression of the male role of leadership in the household environment.

Reason Six: Misalignment in Relationship With Mothers

Can a woman forget her sucking child, that she should not have compassion on the son of her womb? yea, they may forget, yet will I not forget thee (Isaiah 49:15).

This is driven by the rejection received from the father combined with emotional issues that the mother may have.[54] She may really *overprotect* the boy through her affection, thereby becoming a "smother mother." Inadvertently, she may cause the son to have inappropriate feelings toward her. Though they may or may not be sexual, they are emotionally fulfilling and physically stimulating. This arouses that curiosity which may be lived out with someone of the same sex, because at a young age, the same sex is normally who he is exposed to. Often, according to social scientists, there is an introduction and experimentation with masturbation, fantasy, lust, and physical stimulation at this juncture of self-discovery.

Sexual Alteration

The mother is the boy's first female encounter. Therefore, the relationship must be wholesome and physically correct or it will give a distorted image that will serve as a first sexual reference. Distortions obviously result in perversion. This perversion, like a river, will branch into the outlets and inlets of dysfunction and maladjustment. The boy's mother becomes "the pace car" of how he will conduct the race of life and of how he will relate to other women. The mother and father help to form the child's sexual self-image. The image must be well-adjusted, or it will be maladjusted. It must be aligned and in agreement with God's divine purpose or else it will be altered.

Sexual Altercation

When the self-image of sexuality is altered, the person may suffer a soulish altercation and turn to same-sex peer groups seeking affirmation and belonging. In other instances, early childhood peer pressure and being called names like sissy, queer, faggot, fairy, or the like, seek to reaffirm the very low sense of self-esteem. It may seem like harmless fun to the teaser, but is very hurting to the child, further pushing him to seek affirmation from the male sex.[55] Many may remember defiantly uttering the words, "Sticks and stones may break my bones, but words will never hurt me." The truth is this: Words do not harm the body, but they definitely hurt and damage the soul and spirit of a little child. The Scripture says, *"How forcible are right words"* (Job 6:25a). On the contrary, how damaging are destructive words. This is particularly true for the child who is melancholic in his disposition. The sensitive element may make him less *resistant* and *resilient* to this early childhood trauma of rejection.[56] Thus, parental rejection gives homosexuality an inlet into the child's soul. All parents should study parenting and seek to have God's power work through them for the development of a healthy child and for the glory of God. Children raised in an atmosphere of affirmation accomplish great things in life more often than not. They become signs and wonders; they are ten times better; and they become arrows of deliverance (see Is. 8:18; Dan. 1:20). It has been said that *children are living messages that are sent to a time that the parents will not see.* Parental rejection sends the wrong message to the child, and it also confuses and complicates the message that the children themselves will send.

Reason Seven: Transference in the Womb

And it came to pass, that, when Elisabeth heard the salutation of Mary, the babe leaped in her womb; and Elisabeth was filled with the Holy Ghost (Luke 1:41, emphasis added).

In the natural sense, the mother's state of mind and body has a major correlation to the health and life of the unborn child. Unhealthy actions such as smoking, drinking alcohol, and drug usage affect the child in a negative way. This is why many children are born with birth defects, crack cocaine addictions, and even AIDS. An unborn child, though not yet delivered, is directly affected by the mother's contributions and

PARENTAL REJECTION GIVES HOMOSEXUALITY AN INLET INTO THE CHILD'S SOUL.

actions in a positive sense as well as in a negative sense. If she is experiencing proper nutrition, good rest, and regular exercise, it will correlate with the child who is being formed within her.

In a mysterious way, this is also true of spiritual transference. The mother's spiritual and mental state at the time of pregnancy can result in the embryonic environment being conducive to a holy and healthy transference. At Mary's announcement of her pregnancy to her cousin Elisabeth, who was already six months pregnant, the baby literally leaped in her womb (see Lk. 1:44). Elisabeth's child, though he was an embryo, was able to perceive the good news of the Messiah's birth. This is proof positive that in the invisible, unconscious realm of the human spirit, something can be passed on to children, even in the womb. A parent who refuses, disapproves of, or regrets the child can cause a spirit of rejection to transfer to the child in the womb, just as readily as natural disease can be genetically transmitted in the child's DNA while he or she is still in the womb.

A strong desire and subsequent disappointment by the parents for a baby who is not the gender of the child that they actually have, can do enormous damage to the growing young person's psyche, should they be privy to the information. For example, a person's parents may have earnestly desired a son, and therefore decided upon the name John. However, they have a girl instead and decide to name her Johanna. Perhaps they wanted a daughter and were going to name her Kimberly, but because they have a son, they name him the male version of Kim. Inadvertently, in some extreme, and I emphasize *extreme* (not normal) cases, the child will manifest subconscious feminine tendencies or an effeminate spirit, because what has been embodied in his name is his parent's secondary choice and disappointment.

As a boy, he may accentuate effeminate gestures, mannerisms, etc. This is a subconscious identification with the feminine possibilities inherent within his name. Though he is a boy, he has girlish ways. He will receive criticism for this, and the spoken words may reinforce his self-image maladjustment, which may lead him into a closet homosexual inclination, and when he is older, a complete knowledge. As a girl, she may identify with the male gender, become quite boyish, and soon become known as a tomboy. Of course, most "tomboys" per se do not become lesbians; but some of them do, and therefore the possibility cannot be diminished. In either case, the primary cause is disappointed parental expectation.[57]

Many gay and lesbian people assert that they grew up feeling like they were cursed to have the external genitalia of one sex, but the internal gender of the opposite sex. When you combine *disposition* with *temperament, prenatal expectations, parental influence, detachment from father, attachment to mother, spiritual transference,* and *words of rejection,* a child may grow up experiencing *insecurity* about his or her sexual *identity,* thereby leading him into sexual *confusion* and ultimately a *homosexual* lifestyle. Satan gains a *foothold* that becomes a *stronghold* if it is not discerned and dealt with expeditiously. The Church must be prepared to acknowledge and accept that this is indeed the case. Unfortunately, many believers write off the gays or lesbians as if they were a cancer or a plague, and do not really comprehend the degree to which the person's soul has been under assault, even from his mother's womb. Transference in the womb due to prenatal conditions in the parents and in the environment is often a critical feature in the making of some homosexuals.

Reason Eight: Childhood Sexual Trauma

...Arise, and take the young child and His mother, and flee into Egypt, and be thou there until I bring thee word: for Herod will seek the young child to destroy Him (Matthew 2:13).

A powerful case could be made that the most dominant stimuli for sexual confusion and malfunction is *childhood sexual trauma.* This is when a child is prematurely exposed to sex against his or her will or before they can properly process the exposure. The first experience serves to imprint their mind and emotions. The first impression may result in a suppression, oppression, depression, and ultimate possession. Studies reveal that 85 to 90 percent of lesbians were sexually abused by the opposite sex and therefore have always had difficulty relating to men as beings of intimacy.[58] In another 2001 study, it was found that 46 percent of homosexuals and 22 percent of lesbians reported that they had been molested by a homosexual during childhood, compared to 7 percent of heterosexual men and 1 percent of heterosexual women.[59] Ninety percent of all homosexuals were actively recruited by older men.[60] Sixty-two percent of homosexuals are more likely to admit to having sex with children under the age of 13.[61] Five hundred fifty-seven percent more gays report being arrested for sexual crimes.[62]

A young boy who is sexually violated lacks the maturity to distinguish that he is indeed being victimized and is an unwilling participant in the horrific act(s). He may assume that it is natural and that it is something that he is responsible for. In other words, a child can be violated and not even know and understand that he is being violated. This initial imprinting does severe damage to the psyche of the child.[63] Psychologists have discovered that the cause and effect of human behavior can be traced to events that can be lodged in the memories that control conduct, without a person ever realizing the root cause of their actions. One homosexual testified that his earliest memory of oral sex was when he was having sex with someone through the bars of his crib. However, there could be some memories of early homosexual activity that are not retained, thereby leaving the person thinking that they have always been or were born the way they are. This is clearly the trick of the enemy to pervert their thinking and alter their sound judgment. It is critical that parents be very careful concerning who they allow their children to be exposed to in their formative years of infancy and childhood. *A homosexual once told me that after he was molested, he automatically accepted male advances toward him in subsequent years as normal.*

Some parents ignore the evidence of early childhood sexual trauma, even when it clearly manifests before their eyes. In the autobiographical movie *Antoine Fisher*, the main character was sexually abused by his babysitter who happened to be his foster sister. He was greatly traumatized by it. Although he did not become a homosexual, he was deeply pained, somewhat terrified, and filled with inner disgust. Eventually, his life became better and his childhood trauma was overcome.

Not-So-Innocent Childhood Games

The so-called innocent games that children play, like "doctor" and "house," can produce an imprinting in the young person. These situations imprint them with memories of pleasure or, in some instances, even pain. The sadomasochistic inclinations of certain homosexuals may often be traced to this early stage of game playing. In the formative years of a child's life, "experimentation" is a fundamental concept of the inquiring child's mind. He is automatically *classified* by sex upon birth, *identified* by sex every time he uses the restroom, *separated* by sex in school, and *attracted* by sex to various toys, games, mannerisms, clothing, and colors, etc. At the earliest learning stages, all of life is fantasy and the child's body is like an uncharted sea, an unexplored horizon, and an uncultivated garden. Innocent child games may sometimes go too far. Statements like, "You show me yours and I'll show you mine," may result in visual pleasure; and when it progresses to fondling, caressing, holding, and touching, then the imprinting is in full swing. If oral activity is initiated by either one of the parties, fixation may become the result. Thus, the childhood exposure can produce childhood sexual tendencies. If the experiences are painful and unwelcome, they will produce childhood sexual trauma and could possibly become an element in the making of a homosexual. This is precisely what has happened to many homosexuals in the world today.

Reason Nine: Early Interest in Sex

Coupled with one or more of the six previously mentioned factors, the child digresses into the next phase of becoming a homosexual, which is *an early interest in sex*. Exposure to the barrage of sexual images in our society exacerbates the plight of children having difficulty in this area. Studies of homosexuals show that an overwhelming majority of them enter puberty at an early age, thereby experiencing somewhat of a sexual awakening of curiosity. Although the body is developing at this age, the mind is not quite in pace with the physical development. This is a dangerous moment, and even minor events that trigger sexual response have been noted to serve as a backdrop of sexual experimentation.

Even through incidental experiences, such as riding a horse or riding a bicycle, the genital area may become stimulated. This may lead to genital stimulation and fascination. Oftentimes, masturbatory thoughts are indulged and become fixations in the person. A young child in the stage of puberty is normally around children of the same age and does not normally have a lot of interaction with the opposite sex. Behaviorally, he or she is at the age when they do not normally desire or experience much exposure to the opposite sex. Therefore, there is opportunity for experimentation with the same sex. The *curiosity* combined with *convenient* opportunity make a *concoction* that can result in a sexual *combustion*. This is the testimony of many who have been introduced to homosexuality. It started as innocent experimentation, and alas, like a venomous viper, the spirit of homosexuality dug its poisonous fangs into their preference and consciousness. Having been bitten by the beast, their lives became drastically affected and their course was dramatically altered.

Reason Ten: Seducing Spirits

It must be understood that "seducing spirits" are very much involved in planting feelings, subtle suggestions, and in spreading misinformation into the mind-set of individuals who may be unaware of their activity. Thus, the feelings that appear to be *real*, may in fact be *surreal* and satanic in their origin, even though they portray themselves as *homosexual* tendencies and *orientation*. A person who is homosexual may actually have taken on a "demonic spirit of homosexuality." A lying spirit generally accompanies the spirit of homosexuality (see 2 Thess. 2:9). However, to be homosexual does not necessarily mean that one is demon-possessed.

A seducing spirit is not the same as a *homosexual tendency*. A seducing spirit is not the same as *homosexual orientation*. Nearly everyone at sometime in their life is engaged with an onslaught from the deceiver in this area of their psyche. In *Pursuing Sexual Wholeness*, Andrew Comiskey writes:

> The deception is incredibly effective because of the power of sexual bonding. One genuinely feels release, belonging and covering. The warm, sensual acceptance of a lover seems to melt away decades of loneliness and alienation. The enemy knows the yearning and its seeming release. He knows the power of homosexual communion. And he will employ its sensual and emotional returns to deceive us mightily. Many solid Christians have rejected orthodox Christianity due to homosexual unions or, worse, have tried to conform orthodoxy to their deceived status. Once their wills are yielded to the sin, they submit their souls and spirits to the ravages of the evil one.[64]

The devil himself takes on any nature and any perversion that is necessary for the accomplishment of his ends. To satan, the means are justified by the ends. It does not matter to him how old the person is when he attacks him or seeks to devour him. He is hell-sent and therefore hell-bent on deluding, deceiving, damning, dooming, and destroying those who have the mark of the Creator God upon them and whose purpose for them is redemption, righteousness, and hetero-reality.

Reason Eleven: Transference of Spirits

One of the more subtle ways that an individual can become homosexual is to regularly attend a church that is pastored by a gay or lesbian person. I have witnessed this time and again. Social scientists have concluded that *children evolve into the image that they see on a consistent basis*. They are impressionable, and subconsciously they will emulate the behavior that is modeled before them. I know of an instance where a pastor was heavily influenced in his younger years by an older minister, who happened to be a closet gay person. This was confirmed in subsequent years by the testimonies of those who either had been fondled or had engaged in sexual situations to varying degrees. In time, the child grew up and became a pastor himself. Every time that I ministered in the church, I noticed a significant amount of "sissified activity" among the obviously effeminate majority of men. There were two young men, in particular, who grew up to become homosexuals themselves, and one of them died of complications due to A.I.D.S. Though their pastor did not personally solicit or attempt to seduce either of these two young people, I believe that he will be held responsible on the Day of Judgment for what happened to them. Their homosexuality was not a coincidence, nor was it chosen per se, but it was caused by the *transference of spirits.* Whenever a minister opens his mouth, he is either speaking from the *Holy Spirit, the human spirit,* or *the hellish spirit.* Either his tongue is set on fire by God, or by hell (see Jas. 3:6). Words are powerful because they often release spiritual forces—either good or bad—into the atmosphere (see Job 6:25). Images are even more powerful than words. Closet homosexual pastors may portray that they represent Christ, but they reproduce perversion, after their own heart. When I interviewed these two young men as to the root cause of their homosexuality, both of them attested to the spiritual environment that they were raised in. Woe be to the homosexual pastors who transfer their spirit upon unsuspecting souls. The Master Teacher pronounced severe judgment upon those who are responsible for raising up *twofold children of hell.*

> *Woe unto you...ye make him twofold more the **child of hell** than your-selves* (Matthew 23:15, emphasis added).

The Causation Argument: The Conclusion Homosexuality and the Unholy Gay Trinity

The Predisposition Is Formed

The result of all of the noted factors, whether it is disposition, temperament, womb transference, insecurity about sexual identity, detachment from the father figure, childhood sexual trauma, misalignment in their relationship with their mother, early interest in sex, or introduction to masturbation and fantasy, seducing spirits or transference of spirits; there is a predisposition toward homosexuality that is formed and congealed. Eventually, the environment and timing coincide for a homosexual experience. The Family Research Institute surveyed 4,340 adults. Among homosexual men, 85 percent said their first sexual encounter was homosexual. Twenty-nine percent of lesbians said the same. In the same study, the first sexual encounter of 96 percent of the heterosexual men and 97 percent of the heterosexual women was heterosexual.[65]

This initial occurrence may produce a mental obsession with whatever pleasure was derived from the encounter. Even if it caused a lot of pain, it is still embedded as a sexual obsession. Inevitably, the result is a repeat performance and the subsequent guilt that accompanies it. Despite this reality, the behavior is repeated again.[66] As there are more homosexual experiences, more pleasurable or painful results, the conscience is hardened. The literal attitudinal spirit of homosexuality is lodged within the person's soul. Their will, emotions, and intellect are imprinted fully. *Now they are a homosexual. The making of the homosexual is complete. Without deliverance, they are destined for life to be guided by perverted passion and inordinate affection.* Christian psychologist, Dr. Gerhard van den Aardweg describes the initial reaction of a person accepting and labeling themselves as a homosexual.

> A young person who notices homosexual interests in themselves often goes through a miserable time....They may feel ashamed; when the topic of homosexuality is touched upon, they want to hide lest others connect it with them. They suffer in silence; maybe they try to decoy or play down their feelings, even to remember. The moment comes, however, often around the age of eighteen, when the young person has to face the situation. Then he

may conclude, "I am a homosexual." That can give great relief. The acute tension declines but a price must be paid. The youngster hardly ever realizes that they have fixed a rather definitive label on themselves with this "self-identification" and assigned themselves to a second-class and in fact excluded status....They inwardly realize that their "big difference" is an inferior form of sexuality... the toll for this, however, is the depressing fatalism that is implicit in this newly acquired identity. "I am just that way." The young person does not think, "I must have been born the same as anyone else." No, he feels he is a different and inferior creature, who carries a doom: he views himself as tragic.[67]

A Psyche Under Seige

An individual is not a homosexual because he feels like one, or because he has labeled himself as one, and certainly not because he is labeled as such by others. A person is one only if he regularly yields to the impulses and the accompanying feelings of it.

Former homosexual, Frank Worthen, testified that when he was living the homosexual life, "he felt like he was created to be lost."[68] Can you imagine what it feels like to think God created you to be lost? Many homosexuals are prone to commit suicide and to premature death. This person felt that he was like an animal that had been wounded, but not killed. He writes:

> There is a rage inside you that wants to lash out at everything and everyone indiscriminately. How do you gain the trust of a wounded animal? Not by kicking it.[69]

Perhaps this self-loathing that often accompanies homosexuality is the reason an independent study conducted from the year 1998-2001 states that "homosexuals and bisexuals are at least twice as likely to be alcohol dependent than heterosexuals."[70] Sixty-two percent *more* homosexuals are drug and alcohol users. In fact, the study further stated that "most gays do not want their children to be gay." Dr. Gerhard van den Aardweg makes this conclusion:

> AN INDIVIDUAL IS NOT A HOMOSEXUAL BECAUSE HE FEELS LIKE ONE, OR BECAUSE HE HAS LABELED HIMSELF AS ONE...

> ...careful analysis of the fantasy and dream life over the whole course of the life of a person with strong homosexual tendencies

[reveal that] one always finds traces of a moral, deeply hidden heterosexual disposition.[71]

The striking truth is this: There is a heterosexual in the homosexual that is so desperate to come out of the closet of his subconscious mind that he will even appear to that person in his sleep!

If a person accepts the label of himself as a homosexual and endeavors to lead the accompanying life, then the stages of the congealment into the confusion may vary from preteen to a full-grown adult. Nonetheless, the conclusion is the same. They are now a homosexual by their own confession and chosen lifestyle. They may be in the closet; but they are hanging, and they need help. They may have even gone through the outward ceremony of a marriage, but they are inwardly miserable as they either *suppress* this tendency or as they *express* it time and again. Everything they value is at risk with the exposure of their "secret life." It becomes impossible for them to "cleave" to their married companion because they have become one flesh with the *spirit of unnatural affection.* This tearing of their soul leads to depression and self-loathing; and if they are married, often it ends in divorce. Even if it goes undiscovered, this is often the case.

Imagine how difficult it must be to *live a lie* for a lifetime. The adage is correct—"*Oh what a tangled web we weave when first we practice to deceive.*" A life of being true to one's self is a life of *simplicity.* A life that masks the true self is a lie to others. It is called *hypocrisy.* A lie to yourself is called *duplicity.* The attempt to make God a liar is called *apostasy.* A person can wear a mask for so long that it becomes impossible for him to remember who he is, even if he removes it.

A Psyche Above Setback

In 30 years of preaching the gospel, I have witnessed much deliverance of glorious proportions because someone trusted in the power of His great name. Those who heed the lessons of the past will never have to repeat them. In Christ, there is hope for the healing of a wounded soul; there is a balm in Gilead to make the wounded whole. There is still room at the cross for the gay, the lesbian, and the sexually-damaged soul. Plunge in today and be made complete. Surely, the statistics do not lie, and you can truly change if you try. No matter who the person is, he or she is not immune to temptation. It is something that is common to the human experience. The tempter targets the tiny toddler and the teething youngster, titillates the pre-puberty adolescent, tempts the post-puberty teenager, and attempts to take over the adult. The biology, psychology, and sociology arguments fall at the foot of the cross. The gay gene theory and myth is debunked. The making of a homosexual is a process of many stages at different ages. God is greater than one's environment, parents, transference, and disposition. Despite the temperament, overcoming the temptation to be homosexual will cease its proliferation. The causation argument crashes as the unholy gay trinity is crumbled. Inevitably, the acceptance of the debunked argument of the unholy gay trinity will lead an individual into "The Consequential Alternative: The Legacy of Homo-Reality."

> Prayer: Father, look upon these Your children—those who have been plagued all their lives with a predisposition toward homosexuality and who turned to it through the influence of environmental circumstances, various events, and private encounters. Send unto them a strong word of deliverance and the mighty hand of the Deliverer. Redeemer, Savior, Friend, we commend our friends to Your loving and gracious care. Lead them to a stable spiritual atmosphere where they can be fed with the life-sustaining manna from on high until they can truly say, "Bread of Heaven, I want, I lack, I need no more! In Christ's name, Amen!

ENDNOTES

1. Edythe Draper, *Draper's Book of Quotations for the Christian World,* (Wheaton: Tyndale House Publishers, Inc., 1992), Entry 836, Bible Illustrator 3.0 for Windows, Parsons Technology, Inc. 1990-1998, Illustrations Copyrighted at Christianity Today, Inc., 1984-1995, Faircom Corp.

2. Draper, *Draper's Book of Quotations for the Christian World,* Entry 847.

3. Draper, *Draper's Book of Quotations for the Christian World,* Entry 993.

4. Dr. Edmund Bergler as quoted by Briar Whitehead, *Craving for Love,* 122.

5. Ibid., 125.

6. "ELECTION 2004 / Cheneys Fume over Kerry's Remarks," *Houston Chronicle* (October 15, 2004), 10.

7. Jeffrey Satinover, *Homosexuality and the Politics of Truth* (Grand Rapids, MI: Baker Books, 1996), 18.

8. Edmund Bergler as quoted by Briar Whitehead, *Craving for Love,* 122.

9. Whitehead, *Craving for Love,* 203.

10. Ibid., 185.

11. Edward T. Welsh, *Blame It on the Brain* (New Jersey: P & R Publishing, 1998), 165,167,169.

12. Dean A. Byrd, "Governor Howard Dean Misunderstands Origins of Homosexual Behavior," NARTH (January 16, 2004).

13. John Ankerberg & John Weldon, *The Facts on Homosexuality* (Eugene, OR: Harvest House, 1994), 21.

14. Ibid., 21.

15. Alice Ogden Bellis and Terry L. Hufford, *Science, Scripture and Homosexuality* (Cleveland: The Pilgrim Press, 2002), 24.

16. Human Genome Project, 1998. The official Internet information site as of 1999 was maintained by Oak Ridge National Laboratory at http://www.ornl.gov/sci/techresources/Human_Genome/home.shtml.

17. Dave Unander, *Shattering the Myth of Race: Genetic Realities and Biblical Truths* (Valley Forge, PA: Judson Press, 2000), 7.

18. *Webster's II New College Dictionary* (Boston MA: Houghton Mifflin Company, 2001), 570.

19. Tim LaHaye, *What Everyone Should Know About Homosexuality* (Wheaton, IL: Tyndale House Publishers, 1988), 62-63.

20. Jeffrey Satinover, *The Complex Interaction of Genes and Environment: A Model for Homosexuality* accessed at NARTH website http://www.narth.com/docs/1995papers/satinover.html.

21. J.M. Bailey, M.P. Dunne, & N.G. Martin. "Genetic and Environmental Influences on Sexual Orientation and Its Correlates in an Australian Twin Sample," *Journal of Personality & Social Psychology* (2000), 78, 524-536.

22. P. Billings, J. Beckwith, *Technology Review*, (July, 1993), 60.

23. William Byne and Bruce Parsons, The Archives of General Psychology, *Homosexual Orientation: The Biologic Theories Reappraised* (1993), 228-39.

24. LaHaye, *What Everyone Should Know*, 62-63.

25. Ankerberg and Weldon, *The Facts,* 23-24.

26. Ibid., 24.

27. Roger Montgomery, as quoted by Ankerberg and Weldon in *The Myth of Safe Sex*, 159.

28. J.M. Bailey, et al., "Heritable Factors Influence Sexual Orientations in Women," *Archives of General Psychiatry* 50, no. 3, pp. 217-23.

29. Ankerberg and Weldon, *The Facts,* 18.

30. Ibid., 22.

31. Ankerberg and Weldon, *The Facts,* 20.

32. Ibid., 19.

33. Ibid., 19-20.

34. Ibid.

35. Unander, *Shattering,* 97.

36. NARTH website, *Is There a "Gay Gene"?*, retrieved April 2004, www.narth.com/docs/istheregene.html.

37. Byrd, Cox, Robinson, NARTH website www.narth.com/docs/innate. html.

38. *The Reformer* (Independent Publication), Response to the question: "Why do you oppose homosexuality?"

39. A. Dean Byrd, Shirley E. Cox, Jeffrey W. Robinson, *The Innate-Immutable Argument Finds No Basis in Science*, NARTH website www.narth. com/docs/innate.html.

40. Jeffrey Satinover, *Homosexuality and the Politics of Truth* (Grand Rapids, MI: Baker, 1996), 31-35.

41. As reported on NARTH website, *Historic Gay Advocate Believes Change Is Possible*, May 9, 2001, www.narth.com/docs/spitzer3.html.

42. Byrd, Cox, Robinson, NARTH website.

43. Ibid., 147.

44. Whitehead, *Craving*, 131.

45. Donnie McClurkin, *Eternal Victim/Eternal Victor* (Lanham, MD: Pneuma Life Publishing, Inc.), 34.

46. Charles Wahl, *The Myths of Homosexuality*, http://www.usiap.org/viewpoints/Family/Morality/Myths of Homosexuality.html.

47. Whitehead, *Craving*, 122, Dr. Robert Kronemeyer, Clinical Psychologist.

48. Charles Hodge, *Commentary on the Epistles to the Romans*, as cited in AGES Digital Library, 304.

49. LaHaye, *What Everyone Should Know*, 87.

50. Ibid.

51. Ibid., 74-75.

52. Ibid.

53. Whitehead, *Craving*, 113.

54. LaHaye, *What Everyone Should Know*, 72-73.

55. Whitehead, *Craving*, 84, 86.

56. Ibid., 102.

57. LaHaye, *What Everyone Should Know*, 78.

58. "No Place for Homo-Homophobias," *San Francisco Sentinel*, (March 26, 1992).

59. *The Myth of Safe Sex & the AIDS Coverup.*

60. Ibid.

61. Ibid.

62. Satinover, *Politics of Truth*, 106.

63. Ibid.

64. Comiskey, 103.

65. Ankerberg and Weldon, *The Facts*, 31.

66. Whitehead, *Craving*, 98.

67. Gerard van den Aardweg, *Homosexuality and Hope: A Psychologist Talks About Treatment and Change* (Ann Arbor, MI: Servant, 1988), 8-9.

68. Whitehead, *Craving*, 181.

69. Ibid., 203.

70. Ibid., 124.

71. Ibid., 124.

CHAPTER
SEVEN

Many gays reject morality, offering any one of a variety of reasons, rational and emotional, for doing so. But there's a simpler, darker reason why many gays choose to live without morality: as ideologies go, amorality is...convenient. And the mortal enemy of that convenience is the value judgment. It quickly became clear to us that urban gays assumed a general consensus to the effect that everyone has the right to behave just as he pleases...Everyone was to decide what was "right for him"—in effect, to make up the rules as he went along. In fact, they boiled it down to a single axiom: I can do whatever I want, and you can go to perdition... We found that in the gay press this doctrine had hardened into stone.[1]

Homosexual authors Kirk and Madsen
After the Ball

God asks no one whether he will accept life. This is not the choice. The only choice you have as you go through life is how you will live it.[2]

Bernard Meltzer

Apart from Christ the life of man is a broken pillar; the race of man an unfinished pyramid. One by one in sight of eternity all human ideals fall short; one by one before the open grave all hopes dissolve.[3]

Henry Drummond

The man driven by lust loses all sense of reality. He completely forgets the costs involved with sin and will often find himself doing things in this altered state of mind that he would never otherwise consider.[4]

Steve Gallagher

The Consequential Alternative: The Legacy of Homo-Reality

For he that soweth to his flesh shall of the flesh reap corruption; but he that soweth to the Spirit shall of the Spirit reap life everlasting (Galatians 6:8).

—HOMO-REALITY FACT— DANGER IS ALL AROUND IT

Consequences of Perversion and Promiscuity

When I was a boy, a favorite game show of mine was *Truth or Consequences*. Contestants were chosen from the studio audience. The host asked them a trick question, and just moments after they answered it, the contestants were informed as to their correctness or not. If they did not answer the truth fully, they would have to pay the consequences.

Concerning areas of sexuality, all have been given ample opportunity to live according to truth. It is important to do so because otherwise, inevitably, you will pay *the consequences.* It is much easier to tell the truth than to lie because you never have to remember what you said. The lie must be remembered, retold, and recycled until finally someone says, "Aha...the truth at last." A lie is always going to be a lie, and it will never be the truth. *The truth obeyed will keep the consequences from being paid.* The consequences of accepting the argument of homosexuality as having a biological basis leave a legacy of dear souls trapped in this lifestyle that results in danger, disease, death, and divine judgment. St. Paul says, "*Speaking lies in hypocrisy; having their conscience seared with a hot iron*" (1 Tim. 4:2).

Homosexuality is one thing; homo-reality is another thing. The legendary homosexuals have left a legacy of homo-reality. Today's youth often say, "Keep it real." It is a big deal, despite how a person may feel, to keep it real. The reality is that as a group, the homosexual population suffers premature death far more often than the heterosexual culture. Only *nine percent* of homosexuals live to become of old age, regardless of whether they die from

271

AIDS or other causes.[5] Dr. Tim LaHaye describes the homosexual world as polar opposite to the heterosexual world.[6] It is a world that homosexual activists generally hide from the unsuspecting public. The "gay" publications espouse strategies of *selective disclosure* to those who are the voices of the group.[7] Selective disclosure means that the horrific realities of homosexuality are handled by spin doctors who purposely diminish the four D's of its practice.

The antismoking campaign may be considered discrimination against smokers, but the reality is that the government has the responsibility to protect its citizens. It is proven that secondhand smoke is also a first-class killer. Hundreds of millions of dollars are spent in antismoking campaigns in an effort to save hundreds of millions of people's lives from heart disease, emphysema, lung cancer, and the like. Smoking commercials are banned from television. Billboards promoting "Joe Camel" have been removed from the urban areas where the majority of teen smokers live. Lawsuits have been filed and won by supposed victims of the advertising. Why has this happened in a country that boasts of its freedom of speech? It is simply because of the *danger, disease,* and *death* associated with it. Homo-reality is associated with the same thing, but there is one more "D." It is the big one. It is DIVINE JUDGMENT. The consequences of perversion and promiscuity are both futile and fatal. God pity the person who mocks the truth.

In most instances, a homosexual is an individual whose life journey has been a checkered and challenged one that has produced a lifetime of struggle and inquiry. Studies conclude that the preeminent factor which drives the homosexual is the lifelong search of the identity and the love he never received in the same-sex parent.[8] Father detachment and mother misalignment is a one-two punch that threatens to end his divine purpose before it ever gets started.

Homo-reality is a futile search that often leads to a life of promiscuity of incredible proportions. Promiscuity is prevalent and monogamy virtually absent among the homosexual population.[9] In fact, *83 percent* will have *over 50 different sexual partners* in their lifetime. "The expectation for outside sexual activity was the rule for male couples and exception for heterosexuals."[10] This is the conclusion reached by a homosexual couple who did a study on the lifestyle of 156 gay couples who had been together five years or less. Of the 156 couples, none of them were able to maintain monogamy in their relationship.[11] Faithfulness to one's sexual partner is not the norm in the gay community. It is known that the incidence of disease increases among both homosexuals and heterosexuals as the promiscuity among them increases.

Succinctly stated, the more sex one has with more partners, the more chance of massive affliction.

The lack of fulfillment in homosexuality causes homosexuals to be three to four times more promiscuous than heterosexuals.[12] In *Sexual Idolatry*, Steve Gallagher quotes Frank Worthen,

> Very few sexual encounters in the gay lifestyle could be considered great. Almost always, there is an element of wishing it could have been better. Often we'd feel used, short changed and degraded after such an encounter. Satan, however, has a way of throwing flashbacks of previous sexual experiences at us. In the memories he presents, all negative connotations are written out.[13]

Consequences of Profession and Proceeding

Only *two percent* of homosexuals purport to be monogamous. However, it is generally understood that many homosexuals who profess lifetime relationships of fidelity regularly have sex outside the relationship.[14] Those who claim to exist in exclusive relationships are usually older and are no longer considered as "desirable" to the general gay populace. Thus they have more difficulty finding partners.

Obviously, this promiscuity factor increases the risk for sexually transmitted diseases. The preeminent component that propels homosexuals is that they typically look for power and strength in another male, which are the qualities that they should have experienced in their father or surrogate father figure.[15] Thirty percent of the homosexual males in a 1978 study had over 1000 sexual partners.[16] This astronomical amount indicates that the apparent search is quite futile and is never discovered in same-sex relationships. Solomon was right, "*Hell and destruction are never full; so the eyes of man are never satisfied*" (Prov. 27:20).

A road sign that is sometimes seen while driving is "Proceed With Caution." Whenever one proceeds in the practice of same-sex encounters, there is always "DANGER AHEAD." Furthermore, with the onslaught of sexually transmitted disease, this preponderance of illicit sexual activity has literally become a life-or-death matter. Sadly, many in the gay community have chosen to gamble with their lives. A gay man interviewed by Briar Whitehead in *Craving for Love* paints a vivid picture of the homosexual lifestyle with its drive to find the ultimate sexual encounter. He told her, "We look for Mr. Right, but Mr. Rightaway will do."[17]

—UNCLEANNESS: THE— UNCOMFORTABLE TRUTH

The...reason why homosexual acts are contrary to nature is not at all easy to talk about. Perhaps it's because we are too genteel and polite, but we don't ordinarily talk about the kind of sexual activity that most homosexuals practice when we debate about whether we should accept homosexual practices.[18]

Gay activists deliberately paint a picture of homosexual life, especially among men, that is the counterpart of heterosexual life.[19]

CAUTION: Please be advised that the subsequent information is somewhat graphic and should be read with a measure of conservative caution. The Bible refers to homosexual behavior as "uncleanness." Roget's Thesaurus lists *uncleanness* as "dirt, filth, defilement, contamination, soilure, abomination, taint, tainture, malodorousness, and putrescence." Although it is difficult to speak with specificity concerning the acts associated with homosexual activity, it is an essential step toward understanding the homo-reality. The Scriptures warn of those sins that are *"a shame even to speak of"* (Eph. 5:12). The Bible addresses sin in a general sense. It does not individualize the acts. For instance, when the men of Israel committed whoredom with the daughters of Moab, the Bible does not specify the deeds (see Num. 25:1). Also, when they sat down to eat and drink, and rose up to play (see Ex. 32:6), it does not graphically portray details. In such instances, there is no need for graphic description, because the point is well-taken.

When Graphic Portrayal Is Needed

The masses must not be repulsed by premature exposure to homosexual behavior itself.[20]

In the extreme case of homosexuality, *the hideous, gory, and gross details of debauchery* must be made known for the purpose of arming the believer in Christ with necessary information for the sake of dealing with the homo-reality. Homosexual activists claim that several prominent Bible characters were homosexuals, including the Lord Himself. As previously stated, they even have the nerve to call God, the Father, gay.

During Alex Haley's blockbuster miniseries, *Roots*, the American public was riveted by a detailed disclosure of the brutal, beastly nature of the peculiar institution of American slavery by its graphic portrayal of lynching, whippings, axed feet, and overall evil that was suffered by slaves from their sadistic masters. During the O.J. Simpson trial, the public was made aware of the horrific details of the death of Nicole Simpson and Ron Goldman. During the Emmett Till funeral of the 50's, his mother requested that his casket remain open so that "all the world would see what the murderers did to [her] boy." His face had been bludgeoned beyond recognition by a group of men who supposedly were avenging a woman whom he had reportedly "whistled at."

In the movie, *The Passion of the Christ*, incredible effort went into portraying the sadomasochistic, merciless massacre of Jesus Christ through scourging and crucifixion. The director, Mel Gibson, was highly criticized by the media for the "graphic" nature of the film. The movie received an R rating and "warning" signs were placed at the entrance of movie theaters, informing people that the movie was not fit for children to see. This was obviously a biased act, because far more violent movies have been made that have received far less virulent scrutiny. Christians packed the theaters, and they did not turn their faces as the physical torture was depicted. They wept through it.

When one considers the disgusting, depraved, and degenerate sex acts of uncleanness as it reflects primarily (though not exclusively) to homosexuality, they should not turn their heads either. Instead, they should also weep for those caught in homo-eroticism. To justify them in the name of homo-eroticism is a thinly veiled excuse that does not hold water. The Scripture says, *"They are without excuse"* (Rom. 1:20b). The various "unclean" practices are *dangerous*. They almost always lead to *disease* and, in some instances, *death* itself and the ultimate *divine judgment*.

—UNCLEANNESS: THE PRACTICE— OF PERVERSION

And lest, when I come again, my God will humble me among you, and that I shall bewail many which have sinned already, and have not repented of the uncleanness and fornication and lasciviousness which they have committed (2 Corinthians 12:21).

Rimming: This act is a common occurrence during homosexual activity. It involves the application of a man's tongue around and within the anal area of another man. Supposedly, it is done to stimulate the area in preparation for the injection of the penis. The homo-reality is that the mixing of saliva with fecal matter is about as gross as you can get.[21]

Ringing: The male organ is placed in a tight metal ring, which becomes even tighter upon the blood entering it, resulting in its erection. At some point, it becomes tightened to the extent that it disallows ejaculation. The prolonged penetration without this occurrence allows for continuation for a lengthy period. The inherent risk that results is transmitted disease in that the skin may become thinned and the germ microbes can enter in. The deceitfulness of this sin is that to the homosexual it appears, "the more the merrier, but the homo-reality is the more the scarier."[22]

Fisting: This act involves the insertion of a person's fist inside the rectum of another. Both men and women engage in this. Despite lubricants, oils, and creams, this is an exercise that brings bizarre painful sensations interpreted by diseased minds as pleasure. Oftentimes the rectal lining is worn and sometimes torn. The homo-reality result is bleeding and severe infection. Of course, by design, the rectal area is a place for the exit of waste, and not the entrance of another person's fist. To enter it unlawfully is equivalent to going the "wrong way down a one-way street."[23] Wherever excrement exits, the penis or tongue should never enter.

Anal Intercourse: In God's creation of the male gender, the Almighty did not accommodate him with a vagina. Therefore, he is ill-equipped to handle reception of another man's penis. That leaves only one homo-illogical possibility, that being, the infamous anal area. God gave the anus "an exit strategy" and posted an invisible "DO NOT ENTER" sign on its entry point. Those who fail to heed the sign "PROCEED AT THEIR OWN RISK." The homo-reality is that the *mutilation* of the anal canal will *multiply* the adverse possibility of disease and death.[24] A study of the sexual practices of 5,000 gay men came to the conclusion that:

> A significant majority of these men…reported having 50 or more lifetime sexual partners, and over 80% had engaged in receptive anal intercourse with at least some of their partners in the previous two years.[25]

> R.A. Kaslow et. al.
> *American Journal of Epidemiology*

Water Sports: Please brace yourself for this. This unclean activity sometimes goes as far as showering the passive person with urination by the dominant partner.[26] The uncleanness is apparent, and the demonic nature of this unclean spirit is clearly seen as well. Urine is meant for the toilet, not for a shower upon one's face and body.

Sadomasochism: Sexual acts that involve master/slave, dominant/passive positions are common occurrences in homoerotic behavior. It includes whipping, bondage, infliction, and reception of pain. The role-playing and wearing of peculiar clothing normally accompanies the performance of this non-Olympic, disgusting sport. Whips and chains are associated with slavery, not sexual liberty.

Fellatio: This practice is in no way exclusively limited to the homosexual community. However it is a prominent feature of male-to-male or female-to-female (cunnilingus) sex. The mixture of sperm with saliva is an unclean concoction that could possibly coordinate into a disease combustion. Even if the sperm is not ingested, the elements can easily infiltrate areas that have been opened through brushing, smoking, cold blisters, etc. The mouth is not the receptacle for the instrument that expels liquid waste.

Multiple Sexual Partners: When simultaneous sexual intercourse with more than one is participated in, it results in the exchange of seminal fluids and the irreversible effects of transmission. Group sex occurs in homosexual clubs and bathhouses, where there is frequent mass public masturbation. It is quite absurd to suggest that a person engaging in sex with the equivalent of a proverbial football team at one time is not guilty of violations of the scriptural sexual health code. The plan of God for a man is a wife for life, not different dudes on any given day. Ménage à trois, or sex scenes of three or more, often escalate in quadruple bypasses. The heart was not designed to pump and be pumped by more than one person at a time.

Pornography: The use of sexually stimulating material to excite the passions often occurs, resulting in the addictive cycle of sexual bondage. In *Affair of the Mind*, a man with a pornography addiction actually developed a groove on the section of his brain that controls response to visual stimuli. Pornography is widely available today through books, web sites, chat rooms, sex clubs, etc., and studies reveal that a great deal of homosexuality finds its basis in one's exposure to it. A former homosexual prostitute, Roger Montgomery, writes, "Although it is not widely spoken of or acknowledged, pornography plays a prominent place in the life of every homosexual."[27] This produces a corruption in their subconscious and carnal mind which manifests in conscious choices of further corruption. Corruption is another way of saying death. Physical corruption is the result of spiritual corruption. St. Paul said, "*...evil communications **corrupt** good manners*" (1 Cor. 15:33, emphasis added).

—HOMO-REALITY FACT—
DISEASE IS ASSOCIATED WITH IT

Statistics Do Not Lie

"Gay" isn't gay for the majority of homosexuals, not even some of the time. [28]

The relationship between homosexuality and disease, like the practice itself, is not new. This correlation has been around for millennia. In the context of the present, the gay population is estimated to be between two to five percent of the U.S. population. Yet *80 percent of STD cases* are among those who practice homosexuality. That means that four out of five people who have a sexually transmitted disease are homosexual. *Homo-reality statistics do not lie.* God's moral laws of human nature are giving an undeniable message to each of us today. The law of sowing and reaping is simply this: "*You reap what you sow*"—sometimes *more* than you sow and *later* than you sow.

> *Be not deceived; God is not mocked: for whatsoever a man soweth, that shall he also reap. For he that soweth to his flesh shall of the flesh reap corruption; but he that soweth to the Spirit shall of the Spirit reap life everlasting* (Galatians 6:7-8).

Sexually Transmitted Diseases

The entire planet is engulfed in a battle against STD's. The comparison between the homosexual and heterosexual populace reveals the disproportionate amount of exposure and infection in the gay community. Lesbians have syphilis at about a 19 percent rate proportionate to their population. *The Medical Aspects of Homosexuality* reports that homosexuals are:

- Fourteen times more apt ever to have had syphilis

- Three times more apt to ever have had gonorrhea

- Three times more apt to have ever had genital warts

- Eight times more apt to ever have had hepatitis

- Three times more apt ever to have had lice

- Five times more apt ever to have had scabies

- Thirty times more apt to ever have had an infection from penile contact

- Hundreds of times more apt to ever have had oral infection from penile contact

- Over FIVE THOUSAND times more apt to ever have had AIDS.[29]

Dr. Dale Conway, in *Sex in the Bible,* reports that there are approximately 180,000,000 to 220,000,000 spermatozoa in every male ejaculation. That is nearly the entire U.S. population. The HIV virus carried through the blood stream is virtually unstoppable and will oftentimes be transferred with or without a condom. Even the condom manufacturers say that their product cannot guarantee success one hundred percent of the time. The microbe carrying the HIV virus is 450 times smaller than one spermatozoa.[30] Therefore, it is virtually unstoppable. Condom or no condom, the danger is undeniable. The frightening truth is that no matter how one *covers it up or zips it up,* the germs causing the HIV virus will inevitably infiltrate the body's immune defenses. Therefore, the homo-reality statistics are not *coincidental* or merely *accidental,* but rather they are *incidental* and *indicative* of the truth of the consequential alternative.

Sexual Roulette

> Everyone who preached free love in the Sixties is responsible for AIDS. This idea that it was somehow an accident, a microbe that sort of fell down from heaven—absurd. We must face what we did.[31]
>
> Camille Paglia

Having sex outside of covenant has become deadly. During his announcement in 1991 of having contracted the HIV virus, former NBA player Magic Johnson testified that he never thought it would happen to him because he was not a homosexual and he did not engage in unprotected heterosexual sex. Sexual looseness among the gay community is synonymous with *Sexual Russian Roulette!* Unholy living is like pulling the trigger of a loaded gun and pointing it at the "temple" of the Holy Ghost (your body), never knowing which pull can be the fatal bullet.

—HOMO-REALITY FACT—
DEATH ACCOMPANIES IT

*There is way which seemeth right to a man, but the end thereof are the ways of **death*** (Proverbs 14:12).

*But every man is tempted, when he is drawn away of his own lust, and enticed. Then when lust hath conceived, it bringeth forth sin: and sin, when it is finished, bringeth forth **death*** (James 1:14-15, emphasis added).

Wham, Bam, Damned

The response of the church to homosexual persons must be a compassionate one, because they have been created in God's image and, because Christ died for them. As such, they have innate dignity and worth. However, the church must also have the courage to share the truth with homosexuals. The Bible does teach that homosexuality is a sin and that homosexuals, like unrepentant sexual sinners from the heterosexual population will not enter the kingdom of heaven. We recognize that not every homosexual person has the same lifestyle in terms of the potential for sexual excess. But when examined as a whole, the HOMOSEXUAL LIFE IS ANYTHING BUT REALITY.[32]

John Ankerberg and John Weldon, *The Myth of Safe Sex*

The Master Teacher said that all unbelievers are damned (see Mk. 16:16). For homosexuals who participate in much wham-and-bam sex, being damned is the death associated with it. Homosexual men have an average lifespan of about 42.9 years. That is 25 to 30 fewer years than the average lifespan of the average American male, which is around 70 years. The life expectancy of an alcoholic only decreases by 5 to 10 years.[33] Gays are three times more likely to commit suicide than heterosexual men.[34]

AIDS NEVER WAS, NOR IS IT NOW, A CURSE FROM GOD AGAINST ANY PERSON OF ANY SEXUAL PREFERENCE, ORIENTATION, TENDENCY, OR PRACTICE.

The fear of AIDS causes some gays to commit suicide.[35] A lesbian's average lifespan is just under the age of 45. Compared to the heterosexual populace, this is a considerable difference and an undeniable homo-reality.

The disease that we now know as AIDS was first called G.R.I.D. (gay-related immune disorder). Through much lobbying and political pressure, it was renamed AIDS.[36] During the early days of the disease, homosexuals were the chief victims of AIDS, causing many to call it a curse from God against gays. Today, the heterosexual population's contracting of AIDS has greatly increased, and this is probably due to experimentation with bi-sexuality. *Aids never was, nor is it now, a curse from God against any person of any sexual preference, orientation, tendency, or practice.* However, it is true that the gay community still experiences a disproportionate ratio of AIDS cases and other sexually transmitted diseases. A heterosexual male has a 7 out of 10,000 chance of contracting AIDS. The homosexual male has about a 300 out of 10,000 chance. That is hundreds of percent more of a possibility. AIDS is an end-time pestilence that the Master Teacher prophesied would come upon the earth in the end-times.

> *For nation shall rise against nation, and kingdom against kingdom: and there shall be famines, and pestilences, and earthquakes, in divers places* (Matthew 24:7, emphasis added).

The Sham of Safe Sex

If any man defile the temple of God, him shall God destroy; for the temple of God is holy, which temple ye are (1 Corinthians 3:17).

These preceding alarming statistics hold true in spite of the "safe sex" campaign which was later renamed "safer sex." Safe sex and safer sex is a sham perpetrated against an unsuspecting public. Truthfully, the only safe sex is what Dr. T. Garrott Benjamin calls "saved sex." Although they are aware of the dangers of not taking some kind of precaution, homosexuals are compelled by the compulsiveness of homosexuality to have unprotected sex. John Rechy writes about promiscuity in the gay community,

> Once chosen, it's a world that carries him to the pinnacle of sexual freedom—the high that only outlaw sex can bring—as well as the abyss of suicide.[37]

A frightening 30 percent of all gay men who are at least 20 years old will die of AIDS or be HIV positive by the time they are 30.[38] That is one third of the entire gay population. If this statistic was comparable in the heterosexual world, this would mean the death of 80 million Americans. Our hearts should tremble for the same-sex community in America. Though it may go unnoted in the media, this is the *most critically alarming* news of our generation. Again, I repeat, this is indeed a "pestilence," such as the Lord Jesus Christ prophesied in Luke 21:11. The word *pestilence* means "contagious disease." According to prophecy, "the end time" of the world will result in the world's greatest harvest of souls. This is because there are literally multitudes in the valley of decision seeking to escape the corruption that is in the world because of its lustful infatuation and gratification. AIDS is not necessarily a divine judgment upon homosexuals in particular, but it is generally a direct result of the promiscuous lifestyle. Sex outside of covenant has never yielded edifying results of any kind. If AIDS were merely a judgment against homosexuals, then innocent people who have been infected unaware and through various means would be justified to feel that God is cruel to give them something that they did nothing to deserve. The homo-reality is this: *AIDS is the result of a sin-cursed world's sin finding them out.* The patriarch Moses declared,

> *But if ye will not do so, behold, ye have sinned against the Lord: and be sure your sin will find you out* (Numbers 32:23).

Throughout Scripture, at times when there was wanton sexual sin among God's people, He would remove His hand of protection and allow them to reap the immediate consequence of their illicit behavior. He has established the universe by laws, and they are irreversible; and unless it is His sovereign will to usurp them, they are unconquerable and incontrovertible.

The Annals of Internal Medicine, a medical journal, addressed the homosexuality and STD connection by stating:

> In addition to gonorrhea and syphilis, both of which may develop primarily at anorectoral or pharyngeal sites, a number of conditions including Neisseria meningitis urethritis, non-specific wathrites, anorectal herpes, condyloma acuminatun, anebiasis, giardiasis, shigellosis, typhoid fever, enterobiasis and hepatitis A and B have been identified as being transmitted by male homosexual contact. Protologic complications of anal intercourse include allergic reactions to anal lubricants, prolapsed hemorrhoids and festulas and tissues. Restosignoid tears may result from fist, forearm and foreign body penetration of the bowel.[39]

The above list contains no less than 18 health risks and diseases associated with homosexuality. Who would come to eat at anyone's table if they felt they would be at risk for even one disease? Risking 18 is unthinkable. Most of medical science today is constituted to help homosexuals deal with the diseases that are the result of their destructive behavior as opposed to the root causes that precipitate the behavior in the first place. The Word of God does just the opposite. The Master Teacher taught that *"the axe is laid unto the root of the trees..."* (Mt. 3:10). Radical ministry goes to the root and removes it. Homo-reality uproots the false assumptions of asininity associated with homo-eroticism.

The "oil and wine" Church must engage in *radical* ministry if it is to be relevant and if it is to keep it real. The founder of the homosexual Metropolitan Community Churches, a 77,000-nationwide network of gay churches, Troy Perry, readily admits the loose lifestyle of many gays when he says, "I presume we've all been exposed to the virus. I just take the attitude that every gay man has been exposed to the virus, but I refuse to go down there (to take a test) and have my name in a computer somewhere."[40] It is inconceivable that a person purporting to be a minister of the gospel could endorse and make light of a lifestyle that could wipe out the entire gay population. One former homosexual prostitute offers this insight, "Self-deception is the reality of the homosexual community."[41] The reality is, a person who is into it has been imprinted in their erogenous zone with confused data. Despite their pain, they find heterosexual thoughts hard to compute.

Standing Is a Personal Responsibility

Wherefore take unto you the whole armour of God, that ye may be able to withstand in the evil day, and having done all, to stand. Stand therefore, having your loins girt about with truth... (Ephesians 6:13-14).

The term "withstand" or "stand" is used three different times in these two verses. The whole armor of God includes the helmet of salvation (right thinking); the breastplate of righteousness (right affection); the shield of faith (right believing); the sword of the spirit (right confession); the loins girt with truth (right standing); and feet shod with the preparation of the gospel of peace (right walking).

To withstand is to be in a positive defense against a purposed onslaught. The consequences of not withstanding is that you will be *overrun*. When you are *overrun*, you are *overcome, overwhelmed,* and *overtaken*. Whatever a person is *overcome* by, he is brought in bondage to. To fail to stand is to proceed to fall. Some falls do not happen *overnight*. They happen over a period of time. That is why *over* and *over* again, the Scripture refers to the believer as an *overcomer*. Unfortunately, many professing Christians are "barely coming" and not *overcoming*. To stand successfully is to *overcome* obvious *overtures of the enemy*.

St. Paul implores the Church to stand in diametric opposition to the world. There is "standing room only" in the "oil and wine" Church. To avoid falling for little or nothing, the Church must stand for something. The naked truth is something worth standing for. Dr. Martin Luther King, Jr. once said, "If a man hasn't discovered something that he will die for, he isn't fit to live!"[42] The homo-reality of the need to stand is summarized by this powerful poem. No person has to fall to the sin of homosexuality. To be forewarned is to be forearmed.

—THERE IS A DEEP HOLE IN THE SIDEWALK—

I fall in.

I am lost…

It is hopeless.

It was not my fault.

It takes forever to find a way out

I walk down the same street

There is a deep hole in the sidewalk

I pretend I do not see it

I fall in again.

I cannot believe I am in the same place.

But it is not my fault.

It still takes a long time to get out.

I walk down the same street

I still fall in

It is a habit

My eyes are open

I know where I am

It is my fault

I get out immediately

I walk down the same street

I see the same deep hole

I walk around it

I walk down a different street.[43]

Portia Nelson

The Consequential Alternative: In Conclusion
The Legacy of Homo-Reality

As the bird by wandering, as the swallow by flying, so the curse causeless shall not come (Proverbs 26:2).

Those who do not walk around the danger, disease, and death will run headfirst into divine judgment. God's will is that mercy triumphs over judgment. It is not God's will that any should perish, but that all may come to repentance (see 2 Pet. 3:9). However, *God's will for man will not usurp the will of man*. The Scriptures say that there is blessing for obedience and cursing for disobedience. The choice of the Father was to send His Son to bare in His body the curse for human sin. Galatians 3:13 says, *"Christ hath redeemed us from the curse of the law, being made a curse for us: for it is written, Cursed is every one that hangeth on a tree."* Therefore, the presence of divine judgments or cursed consequences is the result of carnal compromise. Any person who is experiencing the fruit of his sin cannot blame God. He must hold himself responsible for himself. Whether a person stands or falls is completely on the individual and not on God.

I. The Divine Judgment of God Upon Cain

Cause: Murder, The Shedding of Innocent Blood

Curse: Marked, Exiled, Vagabond, Infamous, Cursed Seed

Text: Genesis 4:8,11-12

And Cain talked with Abel his brother: and it came to pass, when they were in the field, that Cain rose up against Abel his brother, and slew him....And now art thou cursed from the earth, which hath opened her mouth to receive thy brother's blood from thy hand; when thou tillest the ground, it shall not henceforth yield unto thee her strength; a fugitive and a vagabond shalt thou be in the earth (Genesis 4:11-12).

Cure: If Cain had heeded God's call to repent, his brother's blood would have never cried from the ground.

II. The Divine Judgment of God Upon Egypt

Cause: Idolatry, Hardheartedness, Sexual Sin, Rebellion

Curse: Death, Crop Failure, Insect Plagues, Gross Darkness, Pestilence

Text: Exodus 9:8-11

And the Lord said unto Moses and unto Aaron, Take to you handfuls of ashes of the furnace, and let Moses sprinkle it toward the heaven in the sight of Pharaoh. And it shall become small dust in all the land of Egypt, and shall be a boil breaking forth with blains upon man, and upon beast, throughout all the land of Egypt. And they took ashes of the furnace, and stood before Pharaoh; and Moses sprinkled it up toward heaven; and it became a boil breaking forth with blains upon man, and upon beast. And the magicians could not stand before Moses because of the boils; for the boil was upon the magicians, and upon all the Egyptians (Exodus 9:8-11).

Cure: If they would have ceased to resist the command, "Let My [God's] people go," none of the plagues would have happened.

III. The Divine Judgment of God Against Hophni and Phinehas

Cause: Immorality, Irreverence, Iniquity

Curse: Glory Departed, Simultaneous Death

Text: First Samuel 2:12,17,34

Now the sons of Eli were sons of Belial; they knew not the Lord....Wherefore the sin of the young men was very great before the Lord: for men abhorred the offering of the Lord....And this shall be a sign unto thee, that shall come upon thy two sons, on Hophni and Phinehas; in one day they shall die both of them (1 Samuel 2:12,17,34).

Cure: If they had resigned from ministry altogether and took a position among the people, seeking God for His delivering power, then they would not have been able to corrupt the holy place any longer. Self-judgment often eliminates the need for divine judgment (see 1 Cor. 11:31).

IV. The Divine Judgment of God Upon the Philistines

Cause: Stealing the Ark and Its Holy Content

Curse: Emerods, Bleeding Piles, Dysentery, Bloody Flux, Epidemic of Mice

Text: First Samuel 5:1,6,9

And the Philistines took the ark of God, and brought it from Ebenezer unto Ashdod....But the hand of the Lord was heavy upon them of Ashdod, and He destroyed them, and smote them with emerods, even Ashdod and the coasts thereof....And it was so, that, after they had carried it about, the hand of the Lord was against the city with a very great destruction: and He smote the men of the city, both small and great, and they had emerods in their secret parts (1 Samuel 5:1,6,9).

Cure: Do not ever "take or touch" the glory of God.

V. Divine Judgment Against King David

Cause: Adultery, Murder

Curse: Death of a Child, Family Destroyed, Lifetime of Sorrow

Text: Second Samuel 12:7,10,15,18; see also Second Samuel 11:2-4

And Nathan said to David, Thou art the man. Thus saith the Lord God of Israel, I anointed thee king over Israel, and I delivered thee out of the hand of Saul....Now therefore the sword shall never depart from thine house; because thou hast despised Me, and hast taken the wife of Uriah the Hittite to be thy wife....And Nathan departed unto his house. And the Lord struck the child that Uriah's wife bare unto David, and it was very sick....And it came to pass on the seventh day, that the child died. And the servants of David feared to tell him that the child was dead: for they said, Behold, while the child was yet alive, we spake unto him, and he would not hearken unto our voice: how will he then vex himself, if we tell him that the child is dead? (2 Samuel 12:7,10,15,18)

Cure: Do not be in or on the bed when you should be on the battlefield. Guard your "eyegate," and do not abuse your authority or influence.

VI. Divine Judgment Against Israel

Cause: David's Reliance Upon Troop Numbers, Disobedience

Curse: Thousands Died

Text: First Chronicles 21:1,14

And Satan stood up against Israel, and provoked David to number Israel....So the Lord sent pestilence upon Israel: and there fell of Israel seventy thousand men (1 Chronicles 21:1,14).

Cure: It is not wrong to count your resources, but it is wrong to count on them. Do not count on a cure or medical help while pursuing needless risks to your health and safety. Count on the faithfulness of God to enable you to live free of sexual sin.

VII. Divine Judgment Against Elisha's Servant Gehazi

Cause: Greed

Curse: Leprosy, Death

Text: Second Kings 5:6,25-27

And he brought the letter to the king of Israel, saying, Now when this letter is come unto thee, behold, I have therewith sent Naaman my servant to thee, that thou mayest recover him of his leprosy....But he went in, and stood before his master. And Elisha said unto him, Whence comest thou, Gehazi? And he said, Thy servant went no whither. And he said unto him, Went not mine heart with thee, when the man turned again from his chariot to meet thee? Is it a time to receive money, and to receive garments, and oliveyards, and vineyards, and sheep, and oxen, and menservants, and maidservants? The leprosy therefore of Naaman shall cleave unto thee, and unto thy seed for ever. And he went out from his presence a leper as white as snow (2 Kings 5:6, 25-27).

Cure: In some instances, judgment is final. God is sovereign. God is just. God is God. He has no obligation to change the effect of His established divine laws. If they are violated, He can refuse to terminate a condition. The Scriptures refer to God as *"faithful in praises, doing wonders"* (Ex. 15:11b). His judgments are just, and He is *"altogether lovely"* (Song 5:16).

VIII. Divine Judgment Against King Jeroboam

Cause: Idolatry (always closely associated with sexual sin)

Curse: Leprosy, Death

Text: Second Kings 15:3-5

And he did that which was right in the sight of the Lord, according to all that his father Amaziah had done; save that the high places were not removed: the people sacrificed and burnt incense still on the high places. And the Lord smote the king, so that he was a leper unto the day of his death, and dwelt in a several house. And Jotham the king's son was over the house, judging the people of the land (2 Kings 15:3-5).

Cure: Remove the high places of compromise. God is a jealous God, and He will have no other gods before Him. His jealousy is jealousness personified. He requires leaders to establish purity of worship among the people, or He will hold them accountable.

IX. Divine Judgment Against King Jehoram

Cause: Whoredoms

Curse: Prolonged Illness, Death

Text: Second Chronicles 21:12-15,18-19

And there came a writing to him from Elijah the prophet, saying, Thus saith the Lord God of David thy father, because thou hast not walked in the ways of Jehoshaphat thy father, nor in the ways of Asa king of Judah, but hast walked in the way of the kings of Israel, and hast made Judah and the inhabitants of Jerusalem to go a-whoring, like to the whoredoms of the house of Ahab, and also hast slain thy brethren of thy father's house, which were better than thyself: behold, with a great plague will the Lord smite thy people, and thy children, and thy wives, and all thy goods: and thou shalt have great sickness by disease of thy bowels, until thy bowels fall out by reason of the sickness day by day....And after all this the Lord smote him in his bowels with an incurable disease. And it came to pass, that in process of time, after the end of two years, his bowels fell out by reason of his sickness: so he died of sore diseases. And his people made no burning for him, like the burning of his fathers (2 Chronicles 21:12-15,18-19).

Cure: Cease playing the whore, preying on the whore, or being paid as a whore. Kick the "ho" *out* of your home. Selah.

The homo-reality of homosexuality is that it is dangerous; it is disease ridden; it is deadly; and it is on a crash course with divine judgment. The homo-reality is that the believer is admonished to *"come out from among them"* and to recognize that *"God hath not appointed us to wrath, but to obtain salvation by our Lord Jesus Christ"* (1 Thess. 5:9). "The Consequential Alternative" of homo-reality is cursed when confronted with the truth. No plague shall come nigh the dwelling of those who apply the blood of the Lamb upon their thinking, believing, speaking, feeling, standing, walking, and living. No person has to be another statistic. Life is already short enough. It does not need any assistance in being made shorter.

We must be a relevant Church, providing "reality." I once preached a sermon entitled, "Reality Church." Here is some of what I said:

The New Testament Church was not Protestant or Catholic. It was not even universal or local per se. It was simply a Spirit-filled Church. Not Spirit-thrilled, Spirit-chilled, or Spirit-nil. There is a difference between being Spirit-filled and Spirit-thrilled. When you're Spirit-filled, you are into red-hot praying and radical praise and revolutionary prophetic worship. When you're Spirit-thrilled, you have more of an exhibition than a demonstration of the Spirit. Most believers exhibit our gifts. We seldom demonstrate the Spirit. The Spirit-thrilled person feels God, but he is not filled with God.

"Better is the end of a thing than the beginning thereof" (Eccl. 7:8a). It is true that *"he that endureth to the end shall be saved"* (Mt. 10:22). The term, "to be saved," is the antithesis of being lost. Those who forget history are determined and doomed to repeat it. It has been said that experience is the best teacher. In this instance, learning from someone else's unfortunate experience is an even better teacher. In Acts 5:1-10, Ananias and Sapphira learned firsthand that it is dangerous and deadly to lie to the Holy Ghost. It is also dangerous and deadly to lie to yourself. To avoid the abyss of the consequential alternative, it is as simple as ABC. You must: (A) *Acknowledge that God is able to deliver you;* (B) *Believe that He will deliver you;* (C) *Confess that deliverance belongs to you.* To acknowledge is to say H-E-L-P! To believe is to say T-H-A-N-K Y-O-U! To confess is to say J-E-S-U-S. All those who call upon the Lord, believing, shall be delivered from the "Consequential Alternative" and the "Legacy of Homo-Reality." As the *"oil and wine"* Church becomes spirit-filled, it will function as a reality church and it will cause *The Committed Action of the Militant Gay Agenda* machine to come to a grinding halt.

Prayer: Father, we thank You, because You have said that in all of our getting, we are to get understanding. We thank You for the clear understanding of our origin. We thank You that when You created us in Your image, You created us male and female. Sin entered the world and corruption has affected Your creation. Deliver us from the corruption that is in the world through lust. Deliver us from the propensity to delusion and deception. Reform us, conform us, and transform us to Your holy and righteous will, and we'll be so mindful to give Your name the praise. Keep us from the danger, disease, death, and divine judgment of that which is associated with sin. In the name and authority of Jehovah-Shaphat, the Judge of all saints, Amen.

ENDNOTES

1. Marshall Kirk and Hunter Madsen as quoted by Ankerberg and Weldon, *The Myth of Safe Sex* (Chicago: Moody Press, 1993), 148.

2. Edythe Draper, *Draper's Book of Quotations for the Christian World* (Wheaton IL: Tyndale House Publishers, Inc., 1992), Entry 1140, Bible Illustrator 3.0 for Windows, Parsons Technology, Inc. 1990-1998, Illustrations Copyrighted at Christianity Today, Inc., 1984-1995, Faircom Corp.

3. Draper, *Draper's Book of Quotations*, Entry 1163.

4. Steve Gallagher, *At the Altar of Sexual Idolatry* (Dry Ridge, KY: Pure Life Ministries, 2000), 79.

5. Ankerberg and Weldon, *The Myth of Safe Sex*, 149.

6. Tim LaHaye, *What Everyone Should Know About Homosexuality* (Wheaton, IL: Tyndale House Publishers, Inc., 1988), 22.

7. Jeffrey Satinover, *Homosexuality and the Politics of Truth* (Grand Rapids, MI: Baker, 1996), 52.

8. Briar Whitehead, *Craving for Love* (Grand Rapids, MI: Monarch Books, 2003), 97.

9. Satinover, *Politics of Truth*, 53.

10. D. McWhirter and A. Mattison, *The Male Couple: How Relationships Develop* (Englewood Cliffs, NJ: Prentice-Hall, 1984), 3.

11. Whitehead, *Craving for Love*, 112-113.

12. Ibid., 112.

13. Steve Gallagher, *At the Altar of Sexual Idoltry* (Dry Ridge, KY: Pure Life Ministires, 2000), 86.

14. LaHaye, *What Everyone*, 31.

15. Whitehead, *Craving*, 97.

16. Ibid., 112.

17. Ibid., 112.

18. Francis MacNutt, *Homosexuality: Can It Be Healed?* (Jacksonville, FL: Christian Healing Ministries, Inc., 2001), 28.

19. Satinover, *Politics of Truth*, 52.

20. Marshall Kirk and Erastes Pill, *The Overhauling of Straight America: Guide*, 1987, accessed at http://www.endtimeprophecy.net/~tttbbs/EPN1/Articles/Articles-Homo/overhaul.html.

21. Moody Adams, *AIDS: You Just Think You're Safe* (Baker, LA: Dalton Moody Publishers, 1986), 88-89.

22. Ibid.

23. Ibid., 90.

24. Ibid., 90-91.

25. R.A. Kaslow et al., "The Multicenter AIDS Cohort Study: Rationale, Organization and Selected Characteristics of the Participants," *American Journal of Epidemiology* 126, No. 2.

26. Moody Adams, *AIDS*, 91.

27. Roger Montgomery as quoted by John Ankerberg and John Weldon, *The Myth of Safe Sex*, 150.

28. Tim LaHaye, *What Everyone*, 40.

29. Ankerberg and Weldon, *The Myth of Safe Sex*, 151-152.

30. Dr. Dale Conway, *Sex in the Bible* (Shippensburg, PA: Destiny Image, 1996), 143.

31. As quoted by Tammy Bruce, *The Death of Right and Wrong* (Roseville, CA: Prima Publishing, 2003), 97.

32. For further exposition see Ankerberg and Waldon, *The Myth of Safe Sex*, 108.

33. Satinover, *Politics of Truth*, 56-57.

34. Whitehead, *Craving*, 124.

35. Ankerberg and Weldon, *The Myth of Safe Sex*, 149.

36. Satinover, *Politics of Truth*, 16.

37. John Rechy, *The Sexual Outlaw: A Documentary* (New York: Grove, 1972), 300.

38. E.L. Goldman, "Psychological Factors Generate HIV Resurgence in Young Gay Man," *Clinical Psychiatry News* (October 1994), 5.

39. Willis F. Owen, Jr., "Sexually Transmitted Diseases and Traumatic Problems in Homosexual Men," *The Annals of Internal Medicine*, 92 (1980): 805.

40. Ankerberg and Weldon, *The Myth of Safe Sex*, 155.

41. Ibid., 159.

42. Alex Ayres, *The Wisdom of Martin Luther King, Jr.* (New York: Penguin Books, 1993), 56.

43. Portia Nelson as quoted by Briar Whitehead, *Craving for Love*, 242.

CHAPTER
EIGHT

Instead of being about tolerance and equal treatment under the law, today's gay movement, in the hands of extremists, now uses the language of rights to demand acceptance of the depraved, the damaged, and the malignantly narcissistic. [1]

Tammy Bruce, Lesbian Activist
The Death of Right and Wrong

I feel a deep sense of tragedy for those who are deceived by the activists' lies. Righteous anger is properly directed toward efforts to force the full acceptance—even celebration—of the gay lifestyle upon every aspect of society—in school, in marriage and family, in media and entertainment, even in the Christian church. [2]

Timothy J. Dailey, *Dark Obsession*

And once the church is silenced on the sexual behavior issue, it will not take long before it is silenced on many other issues. Already in Canada, churches and other religious organizations cannot speak out on homo-sexual behavior for fear of finding themselves in violation of hate-crime laws. If speaking out against homosexual behavior is considered "hate," then what about other sexual behavior now called sin, such as adultery? Without moral authority, the church in the United States will become like so many are now in Europe, museum pieces from an era long, long ago. The result will be tragic for the millions of individuals who will be unable to hear and respond to the gospel—the good news of Jesus Christ—because the church may no longer be allowed to proclaim it. [3]

Alan Sears & Craig Osten
The Homosexual Agenda

The Committed Action:
Homo-Activism–The Militant Gay Agenda

---

*And of the children of Issachar, which were men that had under-
standing of the times, to know what Israel ought to do; the heads
of them were two hundred; and all their brethren were at their
commandment* (1 Chronicles 12:32).

—AGENDA ONE: GAY PRIDE—
PUBLIC PROTESTS[4]

*The show of their countenance doth witness against them; and they
declare their sin as Sodom, they hide it not. Woe unto their soul! for they
have rewarded evil unto themselves* (Isaiah 3:9).

In 1985, I founded a church in the basement of the YMCA in down-
town Columbus, Ohio. Today, it is called "All Nations Church," and it is a
diverse gathering of believers of varied walks of life. Over the years, we have
been quite successful in our dealing with gay individuals and sensitive in
our declarations concerning the gay community. We have established a policy of "loving confrontation" that has served to help us navigate the waters
of ministry to the masses of humanity in the 15th largest city in America.
One Sunday afternoon in 1985 the gay community in our city held what is
known as "gay pride day." A man was walking down the street with a sign
that said, "The Lord is my shepherd and He knows I am gay." Another carried a sign that read, "Say It Loud, I am Gay and I am Proud."

The words of Isaiah, the eagle-eyed prophet rings true thousands of
years later. The gay agenda has the *city at heart* and will petition and
parade in the *heart of the city*. Since the *heart of every problem is a problem of
the heart*, the Church has every right to *take heart*. Depravity on display is
the diametric opposite of decency in demonstration. The eleven-fold
agenda of the bold gay exposure must be confronted with blessed gracious
disclosure.

For all the promises of God in Him are yea, and in Him Amen, unto the glory of God by us (2 Corinthians 1:20).

—AGENDA TWO: ECONOMIC POWER—

Money talks in the age of big-budget politics. The bigger the coffers, the bigger is the war chest. The golden rule in the world is, "He who has the gold, rules." In America, there are about 250,000 same-sex households. The average income of a homosexual household is much higher than a heterosexual household. The average income for a gay household is $55,430, and $46,000 a year for lesbian households. For other households it is about $32,144.[5] Men are generally paid more than women, so a man and a woman together average about $23,000 less than a homosexual household.

In addition to household incomes, the militant agenda is propagated by getting millions of dollars, including generous grants, from numerous corporations. The funds that are attained from flourishing organizations such as the Gill Foundation come with specific agendas of their own. The partakers of the foundation's generosity have the implicit responsibility of adjusting their antidiscrimination policies to include homosexuals. As a result of its persistence to provide grant monies to institutions, the Gill Foundation has been very influential in the progress of the militant gay agenda. A significant portion of their donations go directly to companies that actively lobby in support of same-sex marriage and the civil liberties that it represents. If their efforts prove successful, they will join more than one-third of the companies that are already recorded on the Fortune 500 business list.

About 18 percent of homosexual households make over $100,000 dollars annually. That is about one out of five. About three percent of lesbian households make over $100,000 per year. Same-sex households are only one-half of one percent of total households in America, that number has increased from one-tenth of one percent. The number of same-sex households is consistently increasing.

—AGENDA THREE: VOTING BLOCKS—

This creates a voting block that most politicians are unwilling to simply dismiss and ignore. Elections can be won or lost based on minuscule representation of their constituency. The majority of homosexuals vote. Homosexual men vote 87 percent of the time, and lesbians vote 82 percent of the time. Among African-Americans, only about 30 percent vote. Other minority groups are even less. The gay voting practice enables them to defeat those who oppose their agenda, because traditionally they are vehement in an effort to ensure that their voice is heard. Low voter turnout among other groups indicates that the right and obligation to vote is not taken seriously by a great number of Americans.

The Gay, Lesbian, and Straight Educational Network (GLSEN) has undisputedly established a steady momentum of influence with its continual stream of attention-grabbing protest. GLSEN executive director, Keith Jennings, addressed a New York congregation in the spring of 2000 about his organization's strategy for operating amongst those who have strong views about the homosexual lifestyle.

> Twenty percent of the people are hard-core fair minded (pro-homosexual) people. Twenty percent are hard-core (anti-homosexual) bigots. We need to ignore the hard-core bigots, get more of the hard-core fair minded people to speak up, and we'll pull that 60 percent of the people in the middle...over to our side. That's really what I think our strategy has to be. We have to stop being afraid of the religious right...I am not trying to say [explicative deleted] 'em! Which is what I want to say, because I do not care what they think! Drop Dead! [6]

GLSEN purposed to provoke those who stood idle into joining their establishment. They have reached out to adolescents who are looking to involve themselves in the gay agenda. A national "Day of Silence" was organized in public schools by GLSEN in April 2002 to draw attention to the discrimination faced by gay, lesbian, transgender, and bisexual individuals. The protest was also engineered to encourage others to join their cause. The "Day of Silence" gained the attention of elect officials who went on to publicly encourage their demonstration, thus fueling the GLSEN objective.

A Local Gay Backlash

Just recently, a local politician came to All Nations Church and mentioned how he had voted against same-sex marriage. He requested prayer because there was a great campaign organized against him. He lost the election because the homosexual community was irate that he as a Democrat voted for what they say is a conservative Republican perspective. However, he was not voting as a Republican, but as a man of God. He is a minister and an African-American. He said that he could not in good conscience vote for homosexual marriage when he knew the Bible firmly stands against it. His stand caused a fierce backlash by the gay activists, and the churches did very little to assist him.

He lost his reelection bid by 173 votes. The homosexual action committees sent out mailings disguising their agenda by attacking him on his voting concerning a tax issue. They targeted the African-American community portraying him as betraying the Black community by voting for decreased taxes for the rich. They did all this in the guise of opposing the Republican Party and its economic policy. They hoodwinked the Black community into a knee-jerk reaction. They cloaked their true opposition to my ministerial colleague, which was his anti-gay marriage stance. Later, they admitted their agenda in the newspaper. By then, he had already been defeated. As it has been said, for evil to succeed, it is only necessary for good men to do nothing.

—AGENDA FOUR: EDUCATIONAL— ACHIEVEMENT

Generally speaking, homosexuals proportionate to their numbers are an educated group of people. Seventy percent of people who profess to be homosexual are college graduates. Employment among homosexual people is about 97 percent. That is only a three-percent unemployment rate. They control about 19 percent of the discretionary income in the United States. For every five dollars that is spent, one of those dollars is in the hands of a homosexual person. The gay economic power is considerable and can be easily wielded to elect candidates who are favorable to their agenda. They indeed frequently do just that because of the very silent majority in our country. This serves as a subconscious enticement to the gay lifestyle.

—AGENDA FIVE: MILITANT ACTIVISM—

Gay activists are not the majority of the homosexual population. The activists are a small number who vociferously make their demands.[7] They have made their intentions known to administrations regardless of who they are.

First, the gay militant activist agenda is for the gay community to be considered a minority thereby receiving protection from all discrimination. Any civil rights legislation is therefore inclusive of homosexual rights.

Second, the gay militant activist agenda also includes a repeal of punitive penalization of all sodomy laws. The 1986 United States Supreme Court's decision, *Bowers v. Hardwick,* held that states could prohibit same-sex sodomy. The case involved two homosexual men in Texas who were engaged in same-sex sodomy when emergency personnel entered their property in response to a report of a man brandishing a gun. Both were fined for their actions, since same-sex sodomy is illegal in Texas.

As reported in the book *The Homosexual Agenda* by Alan Sears and Craig Osten, Chief Justice Warren Burger said this about sodomy in his 1986 concurring majority opinion in *Bowers v. Hardwick*: "Decisions of individuals relating to homosexual conduct have been subject to the state intervention throughout the history of Western civilization. Condemnation of those practices is firmly rooted in Judeo-Christian moral and ethical standards...To hold that the act of homosexual sodomy is somehow protected as a fundamental right would be to cast aside millennia of moral teaching."[8]

In December 2002, the Supreme Court accepted a legal challenge (*Lawrence v. Texas*) by gay activists to the 1986 *Bowers* decision. Gay activists were seeking an extension of the "right to privacy" law to include homosexual sodomy. In addition, gay activists seek to repeal laws addressing age of sexual consent, sexual soliciting, and prohibition of prostitution.

—AGENDA SIX: PUBLIC— EDUCATION INFILTRATION

Abraham Lincoln once said, "The curriculum of the classroom today will be the philosophy of the government tomorrow." In recent times this has proved true. In the state of Massachusetts, there was a conference sponsored by the board of education in which there were workshops and seminars such as "How to Have Queer Sex." Lincoln would never have foreseen that he would have his life portrayed as homosexual to school children. In Lincoln's case, gay activists claim that he was homosexual because he shared a room with another man for two years.[9]

The gay militant activist agenda is determined to have a *redefining of the family*, making way for homosexual marriage. Homosexuals want the right to the same spousal insurance benefits, spousal retirement pensions, family leave, and adoption rights as any others. The enactment of this agenda will ensure that the traditional view of family is redefined to include gay and lesbian marriages.

Public education preschoolers, elementary and high school students are being exposed to and *educated* about homosexual activities. Students are being exposed to such topics as "fisting" (the thrusting of one's fist into the anus of another for sexual excitement), rejecting parental values, and experiencing sexual pleasure in a less threatening manner (with someone of your own gender), are all discussed in health classes. Junior high students are being questioned about their sexuality by school personnel, and preschool children are also being taught about homosexual behaviors.

A California school district, under the guise of teaching elementary students to accept and even appreciate "diversity" in others, incorporated certain teaching techniques in its classroom curriculum. Adults involved in the gay lifestyle were permitted to address these young students and to share with them from a book entitled *Gloria Goes to Gay Pride*. Additionally, school authorities allowed the students from kindergarten through the fifth grade to participate in the making of a "gay pride" rainbow banner.[10]

The Infiltration of the System

The gay militant activist agenda includes exposure to homosexual-entered curriculum in the public school system. Please note that in some state-funded schools, it is already taking place. Children are required to read *Daddy's Roommate* and *Heather Has Two Mommies* in certain local school districts. Books like these promote the acceptance of the homosexual lifestyle as a viable one and subsequently a gay civil union as an alternative kind of family.

Shocking, yes, but this is what happens as the sleeping giant of the Church in America continues to slumber. *"His watchmen are blind: they are all ignorant, they are all dumb dogs, they cannot bark; sleeping, lying down, loving to slumber"* (Is. 56:10). While the Church is asleep, the enemy has implanted the vineyard of hedonism. The Master Teacher taught, *"But while men slept, his enemy came and sowed tares among the wheat, and went his way"* (Mt. 13:25).

—AGENDA SEVEN: GAIN THE— SYMPATHY OF THE MAJORITY

Alexis de Tocqueville, the 19th-century French statesman and author, visited America during its inception as a nation. He analyzed the greatness of America and concluded that it was not until he went into the churches and heard the preachers preaching the Word of God that he understood the greatness of America. He is well known for his observation that *"America is great because she is good, and if America ceases to be good, America will cease to be great."*[11] There are times when silence is golden, and there are other times when it is just plain yellow. I appeared on the *700 Club* during the time of the Million Man March on Washington D.C. I told the audience that whenever you as a believer shut up, the devil speaks up and proceeds to open up the nation. When the "oil and wine" Church takes the backstage, the adversary takes the center stage, and the will of God is upstaged.

Sympathy is a powerful force. In a democracy, the majority rules; therefore, if you are a part of a minuscule minority, then of course, you have to influence the majority to view things in a sympathetic way that concern your cause. This is the effect of the daily barrage in movies, media, and mediums of communication. Americans love fairness and they hate unfairness. If the victim card is played, then the resistance "house of cards" will come tumbling down. The homosexual lobby is aware that their persistent pressure applied politically and otherwise will affect ultimate sympathetic siding with their same-sex suggestion.

—AGENDA EIGHT:— PUBLIC DESENSITIZATION

> Television can be compared to hypnosis, a tool that is used to put a person in a passive state to accept subconsciously what he would not accept under normal consciousness. Television is a lethal weapon that the enemy is using to desensitize, demoralize and eventually destroy the minds of people.[12]

> Steve Gallagher

In an effort to cater to the homosexual community, television stations Showtime and MTV are making preparations to bring a gay channel to the already overflowing list of available channels. LOGO, the reported name of the channel, was developed to serve the gay community with programming relating to their lifestyle. Showtime, who has had previous success with their show *Queer as Folk*, is confident that the channel will be successful based on its lack of competition.

The Penetration of the Destruction

In 1983, 30 percent of Americans said that they knew someone who was homosexual. By 2000 that figure leaped to 73 percent. In 1985, only 40 percent of those polled said they were comfortable around individuals who practice the homosexual behavior. By 2000, that number had risen to 60 percent. In 1985, 90 percent of Americans said they would be upset if their son or daughter announced they were homosexual. By 2000, that figure was just 37 percent![13] What's happening is desensitization in our society. Television is the leading vehicle in the penetration.

There is a *method* to the homosexual agenda as they work to change the *morals* of a nation to gain acceptance into *mainstream* society. One of their modes of operation is a campaign to constantly parade the homosexual culture and lifestyle before Americans in order to cause *desensitization* to it. It is an application of the old adage of slowly cooking a frog. If you put it in a pot of boiling hot water, it will jump out. However, if you first place it in water at a comfortable temperature, it will not jump out. As you gradually warm the water, the frog does not realize it. Eventually the frog is cooked, having been placated and sedated through the process of desensitization without realizing what was happening all along. The Church in America had better wake up before "we are cooked." After all, it is a poor frog that will not croak in its own pond. Frank Mankiewixz and Joel Swedlow wrote in their book, *Remote Control*:

> Under heavy pressure from organized gay activists, television has for the most part, though, been instrumental over the past decade in helping homosexuals "come out of the closet," individually and collectively. We find dramas, explicit and sensitive, on the subject, as well as a generally dignified treatment elsewhere....[14]

The Escalation of the Construction

The first time people viewed two men or two women either verbally or physically expressing *acts* of intimacy, they were *appalled.* The second time they were *aghast.* The third time they were *alarmed.* The fourth time they were *alerted.* The fifth time they were *aware.* The sixth time they were *accepting.* The seventh time they were *accommodating.* The eighth time they were *anesthetized, apathetic,* and *assured* that it was none of their business. Thus, the desensitization had run its course, and ultimately the person who was once *appalled* has now become an *advocate* for the gay *agenda* themselves.

THERE IS A METHOD TO THE HOMOSEXUAL AGENDA AS THEY WORK TO CHANGE THE MORALS OF A NATION TO GAIN ACCEPTANCE INTO MAINSTREAM SOCIETY.

In recent years, homosexual images have been glamorized or portrayed as objects of sympathy in television and news. The number-one, prime-time comedy has been *Friends*, a show about oversexed heterosexuals, which happens to be produced by an open homosexual. In one episode, the ex-wife of one of the leads marries her lesbian lover in a ceremony officiated by Newt Gingrich's lesbian sister, Candice. The mainstream media outlets have successfully desensitized the nation by exposing the culture to news coverage of gay concerns on a daily basis. Also, the desensitization campaign has caused the nation to tire of hearing about it, until it is ignored altogether. The escalation that results is desensitization.

I remember in the early 90's that America was initially shocked to hear how a mother of two young children had drowned them purposely by driving her car into a lake. After hearing the story over and over, the initial horror wore off and the nation no longer even remotely thought of it. Though, admittedly, the Susan Smith analogy is quite a stretch, be it understood that this is exactly what is happening in the media portrayal of homosexuality.

The goal of the *desensitization* campaign of homosexuals is that America will no longer react strongly against homosexual culture, their demands, or their lifestyle. Before we know it, America could be cooked; and as America goes, so goes the world. The heat is on, and the Church must come to attention and awake out of sleep. A San Francisco pastor wrote a book called, *When the Wicked Seize a City*. He describes a typical gay pride parade. It is as follows:

> The parade begins with an army of lesbians riding motorcycles, proudly calling them selves Dikes On Bikes, in varying degrees of dress and undress. Picture a colorful float slowly moving down Main Street. The float is filled with men and women gyrating to raucous music. The lesbians are smeared with paint and are topless. A gay man is dancing wildly to the music and shoving his hands down into his pants. Another man is clothed only in a g-string. The flap which covers his rear end is a miniature American flag.

> Walking down the street beside the floats are a number of men dressed in women's nighties panty hose and bright blue or red wigs. Dancing among the men is a bald headed woman naked from the waist up, with square pasties over her breasts. Another man stops to pose for a video camera. He is wearing a pink evening gown and has curlers in his hair.

> Lying on the sidewalk near the curb, a long-haired man in shorts has pulled his pants down and is kicking his legs in the air as though he is trying to attract attention. Standing in the crowd, two gay lovers fondle one another, unconscious of the peering on-lookers...Back in the parade, an obese lesbian, naked from the waist up, shows off to the crowd. She is wearing hiking shorts and boots. Walking through the crowd are two men dressed in black leather and silver studded jock straps. These are members of the sado-masochist element in the gay culture. The man trailing behind the first man has a dog collar around his neck. His "master" is holding his "slave" chained to the collar. This is what is called "B&D" for "bondage and dominance," another sex fantasy in the subculture.

A group known as the Radical Fairies marches proudly down the street, and several of them are carrying a ten foot long python or boa constrictor. Another group called NAMBLA (North American Man/Boy Love Association), a group of homosexuals that advocates sex with consenting minors, marches as respectably as every other group advocating sexual lawlessness.

Not long after they pass, a man strolls by with a sign which says, "God is Gay." He is quickly followed by half a dozen lesbians from a group known as SLUTS (Seminary Lesbians under Theological Stress). Various gay church groups pass by identifying their affiliations with traditional mainline churches such as Presbyterians, Lutherans, Roman Catholics, etc.

On the curb, two young men in their twenties lay down in the street and simulate oral copulation with each other. The crowd cheers enthusiastically. Such freedom!

Amazingly enough, in this parade various political candidates for office, state and local, follow these expressions of bizarre behavior, publicly declaring their tacit approval of what "gayness" means in San Franscisco. You ask, "where are the police in all of this?" Most definitely, their presence is seen. For the first time the new police chief is a participant in the parade, riding in an open top car, waving to the crowds, ushered on both sides by his lesbian and gay officers. Indecent exposure laws lapse into outmoded times, far too archaic for the enlightened minds of liberal San Francisco. Laws governing public morality are simply suspended for the day in deference to the gay community. At the end of the parade route, a recruiting table is set up to enlist homosexuals into the San Francisco police department. The police department has a policy of nondiscrimination in the hiring of homosexuals and lesbians, along with racial minorities. All of these events occurred in the light of day on what we Christians call the Lord's Day — Sunday. Is He watching? Or has He abandoned San Francisco to its own little temporal world?[15]

—AGENDA NINE: IMAGE MAKEOVER—

The *desensitization* of the American public has led to a gay image makeover in the motion picture industry's portrayal. A recent example of this is the powerful 1993 movie *Philadelphia,* starring Oscar-winning actors Denzel Washington and Tom Hanks. The movie is about an AIDS patient who eventually died of the disease. Prior to his death, the law firm he worked for fired him because of two improper reasons. The *first* reason was that they feared they somehow might contract the disease while working with him. The *second* reason was because of the apparent embarrassment of being associated with him in their law firm.

At that time in the early 90's, there was a lot less information available about AIDS, and there was a lot of blatant ignorance and sometimes even hostile prejudice against those who had the disease. Consequently, the movie's principle character's victimization at the hand of his colleagues helped to give a sympathetic image makeover to the gay lifestyle. While it is true that his civil rights were violated, the larger purpose of the movie was to reshape the debate and remake the image of the gay lifestyle. On the one hand, the gay community takes great displeasure in being associated with AIDS, and rightly so; but at the same time, it uses the issue to engender sympathy for the cause. This is akin to having your proverbial cake and eating it too." This is the same ploy used by other "minority segments who want complete inclusion and at the same time overwhelming special consideration. Equity is granted, but special preference cannot at the same time be provided.

At the story's end, upon his deathbed, his family was gathered around him. His loving mother laments, "I did not raise my son to sit at the back of the bus." Her son was dying of AIDS, and common sense indicates that it had nothing to do with him "sitting at the back of the bus." However, it is apparent that the script writers were *implicitly* connecting AIDS discrimination with the Civil Rights movement of the 50's and 60's that outlawed segregation in public facilities, education, and transportation.[16]

It was the subtly *implicit* suggestion connected with the *explicit* display of love and support given by his family and his lover that altered views and caused many to rethink their position. The gay agenda of image remaking had accomplished a major coup d'état. Even the core issue was not homosexuality, but AIDS, and it was obscured through intentional blending to influence the American public. The gay advocates purposely connected *supporting one's dying loved one* with the issue of civil rights, and charged anyone in opposition to the gay lifestyle with homophobia and hatred. To think differently is viewed as the exercise of guilty by association with all others who have persecuted the gay community. Whenever you pull on the heart strings of family love and support and connect it with a cause, you are sure to evoke a response; and the movie *Philadelphia* received landmark acclaim as a movie for all times. I thoroughly enjoyed viewing the movie, and I thought very highly of its production and its portrayal of the subject; but I was very aware of its higher agenda and could clearly see the implications and explication underlying its supposed theme.

The entire homosexual community and Hollywood publicity machine got behind the movie *Philadelphia* to ensure its success. Hanks was nominated for Best Actor for the role. In his acceptance speech, he gave tribute to his homosexual drama teacher.

—AGENDA TEN:—
HOMOSEXUAL CIVIL RIGHTS

Black Americans tend to be liberal politically...and yet, Black Americans are among the demographic groups most opposed to gay marriage...The Civil Rights movement of the 1960's was moral. The gay-rights movement is not. It is that simple. Perhaps African-Americans in their churches could start exerting the moral leadership that our whole country desperately needs.[17]

G.E. Veith, Cultural Editor, *World Magazine*

The gay rights agenda is framed in the ERA amendment, which insists that homosexuals should be afforded the same consideration as a minority. By basic definition, a *minority person* in America is someone who is born of an ethnicity of people who do not comprise the numbers of the majority culture. A minority person is a person of ethnicity and not someone who chooses an alternative lifestyle. African-Americans, Latinos, Asiatic peoples, and others so listed did not choose to be born into their ethnic group. Their ethnicity is innate; homosexuality is not. The civil rights of no citizen should ever be violated. The homosexuals are individuals, and not an ethnic group. A minority person is not classified as such because they belong to a sect, a faction, or a group that is not of the majority culture. The homosexuals are a minority of Americans who have exercised a same-sex preference, not a minority ethnicity. Their lifestyle is one of a thousand. They should not be counted as worthy of minority status.

For example, ten percent of Americans, according to statistics, are alcoholics. It is labeled as a disease. The inability to stop drinking alcohol is regrettable, but it is not a minority status; it is a disease that people choose. You cannot call them a minority because 90 percent of the people who are not alcoholics are the majority. To call them a minority and group them with Latinos and African-Americans is just completely wrong and intentionally misleading. However, this is the rationale of the gay agenda for civil rights.

This line of reasoning would qualify a whole host of others for the same classification. As surely as the gay populace is given minority status in our society, credence should also be given to the other chosen lifestyles being credited minority status as well.

A person's civil rights should not be violated because of his choice of sexual lifestyle, but homosexuals should not be allowed to have ministerial positions in religious institutions when it contradicts the core and commonly held beliefs of that particular group. Freedom of religion would be violated if the government ever tried to influence the hiring practice of the institutions of faith. This includes secular positions in institutions where children are preeminent. Children are impressionable; and just as the government is adamant about what it does not allow in schools, such as drugs, forced religion, and convicted criminals teaching our children, it should be just as adamant about undue influence perpetuated upon the young impressionable minds of children as it relates to issues of sexuality. There should be no double standard of the defense of rights.

—AGENDA ELEVEN: HOMOPHOBIC— PORTRAYAL OF OPPONENTS

A major strategy of the homosexual agenda is to profile everyone who opposes them as bigoted and mean-spirited. Therefore, people who speak out against homosexuality are labeled *homophobic*. Statistics are fabricated concerning such things as suicide. They even go so far as to say that the high rate of suicide among homosexuals is aggravated by the antihomosexual lifestyle message. Due to the pressure that they are going through, the shame and the lack of acceptance by their family, many of them are led to commit suicide. They even go so far as to say that if the church opposes the inevitable societal acceptance, then more teenagers will be driven to suicide as a drastic response to the apparent rejection. The truth is that many homosexual teenagers who are committing suicide are doing so from the pressures of being teenagers and not from being homosexual. A study of 266 college men and women found that gay youths were not any more likely than straight classmates to have tried to take their own lives; and a study of 349 students ages 17 to 25

> ANY PERSON FILLED WITH THE LOVE OF GOD WILL NEVER PURPOSELY BE HOMOPHOBIC.

found that those students who are in support groups for behavioral problems and only thinking about suicide was less than ten percent. None said they had tried it due to homosexual tendencies.[18] A Dutch study further corroborates this conclusion. In the Netherlands, where gay and lesbian marriage is accepted, legalized, and affirmed, suicide among its homosexual population is still high.

Any person filled with the love of God will never purposely be homophobic. After all, those of the opposition are not proposing obliteration of homosexual people, just the homosexual agenda.

The Committed Action: In Conclusion
Homo-Activism–The Militant Gay Agenda

The Council Agenda

The "oil and wine" Church in America, having crossed over to a new millennium, has been called to an end-time ecclesiastical council. Having been called to adjudicate the judgments of God in the earth, we must not shirk this auspicious apostolic assignment. The adversary's agenda will annihilate all that we hold sacred and dear if it is granted allowance and accomplishment. The Church must accept the call to arms, recognizing that we wrestle not against flesh and blood, but against the prince of darkness and his demonic cohorts. Individuals, communities, and churches in our country have been summoned to confer—not for flesh-and-blood reasons, but for the apostolic foundation of truth and the prophetic declaration of that same truth to reign. What we stand on and what we proclaim must be one and the same.

Truth should never be divisive. It is our Christian responsibility to protect the little girl who innocently brings home a school library book about two princes who fall in love and marry, and to unite in support of her outraged parents who seemingly can do nothing about it.[19] We must protect the unaware adolescent boy who may be unduly influenced by educational curricula of dogmatic dissertations about *Daddy's New Roommate*. We must aggressively resist the agenda that seeks to entirely infiltrate every aspect of society. Just as there is no area out of bounds with the pro-gay activists, there must be no avenue out of reach of our heavenly Father's outstretched arms. The venue of the gay agenda is everywhere. It is in magazines, on television, radios, computers, at work, in schools, and even in the church. There is no ducking under cover or hiding in the sand. There is no neutral soil, nor is there any middle ground. In the words of General Joshua, you must "*...choose you this day whom ye will serve...*" (Josh. 24:15).

The Compromising Apathy

The story is told that during the war between the states, otherwise known as the Civil War, there was a soldier who did not want to take sides. Therefore, he wore a blue Union topcoat and a gray Confederate pair of pants. In the midst of battle, he was shot at by both sides. The council agenda demands that Christians heed the Mosaic question of the ages, "Who is on the Lord's side?" Passive participants are a parasitic pariah who perpetrate pretense in an effort not to lose their pseudo-popularity. Just as an apathetic person who does not vote should never complain about the decisions reached and legislation passed by elected officials, so should a so-called Christian never complain about the deterioration of the moral fabric of America when they have done nothing to defeat the adversary's agenda for America but compromise. In the eyes of the Almighty God, and in the annals of the angelic abode, the agenda for the hostile takeover is a decided and done deal. The "oil and wine" Church must decisively adjoin divinity's decree before we adjourn the council. Amen.

The Contemptuous Adversary

Every homosexual is in the sights of a satanic scope. Having money, power, and pleasure are not enough to bring peace that passes understanding. The joy of the Lord always comes in fullness, and it is released in proportion to one's acceptance of the will of God. The fact that one *opposes* another person's chosen lifestyle does not mean he does not *accept* them personally. The way of Jesus Christ is simple. He says, "*Come unto Me, all ye that labor and are heavy laden...*" (Mt. 11:28).

No person is rejected when he comes. No person is in a position, whether saved or lost, straight or gay, to reject any human being. The agenda of the Christian community is to see the "*kingdoms of this world...become the kingdoms of our Lord, and of His Christ*" (Rev. 11:15). There is plenty of room in the Kingdom, but there is no room for the things that fall in the Pauline admonition of the "*such were some of you!*" The homosexual agenda must not be allowed to succeed or else what happened to the Roman Empire may duplicate itself in post-modern America. Edward Gibbons, in his classic work, *The Rise and Fall of the Roman Empire*, reports that the great democracy of ancient Rome fell when homosexuality so definitely pervaded the culture that there was a loss of respect for marriage, and consequently a virtual breakdown of the family, which led to a communal, societal, and ultimately national breakdown. You cannot go through the annals of history without seeing the doom and destruction that comes to any nation or civilization that turns its back on God. What we are penning now is the script to the final chapters of American History before the imminent return of our Lord Jesus Christ. The mighty have fallen, as the old cliché states, and history repeats itself. Will we be a nation that forgets God? Will we stand for something or fall for anything? To preserve the union, it is necessary to be aware of the issue of the gay agenda. It is one thing to be sympathetic to gay people, to be empathetic and oppose gay persecution (hate crimes) and gay discrimination (except in faith-based organizations and among children). However, it is another thing to be apathetic to the "Militant Gay Agenda." This is not an acceptable course of action.

The Corrupted Alliance

The Scripture states in Psalm 9:17, "*The wicked shall be turned into* **hell,** *and all the nations that forget God*" (emphasis added). This means that if God's ordinance and divine decree is disregarded in the execution of public policy, the nation has forgotten God's principles and purpose. God will continue to bless America as America obeys and blesses God. Joining other nations in the coalition of the gay agenda is a corrupt alliance. It is a covenant of casualty with grave penalty.

It is very important for America to be right with God. Hezekiah, the king of Judah, "*...did that which was right in the sight of the Lord, according to all that his father did*" (see 2 Kings 14:3). Consequently, his reign was established in peace and given longevity. Longevity does indeed have its place in nation building. The mightiest nations can and will be brought to their knees if they perform the suicidal act of reproaching themselves with sinful choices. Selah.

The Council Adjourns

The court of Heaven has given us the authority to pray for the Kingdom of God to come to the earth. The redeemed and ransomed of the Lord will rule and reign with Him in righteousness in the Kingdom to come. As saints of the Most High, we will one day judge the earth (see 1 Cor. 6:2). As citizens of this *time-limited* planet, we are engaged in a dress rehearsal for eternity. Therefore, we must take the *time* and spend our *time* until the end of *time* helping others to know what *time* it is (see Lk. 12:56). Like the children of the tribe of Issachar, we must "*understand the times and know what Israel* [the Church] *ought to do*" (1 Chron. 12:32). We cannot do everything, but we can do something; and what we can do, by the grace of God, we must do. If we do not do it, it shall not be done. It is a true saying and worthy of acceptation that "If the Church wants something it never had, then it must be diligent to do something that it has never done." We must do something different. We must dare to be different. We must dare to do something different, and in so doing, the consensus will be, "*This is the Lord's doing; it is marvellous in our eyes*" (Ps. 118:23).

We have the authority to bind things on earth even as they are bound in Heaven. There is no homosexuality in Heaven; and therefore, there is no gay agenda either. Accordingly, our prayer is that God's will be done on earth as it is also done in Heaven. Psalm 149:9 declares, "*To execute upon them the judgment written: this honour have all His saints."* Christians are not members of an earthly jury, but we are the judges in the heavenly council who join with our heavenly Father. The Body of Christ in the earth must *hold fast to the Head in Heaven* (see Col. 2:19). The Body cannot act independently from the Head for we are dependent upon His guidance and interdependent as a coregent of Christ. To do so would be a spastic manifestation. Paralysis would be the result of disobeying the signal from the Head. The earthly council must align itself with the heavenly council in a vote of confidence. Imagine such a vote taking place. To do nothing is to favor abolishment of decency in public parades. To do nothing is to favor allowing ministers to preach the Word of God while still living the gay lifestyle. To do nothing is to favor changing the definition of marriage once and forever. The opposite is quite true. If the "oil and wine" Church is in favor of *righteousness* being exalted and justice rolling down like a mighty stream, then we will certainly get involved, not sitting on the sidelines as the homosexual activists run their agenda to the finish line (see Amos 5:24). To do so would most certainly produce *The Confusing Apostasy of Gay and Lesbian Marriage.*

> Prayer: Our heavenly Father, we have a vision for this nation. We share a dream for this land. This country is holy ground. It is the land where our fathers died. It is the land of the puritans, the pilgrims, and the persecuted one's pride. From every mountainside, let freedom ring—not lascivious and licentious false freedom, but true liberating freedom. Confuse the thoughts, plans, and purposes of those who engage in a queer unholy war, and defeat the agenda of those who align against Thee and Thy Son, the Matchless One. Anoint America, the beloved country upon whom You have shed Your grace with a new and glorious morning. We cry, Abba Father, have mercy. We cry, Almighty God, renew us. We cry, Altogether Lovely One, hear our cry, heed our prayer, and turn Thy face toward us once again. Shed Your grace until all can say, surely the Lord is in this place. In Jesus' name, Amen and Amen!

ENDNOTES

1. Tammy Bruce, *The Death of Right and Wrong* (Roseville, CA: Prima Publishing, 2003), 87.

2. Timothy J. Dailey, *Dark Obsession* (Nashville: Broadman & Holman Publishers, 2003), 3.

3. Alan Sears & Craig Osten, *The Homosexual Agenda* (Nashville: Broadman & Holman Publishers, 2003), 148-149.

4. For further exposition of the gay activist agenda see Sears and Osten, *The Homosexual Agenda.*

5. "Overcoming a Deep-Rooted Reluctance, More Firms Advertise to gay Community," *Wall Street Journal* (July 18, 1991). See also "Gays Are Affluent But Often Overlooked Market," *Marketing News* (Dec. 24, 1990).

6. Peter LaBarberay, "When Silence Would Have Been Golden," *Culture and Family Institute* (Apr. 10, 2002).

7. Satinover, 21.

8. Sears & Osten, *The Homosexual Agenda*.

9. Samara, Kalk, "Lincoln Was Gay, Activist Contends," *Madison Capitol Times* (February 23, 1999).

10. Debra Saunders, "Gay-Ed for Tots," *Weekly Standard* (Aug. 19, 1996).

11. Alexis de Tocqueville quote accessed at http://www.zaadz.com/quotes/authors/alexis_de_tocqueville/.

12. Gallagher, 166-167.

13. Alissa J. Rubin, "Public More Accepting of Gays, Polls Find," *Los Angeles Times* (June 18, 2000).

14. Frank Mankiewixz and Joel Swedlow, *Remote Control* (New York: Ballantine Books, 1978), 187-189.

15. Chuck and Donna McIlhenny, *When the Wicked Seize a City* (Lafayette, LA: Huntington House Publishers, 1993), 14.

16. Maxie D. Dunnam and H. Newton Malony, *Staying the Course* (Nashville, TN: Abingdon Press, 2003), 111.

17. G.E. Veith, Cultural Editor, *World Magazine* (July 24, 2004), 25.

18. Marilyn Elias, "Gay Teens Less Suicidal Than Thought, Report Says," *USA Today* (November 26, 2001).

19. Joyce Howard Price, "Gay Princes Book Irks Girl's Parents," *The Washington Times* (March 19, 2004), http://washingtontimes.com/national/20040318-112308-7862r.htm.

CHAPTER
NINE

One thinks of God's institution of marriage—it is to be between one man and one woman. How does the current agenda challenge this design?[1]

James R. White and Jeffrey D. Neill
The Same-Sex Controversy

The gay lifestyle is obsessed with physical appearance because the social life of many homosexuals is closely tied to their sexual attractiveness. Unlike married couples who grow older together and whose value and commitment is not dependent upon physical attractiveness, older homosexuals typically experience harsh rejection by their youthful peers....Married couples look forward to the enduring love and respect from each other and from their children; the gay lifestyle is one of diminishing returns.[2]

Timothy Dailey, The Dark Obsession

Why are Blacks, who know so well the reality of discrimination, so uniformly unsympathetic to the case that the gay community is making...The main reason is that the Civil Rights movement depended on objective moral truth. Homosexual marriage, on the contrary, depends on the rejection of objective moral truth...Blacks know instinctively that the debate on gay marriage is the symptom and not the problem. Without an ultimate standard, Blacks know that the best politics and law even in as great a country as ours, can lead anywhere.[3]

G. E. Veith quoting Star Parker in World Magazine

My experience is that gay men's idea of marriage or any kind of relationship is rather open. That's why a lot of people are a little skeptical. Gay men—they're "together for thirty years": what does that mean? That means they go out and pick up strangers every two weeks. That's a very sophisticated view of marriage.[4]

Camilia Paglia, Lesbian Activist

The Confusing Apostasy:
God's-Eye View of
Gay and Lesbian Marriage

For this cause shall a man leave his father and mother, and shall be joined unto his wife, and they two shall be one flesh (Ephesians 5:31).

The marriage covenant that was established by the everlasting Father is the eternal pattern for what the ancient Greeks called "eros." Homo-eroticism cannot be equated with it because it is not developed from divine decree, but rather the misguiding of genitalia. Everything that feels right is not all right. Anything that seems good is not always good. *Nothing* that violates divine dictate can be considered authentic.

Love is the tie that binds two hearts and lives together. Marriage, based on *agape* and *eros*, is the ship that sails upon the sea called legitimacy. All human beings share in common the basic needs for love, companionship, fellowship, and a sense of belonging. Therefore, it is understood that men and women who are deeply impassioned with one another would desire to continue their commitment under the approving auspices of marriage, which is a beautifully created and a wonderfully designed institution of both ancient and modern times. Indeed, betrothal between those who are beloved is the single thread that unites the garment of society, and it is uniformly held throughout civilization. More than anything, marriage commitment is the most affirming undertaking for a connected couple. Therefore, it is understandable that gays and lesbians would also feel the desire to unite in marriage, the ultimate consummation. In *Dark Obsession*, Timothy J. Dailey writes,

> Many homosexuals–especially young men just entering the gay lifestyle—genuinely aspire to the romantic ideal. But they are invariably—and bitterly—disappointed, as the idealism of finding the perfect man to spend the rest of one's life with eventually denigrates into increasingly transient sexual relationships—culminating in a level of full-blown promiscuity...The unavoidable descent into sexual

immorality occurs because the gay lifestyle is by its very nature inimical to the kind of love and commitment upon which true, heterosexual romance and marriage are based. But by the time it is learned, for many it is too late.[5]

Same-sex couples across the nation are seeking to be joined in *holy* matrimony. By definition, anything "holy" has to follow the "Holiness Code" of the Holy One, for *"holiness, without which no man shall see the Lord"* (Heb. 12:14). Same-sex marriage affords certain legal and financial benefits and a fundamental recognition to no longer be stigmatized by society. Dr. Elizabeth Moberly writes:

> An attachment to the same sex is not wrong, indeed it is precisely the right thing for meeting same-sex deficits. What is improper is the eroticization of the friendship. Such eroticization is secondary, and not essential to the homosexual condition as such.[6]

Same-sex marriage is a demonstrably divisive issue facing our country and the Church. Its ultimate resolution will also affect the entire world, because as America goes, so goes the world. Massachusetts, Vermont, California, and Hawaii, along with parts of Canada, have *judicially sanctioned* same-sex marriage while the United States federal government is resistant and will not recognize these "marriages" with the passage of the Defense of Marriage Act (DOMA) signed into law in 1996 by President Bill Clinton. President George W. Bush, speaking in February 2004, said that:

> The union of a man and a woman is the most enduring human institution, honored and encouraged in all cultures and by every religious faith...Marriage cannot be severed from its cultural, religious and natural roots without weakening the good influence of society. [7]

President Bush's viewpoint is supported by most major religions. Christians are vehemently adamant in their immediate dismissal of same-sex marriage. It is anti-biblical, anti-Christian, and anti-societal. In this writing, we will analyze same-sex marriage *legalization*. Additionally, we will examine the *licentiation* and the *legitimization* of same-sex marriage and the God's-eye view of it. There are definitive teachings in the Word concerning it. What is the divine perspective? The prophet Isaiah declared:

> *Come now, and let us reason together, saith the Lord: though your sins be as scarlet, they shall be as white as snow; though they be red like crimson, they shall be as wool* (Isaiah 1:18).

Righteous Reasoning

Let us not mistake the prophet's reasoning with an intellectual one. Righteous rationale is what the Church must rely upon in seeking answers to the issue of same-sex unions. The Church must utilize rationalization that is based on a proper perception—not opinionated outbursts. An argument is persuasive only when it is produced by the preponderance of pertinent facts. It is the prophetic insight that supercedes hindsight and offers foresight into the humanly "unknowables" of eternal significance. To marry wrongly may indeed put one's soul in danger of hell fire. To marry righteously may put one on the path to eternal peace.

The "oil and wine" Church must communicate a God-conscious conviction to a sin-cursed contemporary society. Contemplations and conversations that reach extrapolations that result in mutilation of marriage are as welcome as the sanitation department dumping the day's stinking, rotten debris on your front porch. It is as welcome as the residue of vomit being re-heaved over and again on any passerby. America needs

> RIGHTEOUS REASONING IS PERSUASIVE BECAUSE IT IS PRODUCED BY THE PREPONDERANCE OF PERTINENT FACTS.

absolutes. The Church in America needs *resolutes*. Moral compromise is convenient, and sometimes coercive, but it is always *catastrophic*. To lie about same-sex marriage is to let down the bloodstained banner. Christians have made a vow that we would serve Him till we die. To live is Christ, and to lie is to die, while you are yet living.

Prophetic Boldness

In 1974, I was saved. My first exposure to public prophecy in operation was given by an elderly saint named Mother Nolan. As she prophesied, her faint and weakened voice grew in strength. By the end of those few minutes, you could clearly hear her all the way from one side of the cathedral to the other. Later that day, I was informed that God had given Mother Nolan the gift to prophesy; the old saints believed that she had been negligent to do so for various reasons, and inevitably her voice had grown weaker and weaker. Whenever she would obey God and prophesy, her voice was restored and she could speak loud enough to hear. The last time I saw her alive, Mother Nolan was speaking as clear as the morning sun is bright.

The Church needs to speak up and out and restore its voice. As we contemplate the *legalization, licentiation,* and *legitimacy* of gay and lesbian

319

marriage, let us take the 360-degree God's-eye view of it. Let us look from every angle until we can see what God sees.

To the revisionist thinker, same-sex marriage is right. To the righteous thinker, it is wrong. The Bible was written to be the moral compass in the midst of chaos, confusion, and collective societal bargaining. It is still a lamp that lights the path of uncertainty. The promises of God are yea and amen (see 2 Cor. 1:20). Despite the cries of discrimination, there are still absolute rights and absolute wrongs. It is always right to obey God. It is always wrong to disobey Him. It is that simple. A fool need not err therein. Pity the person who persists in the paralysis of analysis. There is no need to debate, discuss, dissertate, or dialogue once the God's-eye view comes into clear view! In this chapter, we will see *plainly, predictably*, and *prophetically*. Let God be true and every purveyor of perversion be politely, but pertinently, put in their place.

—LEGALIZATION—

Throughout millennia, marriage has been understood to be between a man and a woman. Just because something may be legalized, does not equate with it being morally right. Abortion is legalized in this country, but it is still not moral. To be legal in the sight of man, does not make it legal with God.

In the biblical story of Jezebel, Ahab, and Naboth, Naboth had a vineyard located in proximity to the king's palace. Ahab wanted his garden. Naboth refused, saying to Ahab, "*The Lord forbid it me, that I should give the inheritance of my fathers unto thee*" (1 Kings 21:3). He understood that he would be worse than an infidel if he were to give away his children's inheritance.

Covert

After this, Jezebel, who was Ahab's wife, *legally* and covertly wrote letters in Ahab's name sealing them with the king's legal seal. She orchestrated a setup that caused Naboth to be murdered, thereby *illegally* obtaining the vineyard of Naboth for Ahab in a way that appeared as if it was *legal*. In the eyes of unsuspecting Israel, the whole matter seemed *legal*, but in God's-eye view, it was an *illegal* acquisition. Through His prophet, Elijah, God revealed that He saw the illegal acquisition and that He is displeased when man violates His laws (see 1 Kings 21:17-19).

King David desired Bathsheba, the wife of another man. To achieve his goal, he orchestrated a setup of Uriah, her husband, which caused him to be killed. In the eyes of man, it appeared that David *legally* married Bathsheba, but in God's eye view, it was an *illegal* acquisition. Through His prophet, Nathan, God revealed that He saw the illegal acquisition and that He continues to be displeased when man violates the authority of His laws (see 2 Sam. 12:1-12).

Martha Stewart, America's domestic diva, was privy to insider information that resulted in her saving a $50,000 investment loss. Initially, her actions appeared *legal*; but after a court case, she was convicted, and a judge sentenced her to a six-month prison term. The appearance of something *legal* does not mean that it actually is. The jury of the Church fathers and the Judge of the court of Heaven have the final say. What appears to be a *legal* acquisition in the sight of men is not always *legal* in God's eyes. In these examples of spiritual *illegality*, death, disease, destruction, and "great shame" were the result. Nothing escapes the One who sits high and looks low upon the affairs of man.

The proposed legalization of same-sex marriage, if passed, will be counted as illegal in Heaven. It will put our nation out of divine alignment. We will be like a wayward child who steps beyond the protection of parents, who are powerless to intervene against defiance of the restrictions set forth. Consequences are the inevitable result to those who defy the divine normative.

Covetous

The Ten Commandments of God culminate with this simple but sacred admonition:

> *Thou shalt not covet thy neighbour's house, thou shalt not covet thy neighbour's wife, nor his manservant, nor his maidservant, nor his ox, nor his ass, nor any thing that is thy neighbour's* (Exodus 20:17).

Jesus, the Master Teacher, taught in Luke 12:15 to "*beware of covetousness: for a man's life consisteth not in the abundance of the things which he possesseth.*" King Ahab and King David exhibited *covetousness* on the highest level. When one covets, one forgets His Creator; and the forces of the *lust of the flesh, lust of the eye, and the pride of life* compel one to step out of the will of God (see 1 Jn. 2:16).

Heterophobic homosexuality is a coercive force that covets the man and woman who are ordained for each other. As was the result for Ahab and David's covetousness, so will be the result for the beloved nation that forgets His precepts: *death* and *destruction*.

America is not a Christian nation, nor is it an infidel nation. However, we are built upon Judeo-Christian principles of life. The distinctive definition of marriage is an inheritance that we should leave to our children's children. As a nation of indisputable Christian heritage, God forbid that we would give the inheritance of traditional marriage, delivered to us by our heavenly Father, our apostolic fathers, and our founding fathers, to a generation of the fatherless.

The revolutionary cry, "Give me liberty or give me death," of Patrick Henry is now become "Give me same-sex marriage and I will give the death of the family that God has ordained." As Rachel demanded of Jacob, "*Give me children, or else I die,*" same-sex couples are saying, "Give us adoptive children and give us the ear of children in schools and universities lest we die for we cannot reproduce." Should the "oil and wine" Church cower silently with fear, induced paralysis, or pride-endorsed arrogance, without any attempt to regain control and turn the family back in the direction of God's divine edicts, our *oil* will surely become rancid and our *wine* will certainly become sour to our generation. Truly, this will set the teeth of the subsequent generations on edge (see Ezek. 18:2).

—LICENTIATION—

Those pressing for gay marriage licentiation often present their cause in a way that is analogous to the civil rights movement. Many traditional family advocates agree that gays and lesbians have the right to live as they choose. But they do not have the right to redefine marriage for an entire society. The statement so freely quoted by gay rights advocates, "I did not raise my child to ride in the back of the bus," is a direct reference to perceived civil rights infractions.

Gays and lesbians have never been forced to ride in the back of any bus, let alone the bus of third-class citizenship. Neither should they be allowed to hijack the bus of the institution of marriage. Hijacking is an illegal enterprise. Yet mayors of cities like San Francisco and Ithaca, New York, and county officials in other cities have illegally allowed or granted homosexuals marriage ceremonies in defiance of existing state and federal laws. This attempt to redefine marriage to include same-sex scenarios is likened to driving without license or authorization. Without a license it is *licentiousness.* This is an Old English word that means wanton lust or desire. Many informed citizens agree that *gays and lesbians have the God-given right to marry; they just do not have the God-given right to marry each other.* Wrong will never be right. License is liberty; licentiousness is depravity. License is granted after examination. Licentiousness is gotten after capitulation. Therefore, the bus analogy may be manufactured, but it is misleading.

Gays and lesbians have illegally taken over "buses" of societal issues, in an attempt to drive America in unauthorized directions. Gay activists have assaulted God's eye view of marriage, which has clearly existed for six millennia. They are attempting to take society hostage and take it down a road that will leave it disheveled and in an upheaval. Whatever your ethnicity, homoeroticism is holding you as leverage in its demands.

Gay Rights—Civil Wrongs?

The first group held hostage against their will is the civil rights movement. To compare the gay rights struggle with the civil rights struggle in America is a civil wrong. With precisely planned, well-organized, and orchestrated activist takeovers, various elements of society and history are being held against the truth in this debate.

Federal protection under civil rights laws are extended to groups that can: (1) demonstrate that they are politically powerless; (2) demonstrate that they are disadvantaged economically; (3) demonstrate that their human characteristics are innate, inborn, and unchangeable. Homosexuals do not meet these stipulations to be extended civil rights. *Former homosexuals exist, but there is no such thing as a former Black American.*

Homosexuals were never subjected to 400 years of cruel slavery, or separate bathrooms and water fountains, Black codes, miscegenation, segregation, and discrimination because of their color. Homosexuals have never had to endure separate and unequal accommodations or education. Homosexuals have never been counted as three-fifths of a person and have never been red-lined by financial institutions because of their sexual preference. Homosexuals are holding by force the history of oppressed people and the blood of their fallen martyrs as they demonstrate for same-sex marriage.

The civil rights leaders of today who are true to the Word of God will not align themselves with wanton disregard for truth. Politics does indeed make strange bedfellows, but civil rights and same-sex marriage rights are in antithesis and not synthesis. Despite this, vociferating voices of dissent are blaring and blasting their bisexual, homosexual, and transsexual triads in a tireless manner. A gracious word of dissent to the gay and lesbian community is the way of the assent of those who hold dear the difference between civil rights and gay wrongs.

Unfortunately, several prominent African-American civil rights leaders espouse the pro-same-sex marriage viewpoint. In part, because it is contained within the Democratic Party's platform, to which they have sworn to what Wayne Perryman refers to as "unfounded loyalty." However, there are other prominent African-American leaders who support traditional marriage. Walter Fauntroy, spokesman of the coalition that supports the Federal Marriage Amendment, is an example.[8]

Children's Rights Versus Parental Wrongs

The second group held hostage are innocent children. Of the studies conducted that examined the effects on children raised in gay and lesbian households, none has shown that children of gay and lesbian couples are unaffected. In fact, an independent review of 14 studies that report favorable data for children in gay and lesbian households shows that these studies lacked external validity as it relates to accepted and practiced scientific investigations.[9]

The jury is still out on the effects upon the children because of the relatively recent occurrence of same-sex parenting and adoption. God Almighty is both a mother and a father to the fatherless. Two moms do not make one dad. Two dads will never equal one mom. Despite the she-she or he-he that same-sex marriage proposes, it is not even remotely equivalent to the model of man made in the image and glory of God and woman being the glory of the man. The glory of God is Christ; the glory of Christ is the man; the glory of the man is the woman; the glory of the woman is her hair (covering); and the glory of the child is his father (see 1 Cor. 11).

No amount of redesigning and redefining the legal aspects of civil unions is going to take away the social stigma of "something not quite right" in the eyes of children.

Children are conceived by males and females and are not meant to be raised in a household that does not reflect their original constitution. Their dichotomous existence will leave them confused about their sexuality. In spite of efforts to tell them otherwise, these misfortunate children may always feel that there is something wrong. The stability of the life and times of a child is found in the environment of their upbringing. Physiology, psychology, and theology serve to witness to the child contrarily to their living arrangement. That is, their *frame*, their *feeling*, and their *faith* will defend the law of nature against the intrusion of the same-sex scenario.

The genetic makeup of a child is not incidental, coincidental, or accidental; and it cannot be ignored. In today's culture of relativism, the absolutism model presented by God in the Garden of Eden still endures as what is needed for children to grow and to develop into well-rounded adults whose charge will be to perpetuate the generations of God-honored, God-ordained,

God-blessed marriage. Those who truly believe in God and His infallible and inerrant Word, hold fast to this realization and do not need further evidence to confirm this. Despite its Hollywood incorrectness, monogamous marriage is the best arrangement for the upbringing of children. Studies by numerous social scientists confirm this conclusively. They have emphatically proven that children who are raised in two-

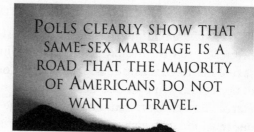

POLLS CLEARLY SHOW THAT SAME-SEX MARRIAGE IS A ROAD THAT THE MAJORITY OF AMERICANS DO NOT WANT TO TRAVEL.

parent male/female households fare much better than those who are not.[10] Same-sex marriage is a contemptuous carjacker, and it has no license to drive the children of future generations. If made a reality and passed over by a passive Church, children will be mercilessly massacred in the same-sex marriage myth.

Children reared in gay and lesbian households love their caregivers, but at the same time, it cannot be denied that these same-sex sleeping arrangements are confusing to impressionable children. Likewise, same-sex marriage is a cruel experiment with the future of children held out of balance. It is an experiment that will yield disappointing results for the adults involved, and children caught up in this quite selfish fleshly foray will be the worst for it.

Gay parents undoubtedly love the children they are raising into adulthood. Abusive parents would argue that they also love their children. One cannot prove or disprove their conviction in either case. We can only look at the result of abuse inflicted on the children. We can only look at the biological and psychological factors that should be in place in their lives.

The environment that children are raised in affects them for life. In the case of sexual, physical, verbal, or emotional abuse, children are indelibly scarred. Therefore the logical course of action when abuse of children is discovered is the removal of the children for safety reasons. Surprisingly, when faced with removal from the home for their own safety, often these children who have been hurt or neglected by parents' negligible practices continue to desire to remain in the home. Yet a child's love for his parent(s) does not preclude the fact that more than likely, the young abused children will grow up to be maladjusted and quite possibly become abusers themselves. The abusive parents' professed love for their children does not nullify the indisputable data that concludes what children need in place in their young lives in order to grow into emotionally and physically healthy adults. The same holds true for children raised in homosexual households.

Civil Rights Versus Conjugal Wrongs

A third group that has been taken hostage is interracial marriage. This is prime leverage for the gay activist. According to them, the debate over homosexual marriage is akin to the prohibition on interracial marriage that existed in our country in past decades. Not so. At no time was the issue of interracial marriage an effort to redefine the marriage as something other than between one man and one woman. If allowed, same-sex marriage will totally and completely change the definition of marriage.

For years, the argument against interracial marriage was that *everything was to reproduce after its kind* (see Gen. 1:24-25). However, the word *kind* means "species." There is no black species, brown species, red species, yellow species, or white species. The complexion of humans is the result of pigmentation, which is directly correlated to the melanin in the skin. In the darker skinned people of the world, melanin exists in all five layers of the skin. In the lighter skinned peoples, it exists in only three of the five layers of the skin. The other physiological differences such as nose, eyes, hair, etc., are the result of environmental adaptation throughout the generations. The teaching against interracial marriage is not biblically accurate. However, the teaching against gay and lesbian marriage is supported by Scripture. When God's judgment resulted in a worldwide flood, Noah took two of every species (see Gen. 7:9).

There went in two and two unto Noah into the ark, the male and the female, as God had commanded Noah (Genesis 7:9).

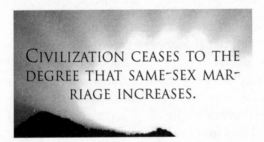

CIVILIZATION CEASES TO THE DEGREE THAT SAME-SEX MARRIAGE INCREASES.

This means that there were two dogs, not two Dobermans, or two German Shepherds. There were two dogs, period. The entire array of the various dog types were contained in the *two specimens* of the *species*. To preserve the human race, God utilized male husbands and female wives. Thus male, Noah, and his female wife, as well as his sons and their female wives, went aboard the ark. Of course, the rest is history and the social streams of humanity stem from those four males and four females. If there had been same-sex marriage, civilization would have ceased to exist. Civilization ceases to the degree that same-sex marriage increases.

Family Rights Versus Societal Wrongs

A fourth group that is taken hostage is the traditional family. Marriage is for the purpose of procreation with loving monogamous companionship included. Same-sex marriage does not fulfill either part of this mandate. Same-sex couples cannot naturally participate in the propagation of the human race. Heterosexual men will be reduced to donors and women's wombs will be merely seen as unconnected incubators that supply children for the gay and lesbian household experiment. The preferred term of derision that homosexuals have for heterosexuals who have children is *"breeders."*[11] Therefore, if homosexuals are licensed to marry each other, not only will the family be jeopardized, but the basic building block of a free, future society will be removed. To intentionally bring a child in this world without that child ever having a sense that he came from both a father and a mother is quite cruel. With the knowledge of mother or father come a sense of pride in lineage and an awareness of genetic inheritance. Even in the case of children adopted and raised in nurturing heterosexual homes, there is often an inner drive that compels them to find their biological parents. Many times there is an inner knowing in adoptive children that a part of them is somewhere else.

Same-sex marriage is a device of death. Gay activists in their unholy heist of holy matrimony are filled with acrimony. The traditional family is being attacked by those driving explosive-packed vehicles parked in front of a passive Church in America. Those of the militancy are detonating bombs that will decimate with destructive results. The gay and lesbian couples who naively march up to city halls seeking marriage are acting out their determination in suicide bomber fashion. These words may appear harsh, but it is the truth anyhow.

When young men and women drive vehicles packed with explosives into a crowded market and detonate them, they truly believe that their suicidal escapade will advance their cause. They are emboldened by the belief that their action will be rewarded by an unending paradise. In reality, unredeemed murderers will have their part in the lake of fire (see Rev. 21:8). The deception dispensed to them causes a prematurely shortened life of potential greatness, while dashing to pieces the lives of so many others.

Gay activists believe they are fighting for the cause of civil rights, but in actuality they are blowing up the basic family unit. The death and disease that they now disproportionately experience will detonate on the future of

America, leaving countless lives wounded and disfigured as the definition of marriage is reconfigured. *Gay marriage undermines procreation. For the Church to sanction and give sacrament to the same-sex would be anathema!* (see 1 Cor. 16:22) Unless the Church wakes up, shakes up, stirs up, and puts a perimeter of prayer around the family, it will be eradicated as we know it today.

—LEGITIMIZATION—

All things are lawful for me, but all things are not expedient: all things are lawful for me, but all things edify not (1 Corinthians 10:23).

Marriage Can't Buy You Legitimacy

There are several reasons why gay marriage is not legitimate and does not edify society or the individuals involved in it. Homosexual activists are spending enormous amounts of money promoting this cause of legitimacy. Their media of transmittal includes pro-gay television programs, advertisements, movies, and the application of political pressure through influence peddling in Congress. However, *their quest to legalize same-sex marriage is setting the movement up for even more miserable results.* On a personal level, they often suffer the misery of rejection and ostracism by family and acquaintances. It is very hurtful and hard to bear. On a communal level, the movement suffers miserably from naiveté. They earnestly assume that societal disdain for their lifestyle will wane if they become legally married partners. Gay activist, Merle Miller, in 1971 mused in his book, *On Being Different,* that he just wanted to be *respected.* Aretha Franklin sang "R-E-S-P-E-C-T; This is what it means to me." She was speaking of a heterosexual relationship. Respect comes after inspection and not introspection. This single thought sums up the feelings of gays and lesbians in America. Homosexuals truly expect their way of life to be respected and accepted by mainstream society after they are allowed to marry. History, however, does not bear this out.

The past issue of interracial marriage will help us see the extent of legitimacy that homosexuals can hope for. We examine this issue simply because gay activists often use it to bolster their case for same-sex marriage. It was not until 1968 that interracial marriages became legal across the entire United States of America. At the time, most Americans were willing to tolerate them, but 72 percent disapproved of them, according to a Gallup poll. It took 23 years for a majority of Americans to view interracial marriage favorably, with 48 percent *for* them and 42 percent *against* them. Ironically, among Blacks in 1991, the approval went down from 70 percent to 63 percent. In 2004, 36 years removed from 1968, 30 percent of Americans still disapprove of interracial marriage. If this is any indication of society's slow adaptation, then homosexuals are in for a rude awakening as they look for legitimacy of their lifestyle through legalized marriage.

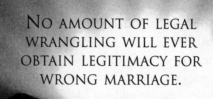

NO AMOUNT OF LEGAL WRANGLING WILL EVER OBTAIN LEGITIMACY FOR WRONG MARRIAGE.

Ultimately, every man's judgment is from the Lord. Opinion polls are shortsighted because they are based on cultural shifts and transient times. The conscience of the majority should be the least concern. Every professed homosexual should be far more concerned about *what the Lord requires of them*. In the end, man does not have a heaven or hell to send anyone to. Those whom God hath joined, are ordained and sanctioned. Those who join themselves are actually dis-jointed, dis-united, and headed for disaster. *Before anyone says, "I do," to another, he should say, "I do" to God's will.*

Simply because it is possible to market the legitimacy of same-sex marriage does not mean that it changes the moral definition. Absolute truth contains no variableness, neither shadow of turning (see Jas. 1:17). God does not change His mind. God says of Himself in Malachi 3:6, "*I change not.*" No amount of legal wrangling will ever obtain legitimacy for wrong marriage. Christianity's influence on millions of people for over two thousand years will forbid it. The "oil and wine" Church is a literal sleeping giant, arising out of its slumber. It is shaking itself from inactivity and apathy, while casting off the bands of carelessness and callousness. It is answering the call to confront the times with a clear word from the Lord.

We can never make the number one the same as the number two, nor can we make a rose be a daffodil. Therefore, two men can unite and be given a certificate if they stand before a judge, but it will never be a union certified in Heaven. Likewise, it is true of two women. Since the inception of creation and the conception of the new creation Church, the definition of marriage has been adhered to by all Christian church groups whether Protestant or Catholic. Some things do not change, and this is one of them. Charles Colson writes, "God has ordained three institutions for the ordering of society, the family for the propagation of life, the state for the preservation of life, and the church for the proclamation of the gospel."[12] These three institutions have a distinctive role and prominence. The family, the church, and the state are God's idea for an ideal society.

Marriage between a male and female has its roots in antiquity. *Homo-eroticism, regardless of being cloaked in any type of union, will always be on the fringe of society in the eyes of the majority of Americans and of the world.* Same-sex marriage for gays and lesbians will be anticlimactic and a huge disappointment because it cannot deliver a legitimacy to homosexuality, because it flies in the face of Truth. With the legalization of same-sex marriage, the despair of gays and lesbians will not be alleviated. *The isolation will not end; the mainstream acceptance will not kick in; and God's blessings on same-sex unions will not begin.*

Marriage Can't Buy Monogamy

Marriage is a monogamous endeavor instituted by a holy and righteous God. At its very core is fidelity, the key ingredient to all successful marriages. There is nothing as heart-wrenching as discovering that one's husband or wife has been unfaithful after declaring their exclusive love before many witnesses. In spite of hopes of living happily ever after, many *heterosexuals* have experienced great pain in marriage. Many couples enter marriage with false expectations that a marriage ceremony will suddenly change the hardened heart and cheating ways of the spouse.

In spite of counsel to proceed with caution, many well-meaning, morally-living young ladies proceed hastily into marriage, thinking it will be the ingredient that will cause a man to be faithful and to honor them. No doubt the high divorce rate is partly attributed to these false expectations of what a wedding ceremony can do. If issues of unfaithfulness, abuse, neglect, and irresponsibility are evident in the dating period, the behaviors will also manifest after the wedding ceremony is over, and they will only be exacerbated within the marriage. It may take a few days or even a few years, but there will eventually be problems. The same is true for the unfaithful female. A woman who dishonors the man before marriage will not suddenly change after saying, "I do."

When examining the gay and lesbian arguments for marriage rights, one will find a *similar false expectation concerning marriage.* There is an earnest expectation of what marriage will do for their ability to live together monogamously. This anticipation and expectation far exceeds any financial windfall. The belief is that *legitimized* marriage will effect a change in their behaviors, enabling them to function within the glorious constraints of monogamy and fidelity, even if they could not live within these boundaries in the past.

Exclusiveness can be quite *elusive* to the gay person. Promiscuity and infidelity is a driving force beyond his control. There are a few gay and lesbian couples who have reasonably stable relationships. However, this is not the statistical norm. One lesbian says this about long-term gay relationships:

> My experience is that gay men's idea of marriage or any kind of relationship is rather open. That's why a lot of people are a little skeptical. Gay men—they're "together for thirty years": what does that mean? That means they go out and pick up strangers every two weeks. That's a very sophisticated view of marriage.[13]
>
> Camilia Paglia, Lesbian Activist

It gives false hope that marriage will cause the other person or themselves to change. One of the most fallacious and often touted arguments of the homosexual is that there is both a "natural" and "unnatural" homosexuality. If this is so (and it is not), *why then do gay activists want to force the monogamy of marriage upon the homosexual community when inherent in the homosexual lifestyle is a "natural" tendency towards promiscuity which "unnaturally" fits into marriage?* The very cloth of holy matrimony is spun from the cohesive thread of fidelity. Same-sex marriage is an unnatural exercise in futility, and if the root of the union is unnatural, the fruit of it will be unthinkable. For this reason, many gay and lesbian persons do not support those who ascribe to this theory. They have rightly concluded that *marriage is not the vehicle that will bring the homosexual to a settling peace within themselves.* However, if legalized, many same-sex couples are poised to enter into a "protest marriage" as a way to add to the demise of the institution.

—LICENTIATION—

For God is not the author of confusion, but of peace, as in all churches of the saints (1 Corinthians 14:33).

A Perilous Scenario: The Bottomless Chasm

The apostle Paul in Second Timothy 3:1 prophesied of this age, calling it *"perilous times."* Paul, in using the term "perilous," was speaking of a troublesome time, because of a slack stand that results from leaving a higher place of belief to live from a lower place of reference, thereby being in danger of falling into a gulf, a chasm, or a gaping opening. The New American Dictionary defines *chasm* as an "abyss," or a bottomless pit or hell. Traditional marriage is a high standard in the midst of cultural compromise. Gay marriage is truly a bottomless chasm. It is a perilous plunge into the piracy of the perfect will of God.

The key to not struggling to keep from sinking to the bottom of quicksand is to not step in it in the first place. America is being driven toward same-sex marriage by operators who have impaired vision. They also have an obstructed view that causes them to see the immediate goal without seeing the implications of changing traditional marriage. Gay marriage, if legislatively and religiously sanctioned, will plunge America and society into a quagmire that will release a quandary of endless relationship scenarios. The traditionalists are looking at the pitfalls in the road ahead as gay activists continue to destructively drive while dragging society kicking and screaming along with them.

> IF SOCIETY APPROVES THE LEGALIZATION...OF SAME-SEX MARRIAGE, THE JUDGMENT OF A JUST GOD WILL BEAT UPON OUR DOORS.

Before sacrificing traditional marriage on the altars of revisionist pluralism, social tolerance, and civil rights, it behooves the serious seeker to ponder deeper into the result of rebelliously realigning the righteous institution of marriage. What are the prophetic implications of gay and lesbian marriage, and where will it lead society and the Church? It is rather unfortunate that the 21st-century Church is being led by the winds of change. The first-century Church was a vessel of change in the world. Oswald Chambers once said, "The church does not lead the world nor echo it; she confronts it. Her note is the supernatural note."[14] If society approves the legalization, the legitimacy, and the licentiation of same-sex marriage, the judgment of a just God will beat upon our doors. The hoofbeats of the apocalyptic horseman will be heard, and the nation will be on a collision course with doomsday. To licentiate gay marriage is to blow up the foundation, burst open the doors, break all the windows, and blast every floor of the family unit, leaving a gaping hole in the once fertile ground of the family that will allow all sorts of living arrangements to become authenticated. Several possibilities will occur.

A Problematic Scenario: Alternative Marriage

The gaping hole left in the family unit would allow the following scenario to be a reality. Two couples are friends. One couple is heterosexual, and the other is homosexual. One of the gay men needs health insurance because he fears that he is gravely ill. The heterosexual couple loves their homosexual friends dearly and do not want them to suffer financial ruin or a lack of health care. Therefore, out of the goodness of their hearts, the heterosexual couple agrees to divorce, and the husband of the wife agrees to marry the homosexual male and extend his benefits to him. The woman does not marry him because her insurance from her own business is not as comprehensive as her husband's. On paper they appear to be divorced, but in reality, the living arrangements have not changed. There is no verifying of the arrangement. Since *Lawrence v. Texas,* the 2003 Supreme Court ruling that struck down a sodomy law in Texas, no one has a right to determine what people do in the privacy of their homes. This is confusion, and God is not in it.

The gaping hole in the foundation of the family unit will mean financial devastation to companies. Small business owners, the backbone of the economy, many of whom already struggle to stay fiscally afloat, will receive the brunt of the blowup of traditional marriage. Large and small businesses will be forced to extend health insurance and other benefits to gays and lesbians who by choice of their lifestyle willfully put themselves in jeopardy for higher rates of physical diseases and emotional disturbances. Ultimately, this will have a devastating effect on the American economy and the taxpayer will pay for it, either in taxes or in higher premiums.

The gaping hole in the foundation of the family unit will benefit only one group of people in America. They are the degrading talk show hosts who indiscriminately spew fecal matter on the unsuspecting American public. With the addition of a litany of legalized living arrangements, they will have a plethora of material to parade before our eyes, exposing innocent children to tainting elements that they would otherwise be oblivious to. Whenever homosexuality is looked upon favorably by a society, young people are more likely to "give it a try," thereby increasing its tolerance and its accompanying distresses. Marriage between a man and a woman will not be viewed as the norm, and children will grow up believing that marriage is merely a consenting contract between any combination of men and women.[15]

None calleth for justice, nor any pleadeth for truth: they trust in vanity, and speak lies; they conceive mischief, and bring forth iniquity (Isaiah 59:4).

Pro-gay activists say, "Not so!" To them, these other arrangements are ridiculous. However, it is quite hypocritical at the worst or naïve at the best, for them to say this. If their so-called "civil right" to "marry" cannot be violated, then neither can the rights of any other segment of society. In a democracy, the majority rules. However, many pro-gay extremist activist judges render decisions that *dictate to us,* rather than decisions that *reflect us.* In a democracy, the *people* make the laws, not federal judges who create new laws rather than interpret the existing constitutionally based laws. Homosexuality in any form falls short of the glory of God, and therefore, it is a sin. Transference of sin upon a society is a serious mistake with serious consequences. This is confusion, and God is not in it!

A Predictive Scenario: Sibling Marriage

Cursed be he that lieth with his sister, the daughter of his father, or the daughter of his mother... (Deuteronomy 27:22).

Society will have forfeited the right to say "no" to siblings who will eventually apply for marriage licenses. The abolition of marriage's foundation means that Bill and Will Harper, two brothers who love each other, will have a right to marry. Why not?—they are the same gender. Since they will not have children, their genetic similarity will not be an excluding factor. You say that is incest. But what if they are not gay and simply want the financial benefits of marriage? This is confusion, and God is not in it.

Any type of same-sex union is confusion. Any such combination is an abomination. We see the unspoken rule of men not copulating with their sisters in the story of Abraham, Sarah, and the Egyptian Pharaoh. When Abraham announced that Sarah was his sister, Pharaoh felt free to take her for himself knowing that there was nothing sexual between siblings. Abimelech took Rebecca, Isaac's wife, because it was understood that Isaac would not copulate with his own sister. We continue to ascribe to the rule of sisters and brothers not marrying today. Aside from the genetic issues involved, it is just plain absurd. God's judgment in both instances was immediate (see Gen. 12:17; 20:3).

The false prophets of today would have us believe that God's Word is not the final authority on homosexuality. If it means something other than what it plainly says, then we can logically conclude that the forbidding of sisters and brothers from having sex and the forbidding of bestiality could also mean something else. We see that the Word of God is not the ultimate authority for those who advocate same-sex unions. Therefore, there is nothing to prevent the sister-to-sister and brother-to-brother same-sex scenario from moving from anomaly to normalcy in the day of perversion.

The Perverse Scenario: Non-Restricted Marriage

In a world of political correctness, those who dare to call wrong *wrong run the risk of being labeled irrelevant relics of an era gone by.* Although it is conceivable that two people of the same sex can feel affectionate love as well as care for each other deeply, it is perversion, and a diversion from the *Revised Standard, New International, King James,* and *New King James Versions.* A person may have many friends of the same sex, but it is wrong for them to marry. It is right to love your children, but it is wrong to have sex with them. Fathers love their sons and mothers love their daughters, but having sex with them is not an option; it is incest. It is fine for an older man to love his young protégé, but it is wrong for him to engage him in sex as the North American Boy Love Association (NAMBLA) advocates.

> THE FACT IS, NO SOCIETY HAS SURVIVED IN GREATNESS THAT HAS SANCTIONED HOMOSEXUALITY AND SAME-SEX MARRIAGE.

It is right to love your pet dog, but it is wrong to copulate with it. That is bestiality. Seventy-five people may love each other deeply and want to enter into marriage together, but you would need the world's largest box spring and mattress. It is wrong for an adult man to have sex with a 14-year-old girl. Society calls this statutory rape. We are free to yell "Fire!" in a crowded theater, but it is wrong to do so if no fire is present. If society has a right to express what is right on these issues, then it has a right to call right or wrong, based on the inerrant, intransigent, and invariable Word of God, the issue of same-sex marriage. The fact is, no society has survived in greatness that has sanctioned homosexuality and same-sex marriage. Those who do not know history are doomed to repeat it. The licentiation of gay and lesbian couples is confusion, and God is not in it!

The Polyluv Scenario: Multiple Marriages

Marriage may become an institution of polyamory. The gaping hole in the family unit will allow Zach, Sharon, Jeremy, and Elizabeth to marry, if they choose to do so. If gays and lesbians marry, society cannot say no to *groups* of individuals who want to marry. What reason would there be left to restrict marriage to just heterosexual couples?

When the *Titanic* hit the gigantic iceberg in the Atlantic Ocean, no one aboard saw the full destructive force that lay beneath the cold dark waters. The captain, however, ignored six warnings, finally telling the bearer of the bad news to "Shut up!" The original sin of Sodom was *pride,* which goes before destruction (see Prov. 16:18). Gay marriage is just the tip of the iceberg. As marriage is recklessly driven toward the inclusion of same-gender couples, the large, shadowy figures of polyamory and polygamy lurk beneath the surface. They will prove to be even more destructive to the traditional family than the sanctioning of same-sex unions. Polygamy and its close kind of polyamory are waiting to sink marriage to a drowning death with no hope of resuscitation. Great will be the fall of the American home.

Not to be confused with classic polygamy of one man and several wives, polyamory can include many combinations of living arrangements that can be heterosexual, bisexual, gay, or lesbian. These arrangements can be open, or they can be closed to others outside the group. Polyamory is not new and can be traced back to the communes of the 1800's. The modern surge in polyamory began in the mid-90's, aided by the confidentiality of the Internet. It is also reminiscent of the "sexual revolution" of the 60's. Both instances have not been beneficial to women, but have been most beneficial to men, giving them an ample supply of women willing to engage in sexual activity outside of covenantal commitment. Regardless of the origins, polyamory, like polygamy, is lethal for marriage and for society for several reasons.

While some gay marriage advocates disingenuously distance themselves from polyamory, some openly admit that they are related issues. Richard Goldstein writing in the *Village Voice* stated that the fate of gay marriage, polygamy, and polyamory "are entwined in fundamental ways."[16] In 2001 the American Civil Liberties Union (ACLU) came to the aid of Tom Green, who was placed on trial in Utah for openly flaunting his polygamy, thereby violating Utah's "do not ask, do not tell" policy concerning polygamy.

Both will sink marriage into non-monogamy. Anything that says that marriage is not between *one man* and *one woman*, only jeopardizes the monogamy of marriage and thereby puts the institution in danger. Ultimately, marriage will come to mean nothing. With the entrance and exit of so many "marriage" combinations, it will lose its original stance in society. This will ultimately achieve the original goal of gay activists and leftist anarchists—the total abolition of marriage.[17]

Both will roll back women's rights in dignity, self-worth, and individualism. Marriage of today is based on companionate love with the complementation of the opposite sexes at its foundation. It is based on individuals' rights to choose their mates.

An examination of societies where polygamy has been and is practiced, will reveal that the women were and are quite subjugated. These marriages are for the purpose of political and economic alliance among family groups. Women are seen as more of a possession rather than a companion. Even in the polygamy of the Mormons, the desire of men for multiple wives is closely tied to the religious belief of a man's status being elevated in eternity based upon the number of wives he has while living. Here again, we see women as a means to an end and not the end themselves. True to the nature of polygamy, Solomon married many of his wives for political alliances. When David married Michal, Saul's daughter, his political and social statuses were immediately elevated. When marriage is not based on individual choice, men benefit more than women.

Men who tout polyamory say that it frees women from ownership. However, women caught in the trap soon realize that instead of accountability with one man, they are the property of many men with no right to hold any of them accountable. For polygamy and polyamory to work, husbands and wives have to be emotionally distant, and women must have little or no rights. In ancient Israel, for example, a man could divorce his wife, but the wife could not divorce the husband. For polygamy to work, there had to be strict rules of seniority among the wives and rules about the distribution of resources among the women and children. Feelings of romance, by necessity, had to be abated.

Polyamory, as well as polygamy of today, is an attempt to combine the group marriage of the past with the present concept of companionate love. The Mormons of Utah have tried to combine companionate love with polygamy and have not been successful with it. A study of 19th-century divorce rates shows that among polygamists, it was triple the rate of traditional marriages. Utter chaos and confusion will ensue as men and women realize the impossibility of combining these practices with romantic love. As dissolution sets in, these legalized groups will fill the courts squabbling over resources and children as they dissolve these contracts. When the dust settles, the result will be that somebody will have to lose some rights to make these marriage arrangements work. History confirms that it will not be the men. Strict rules concerning seniority and the distribution of resources will be once again implemented, and marriage will be for strategic purposes with romantic love less of a factor. This is repeating history. Unfortunately, it will be impossible to go back to traditional marriage as the norm because generations of children will be indoctrinated with these loose-living lifestyles. Those who are pushing for polygamy and polyamory in the name of "sexual freedom" will in fact have led women down the path of the past.

> *...for love is strong as death; jealousy is cruel as the grave: the coals thereof are coals of fire, which hath a most vehement flame* (Song of Solomon 8:6).

One may ask why it is thought that there will be problems in these sexual arrangements. After all, these are all consenting adults, and no one is defrauded because everything is all in the open. One problem that is rampant in polygamy and polyamory is jealousy. In spite of efforts to control *jealousy*, it is prevalent and an ongoing problem in these sexual arrangements.

When couples delve into polygamy and polyamory, they cannot defy what God has placed inside of them biologically and psychologically. After Haggar conceived by Abraham, the Bible says that she despised Sarah (see Gen. 16:4). Leah tried unsuccessfully to win the affection of her husband through her childbearing. Rachel envied Leah because she gave Jacob sons. These are biblical examples of the jealousy that ensued when more than one woman was involved with a man. What caused them to react this way?

For jealousy is the rage of a man: therefore he will not spare in the day of vengeance (Proverbs 6:34).

Both men and women have a pituitary hormone in the brain called oxytocin that is released during intercourse. Women experience a much greater influence of this hormone than men, even though men are also somewhat affected by it to a lesser degree. It is the same hormone that is released during childbirth and during breastfeeding that bonds the mother and the child. This is why a woman can become bonded when she has sex with a man and the man is less likely to bond based on physical encounters. Paul said in First Corinthians 6:16, "*What? know ye not that he which is joined to an harlot is one body? for two, saith he, shall be one flesh.*" It is for reasons beyond the natural ability to control that men and women become jealous in these relationships that ultimately fall apart, pulling apart the lives of the men, women, and children involved in them.

Notice that Hagar came out on the short end as Abraham reinforced Sarah over her. He said to Sarah that she could treat Hagar the way she wanted (see Gen. 16:6). Although he was having a child with Hagar, Abraham had to distance himself emotionally from her in order to maintain peace in his home. Jacob was driven to the point of frustration with the infighting between Rachel and Leah, his two wives. At its most intense point, Jacob asked Rachel if she thought he was God who could keep her from having children (see Gen. 30:1-2). Many women will be highly dissatisfied as they are lured into polyamory and polygamy. *Same-sex marriage must not be allowed to open the door to this.* Rather than looking at polyamory and polygamy as the culprit in their failure, society will begin to look at marriage itself as the blame for their failed polyluv experiments. This could result in the abolishment of marriage altogether.

However, it is not the institution of marriage that is at fault. The greatest fulfillment in marriage is shown between one man and one woman. We hear nothing of Abigail or Michal after David sets his affections on another woman named Bathsheba. The Song of Solomon, a song of eros love, with theological allegory, was about one woman and not the thousand wives whom Solomon married. Abraham, though he had a child with Hagar, loved Sarah. Isaac loved Rebekah, and Jacob loved only Rachel in spite of the fact that he had many children with Leah. True romantic bonding can only occur between one man and one woman. It occurs with a wife for life and a husband with whom a woman can always stand.

The abolishment of traditional marriage, and the participation in polyamory in the name of sexual freedom for women, resembles the same old tired line that satan has been giving women since the Garden of Eden. Unfortunately, women are still biting the bait. Satan painted a picture to Eve that she could be something that she already was and that she would obtain what she already had. He told her that she would be like God. The truth is that she already was created in the image of God (see Gen. 1:27), and made a little lower than the angels (see Ps. 8:5).

"Poly arrangements" promise a certain dignity and control which is supposed to result from "sexual freedom." The truth is that women of today already have unprecedented freedoms and rights in society that originated in the life and ministry of Jesus Christ. Prior to Jesus, women in Jewish and other ancient cultures had little or no rights. Their role was that of mother and nurturer. An often recited rabbinic prayer stated, "Praise be to God that he has not created me a gentile; a woman; an ignorant man."[18]

Jesus was the consummate revolutionary. He elevated the status of women and spoke positively about them. Jesus had such an impact on the status of women that the writers of the Gospels portrayed this in spite of the cultural context that they found themselves living in.[19] Women were consistently portrayed in the Synoptic Gospels as followers of Jesus (see Mk. 15:40-41; Lk. 8:1-3; Mt. 27:55-56). We see Jesus going to the house of Martha, not the house of Lazarus. Women were strictly forbidden to study with a rabbi.[20] Yet, Jesus allowed Mary to take the role that was given to men. She sat at the feet of Jesus, the traditional posture a disciple takes "sitting at the feet" to study with a rabbi. Jesus' words approved of this (see Lk. 10:42). By doing so, He showcased women's capabilities beyond domestic service and hospitality.[21] On more than one occasion, Jesus used women in His parables. The mere fact that Jesus acknowledged women when portraying the nature of God and the Kingdom of God elevated them. Jesus conversed with the woman at the well (see Jn. 4:4-30), and did not rebuke the woman with the issue of blood when she touched Him (see Lk. 8:40-48). It was women who first told of the resurrection.

After Jesus and the onset of Christianity, women did not suddenly go out to get 9-to-5 jobs. Rather, He elevated their status, showing that in addition to motherhood and servanthood, women could be respected as viable members of society capable of contributing more to the community of believers. Jesus Christ paved the way for the rights and freedom that women in free societies partake of today. It is a status that has evolved over millennia through the spread and influence of Christianity.

Same-sex marriage does just the opposite for women. It opens the door for other "marriage" arrangements, which will eventually lead women backward rather than forward. It will lead women to dispossess what they already possess. It will lead to judging women by the content of their body parts rather than the content of their character. When men are afforded a virtual female smorgasbord in polygamy and polyamory, the need to get to know one woman on a deeply personal level will be wiped out of the equation of interaction between the sexes.

Those women who honestly tell about their experiences in polyamorous arrangements speak of being devalued by the men. One lifetime polyamorist writes of being passed back and forth between the men in the group as "sexual chattel."[22] She further states that these practices are "the norm and not the exception" in polyamorous groups.[23] She astutely notes that it is men who are the most vocal for the supposed sexual freedom of women through promiscuous polyamory and polygamy. Yet few if any of these men are seen at a protest for women's rights. Few have actually jeopardized their bodies or their safety for women's issues.[24] Few if any homosexual men protest for women's rights. Ironically, in her article, she comes back to the conclusion that it is best for her to give herself to one man.

True freedom for women, for the homosexual as well as for all peoples, is found in Jesus Christ. He touched the untouchable. He spoke to the shamed and the shunned (women and men). He jeopardized His safety, His reputation, and His life when He acknowledged the women who followed and reached out to Him. For all peoples, all roads lead to Christ and it is through Christ alone that respect for marriage will be *resurrected*. It is through Jesus Christ alone that this onslaught against the home, against women, against children, and against society can be *corrected*.

The Paradigm Scenario: Holy Marriage

Throughout the entire holy writ, there are examples of the God-ordained paradigm of family, marriage, and sexuality. Nowhere in Scripture does God leave a paradigm for a man and man or a woman and a woman to marry. There was real opportunity for Him to do so. An all-knowing, all-wise God, who knows the beginning from the end, and who is the Alpha and the Omega, knew that gay and lesbian couples would seek divine sanction of their unions. To the Omniscient One, this 21st-century debate is not a surprise! Had He intended such scenarios, surely a loving God who is accused of creating people with their purported pre-wired sexual preference would have left some example of same-sex marriage.

Without a model for same-sex union in the Scriptures, gays and lesbians are left naked and exposed, forced to chop down the fruitful vine to find a covering that will convince society to fully accept their practices. They have covered themselves with the fig leaves of dead works (see Heb. 6:1-2).

The reality is that despite the formality of the marriage rite, there will never be covering without covenant. Holy matrimony is not merely a "contract or a conscious decision," but it is a covenant between God, a man, and a woman. The mariage covenant takes three. The whole biblical account is based on covenant with marriage as one of several of its sub-illustrations. God is a covenant-making, covenant-revealing, and a covenant-keeping God.

> HOLY MATRIMONY IS NOT MERELY A "CONTRACT OR A CONSCIOUS DECISION," BUT IT IS A COVENANT BETWEEN GOD, A MAN, AND A WOMAN.

God so honors covenant that even at the breaking of His heart by Adam and Eve, He did not separate their hearts from each other. At that moment and juncture in time, God could have justifiably (according to human-centered justice) abolished heterosexual union and produced a new model for marriage that allowed homosexuality. Yet in such a perilous time, a turning point in human existence, God did not create a new order for covenantal relationship. He honored the paradigm, and He kept the man and the woman together, even as paradise began to fall apart.

God did not separate the two who had become one flesh. Neither did He change to a "Plan B" that included a "homosexual exception clause." Adam said of Eve after God brought them together in Genesis 2:23, *"This is now bone of my bones, and flesh of my flesh: she shall be called Woman, because she was taken out of Man."* This was a covenantal declaration by Adam. Even after His rendered judgment, the heavenly Father still referred to Adam and Eve as husband and wife (see Gen. 3:16-17). From this picture of marriage established in Genesis, we have a pattern that continues to stand today. In all 66 Books of the Bible, the heterosexual paradigm continues throughout. Not one time is homosexual marriage referenced or modeled. There is no evidence of it, and therefore there is no consideration.

The Bible does not paint only a completely rosy picture of marriage. It also shows many challenges to the marriage covenant, just as there are similar challenges today. However, failure or the faults associated with the institution of marriage itself is not God's fault. The fault is with the fallible beings who are participants in this divine paradigm. The Bible admonishes believers in Christ to be perfect. This simply means that we are to strive or move on in the direction of maturity, not infallibility. Among other things, Christians are to strive for maturity in marriage. The high divorce rate in traditional marriage is even found in so-called Christian ones. However, that does not mean that we should abolish marriage as we know it and as it has always been known. Certainly, the introduction of same-sex marriage will in no way help traditional marriage. That is like rubbing salt in a bleeding wound, thinking that it will somehow bring comfort and healing.

> THE IDEAL MARRIAGE IS THAT MAN TAKES A WIFE FOR LIFE...IT IS PARADISE, NOT PRISON. IT IS SANCTIONED SEX, NOT SAME SEX.

It is not enough to stop the bleeding of this wound. We have to seek the total healing and restoration from the scars of cynicism toward marriage. Here is a thought: In addition to answering this revolutionary offensive against marriage and the traditional marriage with a constitutional amendment; America, with the "oil and wine" Church leading the way, should lead a counterrevolution to strengthen marriages and the traditional family. Every informed citizen is aware of the statistics showing the lack of longevity for today's marriages. The "oil and wine" Church should seek to create and maintain existing initiatives that offer premarital counseling to couples that help them deal with and face the preexisting baggage that couples take into marriage. Postmarital services could be implemented to help equip couples to deal with the stresses that arise in marriage. Everyone in society, regardless of what religious affiliation or nonparticipation in religion, has a vested interest in the success of stable heterosexual homes.

God's idea of marriage is ideal marriage. It cannot be improved upon. The ideal marriage is that a man takes a wife for life. It is a lifetime commitment and not a life-term sentence. It is paradise, not prison. It is sanctioned sex, not same sex. It is holy, not holey. It is blessed and not cursed. It is God's will, and not the result of the breakup of Jack and Jill who took a spill while falling down life's hill. Jack did not get up looking for Zach, and Jill did not get up trying to chill with Lil.

—THE CEREMONY—

The marriage ceremony is one of the most powerful things to observe and participate in. I have had the opportunity to participate as the groom to my bride as well as facilitate and minister in hundreds of weddings. Marriage is the beginning of the completion of the human cycle. It is the first key in the fulfillment of reproduction with blessing. It is the awesome climax of a loving commitment between attracting opposites and singular representatives of separate genders. In the presence of family, friends, and Almighty God, that a man and a woman exchange vows and enter into covenant to one another. When the officiating minister says, "By the power invested in me and by Almighty God," at that moment everyone realizes that all of society and Heaven is standing in witness and shouting a resounding, Amen!

Marriage is sanctioned by the State, which is comprised of its individual residents. Therefore, all of society witnesses the legalization and loveliness of heterosexual marriage. When the minister asks, "Who gives this woman in marriage?" it is not only her father, but all of unseen society, who gives her to be wed to her husband. When the preacher pronounces them husband and wife, he is backed by all the witness of the history of human society. When the minister performs the vows, all of society is there saying the words with him. When the minister administers communion, all the hosts of Heaven rejoice at the commencement of the covenant and the pronouncement of the nuptial couple. Marriage is more than just between a man and a woman. It is a threefold cord that shall not easily be broken. It is the commencement of covenant with the witness of society and the approval of the heavenly cloud of witnesses.

No one is neutral on the same-sex marriage issue. If legalized, all men and women in America will stand with every gay couple as state-sanctioned witnesses giving a stamp of approval. As the legislative branch of government decrees and the judiciary branches declare, Americans must agree by compliance with its laws. The "oil and wine" Church will lose the right to righteous indignation over same-sex marriage if it sits and does nothing to preserve traditional marriage. The 2004 Janet Jackson "wardrobe malfunction" will become a regular function of the airways, with mothers and fathers losing the right to complain to any governmental authorities. Televised homosexual weddings will occur regularly with the implied consent for young ones to consider homosexuality. As America goes, so goes its children.

The story is told that some years ago a guide in the Himalayan mountains of Nepal was asked why he risked his life to continue to take individuals to the mountain's summit? He replied, "It is obvious from your question that you have never been to the top!"

Dr. Martin Luther King spoke prophetically of going to the mountaintop on the eve of his assassination. From his pinnacled perspective, he saw beyond the mere present-time circumstances. He saw the end result of his dream. He saw tomorrow, which is today's generation. Today is the tomorrow that was talked about yesterday. The Church sometimes lives so far in the past that the future is gone by the time it gets there. The past should serve as a platform diving board, not a hammock tied between two trees. We cannot acquiesce our apostolic position in fear of the *homophobic* label. The "oil and wine" Church is more than able to live up to its call to be a courageous body that uncompromisingly confronts the issue of gay unions, with *gracious Truth*, and not with rough hate rhetoric. In short, the Church's angle is the agape angle. *There is nothing homophobic about agape love.* Agape love is indeed tough and tenacious, yet tender and unrelenting in its stance. It reaches the hard to reach, by staring in the face of fear, hate, and pain with the flaming eyes of fire of the Lord Jesus Christ (see Rev. 19:12).

As saints of the Most High, the challenge is to live in two worlds while truly existing in one. Jesus said that His followers are in the world, but not of the world (see Jn. 17:14-15). While we descend in love to live in this world below, we take our cues from the world above. We are not to adopt, or accept, or acquiesce to the reasoning of the world. We see farther from the mountaintop. Like Moses, we have to go to the mountaintop to avoid being overtaken by the rise-up-and-play mentality (see Ex. 32:6). Therefore, our answers to the questions surrounding gay and lesbian marriage come not from the world system of logical thought. Worldly thought results in homogenitality, sexuality, reality, eroticism, and phobia. The direction that the Church's moral compass always points is *heavenward.* It is time to go to the top. The view up there is a God's-eye view.

> *Let the words of my mouth, and the meditation of my heart, be accept-*
> *able in Thy sight, O Lord, my strength, and my redeemer* (Psalm
> 19:14, emphasis added).

344

*For the Lord thy God walketh in the midst of thy camp, to deliver thee, and to give up thine enemies before thee; therefore shall thy camp be holy: that He see no unclean thing in thee, and **turn away** from thee* (Deuteronomy 23:14, emphasis added).

A God's-eye view of gay and lesbian marriage is radical and not relative. The Israelites lived in a camp set apart from the peoples around them. Homosexuality existed among the Canaanites that the Israelites disposed, but it was not to be named among His chosen people. The "oil and wine" Church is to live in principle, set apart from the world we live in. Sinful practices such as homosexuality should not be named among us. Sin repels the presence of God. When His power is not present, His approval is absent too.

Though He is aware of it, He does not view same-sex marriage at all, because He does not look upon that which is not holy. He turns His head to those who propagate apostasy in His holy and righteous name. While men are even considering the allowance of gay marriage (an oxymoron), God is not. He does not mention same-sex marriage in His Word, simply because He does not bring it before His sight. Deuteronomy 23:14 speaks of a pre-condition for His presence. If it was not met by the children of Israel, God turned His face from them. With His face comes His countenance and His eyes. God does not see same-sex marriage; therefore, He does not bless it.

—MARRIAGE AND MANIFEST GLORY—

And the third day there was a marriage in Cana of Galilee; and the mother of Jesus was there: and both Jesus was called, and His disciples, to the marriage....This beginning of miracles did Jesus in Cana of Galilee, and manifested forth His glory; and His disciples believed on Him (John 2:1,11).

A God's-eye view of gay and lesbian marriage can be summed up in the actions of Jesus. He went to the wedding in Cana.

It was at the Cana wedding that Jesus first began to show His glory. We find the wine along with water. Jesus turned the water into wine. Water sustains life and in that ancient culture, wine enhanced life. Wine is a type, a symbol of blessing. The "oil and wine" Church is needed to show forth the glory of God to this generation. Not only did Jesus bless the man and the woman, the bride and the groom, with His attendance, but God through His Son sanctioned their heterosexual marriage throughout the generations. The very fact that Jesus went to the wedding sharply contrasts with the words of Paul in Second Timothy 3:1-5:

This know also, that in the last days perilous times shall come. For men shall be lovers of their own selves, covetous, boasters, proud, blasphemers, disobedient to parents, unthankful, unholy, without natural affection, trucebreakers, false accusers, incontinent, fierce, despisers of those that are good, traitors, heady, highminded, lovers of pleasures more than lovers of God; having a form of godliness, but denying the power thereof: from such turn away (emphasis added).

Paul admonishes the reader to *turn away* from that which is unholy. Deuteronomy 23:14 tells us that God *turns away* from that which is unholy. God does not view same-sex marriage at all. It is not the Father's will that any should perish, but that all should come to repentance. Therefore, He looks past it, never ceasing to woo the gay and lesbian persons' hearts to return to His created purpose and perfect will for them. One of the holiest moments in wedding ceremonies is when communion is given to the bride and the groom. It signifies that it takes the divine sanction to make marriage successful. This is made possible by the Lord's sanctioning of the wedding in Cana, which was where He first *"manifested forth His glory"* (Jn. 2:11). His presence in godly unions blesses them and makes them stronger. God will not look upon same-sex unions because it is a direct defiance of His divine decree. It is the embodiment of error. Same-sex marriage mocks God and attempts to make God look like He is oblivious to its occurrence. God placed man's iniquity upon Jesus, causing Him to cry out, *"My God, My God, why hast Thou forsaken Me?"* (Mt. 27:46b) If God forsook His only begotten Son on the cross because He could not look upon the sin that Jesus had literally become, He will not grace same-sex unions with even a cursory glance.

> SAME-SEX MARRIAGE MOCKS GOD AND ATTEMPTS TO MAKE GOD LOOK LIKE HE IS OBLIVIOUS TO ITS OCCURRENCE.

A God's-eye view of gay and lesbian marriage is a heart-to-heart affair. While His very nature does not allow Him to acknowledge the union, His grace continues to reach out to the hearts of those who feel in their hearts they are doing the right thing. God's grace is His ability in our situations. One who is entangled in homosexuality cannot set himself free. With God's grace and with His ability, all things are possible. It is only by His mercy that none of us receives His judgment that we deserve. His goodness and His mercy continue to pursue homosexuals even in their attempt to violate the marriage covenant.

A God's-eye view of gay and lesbian marriage is present in light of the examples of His view of heterosexual marriage. Sacred Scripture abounds with ecclesiastical exhortation concerning the holy ordinance that abounds with divine blessing (see Eph. 5; Col. 3).

The evidence is clear and the proof is there. God does not have a favorable view of gay and lesbian marriage, and therefore, does not voice sanction of it. It is God who joins heterosexual marriage, and the "oil and wine" Church is to be on the vanguard to assure that no man puts it asunder.

> *Wherefore they are no more twain, but one flesh. What therefore God hath joined together, let not man put asunder* (Matthew 19:6; see also verses 3-5).

It is presumptuously arrogant for man to think that he knows better than the Creator. St. Paul had this in mind when he declared, *"Professing themselves to be wise, they became fools"* (Rom. 1:22).

The Powerful Scenario: Reinforcing Marriage

What will stabilize the Body of Christ as it navigates waters muddied by truth mixed with half-truths, a.k.a. lies, construed to seem like *the* Truth? Succinctly stated, it is the power of Truth. Truth is a person and that person is Christ. Christ is the all-powerful Truth who is made unto us in the wisdom of God (see 1 Cor. 1:24). The answer lies in searching the Scriptures, the *holy inerrant Word of God*. In it, we find definitive answers and *absolute* Truth, rooted in God, the Father who is Truth and mercy, just and righteous, holy and wise. God's Word is the principle element that stabilizes the Church in the midst of heart-jolting, bombarding blows to its Christ-centered worldview. In these *perilous* times, the Word of God is the *naked truth that now must be told*. It is the truth that enables the Church to be instrumental in stopping the fray of society's moral fabric. The Word of God is the guidepost.

The Prayerful Scenario: Fighting for Marriage

A war has not breached the shores and borders of America since the mid-1800's. However, America is subject to a daily spiritual warfare on a level that is not necessarily seen with the naked eye. America is in a battle for her soul. The Church in America has historically played an important role in defining the direction of this great nation. Throughout our history, our nation has been directed by men and women of the monotheistic Christian faith. It is time for the "oil and wine" Church to remain constant in its course. What has been effective in America's past will surely prove to continue its future success. The war is not a fleshly one, but a spiritual one, repairing a prayer shield of faith.

> For though we walk in the flesh, we do not war after the flesh: (for the weapons of our warfare are not carnal, but mighty through God to the pulling down of strong holds (2 Corinthians 10:3-4).

The same-sex marriage controversy will not simply be favorably settled in the court of public opinion, nor in the courts of this land. Rather it is that tried, true, and tested medium of prayer that releases God's will to be done in this nation as it is done in Heaven. Prayer is the master key which locks out the devastatingly destructive force of same-sex marriage. Prayer is the combination that unlocks a stable future for this nation. Prayer is the code that the devil cannot decode. Prayer is the secret weapon that releases the ability of the Almighty God to openly reveal His power on earth.

> Who hath heard such a thing? who hath seen such things? Shall the earth be made to bring forth in one day? or shall a nation be born at once? for as soon as Zion travailed, she brought forth her children (Isaiah 66:8, emphasis added).

As traditional marriage is seemingly being flung into deep waters of aversion with submersion seeming inevitable, the "oil and wine" Church has two choices: Either it can sink or swim, or it can watch and pray. To do nothing means an imminent and impending demise of the family and of this country.

The first choice seems like an expeditious action, but how can one traverse an ocean with human effort alone? Same-sex marriage is truly a wide and endless expanse. To attempt to swim its muddied waters means to eventually sink. It is not by might, nor by power, but by the Spirit of God that the tide of this debate will be turned. Rather than utilizing human effort and reason alone, we are to pray, or else the family will surely sink. No one has enough intellect, intelligence, mastery of words, or debate in himself to fight this battle from the humanistic ideology.

> And he said, Hearken ye, all Judah, and ye inhabitants of Jerusalem, and thou king Jehoshaphat, Thus saith the Lord unto you, Be not afraid nor dismayed by reason of this great multitude; for the battle is not yours, but God's (2 Chronicles 20:15).

This clarion call to fall on our knees is a summons to be informed concerning the assault of same-sex marriage. King Jehoshaphat and Judah seemed powerless against Moab and Ammon who gathered themselves together to attack the Israelites (see 2 Chron. 20:1-25). The king of Judah went before the Lord once he knew who the enemy was and where they were located (see 2 Chron. 20:1-4).

Prayer is not like shooting randomly in the dark or discharging a shotgun in an open field. Instead, effectual and fervent prayer on the highest level is pointedly strategic. Knowing the Word of God, being discerning listeners and discriminating readers will enable the "oil and wine" Church to pray with precision. True prayer engages the spirit and body while not ignoring the soul. The intensity of prayer is what can rescue this nation in one day from the hijacking homosexual activists' agenda for America. Out of Jehoshaphat's and Judah's intense and informed prayer before God, came a strategy to defeat their enemies. Prayer changes things. Prayer also changes people. There is no substitute for "knee-ology." It is indeed prayer time in America.

The Proactive Scenario: Weighing Marriage

Same-sex marriage is weighed in the balance with the proactive biblical account and is found...well, it is just not found in the Bible. There is nowhere that we find that God views, acknowledges, blesses, or sanctions same-sex unions. Instead, we see countless affirmations of heterosexual marriage. We see Isaac sporting with his wife, Rebekah (see Gen. 26:8). We have the entire Book of the Song of Solomon depicting a male and female expressing their love for each other, which typifies what the Body of Christ as the Bride of Christ should feel for Christ the Bridegroom. We see Jacob working a total of 14 years to marry Rachel, the woman he loved (see Gen. 29:20). We see Noah, his wife, his sons and their wives, all heterosexual couples, going into the ark with Noah (see Gen. 7:7).

Aside from the Genesis account of a union between a man and a woman, there were other opportunities for God to give the world a model of same-sex unions. As a Book of the Truth, the Bible plainly shows fallible beings failing in the area of their sexuality and in marriage as previously mentioned. The account of David and Bathsheba is a case in point. David committed adultery with Bathsheba and essentially ordered the execution of her husband. After David sincerely repented, rather than abolish opposite gender marriage, God even blessed the seed of their union. I repeat, there are no examples of same-sex marriage in the Bible. God so honors covenantal union between male and female that He never referred to Bathsheba as David's wife. In every subsequent reference to Bathsheba, she is always referred to as the wife of Uriah. However, in His mercy, it is in the lineage of this woman, the mother of Solomon, Israel's wisest being, that the Messiah was born.

The Confusing Apostasy: In Conclusion A God's-Eye View of Gay and Lesbian Marriage

Confusion is the diametric opposite of peace. *A God's-eye view of gay and lesbian marriage* begins with a reverent view of God and ends with a holy view of the institution. The constitution of marriage between a man and a woman is the only model that is in the scope of the blessing of the heavenly Father. Solomon stated it succinctly:

> *The thing that hath been, it is that which shall be; and that which is done is that which shall be done: and there is no new thing under the sun* (Ecclesiastes 1:9).

Marriage as it has been is the way that it will always be. The way that it was ordained by the creation of Adam and Eve is the way that it shall always be done. There is no new marriage paradigm under the sun that God views as holy and acceptable in His sight. Of course, the imagination of man's mind is endless. It stands to reason that if the "Causation Argument" is *accepted* and the "Christological Apologetic" *rejected*, then the "Confusing Apostasy" will be *elected*. Considering the "Consequential Alternative" or "Compassionate Approach," the "oil and wine" Church must be the "Church in Accord" in order to deal with the "Committed Activism" of the "Confusing Apostasy." In Noah's day, the *imaginations* of man's mind became warped, and judgment was the result. Secular writers have also spoken to the powerful effect of imagination and its role in sexual bonding.

> The deception is incredibly effective because of the power of sexual bonding. One genuinely feels release, belonging and covering. The warm, sensual acceptance of a lover seems to melt away decades of loneliness and alienation. The enemy knows the yearning and its seeming release. He knows the power of homosexual communion. And he will employ its sensual and emotional returns to deceive us mightily. Many solid Christians have rejected orthodox Christianity due to homosexual unions or, worse, have tried to conform orthodoxy to their deceived status.

Once their wills are yielded to the sin, they submit their souls and spirits to the ravages of the evil one.[25]

King Solomon said in Ecclesiastes 12:13, *"Let us hear the conclusion of the whole matter: Fear God, and keep His commandments: for this is the whole duty of man"* (emphasis added). The conclusion of the matter is that the inclusion of same-sex marriage should be treated as an exclusion. Though at the present time legalization, licentiation, and legitimacy is sought, same-sex marriage is not to be found in Scripture. Therefore, it should not be sanctioned in society. It should be considered illegitimate, illegal, and invalid. To proceed in it is equivalent to, at worse, driving under the influence of *another spirit,* or at the least, driving without the license of the *Holy Spirit.* The hijacking of the holy institution will result in the decimation of the foundation of the family as we know it and the society as we have known it. It is improper to liken the gay rights movement to the civil rights movement. Marriage between the same sexes will never be right even if society grants the right. Everyone has a right to be wrong, but in this instance, it is wrong to call gay marriage right. Children are born through the biological means of males and females interacting through intimate intercourse. Artificial insemination is the exception, but male/female participation is the rule. Children are not made in monogamous relationships of male and male. They are not fertilized in female/female factories. The divine design has determined that the XY chromosome requires the XX chromosome to make a duplicate human being. Those who disagree with divine design are powerless to alter it. Their arms are too short to box with God. The generation that is raised by two daddies, two mommies, promiscuous partners, and polymorous sleepovers will rise in judgment against their progenitors. Mr. Frank and Mr. Stein will have to deal with the "Frankenstein" they produce. Ms. god and Ms. Zilla will have to deal with the "Godzilla" they produce. *Children evolve into the image they see.* You cannot contradict the chromosomal composition and avoid incontrovertible consequences. Once marriage, a proverbial Humpty Dumpty, has fallen off the wall of the Word of God, it will be impossible to put it back together again. Children need marriage models more than they need confused critics. We owe it to "destiny's child" to preserve the hope of "legacy's child." This can only be done by the children of "accuracy."

The predictive, problematic, probable, prophetic, powerful paradigm and proactive scenarios do not favor the aberration of the institution of heterosexual marriage. The debate concerning polygamy and polyamory was decided over a hundred years ago. Why should we reopen the case? The presence of polyamory is *daunting* and *haunting.* The perversion is *taunting.* Same-sex marriage is a Pandora's Box that is best kept closed—because once it is opened, it will be much worse than a proverbial can of worms. It will extend an open-end lease to the gay serpent, and it will eradicate his eviction from *better homes and gardens* (see Gen. 3:14-15). It will produce a cataclysmic catastrophe upon the continental shores of our country and cause a ripple effect throughout civilized continents and their countries. It will precipitate the "beginning of the end" of America's prominence and guarantee the demise of its glorious greatness. Surely the blood of our ancestors and forefathers who gallantly gave their lives declaring, "Give me liberty or give me death," will cry from the ground saying, "*use not liberty for an occasion to the flesh...*" (Gal. 5:13b). Our leadership among the nations will be lost and the accusations of the degradation of the West will become self-fulfilling prophecies. To vote yes on this issue is to vote for the future confiscation of mankind's created purpose.

The prophetic prognostication is that even if a constitutional amendment forbids legalization of same-sex mariage, it will not stop the same-sex activists, just as blindness did not stop the demonically-crazed Sodomites. They persisted in seeking to tear down Lot's angelically shut, dead-bolted door. The forbidden fruit holds a master-servant appeal. It will not be satiated even if legalized. It will continue to slither into the corridors of government assemblies, the walls and halls of the school system, onto the pages of the educational curricula, and even into institutions of faith, until it has eroded the foundation of all that is akin to the righteousness of God. You cannot legislate legitimacy, nor can you license lust that burns toward another of the same sex. It is still true that: "*Righteousness exalteth a nation: but sin is a reproach to any people*" (Prov. 14:34). It is true that "*the wicked* [will] *return to the grace, all the nations that forget God*" (Ps. 9:17). "*If* [God's] *people, which are called by* [His] *name, shall humble themselves, and pray, and seek* [His] *face, and turn from their wicked ways; then will* [He] *hear from heaven, and will forgive their sin, and will heal their land*" (2 Chron. 7:14).

God's way is the *true way*. God's way is the *only way*. God's *way* is the *only true way*. Therefore, we must shun the *way* that seems right but in reality is the way of death (see Prov. 14:12). Jesus is *the* way, *the* truth, and *the* life; not *a* way, *a* truth and *a* life (see Jn. 14:6). The Almighty offers no alternative ways, but only absolute ones. The "oil and wine" Church must embrace the *resolution* of *absolution* and not suffer the *dissolution* of the transfusion concerning holy matrimony. A God's-eye view of gay and lesbian marriage is that He loves the homosexual, but He loathes same-sex marriage. We must join with the Psalmist declaring, "*Let God arise, let His enemies be scattered...*" (Ps. 68:1) "*...let God be true, but every man a liar...*" (Rom. 3:4). If these words have seemed hard, harsh, hurtful, or homophobic, I sincerely seek the forgiveness of any who have received anything less than the gracious love of God. If these words seem too weak and hesitant to be candid in Christ-like concern, I beg God's forgiveness. May the Lord add many blessings to the reading of His word, as we take up *The Combative Appeal: Evicting the Gay Serpent From God's Garden.*

Prayer: Eternal and All-Wise God of Infinite Wisdom; God whose right and divine decree beggars no disagreement, views no dissent, nor voices any defamation. Look upon the unsavory stench of same-sex marriage and breathe the congealing wind of wisdom. Stop it as it threatens to impede the progress of those who are crossing over to the other side of the Promised Land. Send a healing of hurting hearts that have been welded together in unnatural affection. Bring them into wholeness, we pray. Restore our nation to righteousness. In the name of the Righteous and Holy One, Amen!

ENDNOTES

1. James R.White and Jeffrey D. Neill, *The Same Sex Controversy* (Minneapolis: Bethany House Publishers, 2002), 16.

2. Timothy J. Dailey, *Dark Obsession* (Nashville, TN: Broadman & Holman, 2003), 81.

3. G. E. Veith quoting Star Parker in *World Magazine* (July 24, 2004), 25.

4. Andrew Sullivan, editor, *Same-Sex Marriage: Pro & Con* (New York: Vintage Books, 2004), 141.

5. Dailey, *Dark Obsession*, 3.

6. Dr. Elizabeth Moberly as quoted by Francis MacNutt, *Homosexuality: Can It Be Healed* (Jacksonville: Christian Healing Ministries, Inc., 2001), 45.

7. Sullivan, *Same-Sex Marriage*, 342-343.

8. Dr. James Dobson, *Marriage Under Fire: Why We Must Win This Battle* (Sisters, OR: Multnomah Publishers, 2004), 96.

9. Sullivan, *Same-Sex Marriage*, 250.

10. As stated by Dobson, *Marriage Under Fire*, 54.

11. Eric Marcus, *Is It a Choice?* (New York: Harper/Collins, 1999), 24.

12. Charles Colson, *Do I Have to Join a Church?* http://jmm.aaa.net.au/articles/9668.htm.

13. Sullivan, *Same-Sex Marriage*, 141.

14. Edythe Draper, *Draper's Book of Quotations for the Christian World* (Wheaton, IL: Tyndale House Publishers, Inc., 1992), Entry 1428, Bible Illustrator 3.0 for Windows, Parsons Technology, Inc. 1990-1998, Illustrations Copyrighted at Christianity Today, Inc., 1984-1995, Faircom Corp.

15. Dobson, *Marriage Under Fire*, 47.

16. Richard Goldstein "*Love That Dare Not,*" *Village Voice* (June 5, 2001), Vol. 46, Iss. 22; p. 41.

17. Dobson, *Marriage Under Fire,* 52-53.

18. Quoted in Leonard Swidler, *Biblical Affirmations of Woman* (Philadelphia, PA: Westminster Press, 1979), 155.

19. Barbara J. MacHaffie, *Her Story: Women in Christian Tradition* (Philadelphia, PA: Fortress Press, 1986), 15.

20. Ibid., 15.

21. Ibid., 15.

22. Kimberly Kreutzer, "Polyamory on the Left: Liberatory or Predatory?" *Off Our Backs* (May-Jun 2004), 40.

23. Ibid., 41.

24. Ibid., 41.

25. Andrew Comiskey, 103.

CHAPTER
TEN

To attribute homosexuality solely to a demonic spirit of homosexuality and try to cast it out is as silly as trying to cast out someone's legitimate hunger for gender affirmation, parental love and peer acceptance.[1]

Briar Whitehead

...I have encountered a "spirit of homosexuality" in some homosexuals and they were not free until it was cast out. In saying this, I am not making homosexual activity into a different dimension than the problems heterosexuals experience...Just as some heterosexuals may need deliverance from spirits that drive them toward promiscuous sexual activity, so apparently some homosexuals can benefit from deliverance prayer.[2]

Francis McNutt

...My experience, as well as my understanding of the Bible, has led me to believe not only in the reality of the demonic realm, but also in how commonly these evil spirits influence or control people's lives.[3]

Francis McNutt

Demon influence, at least in its milder forms, is extremely common among the regenerate, not to mention its all but universal prevalence among the unsaved (Ephesians 2:1-2; 2 Corinthians 4:3-4). In an age of increasing moral laxity and spiritual lawlessness, the more serious forms of demon influence are becoming more prevalent among Christian people.[4]

Dr. Merrill F. Unger

The Combative Appeal:
Evicting the Gay Serpent
From God's Garden

Awake, awake, O Zion, clothe yourself with strength. Put on your garments of splendor, O Jerusalem, the holy city. The uncircumcised and defiled will not enter you again. Shake off your dust; rise up, sit enthroned, O Jerusalem. Free yourself from the chains on your neck, O captive Daughter of Zion (Isaiah 52:1-2 NIV).

The seventy-two returned with joy and said, "Lord, even the demons submit to us in Your name."..."I have given you authority to trample on snakes and scorpions and to overcome all the power of the enemy; nothing will harm you" (Luke 10:17,19 NIV).

Adam and Eve were placed in a paradise called Eden. Some translators say that *Eden* means "a moment in time." Eden was a planted garden. It was a little part of Heaven that had come to earth. When the serpent entered it, he threw it into chaos; and through deception, he devastated the garden of God's creation. He emphasized the negative and imparted his pride on the unsuspecting woman and literally "hissed" her right out of the will of God. From that day to this, every perversion known to man has ensued. Deliverance ministry began in the garden when satan was served an expeditious eviction notice. Times have changed, but the serpent has not.

Some years ago, I was in the state of Connecticut in revival when a young girl of about 16 years of age came to me. One look at her countenance and I knew she was very upset. She began to describe her living conditions. She was an adopted child who felt very unloved in her situation. I ministered and prayed with her. Afterwards I left that state and returned home. A few days later, I received a letter from the same young girl. In the letter, she explained that she had a dream, and in the dream the only thing she saw were snakes coming after her.

I noticed that her handwriting was extremely small, and it leaned toward the left down the entire page. As I looked at her handwriting, it was as if the Holy Spirit gave me insight concerning it. He showed me that this young girl had a very serious complex, and it was evidenced by the size of her handwriting. The fact that it was leaning toward the left indicated that her self-esteem was improper. There were other things that were revealed to me, and I soon responded to her concerning her dream, relating to her the meaning of the snakes in it. Throughout the Scripture, snakes are a metaphor for evil and represent the prince of darkness and his demonic hordes.

> MANY PEOPLE WHO ARE ENGROSSED IN SAME-SEX ATTRACTION ARE BESIEGED WITH A DEMONIC PRESENCE IN THEIR LIFE.

Many people who are engrossed in same-sex attraction are besieged with a demonic presence in their life that makes it extremely difficult for them to truly be free as Jesus promised in John 8:32: *"And ye shall know the truth, and the truth shall make you free."* Dr. Merrill F. Unger writes:

> Demon influence, at least in its milder forms, is extremely common among the regenerate, not to mention its all but universal prevalence among the unsaved (Ephesians 2:1-2; 2 Corinthians 4:3-4). In an age of increasing moral laxity and spiritual lawlessness, the more serious forms of demon influence are becoming more prevalent among Christian people.[5]

Harassment, Influence, and Control

Harassment is what St. Paul referred to as being "buffeted," which means to beat, batter, strike, smash, thrash, hammer, pound, or pummel. At this level, the spirit of homosexuality besieges the individual mind on a continual basis. This is more than just being tempted or suggested to by the devil. It is when the thoughts are constant and transfixed in the mind. It is when the images are mentally bombarding an individual and his will to resist is eventually weakened because he is unable to find the strength to stand against the wiles of the literal demons (see Eph. 6:11).

Influence, otherwise known as oppression, is the second level of demonic infiltration. This is when a person consistently yields to the influence, thus forming a pattern of behavior that is woven into his own behavior. An oppressed person is demonized to the extent that he is weighed down and literally bound by the spiritual influence.

Control, otherwise known as possession, is the graduated state of being bound. Very few people are in this category, but nonetheless it is an occurrence in some homosexuals' lives. It is when an individual's will has been overtaken, and he is literally controlled or piloted by the perverted power on a regular basis.

—THE SERPENT DOES NOT CARE—

Be sober, be vigilant; because your adversary the devil, as a roaring lion, walketh about, seeking whom he may devour (1 Peter 5:8).

The serpent does not care how young or how old you are. He has targeted believers for destruction. He is unfair, ungodly, unrighteous, and an unclean devil. The devil is the DEVIL! He targeted this young girl, and it did not matter to him that she was without her natural parents or family and that she was just a teenager who had not really begun to fully live her life. He targeted her. Many of those who are caught in the vice-grip of homosexuality have yielded so frequently that they have become infiltrated by the "seven worse devils" that Jesus referred to in Matthew 12:45. Although this young girl was not a lesbian, she had been targeted at a young age for very serious lifelong issues. She was an adopted child and the victim of molestation. Often in such cases, the will of the victim develops a predisposition to promiscuity or perverted sexual preferences as a result of the mental onslaught against their person. The serpent is a convicted felon that steals, a convicted murderer that kills, and a convicted arson that destroys (see Jn. 10:10).

—THE SERPENT SELECTS—

When passing through airport security, often a person is subjected to a random search. While passing through life, some are randomly selected by the serpent. It is nothing that they have done or anything that they deserve. Nevertheless, the devil has targeted them. He sees the hand of God upon a person who endearingly and sincerely wants to do God's will, and he randomly searches for an opening of attack.

One of the things I noticed about the young girl in Connecticut was that she had an extremely pleasant personality. She was a fair-skinned African-American, and she lived with a family of dark-skinned people. The children teased her and made fun of her because of her complexion. As a result, she developed a complex. A literal spirit of rejection had entrapped her. Satan does not care what gives him an opening to affect a person's psyche and self-esteem as long as he is able to influence him or her toward his purposes. Ephesians 4:27 states, *"Neither give place to the devil."* Sometimes rejection serves as the root of unnatural affection that manifests in same-sex attraction.

There are a lot of mind-sets that people have developed throughout the years—complexes concerning the color of their skin, the texture of their hair, their lack of reading ability, or any number of things. It may seem to them that when God was passing out gifts and abilities, He just passed them by. There are devils, which are represented in the likeness of snakes, that are all around them, trying to harass, influence, and control them. Demons are disembodied spirits, and they require a body to operate. Jesus said that they "roam," seeking rest. Demons find rest when they inhabit a human being. Homosexuality is often associated with unclean spirits.

> *When the unclean spirit is gone out of a man, he walketh through dry places, seeking rest; and finding none, he saith, I will return unto my house whence I came out* (Luke 11:24).

Be Sober

The apostle Peter said that the demonic powers walketh about to and fro, seeketh whom they may devour (see 1 Pet. 5:8). Demon spirits, which are doomed to hell, are desperate to take people with them. They are determined to conquer confused souls. When the serpent engaged the Master Teacher in the wilderness temptation, he was seeking to harass, influence, and control Him. Jesus resisted the devil, and he departed from Him, but it was just for a season (see Lk. 4:13). The nature of the devil is that he is determined to return.

Some people have had to pass through some very traumatic situations that are difficult to diffuse. The results of these "close encounters of the perverted kind" is that varying degrees of demonic presence may operate in their life. Those who profess Christ as their personal Savior are engaged in a threefold spiritual warfare against the world, the flesh, and the devil. Each of these requires a different course of action. A Christian cannot change the nature of the world; however, he is exhorted not to conform to it, nor let it squeeze him into its mold. To fight effectively, one must be sober, serious, sure, sensitive, sincere, sure-spoken, and safe.

> *And be not conformed to this world: but be ye transformed by the renewing of your mind, that ye may prove what is that good, and acceptable, and perfect, will of God* (Romans 12:2).

Be Serious

You cannot cast out flesh, nor can you crucify demons. You must apply the cross to your flesh and crucify it, reckoning it dead to sin but alive to God. You must cast off and cast out demons. Many who suffer from the "gay serpent" have a rough time just keeping their sanity, let alone keeping themselves sexually free. The devil is there harassing them and causing great turmoil on the unseen realm of their psyche. There is an intense internal struggle that takes place in the soulish, volitional, emotional, and intellectual realms of those struggling with same-sex issues. Satan's nature is parasitic. He loves and longs to gain entrance into a person's internal being where he can work in the darkness, while evading discernment. To cast out a devil(s), it is necessary to operate in discernment. Demons must be identified, and demonic strongholds must be demolished. This is why Jesus asked the demon his name in Mark 5:9, *"And He asked him, What is thy name? And he answered, saying, My name is Legion: for we are many."*

Be Sure

Sometimes...there may be a need for us to pray for deliverance from evil spirits; if these spirits are present and we don't pray deliverance, they will tend to block any change...there are spirits that affect some homosexuals–spirits that title themselves, spirits of "homosexuality," of "lust," of "pornography," of "sadism," of "addiction," and so on.[6]

In dealing with the devil, Jesus first discerned him. The Bible refers to various spirits by name. Isaiah the prophet speaks of the spirit of heaviness: *"...the garment of praise for the spirit of heaviness..."* (Is. 61:3). Another name for this is the spirit of infirmity. *"And, behold, there was a woman which had a spirit of infirmity eighteen years, and was bowed together, and could in no wise lift up herself"* (Lk. 13:11). Demons are capable of all manner of evil, but they will generally concentrate on a particular area of a person's life. The devil specializes in causing seekers of God to become enmeshed in trivial pursuits and spiritual civil war.

Many times the people of God war against one another. They war over doctrine, differences, diversities, and distractions. They war over their biblical perspective concerning the particular influences of darkness. For years, there has been a debate as to whether a Christian can have a devil. It is my judgment that the question is wrongly posed. The question is, "Can a demon have a Christian?" The answer is both yes and no. The believer who is filled with the Holy Spirit cannot be possessed (in the sense of ownership) by the devil, but he/she can be oppressed and harassed. The Holy Spirit inhabits the spirit of a man. The Bible says, *"The spirit of man is the candle of the Lord, searching all the inward parts of the belly"* (Prov. 20:27). The Holy Spirit influences the soul and seeks to bring the body into subjection. The body is the temple of the Holy Spirit. However, many times demon spirits infiltrate the soulish or the physical parts of a person's being. The issues of where the devil is, is not the greatest concern. Getting rid of him is. The question, "Can a Christian have a devil?" is answered yes! A Christian can have as many of them as they would like, or none of them if would not like to. The choice is up to the individual. Dr. Francis McNutt says,

> ...I have encountered a "spirit of homosexuality" in some homosexuals and they were not free until it was cast out. In saying this, I am not making homosexual activity into a different dimension than the problems heterosexuals experience...Just as some heterosexuals may need deliverance from spirits that drive them toward promiscuous sexual activity, so apparently some homosexuals can benefit from deliverance prayer.[7]

Be Sensitive

Deliverance ministry requires sensitivity from insistent souls. A gay or lesbian person, who is wholly given to the lifestyle, is oftentimes the receptacle of a demonic depository and definitely must receive strong deliverance while being sensitively freed from the venomous vice-grip. This is only the starting point. After he has been delivered, he will need to be filled with the Holy Spirit and then learn to walk in the Spirit if he is to remain free. Otherwise, the devil returns to the once cleaned house with even more unclean spirits.

The Church needs to stop its demonic debate and start delivering the demon-infected houses. We should never hate and demean one another because we are never one another's enemies (see Eph. 6:11-12). The devil is our common enemy, and he is the one we should always be warring against. The devil is the accuser of the brethren, so he accuses and deceives; and he keeps believers warring against each other because he is the author of confusion (contrary to fusion). (The vision that was shared in the Foreword expounds upon this concept.)

> *The Spirit of the Lord is upon Me, because He hath anointed Me to preach the gospel to the poor; He hath sent Me to heal the brokenhearted, to preach deliverance to the captives, and recovering of sight to the blind, to set at liberty them that are bruised, to preach the acceptable year of the Lord* (Luke 4:18-19).

When the Church can no longer see the needs of their brethren and can only focus on their faults, their shortcomings, and their captivity, it is guilty of failing to preach deliverance to the captives. Jesus inaugurated His ministry with words of deliverance. The "oil and wine" Church must exercise deliverance to evict the gay serpent from God's garden.

Be Sincere

Those who have denounced deliverance have joined ranks with the enemy. They have lost their sensitivity. Those who speak against gay and lesbian people and their struggles are being used of the enemy. Sometimes demon strongholds are formed by loose lips and the incantation of curses from the so-called saints of God. This is accomplished by what they say and do. The apostle James addresses this by saying, *"And the tongue is a fire, a world of iniquity: so is the tongue among our members, that it defileth the whole body, and setteth on fire the course of nature; and it is set on fire of hell"* (Jas. 3:6). The Scriptures abound with this truth (see Prov. 18:21; Ps. 19:14).

Be Sure-Spoken

> As we respond to that love by pledging our allegiance to the rule of Christ Jesus, we are delivered...emotional and relational healing must occur alongside deliverance...deliverance defined as the power of love purging the power of perversion" frees the struggler all the more to grow in grace and truth.[8]

Andrew Comiskey

To serve the gay serpent an eviction notice, the words of your mouth must be acceptable in God's sight. Constructive words bring life; destructive words bring death. In his book, *The Three Battlegrounds*, Francis Frangipane stated, "Victory begins with the name of Jesus on your lips; but it will not be consummated until the nature of Jesus is in your heart."[9] When God has allowed you to discern the demonic presence in some-

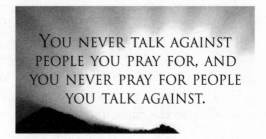

YOU NEVER TALK AGAINST PEOPLE YOU PRAY FOR, AND YOU NEVER PRAY FOR PEOPLE YOU TALK AGAINST.

one's life, you should readily engage in prayer on his or her behalf. God wants His love through you to cover a multitude of faults and sins.

Some sins are easily seen; others are not so easy to see because love never uncovers. God's gracious love never reveals somebody's weakness or shortcomings for the purpose of public berating. Dr. Edwin Louis Cole once said, "You become intimate with the God to whom you pray, and the people for whom and with whom you pray."[10] You never *talk against* people you *pray* for, and you never *pray* for people you *talk against*. You can determine what your feelings are toward someone based upon your prayers concerning them. You would not appreciate someone talking against your child if he was homosexual; and therefore, you should not talk against anyone else's child either. Judgment always recoils on the head of those who judge self-righteously (see Mt. 7:1-2). The gay and lesbian person in your life is placed there for a reason. The believer is exhorted to stand in the gap and intercede on his behalf. This will weaken his resolve to remain that way, as well as weaken his resistance to the witness of the gospel. True love thinks no evil and deliverance can only be wrought by those who truly work with the ministry of love. The path to a person's deliverance is pursued by another person speaking their name in intercession.

> *Charity suffereth long, and is kind; charity envieth not; charity vaunteth not itself, is not puffed up, doth not behave itself unseemly, seeketh not her own, is not easily provoked, thinketh no evil* (1 Corinthians 13:4-5).

Be Safe

Deliverance ministry is hazardous work. It requires safety glasses and the safety helmet of salvation. According to the Scripture, every believer has a personal guardian angel assigned to him (see Mt. 18:10). It is not a stretch to say that there may also be demons that are assigned against them by satan. Paul calls it *"the messenger of satan sent to buffet [you]..."* (2 Cor. 12:7b). The Spirit of God is calling the people of God to begin to rise up in their authority. In spite of a brother's or sister's struggle with the spirit of perversion, the precious people of God must remain steadfast in their convictions, and sympathetic in their communication. There is absolutely no excuse for sin, but there is also no excuse for harshness, high-mindedness, and hard-heartedness either. God, the righteous Judge, sits high and looks low; and He is now as He has always been, slow to wrath, full of mercy, and ready to avenge those who call upon His name in truth. The apostle James says:

> *But the wisdom that is from above is first pure, then peaceable, gentle, and easy to be entreated, full of mercy and good fruits, without partiality, and without hypocrisy* (James 3:17).

Those who have been overtaken in sexual sins need to recover themselves from the snare of the devil, recognizing that they have sold themselves out for much less than God's foreordained best (see 2 Tim. 2:26).

—THE PROCESS OF DELIVERANCE—

Awake, awake; put on thy strength, O Zion; put on thy beautiful garments, O Jerusalem, the holy city: for henceforth there shall no more come into thee the uncircumcised and the unclean. Shake thyself from the dust; arise, and sit down, O Jerusalem: loose thyself from the bands of thy neck, O captive daughter of Zion (Isaiah 52:1-2).

The process of deliverance is made possible by the overcoming blood of the Lamb (see Rev. 12:11). To be free of demonic harassment, influence, and control, it is necessary to submit to the deliverance process. The result of this process is that the person is made whole. The first thing that a person has to do is *wake up* from semiconsciousness of a spiritually comatose state. They have been oblivious to what has been happening to them.

After a person wakes up, he must then *get up.* Many have been lying in that same dust; that is, in the dust of what people say and think, in the dust of their past, in the dust of their fears, etc.

There Is a Serpent in Your Garden

In the sweat of thy face shalt thou eat bread, till thou return unto the ground; for out of it wast thou taken: for dust thou art, and unto dust shalt thou return (Genesis 3:19).

In actuality, man is a glorified mud ball, who derives his physical composition from the dust. Dirt is more than the dust, because the latter is what is left on the top of the dirt. Left to one's old nature, one will return to a dusty and dirty life. The serpent dines in an environment of dust. Therefore, those who yield to the dust detail will have to pick the serpent up by the tail, look him straight in the eye, and declare, "I serve you an eviction notice from my garden."

This is what Moses did when he threw down the rod in the presence of God. It became a serpent (or a snake). Serpents always get thrown down in the presence of the Holy One. The rod was merely a dead stick that Moses picked up in the wilderness. Dr. Mark Chironna says that you survive by what you pick up, but you thrive by what God gives you.[10] The dead stick manifests a living reality. There was a serpent nature living in Moses, and he had to deal with his own personal devils before he could deliver God's people from the Pharaoh devil. Moses took up the serpent by the tail, meaning that he looked it squarely in the eye. Whenever you look the devil squarely in the eye, he will blink. Even though the serpent is a formidable foe, his nature is that of fear, and he will flee (see Jas. 4:7). Once the serpent was stared down, it once again became a rod. This time, however, it became the rod of God (see Ex. 4:4).

The demons of the past were dealt with, defeated, and were delivered a death blow. Moses went on to greatness in God from that moment on. The believer, who yields to the dust nature, feeds the serpent. In the Genesis account, satan is depicted as a serpent; but by the Book of Revelation, the last Book in the Bible, he has become a "dragon." A *serpent* will become a *dragon* when you feed him enough *dust*.

> When we find a person compelled by such an incredibly strong drive towards promiscuous, risky, sexual behavior—whether heterosexual or homosexual—we often find that they are driven by evil spirits of addiction and lust which fill them with an almost uncontrollable urge to have sex at any cost.[11]

Every person who is sincerely seeking to do God's will must, in the words of C.S. Lovett's book, *Deal With the Devil,* or A.W. Tozer's book, *Talk Back to the Devil.* The human spirit is a building that cannot exist without maintenance. The temple of the Holy Ghost cannot make it without continuous deliverance ministry.

Another Serpent Bites the Dust

To overcome the evil one and make him sing, "Another One Bites the Dust," you need to *wake up* from sleep, *get up* from the dust, and *take up serpents.* St. Mark 16:18 says:

> *They shall take up serpents; and if they drink any deadly thing, it shall not hurt them; they shall lay hands on the sick, and they shall recover.*

This verse does not mean that you should go searching for demons. In fact, if you are a spiritual-minded person, they will probably seek to avoid your presence, which represents anointed interference. They will probably *go on the down low* around you. There are many who have *latent legions* and *dormant devils* that do not necessarily leave, but just go undercover. That is the very reason that there are so many closet homosexuals.

The Master Teacher said, *"Men loved darkness rather than light, because their deeds were evil"* (Jn. 3:19). In dealing with the devil, it is important not to commit the error of demon *inspection,* or secondly, demon *ignorance.* To deal with devils, you do not need to have ongoing conversations with them. After all, they are liars, and the truth is not in them. Therefore, they would probably lie to you anyway. Simply discern them and evict them.

Never be a demon inspector. Also, never be a demon ignorer. It is not true that if you leave the devil alone, he will also leave you alone. He is doomed, despicable, and determined. Therefore, the devil emulates the famed General Douglas MacArthur, who upon leaving the Philippines vowed, "I shall return." The devils that are evicted always vow to return. You should never be a demon ignorer. To ignore their deeds is dumb, and it is dangerous.

To take up serpents means to remove them. The picture is that of clearing the way. The process of deliverance must be made possible by the progress of the delivery. To take up serpents prevents them from ever becoming a fire-breathing, mythological dragon of demonic proportions. The best time to kill a rattlesnake is when it is still an egg. Many years ago, we sang a song in the Pentecostal church, "Do not let the devil ride, because he will want to drive. Do not let him be the boss, because he will make your soul be lost. Do not let him ride."

THE BEST TIME TO KILL A RATTLESNAKE IS WHEN IT IS STILL AN EGG.

A renowned minister tells the story of when he was in a great series of meetings held in a local church. Towards the end of the scheduled services, a woman approached him and said to him, "You should be dead by now." He inquired, "Why?" She replied, "Because all this week we [witches] have been working roots [black magic] on you." The man of God, who was then in his early 20's, retorted, "The reason that your roots did not work is because your roots are not as great as my root. My root is the root of Jesse; the root out of a dry ground; the root and offspring of David."

If you do not know how to *wake up, get up,* and *take up* serpents, and serve them an eviction notice, they will move in and take over. They will have you tossing and turning on the couch of complacency while they lounge in the master suite of manipulation.

When it comes to personal deliverance, you must actualize the phrase, "You da Man." The command is to *you. You* have the authority to take up. *You* have the authority to get up. *You* have the authority to wake up. *You* have the authority to shape up, and cast the band off your neck.

Loosed From Bondage

The neck represents your strength. It receives the signal from the head, which turns it. The neck connects the head to the body. If something happens to your neck, it will paralyze you and immobilize your entire body. Your head, your "control system," operates through your neck. If your neck is impaired, you cannot turn your head, and you cannot have your nervous system operating at its optimum.

Those who have yielded to the "gay impulses" of the dust nature in the dirty environment of low living have been yoked by it. To the extent that they are overcome by the proclivity, it becomes a practice and the behavior pattern of their life. Deliverance ministry is needed when they keep stumbling on the same things over and over again and cannot seem to shake off the shackles of their youth or childhood. There seems to be a dark cloud of oppression that continues to hover over them. They may have been attending church consistently, but now they are engaged in church-hopping, just like many people engage in club-hopping before they become Christians. They try different scenarios, male-male, male-female, female-male, female-female, or whatever else they imagine, and it does not satisfy them. The reason is simple. Sex is not the answer. The Savior is. Those who are incarcerated, imprisoned, and impaired in their pursuit of deliverance are bound by demonic influences that have delved into the depths of their being. They are captives; and if they are not delivered, they will become trophies of hell.

A Lifetime of Bondage

...ought not this woman, being a daughter of Abraham, whom satan hath bound, lo, these eighteen years, be loosed from this bond...? (Luke 13:16)

This spirit of infirmity caused the woman's back to be bent for nearly two decades so that she *"could in no wise lift up herself"* (Lk. 13:11b). When Jesus, the Master Teacher, came on the scene, He liberated her, causing her back to be as straight as it was in the days of her youth. She had spent 18 years looking at the ground.

When a person's back begins to straighten up, he can begin to see clearly. When his back begins to straighten up, he is well on his way in the process and progress of deliverance. Dr. Martin Luther King, Jr. once said, "Whenever men and women straighten their backs up, they are going somewhere, because a man can't ride your back unless it is bent."[12] When your back begins to straighten up, the devil cannot hitch a ride on it. If you do not let the devil ride, then there is no way he will be able to drive.

Gay and Lesbian Deliverance

Jesus called the woman a daughter of Abraham. He was saying to her that by virtue of her being a daughter of Abraham, she had covenantal rights of deliverance. As those who put their faith in Christ, because of the blood of Jesus, you have covenantal rights; you have power and authority through the blood. You overcome by the blood of the Lamb and by the word of your testimony (see Rev. 12:11).

You have authority in the name of Jesus as well as in the blood of Jesus. Mark 16:17 states, "*And these signs shall follow* [walk with, accompany, be by the side of] *them that believe; In My name shall they cast out devils; they shall speak with new tongues.*" To take up serpents does not mean that Christians should engage in snake handling, but rather, that we shall remove them from impeding our spiritual progress. To take up serpents means that even though the enemy has afflicted a person's life for years, he has to go. He cannot stay there. The gay lifestyle, lesbianism, and any other deviations must flee at the powerful presence of the Holy One. When a person takes up the serpent, he immediately sends him to the perilous pit where he will ultimately be confined. Shake it off and make the devil take it back. Tell him boldly, "Get back, Jack, and don't you come back no more, no more, no more, no more." Deliverance ministry is needed to shake the snake and to evict his lies of tendencies, preferences, inclinations, and orientation. They are depraved machinations of his deviant, despotic, demonic, and disembodied being.

Regional Deliverance

And the seventy returned again with joy, saying, Lord, even the devils are subject unto us through Thy name. And He said unto them, I beheld satan as lightning fall from heaven. Behold, I give unto you power to tread on serpents and scorpions, and over all the power of the enemy: and nothing shall by any means hurt you. Notwithstanding in this rejoice not, that the spirits are subject unto you; but rather rejoice, because your names are written in heaven (Luke 10:17-20).

When Jesus declared that He saw satan fall as lightning from Heaven, many people think that He was talking about the time when satan was kicked out of Heaven by God. As the disciples began to exercise their spiritual authority, the spirits were subject to them in Jesus' name. At that time satan and those demons that were in the heavenly places were literally dethroned and prevented from operating and occupying those strongholds. The principalities of regions that form strongholds, such as homosexual ones, are not allowed free reign when believers exercise authority in powerful intercession.

When the Wicked Seize a City, a book by Chuck and Donna McIlhenny, details how this takes place as it relates to defeating homosexual strongholds. Satan was defeated at the cross; however, he still operates in the earth realm.

And despite intense spiritual warfare, he will be allowed to do so until God serves him his ultimate eviction papers. No matter how many Christians pray, you cannot altogether keep the devil away. He is the god of this world (see 2 Cor. 4:4). The world lies in the lap of the evil one (see 1 Jn. 5:19). He is the prince (ruler) of the power of the air (see Eph. 2:2).

In order to completely dislodge his influence over a region, the people of that region have to evict him. This is not a simple accomplishment. It is impossible for any group of Christians, no matter how large or small, to completely evict him out of a city such as San Francisco, Los Angeles, or Charlotte, North Carolina. Satan has a legal right to stay because people have opened themselves up to him, which essentially extends his lease and liberty. Therefore, he continues to set up shop. The Christian's authority is primarily a personal one, exercised on a personal level. John Paul Jackson, in *Needless Casualties of War*, points out that engaging regional principalities and powers can have a reverse boomerang effect, in that the people who ignorantly attack the demons become targets for counterattack. They may become casualties and fatalities needlessly in spiritual warfare. As a rule, a person should never fight a war that he cannot win. It is a losing strategy. Counting the cost before engaging in battle is the wise method of deliverance.

Personal Deliverance

Furthermore, satan's lease is only temporary. Jesus already defeated him at Calvary. We do not have to defeat him because he is already defeated. We simply deal with him and remind him of his defeat. *Whenever you have been freed from same-sex attraction and he reminds you of your past, you should remind him of his future.* Satan will get behind you when you operate knowing that Jesus engaged him on your behalf and said, so to speak, "Satan, your behind is Mine, and I am going to send your behind to where the sun does not shine for all time." *He has been cast out and cast down, and it is up to you to cast him away.*

WHENEVER YOU HAVE BEEN FREED FROM SAME-SEX ATTRACTION AND SATAN REMINDS YOU OF YOUR PAST, YOU SHOULD REMIND HIM OF HIS FUTURE.

Jesus said that He has given the Church power to tread on serpents and scorpions. Therefore, you do not have to duck tail and hide, or hang your head. To the gay and lesbian person, there may be areas in your life which satan has held for a long time. But, even now, God is loosing your faith and causing you to become militant. Soon, you are going to cause satan to fall like lightning from those areas of your life where he has had a stronghold. No matter how long the same-sex attraction has been there, Jesus is ready to move within your inner man and establish His reign as the Sovereign of your soul, but you must *shake it off and make the devil take it back.*

Deliverance Through Praise

The Bible says that Judah's *"hand shall be in the neck of* [his] *enemies,"* and that Judah's *"eyes shall be red with wine, and his teeth white with milk"* (Gen. 49:8,12). The name *Judah* means "praise now," and praise always wrings the serpent's neck. The wine and milk typify the Spirit and the Word. God is saying that you are going to be full of the Spirit of God and full of the Word of God. You will have your hand in the neck of the enemy whenever you decide to cast the band from off your neck. The anointing makes this possible because it is designed to effect deliverance.

> *And it shall come to pass in that day, that his burden shall be taken away from off thy shoulder, and his yoke from off thy neck, and the yoke shall be destroyed because of the anointing* (Isaiah 10:27).

Executing God's vengeance is an honor that all the saints have (see Ps. 149:9). God wants all those who love Him to be so honored. He does not want your faces sad; He does not want you feeling bad; He does not want you to meditate on your mother and get mad; He does not want you dysfunctional because of your dealings with your dad. God has said that He has given you power over all the power of the enemy. It is power to make snake rugs out of serpents and scorpions. The serpents are not imaginary, but they operate with optical illusions. They make things appear a particular way when in reality they are another way. Despite how long you have been caught in a stronghold, *dare to believe* that the Greater One still possesses all power. The saints of old sang: "Let Jesus fix it for you, for He knows just what to do; and wherever you pray, let the Lord have His way. He knows just what the problem is; let Jesus fix it for you." God will fix it if you stop faking it and start fighting it. The formula for "shaking it off" and "making the devil take it back" is this: *Admit it, quit it, submit it, forget it, and split it.* It is easier said than it is done, but you *must do it.* Shake yourself from the dust of earthly entanglement and enticement and embrace your entitlement. *"If the Son therefore shall make you free, ye shall be free indeed"* (Jn. 8:36). Victory is yours. The songwriter exclaimed,

> *Victory is mine, Victory is mine, Victory today is mine.*
>
> *I told Satan to get thee behind. Victory today is mine.*

—THE VIPER AND HIS VICE-GRIP—

*And when Paul had gathered a bundle of sticks, and laid them on the fire, there came a viper out of the heat, and fastened on his hand. And when the barbarians saw the venomous beast hang on his hand, they said among themselves, No doubt this man is a murderer, whom, though he hath escaped the sea, yet vengeance suffereth not to live. And **he shook off the beast into the fire**, and felt no harm. Howbeit they looked when he should have swollen, or fallen down dead suddenly: but after they had looked a great while, and saw no harm come to him, they changed their minds, and said that he was a god* (Acts 28:3-6, emphasis added).

The viper seeks a victim, whom he may devour. His vice-grip hold is very formidable, but he has already lost the battle by virtue of the cross (see Col. 2:14-15). The *triumph* was on when the *trump* began. The serpent is destined to be *incinerated* in the *incendiary* of *red-hot* prayer, *radical* praise, and *revolutionary-prophetic* worship. He cannot help himself. He is a depraved devil. He is determined to bring you down with himself. That is why he seeks to get men and ministers on the down low. Misery has always loved company, and diablos (the devil) is no exception. Therefore, you must be even more determined than he is. Although the demon may have attached himself to you in the form of a perverse preference for the same-sex, you must not delay in shaking him off and making the devil take him back.

In Acts 28, St. Paul's journeys took him to the island of Melita, known today as Malta. He encountered the *storm*, survived a *shipwreck* having escaped on broken pieces, and was attacked by a *snake*. The snake came after two previous troubles. Sometimes, trouble comes in three's! The patriarch Job had family, business, and health troubles hit him all at once. He survived his ordeal by remembering that *trouble does not always last*. Problems are never permanent, unless you allow them to pull up into your driveway, park their vehicle, put their keys into the locks of your home, and plant their derriere on the sofa in your living room.

Shake It Off

The snake that fastened onto St. Paul was of a serpentine origin. Normally, venomous viper bites knock one down; but in his case, he simply *shook it off and made the devil take it back*. The homosexual impulses must be treated as rudely, crudely, and inhospitably as the man of God treated the snake. The snake came out of the fire, and it was shaken off into the fire. The spirit that brings homosexuality cannot stand the fiery presence of fervent effectual prayer. Shaking is a demonstrative action. It is a physical expression. There is a whole lot of shaking going on, but unfortunately, it is the Samson type of shaking. The Scripture says that he shook himself and did not know that the Spirit of God was gone (see Judg. 16:20). The loss of feeling is a result of the capture of one's soul or psyche, which contains the feelings of an individual. Deliverance ministry will result in the restoration of one's soul and sensation.

Into the Fire

Paul shook the snake off into the fire and so must the believer. "What fire?" one might ask. It is the fire of prayer, praise, personal discipline, dedication, perseverance, powerful resistance, and of patience. *To shake* means to churn, convulse, joggle, jolt, jog, jounce, rock, jar, agitate, brandish, totter, dodder, flutter, palpitate, throb, quaver, quiver, twitter, twiddle, flicker, vibrate, shiver, shudder, and quake. *Whatever it takes, you have got to shake the snake.* Selah.

Feelings or sensations are in the soulish (emotional) realm. Whenever a person's soul has been tied, it handicaps his ability to feel after God (see Acts 17:27). If you cannot feel God, then how would you sense whenever He is near or far from you? St. Paul shook it off, and immediately, he felt no harm. Whenever a homosexual person truly shakes the snake, he

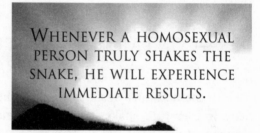

WHENEVER A HOMOSEXUAL PERSON TRULY SHAKES THE SNAKE, HE WILL EXPERIENCE IMMEDIATE RESULTS.

will experience immediate results. To shake the snake implies dealing with the root causes of the demonic stronghold. No snake can stay if you say, "No way." No matter how the proclivity toward perversion haunts and holds to one's soul, when you deal with the issue before it becomes deadly, you defeat it. Deliverance ministry uproots it at its source and destroys its course.

A Snake Is a Snake Is a Snake

What is a snake? Also, how does it apply to the gay and the lesbian? Consider this acronym for a snake. (S) — It is sly, slick, and sneaky. (N) — It is noticeable. (A) — It is an antagonist and an adversary. (K) — It is a killer. (E) — It represents evil. A snake is a snake, has always been a snake, and will be a snake as long as he is a snake. It is the nature of a snake to kill and destroy; you cannot tame a snake. The devil has not always been the devil; but now that he is the devil, he is full of the devil, and he is going to be the devil as long as there is a devil. It does not matter whether you are an innocent infant, an unaware adolescent, in your roaring 20's, your tantalizing 30's, your feeling-fine 40's, your primetime 50's, your sizzling 60's, your sit-down 70's, your aching 80's, or your nostalgic 90's—the devil is still on your trail. But as long as he is on your trail, he cannot block you, stop you, or defeat you.

A Snake Is Always a Snake

I remember reading some years ago, the story of a man who had raised a baby snake. He had taken it close to himself and held it against his chest. One day, after the snake had grown up, the man picked it up and began to hold it. The snake turned on him and with crushing strength, he squeezed the man to death. Some might ask, "Why would the snake do that? After all, it was trained by this man. It was raised up and nurtured by this man." However, one thing must be remembered: A snake is a snake, and it will always be a snake! The fictional story says that the snake looked at the man and said, "I was a snake when you found me and raised me. A snake's got to do what a snake's got to do."

—COMPARING SPIRITUAL SERPENTS—
WITH NATURAL ONES

In the natural, a snake is a reptile that crawls along the ground on its belly. In literature, snakes are used as metaphors of evil. In American classics, snakes represent evil and are associated with witchcraft. Satanism uses snakes as its symbol. Culturally, snakes represent the music of our generation. The group, KISS (Kids in Service to Satan), uses a snake as their logo. Before her untimely passing, young Aliyah featured snakes in one of her videos. Soon thereafter, she died in a fatal airplane crash. Britney Spears began her music career singing lyrics such as, "I'm not that innocent." She was heralded as a young emblem of innocence. Soon thereafter, she performed in a video with a snake draped around her body. Before long, her innocent image was purposely shattered, and now she is an open purveyor of sexually explicit innuendo in her music and lyrics. The same is true for LaToya Jackson, who has often been photographed in snake adornment. Her life has been decimated by her own account as one of being a victim of childhood molestation at the hands of a family member. A snake is a snake, is a snake, is a snake! The dictionary gives various adjectives to describe a snake. A snake represents being *low, groveling, despicable, evil, hideous, crafty, cunning, strange, and deceptive.*

—THE SUBTLETY OF THE SERPENT—

Now the serpent was more subtle [more deceptive, more crafty, more strange] *than any beast of the field...* (Genesis 3:1).

Serpentine Weapons

Basically, in sexual seduction, the serpent has only two weapons, and they are to accuse and to deceive. He accuses much like a prosecuting attorney. He seeks conviction and ultimate condemnation. He deceives much like a magician who employs optical illusions. His methodology of penetration is through subtlety, and he primarily works through wanton sexual suggestions. Second Corinthians 11:3 says, *"But I fear, lest by any means, as the serpent beguiled Eve through his subtlety, so your minds should be corrupted from the simplicity that is in Christ."* Satan specializes in convincing a person that he is homosexual when he is not. An act does not necessarily make a habit. He knows how to get a person's attention and his affection. He knows how to talk to someone when he is all by himself. He took time with Eve; he talked to her. And when she listened to him, he lit her up. The serpent's game is a *tongue* that is not tamed. He always preys upon people's pride, because pride is his principle weapon of mass destruction and deception. The Scripture says that *pride is the condemnation of the devil.* There are six spiritual serpent skins in the Scriptures. First Timothy 3:6 declares, *"Not a novice, lest being lifted up with **pride** he fall into the **condemnation** of the devil"* (emphasis added).

> SATAN SPECIALIZES IN CONVINCING A PERSON THAT HE IS HOMOSEXUAL WHEN HE IS NOT.

—SIX SPIRITUAL SNAKESKINS—

One: The Serpent Is Wise

Behold, I send you forth as sheep in the midst of wolves: be ye therefore wise as serpents, and harmless as doves (Matthew 10:16).

Two: The Serpent Is Toxic

At the last it biteth like a serpent, and stingeth like an adder (Proverbs 23:32).

Three: The Serpent Is Deadly

He shall suck the poison of asps: the viper's tongue shall slay him (Job 20:16).

Four: The Serpent Hides

As if a man did flee from a lion, and a bear met him; or went into the house, and leaned his hand on the wall, and a serpent bit him (Amos 5:19).

Five: The Serpent Lives in Dry Places

Who led thee through that great and terrible wilderness, wherein were fiery serpents, and scorpions, and drought, where there was no water; who brought thee forth water out of the rock of flint (Deuteronomy 8:15).

Six: The Serpent Crawls

The way of an eagle in the air; the way of a serpent upon a rock; the way of a ship in the midst of the sea; and the way of a man with a maid (Proverbs 30:19).

The prophet Isaiah records that prior to being served an eviction notice by the heavenly Father, lucifer, the serpent, declared "*I will*" on five separate occasions.

*For thou hast said in thine heart, **I will** ascend into heaven, **I will** exalt my throne above the stars of God: **I will** sit also upon the mount of the congregation, in the sides of the north: **I will** ascend above the heights of the clouds; **I will** be like the most High* (Isaiah 14:13-14, emphasis added).

Satan's "*I wills*" are meant to break a person's will. His *I wills* against the gay and lesbian community include, "*I will never let you go; I will not come out; I will kill you; I will expose you; I will be your god.*" He persistently proclaims, "You were born like this. You do not have to hear this. You do not need this. You are who you are and you do not have to change. You can stay this way." The serpent is determined to *harass, influence,* and *control* you. He is a lethal liar. He is a venomous viper. Serpents are purveyors of perversion. Their presence is problematic. Deliverance eviction is the only recourse.

Dominating sinful fruit is often the result of demonic sinister roots. When demonic roots are removed, their fruit is destroyed. The authority of the believer is exercised when you wake up, take up, and shake up demonic strongholds. Moses demonstrated this authority in the wilderness experience.

And the people spake against God, and against Moses, Wherefore have ye brought us up out of Egypt to die in the wilderness? for there is no bread, neither is there any water; and our soul loatheth this light bread. And the Lord sent fiery serpents among the people, and they bit the people; and much people of Israel died. Therefore the people came to Moses, and said, We have sinned, for we have spoken against the Lord, and against thee; pray unto the Lord, that He take away the serpents from us. And Moses prayed for the people. And the Lord said unto Moses, Make thee a fiery serpent, and set it upon a pole: and it shall come to pass, that every one that is bitten, when he looketh upon it, shall live (Numbers 21:5-8, emphasis added).

A Brass Serpent

Numbers 21:9 records:

*And Moses made a **serpent** of brass, and put it upon a pole, and it came to pass, that if a **serpent** had bitten any man, when he beheld the ser-pent of brass, he lived* (emphasis added).

The murmuring of the people unleashed a serpentine attack. Death ensued. Moses constructed a brass serpent. He told the people to look upon the serpentine object. It sounded like a crazy commandment of a crazed leader. However, what Moses was doing typified that one day the Messiah would be lifted up, and He would nail the serpent's power to the cross. The serpent that was lifted up represented that the people's sins were being lifted up to God. Despite what a person has done, whether it is licentious or lascivious sin with the same sex, the saved life will start by *shaking it off* and *making the devil take it back*. By looking to Christ upon the cross, the gay and lesbian serpent is served an eviction notice. Snake eyes are normally menacing; but when you look the snake in the eye, you will not die—he will.

In the Scripture, brass is a symbol of judgment. In St. John's Revelation, brass was the depiction of the feet of Christ (see Rev. 1:15). In the tabernacle of Moses, two articles were made of brass. They were the brazen (brass) altar and brazen (brass) laver, both of which dealt with sin. The brass altar was where the sacrificed animals were slain and their blood was shed. It was the place of a bloody mess. The brass laver was the next article of furniture that was passed en route to the holy place, the second compartment of the tabernacle. Brass is a metal alloy. It is a mixture. The serpent of brass also represented the mixture of idolatry in the people's hearts. When people's lives are mixed up, the mix-match manifests in sexuality, which corrupts their worship. Dr. Judson Cornwall once said that cheap instruments will always produce counterfeit worship.

Serpent Bite

To those who are homosexual, the Lord has already judged your sinful situation, at the cross. If you have been snakebitten throughout your lifetime, get ready to get your soul back. The snakes that are still operating are seducing spirits. Refuse disobedience and you will release deliverance. Israel's disobedience, unbelief, rebellion, and refusal to submit to God's delegated spiritual authorities caused the judgment of the plague. The children of Israel began to murmur and to complain against Moses. There are many homosexuals who speak against the Church, not realizing that the Church is the only *true agent of deliverance that they have left*. All persons who attend church are not angels, but neither are they demons. The church is a house of prayer and deliverance, not perfection and debutantes.

Serpentine power is released wherever a person speaks against the authority of Scripture and spiritual authorities. The so-called gay church does both of these two things. They attack the authenticity of Scripture and the authority of the ministers of God. Always remember, godly leadership is the covering of the people. Without covering, there is insufficient protection against the elements of demonic oppression. The Bible says that *"whoso breaketh an hedge, a **serpent** shall bite him"* (Eccl. 10:8b, emphasis added). A hedge is an all-encompassing encirclement, a compassing security. As long as you stay in the hedge of godly leadership, there will be protection from demonic onslaught. Accountability, transparency, and honesty are key ingredients in spiritual covering. Having someone available to share your journey, your struggles, or your temptations, will serve as a hedge that will keep you protected from spiritual snakebite. The hedge in the New Testament Church is the blood of Jesus and also godly shepherds after God's own heart.

> ACCOUNTABILITY, TRANS-PARENCY, AND HONESTY ARE KEY INGREDIENTS IN SPIRITUAL COVERING.

The demons are like wolves that love flesh, that run in packs, and that work at night. They do not really fear the particular sheep as much as they fear the presence of the shepherd. If you "smite the shepherd" with your mouth, a spirit of discombobulation and disorientation will come upon your soul, resulting in scattering. Many individuals who were turned out into the gay and lesbian lifestyle were vulnerable to the spirit because their hedge was broken when they were a child. Desertion, divorce, discrimination, and disengaged dads, normally result in broken homes, hearts, and hopes. Without the man making up the hedge (see Ezek. 22:30), the serpent is free to interject poison, unless the child receives divine intervention. The shepherd of the home is its godly covering. This is true whether it is male or female or both parents at once. This is the divine design for a family. The enemy seeks to smite the shepherd (covering) and scatter the flock (family). The prophet Zechariah says,

> *Awake, O sword, against My shepherd, and against the man that is My fellow, saith the Lord of hosts: smite the shepherd, and the sheep shall be scattered: and I will turn Mine hand upon the little ones* (Zechariah 13:7).

Before the serpent attacked the patriarch Job, he had to first go through the hedge that surrounded him (see Job 1:10). It was not until the hedge was broken that he was able to attack him. A perusal of Job reveals that the first thing satan attacked was all the animals because they were used as sacrifices. Their blood was used as a covering for the sins of Job as well as his family. The serpent knew that the first thing to attack was the blood covering. The demon that influences one towards homosexual harassment, influence, and ultimate control is a renegade without respect for spiritual authority. He is out to undermine the covering because it serves as the hedge that the serpent cannot penetrate. It is the one thing that impedes his plot to persuade people into the gay lifestyle. Godly shepherds are a terror to gay serpents. Serpents are not afraid of solitary praying sheep, but they are terrified of the presence of the shepherd. When the sheep are praying and the shepherd is present, the serpent goes on the down low. The songwriter sings it this way:

Higher — Higher — Higher — Lift Jesus higher.

Lower — Lower — Lower — Stomp satan lower.

Super — Super — Super — Supernatural power.

—FOUR KINDS OF GAY SNAKES TO SHAKE—

Shake the Rattlesnake

First, there is the rattlesnake, which makes a very distinctive noise that affects the hearing. The rattlesnake signifies those demons that affect what you hear. They try to intercept the truth by creating a noise of doubt and unbelief in your ears. If you check your *confessions* that come out of your mouth, you will discover whether or not you have been bitten by a rattlesnake. Many Christians have a hearing problem. The noise of the rattlesnake in their ear is the noise of the lying spirits, carnal imaginations, and the spirits of slander and negativism. A rattlesnake's sound is any noise that exalts itself against the knowledge of God (see 2 Cor. 10:3-6). The rattlesnake says to the young victimized child, "*You are not like everybody else. You are a homosexual. You were born this way.*" The child is vulnerable and unable to discern, deal with, defeat, and deliver his soul from the devil.

You must guard your ear-gate. The Master Teacher taught, "*...Take heed what ye hear...*" (Mk. 4:24, emphasis added). *We must be swift to hear God, slow to speak, and slow to extreme anger* (see Jas. 1:19). The fruit of this spiritual discipline is *self-control*. The serpent seeks to influence your hearing, which affects your believing. Therefore you must "*study to be quiet*" (1 Thess. 4:11a). Trusting in God and His ability to help you *shake it off and make the devil take it back* comes by faith. Demonic influence, like the rattling of the rattlesnake, constantly competes for your attention. Whatever you hear is what you believe, and what you believe about yourself, you will eventually come to see in yourself. If you believe that you are forever resigned to be homosexual, then you will come to see yourself as unable to be otherwise. Only a resolute faith in what God has said is the hope of a new belief system about yourself. Paul says in Romans 10:17, "*So then faith cometh by hearing, and hearing by the word of God*" (emphasis added). The rattle of the demons that affect the hearing must be truncated so that the deadliness they inject can be eradicated by the Word of God. You must evict the rattling serpent from God's garden.

Shake the Copperhead Snake

The copperhead signifies demons that attempt to destroy you by injecting the deadly poison of sin or unbelief into your bloodstream. The foundational sin is unbelief. The Word of God is made of none effect to those who do not mix it with faith. Poison in your spirit will act as a weight upon your spirit and will wear you down, causing the light of your spirit to grow more and more dim. No matter how bad it seems, always believe. If you have fallen over and over again, get up still believing. Spiritually speaking, if your blood has been poisoned, you need a blood transfusion. You need to plead the blood of Jesus. His blood will counteract and destroy any poison the copperhead has injected. Evict the poisonous serpent from God's garden.

> LET NOTHING REMAIN WITH YOU THAT CRAWLS IN THE CREVICES OF SECRECY, DARKNESS, OR HARD AND DRY PLACES.

Shake the Python Snake

The python signifies those demons sent against you to squeeze the life of God out of you. Sometimes it seems that the enemy has come in like a flood; but that is when the Spirit of the Lord lifts up a standard against him (see Is. 59:19). Serpents will squeeze natural affection and life out of you unless you evict them from God's garden.

Shake the Cobra Snake

The cobra signifies those demons who enter in through the eye-gate. They know how to get your attention. When they do, they gain your affection. You become hypnotized, mesmerized, anesthetized, and stupefied in a state in which you are open to the influences and suggestions of the devil. In such a state, you are no longer aware of the danger you are in. Evict the attention-seeking serpent from your visual screen, and he will no longer inhabit God's garden.

The Combative Appeal: In Conclusion Evicting the Gay Serpent From God's Garden

---

To another the working of miracles; to another prophecy; to another discerning of spirits; to another divers kinds of tongues; to another the interpretation of tongues (1 Corinthians 12:10).

Discerning the Demon Spirit

The body is the temple of the Holy Ghost. It is God's garden. The subject of deliverance requires that Christians look at the entire picture when reaching out to assist the afflicted with shifting into an aligned lifestyle in pursuit of their destiny. Too often the Church has tried to piously pray away the manifested symptoms, leaving those who are demonically harassed, influenced, and controlled to exit the doors of the church in the same condition in which they entered. Often, the Church mistakenly underestimates the subtle schemes of the serpent and somewhat shuts their eyes to that which is obvious. Our deliverance attempts are often superficial and fall short of engaging the hidden roots that have deeply entangled entire generations in snares which have kept them sequestered from their God-given destiny. Examination of any ensnarement will uncover the strategies of the enemy, who is roaming up and down, literally to and fro, seeking whom he may devour. He lurks and looks for someone who will open the door and let him in. Selah. Evictions last only if they are enforced by the law. Demons do not willingly depart. Their comfort zone is in the confusion of same-sex perversion.

—DEMONIC ENTRANCES—

But if I with the finger of God cast out devils, no doubt the kingdom of God is come upon you (Luke 11:20, emphasis added).

How Demonic Strongholds Develop

Demons enter in through many of the openings, which are listed in "The Making of a Homosexual in chapter 6." They do not care how they come in. They just want in so that they can bring their cohorts with them to set up camp. They erect their tents in the minds of their victim and operate as blockades to steal, kill, and destroy anything that represents Jesus before it gets into the heart of the hearer. The enemy cannot enter in without legal access into the bloodline. Legal satanic entrance occurs through several common vulnerable situations. These openings apply beyond the scope of gay and lesbian persons.

First, the worship of false gods–through family background in the occult or false religions–opens the bloodline for demonic destruction. The entrance into the bloodline could exist three to four generations back as the door-keeper demon steps in to let the plans from the underworld begin to unfold. As this relates to homosexuality, we must be cognizant that the doorkeeper demon is not always the demon that manifests with outward symptoms. The doorkeeper may be rejection, while the outward symptom is lustful behavior.

Second, negative prenatal influences set the plan for the life of the unborn so that demons have legal access by way of rejection. The demon of rejection stands as the doorkeeper who allows entrance of other demons to assist in continually constructing scenarios that reinforce rejection to the point that the individual becomes ready to do whatever it takes to gain acceptance. This is common in homosexuality.

Third, pressures in early childhood open the mind of a child to be respon-sible for dealing with life situations that they are not yet ready for. This leaves them wide-open targets for demonic entrance. Young children who witness or experience sexual abuse may turn to homosexual relationships to avoid the painful memories of toxic heterosexual encounters.

Fourth, sudden surges of emotion of shock or passionate sexual desire, and/or sustained emotional pressure, open a pathway for demons of fear, lust, anxiety, hopelessness, and anger to have legal access to lure its victim to com-mit behaviors that keep the door to satanic influence open. Homosexuality is a combination of manifestations of fears, lusts, anxieties, hopeless emotions, and anger about life circumstances that is masqueraded in the clothing of a toxic expression of perverted individuality.

Fifth, sinful acts or habits give open entrance for demons to access an individual. Persistent practice of lustful acts keeps the door open for many demons to traverse and influence the mind of its inhabitant. Inordinate affection starts out as a sinful act, but then becomes a habit that cannot be stopped without confession and renunciation of the demon.

Sixth, transference of spirits can take place by the laying on of hands. When the hands of a sexual sinner touch an innocent person, their spirits are interacting. Negative supernatural power is released into an innocent life to begin its destruction. Homosexual encounters are a continual releasing of demonic transference with demon seeds that perpetuate inordinate interactions.

Seventh, idle words spoken open the door for demons to carry out what is said. They often get their assignment from words we speak when engaging in idle conversations, speaking words that bring negative circumstances to fruition. Idle conversations have activated many homosexual relationships as perverted words of attraction are released for demons to travel on into the heart of a wounded spirit and trap them in darkness. Demons enter in a person's life with an organized plan of action that, when carried out without resistance, will strengthen their domain. They come to carry out a subtle takeover through methodical diabolical planning that locks their victim into an invisible prison of the underworld. They do not hang out a sign and tell you where they are hiding out. Their lying tactics and luring language are laced with counterfeit messages that are designed to cut one off from their destiny in the Kingdom of God.

Demons come to entice, to do evil, to harass weak areas, to compel into compulsive habits, to torture the mind and physical body, to enslave into sinful behaviors, to defile the mind and speech, to deceive into false beliefs, to cause addictions, and to attack the physical body. Entanglements in homosexuality are inclusive of all of the above tactics. The spirit of lust comes to entice its victim. The major objective is to entice its victim to commit evil in the sight of the Lord. Its goal is to provoke an affection that is out of order. This spirit knows the weak areas to push through to gain its entrance, and will work at those areas until it breaks resistance. Once the spirit of lust breaks through resistance, it will work at compelling its victim into habitually carrying out lustful compulsions without giving it any thought. It sets up a torture of the mind and physical body through sending signals of lustful desire, followed by an inability to fight off enslavement

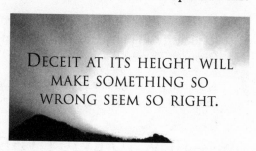

DECEIT AT ITS HEIGHT WILL MAKE SOMETHING SO WRONG SEEM SO RIGHT.

to sinful sexual behavior. At this point, the mind and speech are defiled with thoughts and expressions of lustful acts as the victim is deceived into believing that the lustful interaction is right because it brings them a false acceptance that "feels right, so let's do it again." This affection that is out of order now progresses to an addiction that dictates their every move. The finale of the spirit of lust is to take its victim to his death. This is the making of a sex addict that acts out homosexually. Sexually transmitted disease is the grand finale. There is a way that seemeth right to a man, but its path leads to death (see Prov. 14:12). Deceit at its height will make something so wrong seem so right.

—DEMONIC EXITS—

He that committeth sin is of the devil; for the devil sinneth from the beginning. For this purpose the Son of God was manifested, that He might destroy the works of the devil (1 John 3:8).

How Demonic Strongholds Are Destroyed

The counterfeit diabolical activities may not always proceed with outward proof to the human eye that a demon is on board. Accurate discernment of the behavioral manifestations and language of demons will alert one to see the presence of demonic spirits and/or learned toxic human behaviors. Bodily contortions, changes in voice, changes in facial expression, rolling eyes, unpleasant odors, and changes in room temperature are signs that a demon or demons are rising to outward manifestation. Eviction of the gay serpent and deliverance from any sexual acting out requires a multifaceted approach.

1. First, homosexuals must admit their same-sex attraction and engage in an immediate plan to curtail the sexual acting out. They must embrace the complete deliverance. Accountability factors must be worked into the plan of recovery and rehabilitation.

2. Second, a nouthetic approach to counseling must be established to identify the areas where the demons have gained access. (See Chapter Three.)

3. Third, homosexuals must submit themselves for deliverance from mind-sets, toxic beliefs, unstable behavioral reactions, and demons.

—HOW TO EVICT THE GAY SERPENT—

First, admit it.   *For the grace of God that bringeth salvation*

Second, quit it.   *hath appeared to all men, teaching us that,*

Third, forget it.   *denying ungodliness and worldly lusts, we*

Fourth, submit it.   *should live soberly, righteously, and godly,*

Fifth, split it.   *in this present world* (Titus 2:11-12).

Eviction of the gay serpent requires a preparation for deliverance from demons. God's trained deliverers must assist afflicted individuals to affirm their faith in Christ, humble themselves, confess any sins, repent of all sins, forgive others, break with the occult and all false religions, prepare for release from curses, take their stand with Christ, and expel every hindering demon. Eviction of the gay serpent requires that the Church be willing to address the issue of homosexuality without rejection. Dysfunctional families are great at rejection. Functional families operate from a position of wholeness, pouring out understanding and confidentiality. The compassion of Christ will pour out the doors of the church when the Church at large begins to embrace the fullness of recovery modalities, understanding that people who sexually act out are wounded and need love to heal their wounds. Sexual sin is enmeshed in rejection issues that become only more predominant when the Church stands in the place of judgment instead of the place of a re-presentation of Christ. The deliverance process is: *God, I admit it; God, I quit it; God, I forget it; God, I submit it; God, I split it.*

Evicting the gay serpent is an exercise in spiritual authority. To be in authority, you must be under authority or in submission. The first thing in a person's life that the serpent seeks to remove is spiritual covering. Be careful not to violate your own spiritual covering by speaking against them. To survive a snake attack, you must recognize that the weapons of your warfare are not carnal, but they are mighty through God (see 2 Cor. 10:4). You pull down strongholds by not being slack in counterattack. Do what Paul did—*he shook the snake off and made the devil take it back!* Do not let the venomous, homosexual viper hang on to you. The gay serpent cannot stay when you line up with the Lord Jesus, the living Word, and the Love of God. Let nothing remain with you that crawls in the crevices of secrecy, darkness, or hard and dry places. Uncover the rocks and step on the snake by full disclosure, and watch the power of God in operation. Do not let depression and oppression hang on to you. Do not let complexes and fears hang on to you. Do not let past failures pull you down. Stay lifted up. If you have love and are under spiritual covering, operate with boldness against the gay serpent. The righteous who know their God shall be strong and do mighty exploits in their God (see Dan. 11:32). *You have spiritual authority—start exercising it now!* For this to happen among the ranks of the "oil and wine" carriers, we must hear *The Comprehensive Admonition.*

Prayer: Lord of life, God of glory, Creator of Eden, help us to walk in the liberty wherewith Christ hath made us free. Grant us discernment of spirits as we exercise Your authority over the adversary. As we deal with the devil and evict him from Your garden, grant that we might easily defeat him, delivering the damaged souls from his determined grasp. Help us to shake him off and make him take back every serpent that has risen against us. We thank You for deliverances from harassment, influence, and control. We thank You for freedom from oppression and regression. Amen.

Confession: Satan, I rebuke you and all of the demonic spirits that you have assigned against my life and destiny in Christ. I resist you and remove you. I declare that I am free of you and that I am free indeed. I command you to leave God's garden, God's property, my body, my soul, and my spirit, the temple of the Holy Ghost. In Jesus' name!

ENDNOTES

1. Briar Whitehead, *Craving for Love* (Grand Rapids: Monarch Books, 2003), 252.

2. Francis McNutt, *Homosexualiy: Can It Be Healed?* (Jacksonville, FL: Christian Healing Ministries, 2001), 51.

3. McNutt, *Homosexuality*, 50-51.

4. Merrill F. Unger, *What Demons Can Do to Saints* (Chicago, IL: Moody Press, 1991), 56.

5. Ibid., 56.

6. McNutt, *Homosexuality*, 66.

7. Ibid., 51.

8. Comiskey, 104.

9. Francis Frangipane, *The Three Battlegrounds* (Marion, IA: Advancing Church Publications, 1989), 8.

10. Edwin Louis Cole: A sermon preached in Columbus, Ohio, in 1989.

11. Dr. Mark Chironna, *Let the Prophets Speak* (Tulsa, OK: Vincom Publishing Co., 1996), 43-44.

12. McNutt, *Homosexuality*, 53.

13. Dr. Martin Luther King, Jr., "I've Been to the Mountaintop," delivered April 3, 1968, in Memphis, Tennessee, accessed at http://www.american-rhetoric.com/speeches/mlkivebeentothemountaintop.htm.

CHAPTER
ELEVEN

"To the extent that our unwillingness to become 'community' to persons whose lifestyles we see as abhorrent has contributed to their fleeing to unwholesome communities for fellowship, we contributed to the spread of the epidemic." In other words, *"to what degree are homosexually oriented persons driven to the gay community, even to impersonal sex practices and promiscuity, because they are unable to find community within the wider society and more specifically, within our churches? To what extent have we as Christians been guilty of sinning against persons with a homosexual orientation because of our failure to show love and to offer them the true fellowship they are seeking?"* The church must show both compassion and mercy on the one hand and exercise a call for repentance to the wider society on the other. [1]

Wendall Hoffman and Stanley Grenz,
quoted by John Ankerberg and John White in The Myth of Safe Sex

There is no such thing, strictly speaking, as a homosexual or a lesbian. There are only people who need healing of old rejections and deprivations. [2]

Leanne Payne, Crisis in Masculinity

...Homosexuals' willingness to confess their struggles and seek freedom may depend in part on the values and attitudes around them. Do church members confess their faults and failures to one another? Does one uphold for the other a word of encouragement and a vision of wholeness that enable him to walk uprightly? In short, is Christ's law fulfilled in the church by bearing one another's burdensome sins and weaknesses... [3]

Andrew Comiskey, Pursuing Sexual Wholeness

The Comprehensive Admonition:
Are Homosexuals at Home in the Church?

Come unto Me, all ye that labour and are heavy laden, and I will give you rest (Matthew 11:28).

The eternal question is, "Are homosexuals at home in the church?" In fairness, when asking this question, we cannot isolate homosexuals as if they are some *gangrenous* or *cancerous* sore. Not only must the Church ask if the homosexual is at home, but we must also ask if the fornicator, the murderer, the backbiter, the disobedient to parents, the covetous, the wicked, the malicious, the envious, the one full of strife, the deceitful, the evil-minded, the gossiper, the prideful, and the boasters are at home in the church (see Rom. 1:29-31). We must ask if those with a proud look, a lying tongue, hands that shed innocent blood, a heart that devises wicked imaginations, feet swift in running to mischief, a false witness who speaks lies, and those who sow discord among brethren are at home in the church (see Prov. 6:17-19). *The truth is, no sin is welcome in the church, but without "sinners" there is no need for the church.* The church is a "saving station for sinners" and not simply a "social center for saints." The "oil and wine" Church must adhere to the comprehensive admonition if it is to be a habitation where those who have delved into deviation are to be at home. The Bible is a blueprint for building the Church. It provides gracious goals that will help the "oil and wine" Church *get itself together so that God can bless it.*

The story is told of a man who was walking in a park one night. As he was turning the corner along the path, he heard what sounded like the screams of a woman coming from a thicket of bushes. He froze in his tracks, not knowing what to do. Fearing for his own safety, he thought that he should not get involved. Then he thought that he should try to help her because there was no one else around. Before he could debate within himself any longer, he found himself compelled into action. He ran toward the voice of the woman and pulled an assailant off her. Shocked and startled, the attacker immediately ran away. After the man was sure that the assailant was gone, he went back to help the woman. He called out to her, "Are you all right?" The woman thought that she heard a familiar voice and called out, "Daddy, is that you?" With a flood of thoughts and emotions coursing through his heart and mind, the man helped his own daughter from the ground. In that moment of reunion and embrace, the man could not help but ask himself, "What if I had kept going?"

What if the Good Samaritan had kept going? What if Jesus had decided to keep going past the screams of humanity for redemption and reconciliation? What if He had turned away from the cross as He passionately prayed in the Garden of Gethsemane? Like the man in this story, the "oil and wine" Church must let compassion compel it into action. The Church cannot keep going past the gay and the lesbian, pretending and pleading obliviousness to the cries of imprisoned souls. The "oil and wine" Church must consciously choose to get in the fray.

The Church: A Haven or a Hangout?

God has called the church to be a haven for hurting homosexuals and not a hangout for practicing ones. In *Lesbian No More*, Susan McDonald recounts an incident at the University Redlands at an annual conference. A skit was performed that was designed to showcase the need for the ministries of the church to meet the needs of different classifications of people. An elderly person came to the stage. She said that she was alone and did not have anyone to come to see her. Then another person from the audience got up and put their arm around her and walked out with her. This demonstrated that the church should have a ministry to the elderly. The point was well taken.

Then a child got up. He said that he got out of school at three o'clock and his mother worked and he did not have a father in the house. There were all kinds of things there to entice him into trouble. He said that he needed someone to help him and to take time with him. Suddenly someone got up and put their arm around the kid and took him to a program of sorts for children. Again, the point was well taken.

Then a woman got on the stage. She said that she needed help. She was by herself, she loved God with all her heart and she was studying for the ministry. She said that she could not change the way that she is. She then acknowledged that she is a lesbian and complained brokenheartedly that her particular denomination would not ordain her. It just so happens that the jurisdictional Bishop was in the audience. He wore a ribbon on his clerical collar that is the emblem of the gay movement and indicated his sympathetic identification with the homosexual agenda. The woman received acceptance in the skit as the others had and the audience once again understood the apparent point. The message was simply that the church should accept homosexuality and lesbianism as a legitimate lifestyle and that it should not deter one's ordination to ministry. The Bishop's silence and ribbon gave credence to this perspective.[4]

At the same time a woman arose to address the gathering. She was not a part of the cast, but was a lay member and felt that she could hold her silence any longer. She reverently addressed the Bishop saying that she still believed in the Church and in the Bible. She testified of having been a lesbian for 10 years earlier in her life and had been free from the indulgence for the past 20 years. She indignantly asked him why he let people *propagate the lie that homosexuality is acceptable and that homosexuals cannot change.* She went on to say that her change was not overnight, but was eventual and full. Her conversion to Christ was in an instant, but the reality is that it took a long time to completely embody the truth of transformation. She said that she had to learn to overcome her pre-dispositional programming. She had to be willing to be celibate rather than to be homosexual. She testified that God brought her back to the path of wholeness and later restored her relationship with her family and brought a husband into her life. She was now living a life of fulfillment. *She concluded that the Church should not compromise its convictions for the convenience of appeasing adamant opponents.* Her stand upon the truth was the right thing to do and it is the right thing for every believer in the life-changing, soul-transforming power of the blood of the Lamb of God to do also.

—THE CHURCH IS ADMONISHED— TO "GET INTO THE FRAY"

The wicked flee when no man pursueth: but the righteous are bold as a lion (Proverbs 28:1).

The first thing the "oil and wine" Church must do is: *Get into the fray.* To boldly speak out against accommodation and in favor of transformation is not homophobic, nor is it unwise in winning souls. To do so is to say you are agreeing with what is admonished in His Word. To love the holy Church, the human community, and the heartland country, and yet remain silent

> SINCE GOD'S CHURCH IS NOT A GAY CHURCH, NO BELIEVER WHO HAS ACCEPTED CHRIST SHOULD CLASSIFY HIMSELF AS A GAY CHRISTIAN.

about homosexuality, is to live in contradiction to the cross and cause of Christ.

The Christian way is the vocal way. The Master Teacher modeled God's method of the ministry of reconciliation by boldly confronting human concerns. Jesus never looked for a fight, but He never avoided the fray either.

Speaking Up and Out

Silence perpetuates the hurt for all those who are caught in homosexuality's closing tentacles. Since God's Church is not a gay church, no believer who has accepted Christ should thereby classify himself as a gay Christian. The Church cannot push the mute button on this bothersome issue. The Church is called to speak to the society. Despite rejection, we must realize that an initial reaction of denial and self-justification could possibly become acceptance. Those who are redeemed should say so (see Ps. 107:2). Loving confrontation, spoken through vessels of compassion and clarity, is the way. Homosexuals are at home in the church, but only if they are willing to abide by the rules of the house.

—THE CHURCH IS ADMONISHED— TO "GET A TRANSFORMED MIND"

...Be not conformed to this world: but be ye transformed by the renewing of your mind, that ye may prove what is that good, and acceptable, and perfect, will of God (Romans 12:2).

The second thing that the "oil and wine" Church must do is: *Get a transformed mind.* The Church has to commit itself to being the conduit of change, always believing that people are capable of being transformed no matter what they conformed to in their past (see Rom. 8:11). The word *trans* means "to go from one date or place to another." To *form* is to mold or to make. What good is getting into the fray if you are powerless to deliver those bound by the same-sex force? Far too many churches use people to build buildings, instead of using buildings to build people. This must change if we expect to change homosexuals.

Transforming Sinners Into Saints

The pious fellowship permits no one to be a sinner. So everyone must conceal his sin from himself and from the fellowship. We dare not be sinners. Many Christians are unthinkably horrified when a real sinner is suddenly discovered among the righteous. So we remain alone in our sin, living in lies and hypocrisy. The fact is we are all sinners![5]

Dietrich Bonhoeffer

The Greek word for *transformed* is *metamorphoo*. It is the same word that is translated in the English as *metamorphosis*. It means "to change from within." The hard core homosexual does not want to be transformed. Change is a word that a person who is comfortable in their present state of being is unable to receive with gladness. If a person is not interested in being changed, they interpret your insistence upon it as rejection. In their psyche, their identity is predicated upon their sexuality. They see themselves by a sexual measuring stick, and they monitor society by its acceptance of their mind-set.

Therapeutic healing will result in tremendous change. Years ago, I preached in a church in Pittsburgh. As I left the sanctuary, I overheard the pastor publicly stating that he agreed with what I had supposedly said during the message—"Once a homosexual, you are always a homosexual." As God is my witness, I never said anything like that. In fact, I completely disagree with him. Countless numbers of people have changed. With God, nothing shall be impossible.

Although society and the church are separate, to some degree they go hand-in-hand. Church members are citizens of the greater society. The unchurched of the streets are the same ones who will eventually pack the church pews. In God's eyes, the division between the sacred and the secular merge at the cross. *Your public and your private life should be synonymous with each other. The distance between the two sides of yourself is the actual measure of your character.* If there is a gaping hole or a holy gap, then your character is in definite need of a makeover. Sinners become winners when they change their ways.

> THE DISTANCE BETWEEN THE TWO SIDES OF YOUR-SELF IS THE ACTUAL MEASURE OF YOUR CHARACTER.

Transforming the Situation

The job of the Church is not to *conform* to the culture, but to *transform* the culture. If you freeze water in a square ice tray, it comes out square. If you put it in a round ice tray, it comes out round. Christians are not to let the world squeeze us into its mode of thinking. We do not change our views and philosophy of life simply because it is acceptable, the culture is changing, or because we want to be politically correct. We stand for God and for God alone. However, while being resolute, we should not be self-righteous and harsh toward hurting people who are sincere in their search for God. *The "oil and wine" Church is God's Church and God is Love.* God is just and God is good all the time and even beyond time. The homosexual is not an alien. Glory, glory, hallelujah! It is time to lay the homophobic burden down.

It is wrong to preach one thing and then practice another, and it is wrong to pretend that "nothing is wrong, and therefore, we should all just perpetrate getting along." After Rodney King's 1992 beating at the hands of the Los Angeles Police Department (LAPD) and the subsequent riots, the reporters questioned him and his reply was, "Can't we all just get along?" The Church has taken such a bad beating at the hand of the L-licentious, A-anything goes, P-perverted, D-dumb-dogs crowd, that we now apologize for being apostolic. The Church must not apologize, but instead offer an apologetic that transforms people's lives by the truth. We cannot do it saying, *"I'm okay, you're okay,"* or by singing, *"Kum Ba Ya"* while eating proverbial popcorn together. *Transforming ministry is challenging ministry.* It is bold, in your face, and it is filled with the gracious love of God. It is the *oil* and the *wine* that is applied to lives that transforms them from losing ones to winning ones, from sinning ones to grinning ones, and on to new beginning ones. Everyone has access to the throne of grace no matter what their state of disgrace. Unless a person evidences a new lifestyle in Christ, there's no evidence of conversion. The Scripture says, *"Therefore if any man be in Christ, he is a new creature: old things are passed away; behold, all things are become new"* (2 Cor. 5:17).

Transforming the Scene

The accusatory question of the pro-gay activist is this: Why is the Church making an issue of homosexuality if Jesus did not? I contend with the premise of the question. The Church, in the process of preaching the gospel, must engage the culture in which it is placed with the relevant truth of God's Word. To fail to do so is to make the "Great Commission" the "late omission." Preaching the gospel and teaching those things concerning the Kingdom of God is judgment work. Failure to warn society of inherent and impending judgment is irresponsible, inexcusable, and an indisputable dereliction of Christian duty. The result is that the blood of the lost will be required at someone's hand. The prophet Ezekiel declared, *"When I say unto the wicked, O wicked man, thou shalt surely die; if thou dost not speak to warn the wicked from his way, that wicked man shall die in his iniquity; but his blood will I require at thine hand"* (Ezek. 33:8).

For the Church to transform lives, it must reexamine its apostolic roots and also its fruit toward the homosexual for the last two millennia. The history of the "old way" church's attitude toward homosexuals is quite shameful. A great deal of what the Church has done falls into the category of inhospitality, to the infinite degree. It is impossible to transform the soul of someone whose basic person has been maligned and maliciously murdered in the name of God. The Church has at times been guilty of hostile treatment and hateful homophobic behavior against gays and lesbians. It is no wonder that many of them have *rejected* the Christ of the Christians as well as the church they attend. They have *elected* to have the same-sex life, and they have *selected* to attend the so-called gay church. A homosexual was once invited to a church worship service and he replied flippantly, "Church? Isn't that where God hates me?" The answer is, "*Of course not!*"

Transforming the Sanctuary

Where there are no gays, lesbians, whoremongers, adulterers, bisexuals, or pornographers, the sanctuary may be clean, but more than likely it is not full. The Master Teacher said, "*Go out unto the highways and hedges, and compel them to come in, that My house may be filled*" (Lk. 14:23b, emphasis added). An empty sanctuary makes of none effect the message of the empty tomb. St. Paul said, "*Christ Jesus came into the world to save sinners; of whom I am chief*" (1 Tim. 1:15b). He further stated, "*But if our gospel be hid, it is hid to them that are lost*" (2 Cor. 4:3). A pastoral colleague shared with me that in the days following 9/11, his sanctuary was used to house those who had been stranded in the Denver Airport. Literally hundreds of people

> WHERE THERE ARE NO GAYS, LESBIANS, ADULTERERS... THE SANCTUARY MAY BE CLEAN, BUT MORE THAN LIKELY IT IS NOT FULL.

slept, ate, and were cared for in the sanctuary of his local church. Accordingly, the sanctuary was transformed. People from different parts of the world and those of different religions graced the place with their presence. It was the most beautiful thing that they have ever seen in their church. The transforming of the sanctuary is par for the course when the Church embraces the call to reach out to the down, out, wounded, hurting, and those in need of hospitality by the saints.

—THE CHURCH IS ADMONISHED— TO "GET BACK TO THE CROSS"

For the preaching of the cross is to them that perish foolishness; but unto us which are saved it is the power of God (1 Corinthians 1:18).

The third thing that the "oil and wine" Church must do is: Get back to the cross. There is no way to preach the death of Christ without preaching the cross of Christ. The cross is a vicarious and victorious way. The Christian life evolves around crucifixion while resolving lustful mortification. The cross is the cure-all for the flesh. Crucifixion to the world is the call of the Church. Friends of God are not friends of the world. To be in the "oil and wine" Church, you must be prepared to be persecuted. It is the cost for taking up the cross and being perversion's boss. Showing yourself friendly is right, but never at the expense of selling out the Friend who sticks closer than any brother.

> THE DEEPNESS OF GOD CALLS TO THE DEEP PAIN, HURT, AND PREDISPOSITION OF THE HOMOSEXUAL.

Satan always goes up and down, to and fro, seeking whom he may devour (see 1 Pet. 5:8). The direction of up and down forms the *vertical* bar, and the direction of to and fro forms the *horizontal* bar. Together, they form a cross. The cross is his biggest nightmare. It reminds him of his greatest defeat. The early Christians gloried in the cross and followed it into battle. They marched onward as Christian soldiers, "marching on to war, with the cross of Jesus going on before." The Church was *confrontive* and *combative*, and eager to fight fictitious fables with sound doctrine. The Church stood for something. Too often today, the Church is *content* with the presence of *malcontent* in ministry.

Getting Back for Christ's Sake

For Christ's sake, the "oil and wine" Church must get back to the cross as it faces this 21st-century crisis of crossover. What shall we do? What shall we teach? Who shall we believe—God or the world? Shall we submit to the lordship of Jesus or succumb to the current culture? These questions were answered long ago in the apostolic commission. We must preach that "*holiness, without which no man shall see the Lord*" (Heb 12:14). If we fail to preach *holiness*, it will result in an *unholy* mess! The "oil and wine" Church is a *holy* nation, serving a *holy* God, worshiping Him in the beauty of *holy* lives and perfecting *holiness* in the fear of God. What we demand of others we must demand of ourselves. Regardless of what a professed homosexual perceives as his orientation, he must be holy. The Christian Church is referred to as a *Holy Nation* in its constitution, *The Holy Bible* (see 1 Pet. 2:9). St. Paul wholeheartedly exhorts his son, Timothy, to "*lift up holy hands, without wrath and doubting*" (1 Tim. 2:8). Hands that are uplifted should not be let down to do down low deeds of disobedience. One is reminded that when the Patriarch Moses' hands were let down on the mountain, there was defeat in the valley (see Ex. 17). As long as they were raised in praise, the enemy was routed throughout the day. In the old western movies, the sheriff was known to say, "Come out, with your hands up!" As the Church identifies with the cross of Christ, it may not increase in popularity, but it will never decrease in power either. Without the cross, the Church has lost its compass. Without it, the Church will never find its way through the man-pleasing, materialistic, mind-set that meddles with its mission.

Getting Back for the Generations' Sake

One generation shall praise Thy works to another, and shall declare Thy mighty acts (Psalm 145:4, emphasis added).

And also all that generation were gathered unto their fathers: and there arose another generation after them, which knew not the Lord, nor yet the works which He had done for Israel (Judges 2:10, emphasis added).

This generation will remain degenerate, unless they are regenerated by the cross. It is at the cross where everyone first sees the light. Many nations today are losing their sin-consciousness because of the Church's losing the notion of cross-centeredness. Rampant-running impurity is the sinful result. The voice of the Father speaks resoundingly, *reaching* us and *revealing* to us His heart for the nation and the generation. The fathers have already praised Him; the children must praise Him; and the generation yet to be born is destined to praise Him. It is the job of the baby-boomer generation and the X generation to prepare the way for the next generation, which is the one who will seek His face (see Ps. 24). This is our watch. The prophet asked, "Watchman, what of the night?" The answer came, "The morning cometh, and also the night" (Is. 21:11-12). Watchmen are compared to watchdogs in Isaiah 56:10. A dog may not always bite, but the least it can do is bark. A dog that *cannot*, or even worse, *will not* bark is a poor specimen of a dog. A minister may not bite, that is, he may not be very effective in the demonstration of the Spirit of God, but at least he can bark.

Getting Back for Our Sake

Many of the sermons in the church speak of "taking it back," but only a few speak of "getting back." Today's "oil and wine" Church must sing, "Take us back to the place when we first believed [the cross] to get back what we first received [salvation]." The heavenly council has been adjourned. The text has been read, and the agenda, as well as the arguments, have been made known. The votes are cast; the yeas have it. The gay and lesbian agenda has been denied.

The past will not be held against them, and all will be forgotten and forgiven. The church is as much their home as any other sinner's who is saved by God's grace through faith in the blood of the Lamb. The blood will bring diffusion of the confusion by way of transfusion. Sin must be judged without judgmentalism. We must provide a way of escape that is one of insulation and not isolation. We must critique our words before we seek to criticize God's world. The Church must be the Church, because the world will always be the world. *The Church produces saints. The world produces aints.* Saints should live, because the aints ain't trying to be a saint above taint. The saints will go marching in, and those who faint will go falling out.

Homosexuals need mighty change, and the Church needs major change. The doctrine and demeanor do not change, just the dogmatism and ostracism. We must get back to the cross, which takes us to the throne. In so doing, we are truly *being* the Church and not simply *doing* church stuff. Religion, by itself, never saved anyone. For Christ's sake, for the generations' sake, and for our own sake, we must get back to the cross.

—THE CHURCH IS ADMONISHED— TO "GET WITH ONE ACCORD"

These all continued with one accord in prayer and supplication (Acts 1:14a).

The fourth thing that the "oil and wine" Church must do is: *Get with one accord.* The Church is not Democratic; it is not Republican; it is not Black; nor is it White. The Church is not American; it is not European; it is not male; it is not female. The Church is one. Where there is a unified stand, there will be strength to stand against the fiery darts and the bogus charge of homophobia. Being in one accord will prevent dissonant discord, and it will afford complete concord. The Bible is concise on this.

1. *And they, continuing daily with **one accord** in the temple...* (Acts 2:46, emphasis added).

2. *And when they heard that, they lifted up their voice to God with **one accord**, and said, Lord, Thou art God...* (Acts 4:24, emphasis added).

3. *...and they were all with* **one accord** *in Solomon's porch* (Acts 5:12, emphasis added).

4. *And the people with* **one accord** *gave heed unto those things which Philip spake...* (Acts 8:6, emphasis added).

5. *...having the same love, being of* **one accord**, *of* **one mind** (Philippians 2:2, emphasis added).

6. *...all the people answered with* **one voice**, *and said, All the words which the Lord hath said will we do* (Exodus 24:3, emphasis added).

7. **One Lord, one faith, one** *baptism* (Ephesians 4:5, emphasis added).

8. *There is* **one body**, *and* **one Spirit**, *even as ye are called in* **one hope** *of your calling* (Ephesians 4:4, emphasis added).

9. *...that ye stand fast in* **one** *spirit, with* **one mind** *striving together for the faith of the gospel* (Philippians 1:27, emphasis added).

The Church Has Game

I once preached a sermon entitled, "Church Got Game." This is an urban slang expression which means that one is quite capable of representing who they are. The Church is a shining city, not a hushed hamlet. The Church is the real deal. The Church is "all dat and a bag full of chips." Two believers coming together can put ten thousand homosexual, agenda-promoting activists to flight. Let the Church be the Church. Let God be true, and let the damnable heresies of God's acceptance and accommodation of homosexuality be revealed as a regurgitated end-time lie. The Bible exhorts the believer to *"come out from among them, and be ye separate..."* (2 Cor. 6:17). The Church that is "called out" must "come out" or else it is not a Church. Just as there are some gays who never went into the closet, there are other gays who have come out of the closet. The Church should come out of the corner. Whoever heard of a lion hiding in a broom closet? Selah.

The Church Has Differences

Among the various protestant denominations, there have always been sundry doctrinal differences. However, on major issues such as the sacred sacraments, there has always been a widespread consensus. For example, the essential doctrine of water baptism is fairly consistent throughout Christendom, even though there may be a variance in the methods. The basic tenet is generally consistent throughout all denominations. Differences should be celebrated; dirty sex sin should not be tolerated any more than drunks who are inebriated.

The Church Has Life

The Church is a living organism, not merely a liturgical organization. The Church must be lively stones that build lives recycled for newness in Christ. The unclean thing should not be seen if it refuses to be *re-gened*. Unclean garments should not be worn; unclean lives should not be lived; unclean hearts and hands should not be lifted up. The Church must be the Church and we must get with one accord. A person, whose sexual practice is contrary to providence, should have no access to the practice of a ministry. He should have access to marriage only if he respects the ordinance, changes his ways, and marries someone of the opposite sex. Biblical mandates discriminate against those who mate without marriage. It is called fornication. The Bible is clear. No fornicator shall inherit the kingdom of God (see 1 Cor. 6:9). Selah.

—THE CHURCH IS ADMONISHED— TO "GET RIGHT WITH GOD"

...Homosexuals' willingness to confess their struggles and seek freedom may depend in part on the values and attitudes around them. Do church members confess their faults and failures to one another? Does one uphold for the other a word of encouragement and a vision of wholeness that enable him to walk uprightly? In short, is Christ's law fulfilled in the church by bearing one another's burdensome sins and weaknesses...?[6]

Andrew Comiskey, *Pursuing Sexual Wholeness*

The fifth thing that the "oil and wine" Church must do is: *Get right with God.* The songwriter said, "Get right with God and do it now. Get right with God, He will show you how. Down at the cross, where He shed His blood. Get right with God. Get right, get right with God." As the Church itself is right with God, it maintains authority to speak into the post-modern, hedonistic, and humanistic culture. Young Christian men must guard themselves and gird themselves up in the loins of their mind. Young women of God are encouraged to marry without hurry and to raise up a godly seed who experience transgenerational covenant. Those ensnared in same-sex attraction must recognize it as a distraction and sinful infraction. Those who refuse to get right should get moving.

Getting Right Is Reasonable

To get *right* with God is only reasonable (see Rom. 12:1-2). It is not exceptional. The Church that is not *right* with God is unqualified to represent Him. Being *right* means being on the *right* side of the issues, being on the *right* hand of power, and being *right*-side up. It means to have *right* thinking, *right* believing, and *right* speaking. It means to walk right and talk *right*. It means to embrace *righteousness* and be in *right* standing with God. It means to do the *right* thing the *right* way for the *right* reason. It means to have the *right* stuff and to exercise your *rights* in Christ. Righteousness is a *force* that is greater than the sword of the armed forces (see Prov. 14:34). America has arguably the greatest armed military force in the history of known civilization. With lightning-strike immediacy and precision-point accuracy, its military forces are poised to defend America against adversaries within and without its continental shores. The "oil and wine" Church in America must stand as an invading force of righteousness enlisting supernatural help. Practicing the love of Christ, the Church will help to save our nation's very soul.

Getting Right Is Rational

Josiah, Israel's young king, exercised his rationale by doing what was right. "*And he did that which was right in the sight of the Lord, and walked in all the way of David his father, and turned not aside to the right hand or to the left*" (2 Kings 22:2). His actions included dealing with sexual idolatry in the temples and in the groves (prostitution houses). God blessed him because he dealt a radical blow to the root of homosexuality which is homo-genitality. Since the body has long been considered a temple of God, men worshiped Him with their temple's altar, namely their sex organs or genitals. Those who sat in darkness became irrational in thinking they could copulate with their god indirectly by having sex with male and female prostitutes directly. Godly kings always did the right thing and kicked the idols right out. *Homo-genitality* is a term that speaks of people of the same sex relating physically to one another, but not because of a predisposition or orientation. Primarily, it was in a religious context of idolatry. History reveals that many men who participated in homosexual acts also had wives and an active heterosexual life. They were not bisexual, but they were engaged in homo-genitality in the context of their religion.

Getting Right Is Rewarding

Hezekiah, another of the illustrious kings, did the same thing as Josiah: "*And thus did Hezekiah throughout all Judah, and wrought that which was good and right and truth before the Lord his God*" (2 Chron. 31:20). As long as he did what was right, God blessed the nation. If the Church loves the nation, it

MINISTERING GRACIOUSLY TO THE GAY AND LESBIAN COMMUNITY

must do what is right. Sovereign intervention will result from a right spirit. Church-wide repentance will lead the way to a rewarding national move of God. Toward the end, Hezekiah forgot God, and when he did, his reward became short-lived. Strangely, Balaam, while riding a mule, was subjected to a hesitation on the beast's part to proceed further. The "thing between his legs" (the mule) started acting "crazy." Whenever this happens, in a genital sense, the private parts become purveyors of perversion, and pain is the perpetual result. Balaam was wrong, and the mule was right. The truly crazy one was Balaam himself. He never did get right with God. The thing between his legs acted the way it did only because the one who was supposed to be in control, lacked control.

—THE CHURCH IS ADMONISHED— TO "GET ITS HOUSE IN ORDER"

While the Church remains respectable, many of us will remain hypocrites, people who look good on the outside but keep our compulsions on the inside.[7]

Briar Whitehead

The sixth thing that the "oil and wine" Church must do is: *Get its house in order.* Apostolic ministry always sets things in order. Too many churches have become diss-ordered. Know this: God does not pay for what He does not order. It is a bad thing to be *dissed* by God. This happens when one gets out of order. The songwriter said it well, "Sweep around your own front, before you try to sweep around mine." As the Church reexamines its soul, it will reach the homosexual soul. In the BKW Young Preachers Institute, I have trained nearly 300 young ministers to know that a "minister must preach from the *depths* of his *soul* to reach the *depths* of people's *souls*." You cannot lead people to a place where you are not willing to go to yourself. *Deep calls unto deep*; and if a move of God is to have depth, it must *penetrate* the soil, *permeate* the soul, *procreate* the spirit, and *germinate* the seed. It must *irritate* the flesh. It must *agitate* the carnal mind, and it must *devastate* human self-will. In so doing, it will be blessed. The thing that is weakening the Church's ability to speak into the moral conscience of our nation is the spirit of compromise. It has infiltrated the righteous ranks.

When David committed adultery with Bathsheba and ordered her husband placed on the frontline of battle to cover up his misdeed, sin entered in. Some time later, his son Absalom killed his own brother Amnon. He was avenging the rape of Tamar, their sister. David's earlier adulterous compromise disabled his ability to deal properly with Amnon and Absalom. The previous lack of integrity in his own life had neutralized him. Absalom defied his father even further by committing adultery with David's concubines in the sight of Israel (see 2 Sam. 16:22). David's house was out of order because of the latent and unresolved issues of his past. He recovered his integrity by never making the same mistake twice. To err is truly human and to recover all is truly the work of the divine. First Samuel 30:18 says, "*And David recovered all that the Amalekites had carried away....*" Without prophetic ministry, the lapsed masses meander in a meaningless morass that is otherwise known as a major mess. These things will not happen when the house is in order.

The Church of the Open Door

To get its house in order, the Church must repair its altars and then open the doors. This is not introspection. Of itself, that only leads to depression. When you look down, you are *depressed*; when you look within, you're usually *distressed*; but whenever you look up, you're *blessed*. The *examination* is for the purpose of *location*. To get direction, you first determine *where you currently are*. The Church must rediscover *who we are, what we are* to be about, and *where we are*. The Church has to be open and *teachable* if the gay person is going to be opportunely *reachable*. Homosexuals will not try to climb through windows if the Christians keep the door of the house locked. The Church of the open door soars.

The Church That Soars

To soar, the Church must rediscover its soul and resubmit to spiritual surgery. This will remove all the worldly soul ties that practice cowardice. It is a shame, a low-down dirty shame, that "boldness" is no longer considered a virtue in the Church. The righteous are to be bold as a lion (see Prov. 28:1). It is time for the Church to clean up its act; spread its evangelistic wings and soar; and clear its prophetic throat and roar. *The effeminate spirit will bow before the masculine sound. The mannish spirit will fall before the feminine sound.* It is time for the lion and lioness of God to accomplish the MISSION POSSIBLE. The Church that soars will also roar.

The Church That Roars

The return of the roar signifies *four*. *Four* is the creative number of God. After four days, Lazarus got up and got going. *Four* directions will take you anywhere you want to go—north, south, east, or west. Four seasons will have you cold, warm, hot, and chilly. When the Lion roars, four things happen:

1. He *creates* fear (panic).

2. He *gathers* his family (pride).

3. He *intimidates* foes (predators).

4. He *declares* his territory (property).

The Church that reexamines its soul will recover it and receive a return of their rooaaarr! When the roar returns, the Church will no longer whimper, waddle, and merely wade in the water. It will launch out into the deep, because the "oil and wine" Church is a revolutionary Church. It moves by revolution more than evolution. A revolutionary Church is no longer *pathetic, apathetic, under the influence of an anesthetic, but is apostolic* and *prophetic*. A revolutionary Church bears the yoke, but it does not yoke others.

The yoke of Christ is easy, but the yoke of judgment makes everyone uneasy (see Mt. 11:30). Lionel Ritchie once sang, "Easy Like a Sunday Morning." The Lord's Day should be an easy day, free of judgmentalism. There are those in the Church who claim they have *the gift of discernment*, but it is really *the gift of suspicion*. The only anointing they have is a Dick Tracy or Sherlock Holmes anointing for nosiness. As the Church mends the nets of prejudiced thinking, it will draw in all manner of fish (see Mt. 13:47). As the Church deals with its preconceived notions, nothing will be able to preclude the glory of God from being revealed (see Is. 60:1-4). Isaiah 58:9 says that we are to take away the pointing of the finger at people who are bound by sin. Whenever you point your finger at someone, you are yoking yourself to it. The yoke of someone else's sin is even harder to bear than the yoke of your own sin. The judgment you give to others is what you receive yourself. There are three fingers pointing back at you. The putting forth of the finger will put people out of the house of God. In all their getting, some people need to get out of people's business and stay out.

> THE CHURCH MUST BE DELIVERED FROM PARANOIA, WHICH MANIFESTS IN HOMOPHOBIA.

We recognize that same-sex attraction, marriage, or orientation is not the way, truth, or life. We also recognize that the gay, the lesbian, and the bi-sexual are not the beast, the antichrist, or the false prophet either. The Church must be delivered from paranoia, which manifests in homophobia. If we minister to a sinner, what he has will not get on us. The issue of transference needs to be settled. In order to reach others in their issues, we must first deal with church issues. As we judge ourselves and set our house in order, we become qualified to minister grace, mercy, and peace to others.

—THE CHURCH IS ADMONISHED— TO "GET ITS HEAD ON STRAIGHT"

...the whole head is sick...there is no soundness in it... (Isaiah 1:5-6).

Crookedness

The seventh thing that the "oil and wine" Church must do is: *Get its head on straight.* A notable man of God reportedly surmised that 75 percent of God's best preachers are destroyed by sexual sin. Although there is no way to prove the validity of the above claim, it certainly can be viewed as credible. The pastors and preachers are the leaders. Leadership must shoot straight. They must not vacillate. Today, the heads of the Church are either saying nothing or saying so many contrary things that it has resulted in an uncertain sound. The head must be on straight, or else the body does not move. As the head goes, so goes the body. When the cedar tree falls, the fir tree follows (see Zech. 11:2).

Contempt

Some years ago a minister fought the homosexual agenda in the school system, and he was subjected to a smear campaign. It was intense and on the magnitude of the $100 million investigation of former President Bill Clinton. The homosexuals were determined to find a chink in the armor, and they did. Unfortunately, in time, it was reported and ultimately confirmed that while this person was vehemently opposing the gay agenda, he was secretly involved in an adulterous affair. Needless to say, the enemies of righteousness ridiculed and held this person and the church in contempt. They paraded his failure before the American public like Samson was paraded before the drunken Philistine mob (see Judg. 16:25).

Contamination

Sinful heterosexual activity is periodically indulged in the personal lives of the membership of the local church. The challenge of the leadership is to get its head on straight, and to decontaminate the Body of Christ. Recently, it was reported by a leading hotel chain that whenever church conventions are held in their facilities, there is a marked increase in the pornographic pay-per-view movies ordered. This is a shameful, but needful admission. Simply stated, *the ministry is sexually awry.* There is much homosexual activity and non-covenantal heterosexual activity in church today. Both, according to the Scriptures, will disqualify one from the Kingdom of God (see 1 Cor. 6:9-10). It seems that the oil of holiness has run very low, and the light is almost out in the Temple. The Church must get its head on straight to confront the crookedness, the contempt, and the contamination.

—THE CHURCH IS ADMONISHED— TO "GET HOLY HELP"

The eighth thing God's "oil and wine" Church must do is: *Get holy help.*

THE POWER OF THE CHURCH IS IN ITS PURITY.

Oftentimes, the older preachers could be heard preaching and saying, "I feel my help coming on." The old saints would pray, "Lord, send help from Your sanctuary." The Church is called to function as a peculiar people who are called out of darkness and into the marvelous light (see 1 Pet. 2:9). Light requires a power connection. When there is a disconnect from the source, power is lost. It is a small wonder that gays and lesbians do not view the Church as their "divine connection" for holy help. Getting help is an acknowledgment of need. We need God's help, and He will send it if we seek it. *Help* is a four-letter word, but when it is uttered, it keeps Peter from drowning; it keeps the Syrophenician's daughter from losing her mind; and it keeps David from being pierced by Saul's javelin. With His help, our authority is intact; but without it, attempting ministry is a mere exercise in futility.

A Change in Perception

Perception is the basis of reality. Just as the (Iraqi) Abu Gharib prisoner abuse scandal undermined America's moral authority by altering the perception of America in the Middle East and indeed the world, unrighteousness in our ranks undermines our authority. *The power of the Church is in its purity. A loss of purity is equivalent to the salt losing its savor or the light being put under a bushel. As the Church, our authority is the written Word, but also the living Word, which is the Word made flesh.* Influence is a gift from God, and it should not be taken for granted. Even if others are not aware of the so-called Christian's secret life and closet homosexuality, it is known by the hosts of Heaven and the hosts of hell. Their actions will affect things for good or bad. Whatever affects one directly, affects others indirectly. The spirit world spectates into the human sphere on earth and will not hesitate to relay the information to other cohorts, who in turn will broadcast it until reproach is placed upon the name of Christ. Acts 19:15 says, *"And the evil spirit answered and said, Jesus I know, and Paul I know; but who are ye?"* Demons know whether the Church has the fire of God. The demons know when it's just sexual organs that are on fire. They know what's up! The Kingdom of God is in operation. Demons are cast out by the finger of God (see Lk. 11:20). The Kingdom of God is not merely in word, but it is also in deed.

A leader can say all the right things—*you teach what you know; however, you reproduce what you are.* This is true in all phases of life itself. It is very difficult to deliver someone from something that you yourself are bound by. The Church must get holy help by getting back to the basics of prayer, praise, preaching, and practicing what is preached. The Church must get holy help and escape in prayer to the hills much like Lot did when he fled for his life from the city of Sodom, a homosexual haven. The charge to keep can only be kept by those who have helped themselves to a recharge of the power supply. God's power to heal the homosexual is present in the Church. It is in the charged atmosphere of reality Church that the temperature is changed. Without the renewal, the current charge will not last. If the Church *fasts*, the power will *last*. When the Church *prays*, the anointing will *stay*. There is power to pull the perverted out of the fire, but we must pursue it to partake of it.

> *And others save with fear, pulling them out of the fire; hating even the garment spotted by the flesh* (Jude 1:23).

Changing Times

Though times have changed, the Church has stubbornly resisted change. The Church is in a peace mode, a "che sarà sarà" mood, and a hush-hush mind-set. A military policy that says, "Don't ask, don't tell," has become the church policy as well. We see it, smell it, and even know it, but only a few are asking or telling it. We need help to deal with the sexual concerns. When holy help is received, it will result in a quantitative leap of ministry and a qualitative leap of membership. The lingering dysfunction that causes the Church to *dis-function* will be disabled. The explosive bomb of evil will be disengaged, and the hurting homosexual will finally have a place to be healed.

—THE CHURCH IS ADMONISHED—
TO "GET HEALED OF DYSFUNCTION"

*And they continued stedfastly in the apostles' doctrine and fellowship,
and in breaking of bread, and in prayers* (Acts 2:42).

The ninth thing that the "oil and wine" Church must do is: *Get healed of
dysfunction.* The word *dysfunction* simply means something that does not function correctly. Church dysfunction is much like family dysfunction. This dysfunction results from having our sanctified soul planted in the soil of
contradictory preaching and practice. Spiritual schizophrenia or having a double soul is the result. We sing, "Holy, Holy, Holy," and too often we live holey,
holey, holey. Even worse, many live ho-ley. The term "ho" is short for whore, or
whoremonger. The "old-way" church needs to become an "oil and wine" Church
that repairs what is broken, replaces what is irreparable, and reforms what has
been revived. The founders and fathers fulfilled their assignment; the apostolic
authorities today must finish what was faithfully started. They must author
creeds and canons that curtail the cresting tide of the critical assault of our articles of faith.

The Westminster Catechism and the Apostles Creed are great. However,
today, we also need 21-century ministry modems that synchronize our faith in
these chaotic endtimes. There are too many conflicting views that cast discrep-
ancy on the varied voices, and people do not know who to believe. Like the
dysfunctional family where people fail to communicate and talk things out, the
Church often does the same. Those outside see the conflict on the inside, but
no one talks about it. We must talk, both in prayer to God and to each other.
There is a conspiracy behind the silence. A dialogue with the disconnected is
needed. A dialogue will end the dysfunction. Dysfunction will not just disappear on its own. Sexual discussions are uncomfortable, but they are essential.
Imagine parents never discussing the subject of sex with their children. A
child left to himself will be in disarray by the end of the day. It is foolishness
to expect a child to raise himself. It is equally foolish to try to help the gay and
lesbian unless the Church gets over the phobia surrounding the subject of sex
in general and homosexuality in particular. The Church must deal with
deviant sex and erase the error of its deification in this generation. *Sex is not
king. Christ is King and Jesus is Lord.* The Spirit is still speaking to His Church.
Our dialogue must be moderated by the spirit of determinative justice that
replaces dysfunctional judgmentalism. Care will overcome condemnation, and
mercy will triumph over judgment (see Jas. 2:13). As the Church overcomes its
judgmental tendency and provides a healing haven, it will become a renewal
refuge. As it is willing to heal everyone, regardless of the person's *orientation,
station,* or *determination,* it will experience its own healing. Something on the
inside will work on the outside, the congregation of the righteous will become
more concerned, and their lives will become more clear.

The Comprehensive Admonition:
In Conclusion
Are Homosexuals at Home in the Church?

The Concerned Congregation

There is therefore now no condemnation to them which are in Christ Jesus, who walk not after the flesh, but after the Spirit (Romans 8:1).

In conclusion, consider the following scenario. If a person came into the average church on a Sunday morning and publicly asked for prayer for his son who has cancer, everyone's heart would go out to him. It would not matter if he was rich or poor. The fact is human empathy flows heart to heart. The church would pray fervently for him. But what if a lady stood up right after that and requested prayer for her children because her son is a homosexual and her daughter is a lesbian? Suddenly, most would not have prayed outwardly, but perhaps displayed smirking faces of pity, disdain, and disgust, not necessarily at the suppliant, but at the homosexual son or daughter. After church, her prayer request was probably the dinnertime topic of discussion. Very few prayed for her, but a lot talked about her. This is dysfunction, and far too often it is in the church. The "oil and wine" Church is to be a house of prayer, where you can cast your care. It is not gossip central where a person feels stripped bear.

Continuing the imaginary analogy, another person stands up saying, "Please pray for me; I was diagnosed with leukemia." The congregation, knowing the terror of this disease, would be willing to immediately and fervently pray for healing. However, if in that same meeting, someone who has been diagnosed with AIDS stands up and publicly acknowledges that he has the dreadful disease and requests prayer, a great deal of people around him would become uncomfortable at his presence and begin instinctively protecting themselves and their children from contamination. Second Timothy 1:7 says, *"For God hath not given us the spirit of fear; but of power, and of love, and of a sound mind."* Gayness is not a pestilence. *Homophobia* is not an acceptable way for God's Church to conduct itself. The question, "Is the homosexual welcome in the Church?" is best answered, "Yes!" The altar work and the follow-up ministry of the "oil and wine" Church is its service department. Just as broken appliances, automobiles, and other accessories need to be serviced, so do human beings. Those overcome in sexual sin need help to be healed. The above-mentioned illustration may seem atypical, but in my view it is quite often par for the course. Concerned Christians are not a delicacy; they are a necessity. Concerned Christians possess a clean spirit, without which it is impossible to reach the window.

The Clean Congregation

Solomon said, *"Where no oxen are, the crib is clean"* (Prov. 14:14). It is another way of saying there is no mess. Of course, you know what "mess" is, don't you? Mess is the bent wrist, the high-pitched voice, the effeminate walk, the corrupted musician or choir leader, the lust-filled usher, the unclean preacher, the closet homosexual, and the struggling worker. The Church, like Noah's ark, must be inclusive and exclusive. Where there is no struggling sinner, there is no true Church. Where there is no standard of saintliness, it is a false church. The church that is totally clean is totally out of touch with the corruption that is in the world. The church that is filthy and dirty is out of contact with the purity that is in Heaven. The Master Teacher taught us to pray, *"Thy will be done in earth, as it is in heaven"* (Mt. 6:10b). The church that is filled with dirty souls who are being cleaned is Heaven on earth. The church that is filled with clean souls who refuse to reach out to those who are dirty is not Heaven at all. Christians must learn that they can touch the victims of the leprosy of sin without touching the sin itself. Only those with clean hands are qualified to operate on dirty souls. Where there is mess, there needs to be a consistent message. The message is: "Do not bring your mess in here. Do not bring your evil intentions into the house of God unless you intend to repent of them and change your ways." The Church must not throw dirt at sinners who are already dirty, but it must not try to sweep over it either. Dirt should be buried, not swept over. If the homosexual insists on the perpetration of male-to-male penetration, he must be served a decree of evacuation. Such things should not be, once named, among us as becometh saints (see Eph. 5:3). Selah.

> OPEN THE GATES AND BOLDLY DECLARE HOMO-SEXUALS ARE WELCOME... AND SO IS EVERY OTHER SINNER, TOO!

The "oil and wine" Church is not a museum for polished saints painted on the canvas of perfection. It is not a monument for only those whose faith has never faltered or who feel that they are better than everybody else because they have never fallen on their face.

The "oil and wine" Church is not a mausoleum of marble containing dead men's bones of past glories and achievement in an age of antiquity. It is a place like the Heritage Christian Center of Denver, Colorado, where Bishop Dennis Leonard is senior pastor. On the outside sign a very pronounced and powerful message is inscribed. It simply states: "Sinners Welcome Here." Those who open their arms and are ready to embrace those who have been closed out of the church are those who will harvest the disenfranchised and dis-fellowshipped of society. Legalism will keep a church as small as its thinking. Sinners should be able to go marching in, until eventually they are saints who go marching out. Love will enlarge our borders, enhance our impact, and increase our end-time importance. Open the gates and boldly declare homosexuals are welcome...and so is every other sinner, too! When the glory of love comes, no person will leave the gloomy way they came. When the wise men came bringing gifts to Jesus, they saw His star and fell down and worshiped Him. That night God warned them, through a dream, of King Herod's evil intentions toward them. They decided to take a different route back home to the East than the way they had come. *"And being warned of God in a dream that they should not return to Herod, they departed into their own country another way"* (Mt. 2:12).

When the gay and lesbian person comes in contact with the true and living God, his chance for help and healing increases exponentially. God's presence contains an atmospheric contact. Edward T. Welch, in *Blame It On the Brain,* candidly addresses homosexuality in the church.

> To make steady progress...one-time homosexuals need more than a counselor. Like us all, they need the larger body of Christ and its varied relational opportunities. Men need other men who love, listen, and model brotherly relationships. Women need other women with whom they can have close but not obsessive or sexualized relationships. Both men and women need elders and pastors who can faithfully pray, and, if necessary, bring church discipline as a means of God's loving correction...An effective church should *attract* homosexuals! That is, because of the love of Christ, the church should *pursue* them...The church should also welcome and draw the attention of those who struggle with homosexuality but have never been a part of the church. It should minister by surprising such people with love, a sense of family, and the absence of self-righteous judgment. It should offer truth in such a way that is convicting, winsome, and radically different from anything else the homosexual has ever heard. Has the church been, at times, self-righteous in its attitude toward homosexuals? Is there homophobia

in some of our congregations? Do we tend to think of homosexuality as worse than the gossip and private idolatries that are rampant in the church? Has the church been unwelcoming to unbelieving but spiritually searching homosexuals? The answer to these questions is certainly yes. More specifically, the answer is, "Yes, we have sinned."[8]

—COMPREHENSIVE MANIFESTO—

The word *comprehensive* suggests a complete and thorough coverage; and an *admonition* is a warning to proceed with caution. Throughout the Pauline Epistles, this word is used several times and always with a sense of urgency (see Rom. 15:14; 1 Thess. 5:12). Karl Marx penned the Communist Manifesto, and it ruined an entire continent for nearly a century. Dr. Francis Shaeffer wrote the Christian Manifesto, and it has blessed the Church for the last quarter of a century. To reach the gay and lesbian in our land, we need to heed the words of this brief comprehensive manifesto, throughout this 21st century. It contains a sixfold plan of action.

*The Church must comprehensively **expose** the myth that God made homosexuals like they are.* We can only do this as we are informed about the heresy the enemy is promoting under the guise of truth. *The Church must comprehensively **express** friendship to those who are victims of sexual brokenness.* We cannot call them faggots, perverts, whores, and sluts. The gospel group, the Williams Brothers, sings a song that says, "The only time you look down on someone is when you are picking them up." To have friends, we have to show ourselves friendly. First Corinthians 6:11 says, "*Such were some of you.*" To stay compassionate is our goal. To remain sensitive is the key. The Church must remember what it is called to be. We must show ourselves friendly, because without finding new friends in the Church, gay and lesbian people will most certainly return to their old ones. Thus, they are fulfilling their social and communal needs.

*The Church must comprehensively **effectuate** change over time.* It takes only a second for a person to give and receive forgiveness, but it may take a lifetime for deliverance in every way to occur. The process is both immediate and ultimate. It may take months and years of recovery to become reconstituted in one's internal being. Therefore, there has to be intentional reaching out to others by believers, even if it disturbs the comfort zone of your preferential circle of friends. *The Church must comprehensively **encourage** intentional relational development.* The persons whom we seek to reach must be those who seem out of reach. The perverse sin, we must hate; the sinner we must love.

We must be sensitive to decry the sin without denouncing their self-worth. We do not know their stories, their journeys, or what they have gone through to get through. We do not know their lifelong struggle. We have not sensed their pain. We have not seen their tears. We did not shed our sinless blood for their souls. Our Savior is also their Savior, and He took care of that. He has heard their groan from His throne. His *gracious Word* is the long-awaited Word. Since the righteous will scarcely be saved, we should be seriously scared of scarring the soul of the unsaved. Legitimacy in ministry is a mentality of humility, based in self-consideration, lest you also are tempted (see Gal. 6:1). A bigot of any sort should not wear the holy garments, and a believer bound by homophobic hysteria should not have a haven in which to hide. *"Let brotherly love continue"* (Heb. 13:1).

*The Church must comprehensively **endure** opposition.* Jesus stood before Pilate and said, *"I came to bear witness of the truth"* (see Jn. 18:37-38). Those were the next to last words before His execution. Pilate retorted, *"What is truth?"* Jesus never responded, because truth is not a thing, but a person. He said, *"I am the truth."* Herein the truth is manifested. *The church must comprehensively **envelop** change.* As disgusting, loathsome, reprehensible, despicable, and as *abominable as* the homosexual lifestyle is to all of the "so-called" straight saints, do not forget that all people have issues and stand in desperate need of God's grace. It is not enough to encourage "sinners" of all types to come to church; we must create an enveloping *atmosphere* of transformation. People should feel free to come in one way to the church, and be able to leave another way. They should exit on a street called straight. No longer will they be on the mean street, but rather the lean one. In so doing, the Church will have fulfilled its mission of loving people to life.

> PEOPLE SHOULD FEEL FREE TO COME IN ONE WAY TO THE CHURCH, AND BE ABLE TO LEAVE ANOTHER WAY.

With Christ's love, the ability to remit sins, the strength to deliver souls, and the wherewithal to provide counseling and prolonged therapy, we will effect change (see Jn. 20:23). We are the Church; we are not the answer. Jesus is! We are the Church. We are not the solution. Jesus is! We are the Church. We are not the Savior. Jesus is! He is the Lawyer who has never lost a victimized client; a Doctor who has never lost an AIDS patient. He is a good God; yes, He is. He is a good God. I know He is. God's gracious word to America is: The homosexual seeking change is at home in the Church! The homophobic is at home too. Only the merging of *fact* and *fear* will produce *force*. When

417

each of these sees up close what they have been afraid of, they will realize that *"perfect love casteth out fear: because fear hath torment..."* (1 Jn. 4:18b). *This is indeed a gracious word to the gay and lesbian community. The Comprehensive Admonition is that we need to make sure the Homosexual (seeking help)* is at home in the church. This is because of *The Caring Affection: The Gospel of Gracious Love.*

Prayer: Dear Lord, God of Abraham, Isaac, and Jacob. We are the Church, your Body in the earth. The government rests upon Your shoulders. Help us to stand shoulder to shoulder with Thee. The keys of hell and death are with Thee. The keys of Heaven and earth are with us. Help us to use the keys as faithful servants of Your cause and call. Help us to truly be comprehensive in our admonition, and compassionate and caring in our affectionate approach. Help us to speak into society a word that transforms lives. Renew our vision of the cross, and of ourselves, that we might be right with You and be the prophetic Church that You have called us to be. Heal our dysfunctions, recharge our power supply and challenge our leadership until we can truly say that the Church is Your Church and not our own. We need Thee; every hour we need Thee. O bless us now, our Savior, we come to Thee. In the name of Christ, our Rock, Amen and Amen!

ENDNOTES

1. Wendell Hoffman and Stanley Grenz, quoted by John Ankerberg and John White in *The Myth of Safe Sex* (Chicago, IL: Moody Press, 1993), 189.

2. Leanne Payne as quoted by Briar Whitehead, *Craving for Love*, (Grand Rapids, MI: Monarch Books, 2003), 96.

3. Andrew Comiskey, *Pursuing Sexual Wholeness* (Lake Mary, FL: Charisma House, 1989), 78.

4. Maxie D. Dunnam and H. Newton Malony, *Staying the Course*, (Nashville: Abingdon Press, 2003), 170-171.

5. Dietrich Bonhoeffer as quoted by Whitehead, *Craving for Love*, 303-304.

6. Comiskey, *Pursuing Sexual Wholeness*, 78.

7. Whitehead, *Craving for Love*, 305.

CHAPTER

TWELVE

Some people believe that there is already enough teaching that God warmly embraces everyone, and not enough teaching about God's justice and hatred of sin. This may be true, but it is no reason to sacrifice the greatness of the doctrine of grace...To know the grace of forgiveness, homosexuals must know the truth about themselves: they are sinners in need of grace.[1]

Edward T. Welch
Blame It on the Brain

A judgmental, uncaring attitude has driven countless people deeper into homosexual pattern and behavior. Few groups in society have faced as much condemnation from the church as homosexuals. We all know that Christ came into the world to save sinners, but often the impression is given that homosexuals are excluded from His love and grace. Such a gospel is unworthy of the name![2]

Erwin W. Lutzer
The Truth About Same-Sex Marriage

Christian love links love of God and love of neighbor in a twofold Great Commandment from which neither element can be dropped, so sin against neighbor through lack of human love is sin against God.[3]

Georgia Harkness (1891-1974)
Ecumenical Theologian

The Caring Affection:
The Gospel of Gracious Love

*And all bare Him witness, and wondered at the **gracious** words...*
(Luke 4:22, emphasis added).

It's All About Perspective

The fictional story has passed down through the generations that a king, who happened to also be a religious leader, decided that all the peasants would have to leave his country. This resulted in an enormous lamentation throughout the land, and the peasants petitioned him to change his mind. The religious king remained steadfast in his decision, but he proposed a debate with a peasant representative. If the peasant won, the others could stay. If he won, they would leave immediately. The peasants accepted his challenge. There was just one problem. No one would volunteer. All were afraid. Finally, they drafted an old woman named *Grace*. She was a domestic and had spent her life cleaning up after everyone's messy dirt. She was old, overlooked, and not outwardly rich. She had nothing to lose. So she agreed. She asked for only one consideration. Having been used to cleaning up after others, she was not used to talking much, and she asked that no side be allowed to talk. The religious ruler agreed.

The day arrived for the debate, and all the townspeople assembled at the site. The peasant and the king sat across from each other in complete silence for several minutes. Then the religious ruler raised his hand in the air and showed three fingers. *Grace* looked back at him and raised one finger. The religious ruler waved his fingers in a circle above his head. *Grace* pointed her finger at the ground. The religious ruler pulled out a wafer and a glass of wine. *Grace* pulled out an apple. The religious ruler stood up and said, "I give up. This woman is too good. The peasants can stay." The peasants let out a tremendous shout.

An hour later, the magistrates surrounded the religious ruler asking him what happened. He said, "First I held up three fingers to represent the Trinity. She responded by holding up one finger to remind me that there was still one God. The three are one. Then I waved my finger around me to show her

421

that God was all around us. She responded by pointing to the ground, showing that God was also right here with us. I pulled out the wine and wafer to show that God absolves us from our sins. She pulled out an apple to remind me of original sin. She had an answer for everything. What could I do?"

Meanwhile, the peasant community had crowded around *Grace*. They were amazed that this old, unheralded woman had done what all the king's scholars had insisted was impossible! "What happened?" they asked. "Well," said *Grace*, "first he said to me that the peasants had three days to get out of here. I told him that not one of us was leaving. Then he told me that this whole city would be cleared of the peasants. I let him know we were staying right here." "And then?" asked a man. "I don't know," said *Grace*. "He took out his lunch and so I took out mine."

The moral of the story is: *It's all about perspective!* I have learned in life that perspective is everything. A clear perspective eliminates confusion. An unclear one exacerbates delusion. In the previous eleven chapters of *Ministering Graciously to the Gay and Lesbian Community*, it has been our endeavor to present a Kingdom perspective of homosexuality. It is a thin line between love and hate, and a fine line between peace and war. Both of these conflicting concepts must be kept in balance or else the scale could tip on the side of leniency or the opposite side of legalism. In the ensuing pages of this conclusive chapter, we will shift in reverse before we shift into drive. We will review before we proceed.

Shifting Into Reverse

In Chapter One, we concluded that the *Confrontive Appeal* demands that the *Naked Truth Must Now Be Told*. The truth is that there are *men, married men, church members, and ministers on the down low*, and sisters *laying low*. To see deliverance, we must address the predatory culture and stop the vicious cycle of victimization. People need deliverance from the spirit of perversion, before it pulverizes their present state. This can be accomplished through *restoration, righteousness, reality, reproduction, reformation, removal,* and *reckoning*.

In Chapter Two, we concluded that the *"Church of the Apostles"* must recognize that *"God's Church Is Not a Gay Church!"* The Pauline, Petrine, and Johannine Epistles, as well as the apostolic fathers, provide no substantiation for the subjugation of God's Church. Over two millennia of church history reveal that the heritage of the church is in its differentiation and delineation from the world. Despite the differences concerning particular doctrines, the Church must facilitate the faith of the fathers and honor the time-tested teaching that they bequeathed to the Church. They opposed same-sex relationships and so must we.

In Chapter Three, we concluded that the *"Compassionate Approach"* in ministering *"Prophetic Solutions to Pathetic Situations"* is the only acceptable one. Gay bashing will not work. The homophobic hysteria has never worked. The derogatory demagoguery surely will not work. "I'm okay; you're okay" is bound to fail, as is the "God hates gays" approach. The calling of names such as fags, queers, etc., should be shunned. We also learned that whatever you point your finger at, you are yoked to. A popular children's movie includes a scene where an antagonist calls the lead character a slanderous name. He answers back, "I know you are. So what am I?" People who denigrate others do not like themselves, and they project their negative self-esteem onto others. We learned that the Good Samaritan, who helped the bleeding, half-dead man, typifies the Lord Jesus or the consecrated Christian. The injured man represents the sinner, the hurting saint, or even the wounded homosexual person. The priest represents the ministry; and the Levite, the membership. Their concern was for their own safety, whereas the other was concerned for the victim's safety. The ten acts of kindness provide the formula for the restoration of a homosexual person.

In Chapter Four, we concluded that the *"Composite Anointing"* is the only means of meaningful *"Ministry in the New Millennium."* Prophet Keith Grayton, before he died of AIDS, asked, *"Will the Church have oil for the 21st century?"* We answered his question with a resounding, yes! The oil that was applied to the wounded traveler is available to those who are pilgrims traversing through this world. The oil is for *ministry, vision, knowledge, good deeds, establishment, domination, receiving, delivering, healing, yoke destroying, wounds,* and *preaching.* We explored two types of oil, namely, synthetic and anointing oil. The synthetic oil provided spiritual parallels that it must be weighty, changed often, and kept fresh for maximum mileage. The anointing oil is needed for our worship, our preparation, and our healing of the homosexual.

In Chapter Five, we concluded that the *"Christological Apologetic"* will *"Set the Gay Record Straight."* Beginning in Genesis and progressing through the Epistles of the New Testament, we have defended against the revisionist post-modern teaching concerning the rightness of same-sex activity. We discovered that Sodom was destroyed in part, though not totally, because of homosexuality. We debunked the gay myth that Saul, David, and Jonathan were caught up in a love triangle of jealousy and attempted murder. We countered the charge that Jesus never addressed homosexuality directly, by stating that He never had to. He was never on the defensive concerning the subject. He was on the offensive in His teaching concerning God's order for marriage. We established that there are 25 gay-straightening reasons. They include reasons such as *it dishonors and devalues* the physical body through uncleanness and *it rearranges creation, but it cannot change procreation.*

In *Chapter Six*, we concluded that the *"Causation Argument"* seeks to justify *"Homosexuality and the Unholy Gay Trinity."* The biology argument does not support a predetermination for homosexuality, and the psychology and sociology arguments have nothing to stand upon, once this is removed. We examined several gay gene studies and established that they are inconclusive and have not been replicated in subsequent studies. We looked at the *"Making of a Homosexual"* by laying out the areas of *"Tendencies, Orientation, and Preference."* We proposed that homosexuality is attributed to a number of *heritable* factors, various exposures, and the upbringing of a child, rather than in the nature of his/her biological constitution.

In *Chapter Seven* we concluded that the cause of the *"Consequential Alternative"* results in the *"Legacy of Homo-Reality."* Statistics conclude that this chosen way of living results in grave and sometimes fatal tragedy. We categorized the *dangerous*, the *disease*-ridden, the potentially *deadly* and *divine* judgment that accompanies homosexuality. We discreetly itemized various homosexual activities that are best described as unclean and unholy. We asserted that though AIDS is not a gay or lesbian curse, it is disproportionately found among same-sex practitioners. Therefore, the "at risk" possibilities of participants is extremely high. We established the irrefutability of God's *law of sin and death* (see Rom. 8:2).

In *Chapter Eight*, we examined the *"Committed Action"* of the *"Militant Gay Agenda."* We exposed 11 pro-gay agenda items designed to covertly change the American public's perceptions of homosexuality. The areas of education, politics, and entertainment are three of these targeted areas. We exposed that no segment of society is off-limits to *homo-activism*, including many unsuspecting schoolchildren, who are sometimes exposed through curricula, to the "gay and gory" agenda and the loose and lesbian lifestyle. Often this is done without parental consent.

In *Chapter Nine* we saw the *"Confusing Apostasy"* of *"Gay and Lesbian Marriage."* We examined the potential hazards of its *legalization, licentiation,* and *legitimization.* We concluded that same-sex marriage is a horrendous hijacker of traditional marriage. We also pointed out that children, the civil rights movement, and the traditional family are unwilling hostages and convenient contraband in this attempted hostile he-he, she-she takeover. We further concluded that by virtue of its absence in the Bible and God's undeniable affirmation of heterosexual marriage, God has an opposing view. God is against same-sex marriage, and He will judge both it and the nations that support it. We discovered that though traditional marriage is oftentimes unsuccessful, it is not the institution that is at fault. It is the persons involved. Despite human failure, the Creator never scrapped the original plan. He never introduced a new paradigm for marriage. Additionally, we uncloaked the shadowy figures of polygamy and polyamory, as the twin offspring of the potential gay intrusion.

In *Chapter Ten*, we made a "*Combative Appeal*" to "*Evict the Gay Serpent From God's Garden.*" We concluded that harassment, influence, and control of individuals dealing with same-sex attraction, oftentimes, is demonic. Those targeted by the gay serpent must *be sober, serious, sure, sensitive, sincere, sure-spoken,* and *safe.* Using St. Paul's encounter with the vice-gripping viper, we illustrated what it means to evict the gay serpent. We paralleled spiritual serpents with natural ones, encouraging gay and lesbian persons to *shake the evil snake* and *make the devil take it back.* We gave several practical steps for attaining and maintaining deliverance from the spirit of homosexuality.

In *Chapter Eleven*, we answered the question of "*The Comprehensive Admonition*," namely, "*Are Homosexuals at Home in the Church?*" The answer was a cautious, yes! We concluded with nine admonishments to the "oil and wine" Church, designed to prepare it to welcome the gay or lesbian person who is in pursuit of God, into the house of God. We emphasized that practical ministry to homosexual populace will happen as the Church *gets into the fray, gets back to the cross, gets right with God,* and *gets in one accord.* We provided a *comprehensive manifesto* that reiterates the call for the Church to *get its house in order* so that the transformed *homosexual can be at home in the Church.*

—THE CONCLUSION OF THE MATTER—

Shifting Into Drive

In *Chapter Twelve*, we shall consider the *conclusion of the matter* by presenting the "*Caring Affection: The Gospel of Gracious Love.*" The word *gospel* means good news. It is a proclamation, a pronouncement, and a presentation of information that provides a way of escape. The term *gospel* is found in the New Testament 101 times in 95 verses. In each instance, it is distinguished as being representative of the Father's heart for fallen humanity. The Master Teacher often referred to the "*gospel of the Kingdom*" (see Mt. 24:14). It is in the dominion of the King that the good news finds its impetus. Without dominion, there is dreariness and blurriness. There is depression and defeat. There is mal-alignment and maladjustment. If we ever needed the gospel before, we sure do need it now. The good news is a divinely spiritual edict with dynamic social effect. It is a social gospel that has society-altering potential. The old adage of "If you can't beat them, join them" seems to rule the day. This is a counterfeit gospel. It sounds good. It feels good. On the surface, it even looks good, but it is woefully bad. It is poison!

It has been said that rat poison is 90 percent cornmeal and only 10 percent strychnine. It is not the cornmeal that is the problem; it is the additive that contains the killer ingredient. The Synoptic Gospels of Matthew, Mark, and Luke contain parabolic teaching concerning the true and the false, the wheat and the tares, the goat and the sheep. The Messiah promised that harvesttime will result in a separating of these various entities. The harvest is the end of the world (see Mt. 13:39). This suggests that the identificational lines of demarcation will be obscured until then. In a day, such as today, discernment is needed to know the difference. This is the generation that wants to "have its cake and eat it too." They want to be saved, sanctified, and satisfied from God's table, while dualistically dining on the dainties of deviance, while committing malice and sipping from the chalice of same-sex sensuality. They want to be considered as gay and Christian. In a very thoughtfully written work, a self-professed gay Christian, Herndon L. Davis writes:

> Black Gay/Lesbian Christians are alive and well and in many instances thriving beyond belief within the Black church!! Sadly, most are still deeply closeted, afraid of the retribution awaiting them from their congregations, fellow clergy, co-workers, family, neighbors, and friends. In actuality, Gays/Lesbians have always existed in the church, but have never been fully recognized or openly accepted across all spectrums of the Black mainstream. Contrary to popular belief, Black Gays/Lesbians do far more than just sing, shout and direct the church choir. We also serve as church pastors, preside as bishops, work as deacons, minister to the sick-and-shut-in, preach, teach, feed the homeless, and manage the church finances in the accounting and budgeting of church member tithes and offerings, many of whom are gay/lesbian. However, when the term Gay Christian or Homosexual Christian is dared uttered into existence, it usually evokes scorn, rebuke, fiery criticism, laughter, and questions, lots of questions. The most frequently asked are how can one be both Gay and a born again Christian?? Isn't that oxymoronic?? Must an individual rebuke one and accept the other?! How can you be both??? How can you

serve two masters?! How can you say you love God and do what you do??? How can you inherit the Kingdom of Heaven?!?!⁴

Greatly Challenged

Upon reading the entire book, one is greatly challenged by its contents. Rarely does one encounter writing by someone with an obvious knowledge of God, but with such a misapplication of that knowledge. Throughout the book, Davis even proceeds to give instructions on how to have sex with someone you pick up and take home with you. He instructs extensively on foreplay, oral, anal, and friction sex.⁵ He proceeds to advise the so-called gay Christian in dating procedures. He states that they should, "please masturbate before he/she comes around so that you won't be so quick to fall into lustful unprotected sex!!"⁶ However, he warns against the person becoming "addicted to masturbation, because too much of anything is bad."⁷ Furthermore, he cautions the so-called gay Christian to beware of physical matters getting out of hand and suggests that the initial date be at your house so that you will have knowledge of the whereabouts of all the various weapons that may be stored there. The weapons that he suggests include "steak knives hidden between the sofa cushions, a hammer hidden underneath the bed, or a brick hidden under a pile of clothes...." He further admonishes that such actions may appear to be the result of paranoia, but then he reminds the reader, "Satan has a way of striking you when you expect it least." Amazingly, he asserts that if you meet this person in a club, you should not leave with them "unless you want sex." He gives spiritual instruction that the person seeking this sexual rendezvous should first "make sure that you pray and listen to the Holy Spirit guide you about a certain person...."⁸ There is much more that the book addresses, including an admission that "Fidelity or the lack thereof is a major problem among gay men. No one seemingly trusts anyone because everyone appears to be always on the prowl looking for something younger, more attractive, more fit, more DL, more this more that."⁹

To his credit, the author does acknowledge the inherent dangers of such a lifestyle. This is precisely the idea that we have presented in Chapter Seven, entitled, "The Consequential Alternative: The Legacy of Homo-Reality." Davis states, "It's the idea of the grass being greener on the other side; that is of course until you finally get to the other side and suddenly realize that it's actually brown and dry." Contained within his attempted theological treatise is a quote from Candace Chellew whose purported website comment serves as a basis for the author's point of agreement. He quotes her as saying, "I don't worship God with my genitals."¹⁰ Davis makes a sincere and scholarly attempt at the exposition of homosexual-related Scriptures and instruction concerning other aspects of life, but each instance is a repeat of the standard revisionist argument.

Finally, he even quotes renowned Christian writer, Max Lucado. The author testifies of having read the book, *Just Like Jesus*. He states that "this book has so transformed my life that while reading it I felt the internal waves starting to churn and the veil of confusion and misunderstanding lifted...."[11] Supposedly, the teaching of this book helped him comprehend God's unconditional and sanctifying love. He encourages fellow homosexuals that as they pursue the Christian life that "many of the old habits, vices, attitudes and practices that you once clung to in the homosexual world will no longer retain its flavor."[12]

I have heard of many things in the 30 years that I have been a Christian and in the 40 years that I have been a church member, but I have never heard of *sanctified HOMOsexuality!* First Thessalonians 4:2-5 and 7-8 says, *"For ye know what commandments we gave you by the Lord Jesus. For this is the will of God, even your sanctification, that ye should abstain from fornication: that every one of you should know how to possess his vessel in sanctification and honour; not in the lust of concupiscence, even as the Gentiles which know not God....For God hath not called us unto uncleanness, but unto holiness. He therefore that despiseth, despiseth not man, but God, who hath also given unto us His holy Spirit."*

This Pauline passage is so plain that, as Isaiah 35:8 says, *"Fools shall not err therein."* It requires no at-length explanation or exposition. St. Paul refers to his forthcoming statement as a *commandment*. It is not a suggestion or recommendation. Secondly, he says that it is the *will of God*. Thirdly, he teaches complete *abstinence*. Fourthly, he distinguishes the pre-marriage, celibate lifestyle as *sanctified* and *honorable*. Fifthly, he uses the expression, *"lust of concupiscence,"* inferring that it is not just normal sexual desire, but rather, it is blown out of proportion and exaggerated. It is *concupiscence*. Sixthly, he insists that those who behave as such *do not know God*. Seventh, he labels it as *uncleanness*. Eighth, he is aware of the opposition to his teaching of purity and alerts the Thessalonians that they will be *despised*, accused of intolerance, and looked down upon, because of their stand. Lastly, he says that those who despise them are despising the *Holy Spirit*. The expression, *"sanctified HOMOsexuality,"* is clearly oxymoronic, and the idea (not the person) is moronic. The idea is an iconoclastic, insidious, bombastic, bellicose bludgeoning of verbosity. Simply stated, *It ain't so!* In fact, it ain't so, no matter who says it is so! The debate of ideas should never result in the destruction of a person. That is precisely the problem with the church world. Whenever we perceive that someone's teaching is wrong, we should seek to recover them from the snare of the devil and not hand them over to the devil. They should be given space to repent, recant, and retract. If they refuse to discontinue spreading untruth in the name of God, their ultimate judgment is in the hands of God. It is a fearful thing to misrepresent the Master Teacher.

Great Sadness

Then Jesus beholding him loved him, and said unto him, One thing thou lackest: go thy way, sell whatsoever thou hast, and give to the poor, and thou shalt have treasure in heaven: and come, take up the cross, and follow Me. And he was sad at that saying, and went away grieved: for he had great possessions (Mark 10:21-22).

Reading this intellectually gifted young man's writing left me with great sadness. This is the feeling that the Lord Jesus had for the rich young ruler, who could not part with his possessions and follow the Master Teacher. The Scripture says, "*Jesus beholding him loved him*" (Mk. 10:21a). The Greek word for *beholding* means "to become transfixed, to stare, to look deeply into." Just one look was all that it took for Jesus to love him; however, He did not change His word to accommodate him. Compromise and accommodation will always do injustice to the cause of Christ and injustice to those who need a "*sure word of prophecy*" in the gay and lesbian community. Is it possible for a person to have been raised in the church and having genuinely met the Lord at some point in his life, to become so accepting of the orientation and the inclination for sensual gratification from the same sex, that he develops a *doctrine that borders delusion*? Judging from the various writings by self-professed gay Christians, it seems that it is quite possible. It reminds me of the mirage in a desert. It gives the appearance of refreshing water, of a hope of survival, but it delivers a cruel blow. It promises deliverance, but it can never deliver. There is no overnight service, first-class, second-day air, or even four-to-six-week service. It is a farce. The water is not sparse. It simply does not exist. The person is left parched. It promises survival, but it provides sabotage. It promises life, but it delivers the loss of one's body and soul. What a tragically sad scene. I counter the revisionists' claim by suggesting another consideration.

If the writer's assertion is true that homosexuality is natural and that it is possible to be a "practicer" of it and still be considered a Christian, then one must ask this follow-up question: What else is it possible to be and do and still be considered a Christian? Is it possible to be a practicing fornicator and be a Christian? Is it possible to be a serial adulterer and still be a Christian? Is it possible to be a pornographer and publisher of perversion and still be a Christian? Is it possible to have any sort of sex with one's own child and call yourself a Christian? Is it possible to be filled with the Holy Spirit and regularly go out from church, go into the gay bar in order to go home and sleep with somebody you don't know from Mutt or Jeff, and consider yourself a Christian? The answer to these questions that I have proposed should be shouted from the housetops, *"No, No, No, No, No, No!"* The Holy Bible says, *"Whosoever is born of God doth not commit sin"* (1 Jn. 3:9a). A person truly born of God does not continue to practice sin. The seed of God's Word shall not be mixed with the seed of men. Selah.

The sexual practice of homosexuals is fornication. The term *fornication* is from the Greek word *porneo*, and it means "all manner of sexual sin." As we have afore stated in Chapter Five, entitled, "The Christological Apologetic: Homo-ology—Setting the Gay Record Straight," nearly every scriptural list that addresses sexual sin uses the terms associated with homosexuality, such as "unnatural, inordinate affection, effeminate, abusers of themselves, and male prostitutes." This is not a coincidental occurrence. It is quite probable that St. Paul would have considered the teaching that a person could be a practicing gay or lesbian and still be considered a Christian as a *"doctrine of devils"* (1 Tim. 4:1b). The very fact that a proponent of this line of reasoning has to instruct one-night-stand partners in the art of self-defense is an admission of the satanic presence in all of the activity. This book that further instructs so-called gay Christians concerning *the manner, the place,* and *how long* to maneuver their private parts into someone else, or vice versa, to the avoidance of AIDS, is the epitome of errant exegesis. To teach so-called gay Christians that, in the process of oral-anal or oral-genital stimulation, withdrawing the sexual organ should be done in a timely fashion, but it is no guarantee against contraction of the AIDS virus due to "pre-cum," is not exactly a righteous exhortation.[13] At the very least, you would not expect a book written by a Christian to essentially teach someone how to get their groove on without getting their lights turned out. Some things do not mix. Holiness and homosexuality is one of them. Living for Jesus and lesbianism is another one.

Great Grace Upon the Genitals

Contrary to the majority opinion that a person needs to give God his heart and not his private parts, the entire canon of Scripture teaches a consistent sexual standard. The proof that great grace is upon a person is when God has his heart as well as the control of their sexual organs. When God established His covenant, or binding legal agreement with the patriarch Abraham, He introduced the rite of circumcision. The ceremony was to be enacted on the eighth day of a male child's life. *Eight* is the number of new beginnings and thus signifies the inception or initiation of a claim of God upon the child. Male circumcision involves the cutting away of the foreskin of the male sexual organ. Spiritually, it represents a cutting away of anything that hinders communion with God. To the ancient Hebrews, it typifies what Christians experience in water baptism, which is new life in Christ Jesus (see Rom. 6:1-3). It typifies the outward evidence of an inner expression. Also, it typifies the initiation ceremony into the Kingdom of God. God's covenant was established with Abraham when He made a mark on the organ that would be used to procreate the seed. God said to him: *"And ye shall circumcise the flesh of your foreskin; and it shall be a token of the covenant betwixt Me and you....and My covenant shall be in your flesh for an everlasting covenant"* (Gen. 17:11,13b). The evidence that God had Abraham's heart was the covenant that was cut on Abraham's body.

When God has control of the private parts of a person, more than likely, He has control of every other part of a person as well. When God has marked a man, that man will avoid being marked up by miscellaneous hit-and-run sexual encounters that leave the soul de-shielded, devalued, and destroyed. The body is the temple of the Holy Spirit. Every temple has an altar. The altar of our body is the place where God cut His covenant with man. Therefore, despite the assertion that one *does not worship God with their genitals,* I would adamantly attest that if you worship with your spirit, soul, and body, you cannot exclude your *genitals* (see 1 Thess. 5:23). In other words, you must be sanctified in your sexuality as you possess your vessel in honor. No matter how much a person prays before he has sex with somebody he met in the club, a bar, or even the church for that matter, he will never be able to say that the Holy Spirit was involved in guiding him as he practiced perversion. To say that the Comforter, who guides into all truth, is an active participant in someone's homoerotic carryings-on is a really sick thought. At worst, it is borderline blasphemy. At best, it is unintentional ignorance. A person who truly knows God would know this to be true.

Grace Not to Be Gay

A person's skin color may identify him as Black, Red, White, Brown, or Yellow. A person's sexual preference may identify him as gay or lesbian. Homosexuals, like their heterosexual counterparts, come in all colors, shapes, and sizes. There are more deviations in the area of sexuality than ice cream companies have flavors. Color, gayness, and lesbianism does indeed go together. No singular race has a monopoly on its far-reaching tentacles. The tendency knows no prejudice and prefers no denomination or religious affiliation. It is an equal opportunity de-ployer. There is a select group of committed Christians who happen to struggle with the bombarding temptation to yield to gay or lesbian impulses. However, there is *no practicing gay or lesbian* who is living a true Christian life. A Christian is Christ-like. To be gay is to be man-or boy-like. To be lesbian is to be lady-or girl-like. To be homosexual is one thing; to be Christian is another. Christians are new creations who are compelled to obey the command against practicing compulsive sex outside of marriage (see 2 Cor. 5:17). If any person lives in direct violation of this simple directive, he is in disobedience. All disobedience is sin. The disobedient shall not inherit the Kingdom of God. *They may have a form of godliness, but they have denied the power thereof* (see 2 Tim. 3:5). They may be as creative, sensitive, remarkable, and as likable as one could ever imagine. Despite this, they must surrender the directorship of their sexual preference and purported sentiment to the lordship of Jesus Christ. If they do not do this, then they have received the grace of God in vain and *they have turned the gospel of gracious love into lasciviousness* (see Jude 1:4). They have done this whether they intended to or not.

—WHAT IS THE GOSPEL OF GRACIOUS LOVE?—

...having loved His own which were in the world, He loved them unto the end (John 13:1).

Loved Unto the End

The gospel of gracious love is loving unto the end with an unending love. There is a difference between loving *until the end* and *unto the end.* To love *until* the end implies an *end* that is independent of the condition of the recipient of love. It is limited love. To love *unto* the end extends to the completion of the other person's expected end. A motion picture will end whether you viewed all of it or not. This is akin to loving until the end. On the other hand, loving *unto* the end is a love that never ceases, even if the recipient of that love has not responded. It is "stic-tuitive" and unlimited love. It is postage-stamp love. It sticks to a thing until it gets to where it is going. Consider this premise of love and its relationship to the gay or lesbian person.

His is a lifetime of pain that needs to be ministered to in love. He may not respond positively or immediately to that love. He may not desire to be transformed and reformed to the uniform of the creative conform. Yet the Church must not stop the overtures of God's love, despite its apparent rejection, just as law enforcement officials would not desist in their efforts to bring resolution to a man threatening to commit suicide by jumping off a bridge. They would persist, and they would say whatever it took to bring that person out of their apparent dilemma and despair. I am not suggesting that homosexuals are deranged, drastic, or in suicidal despair, but the person in such a condition should be personally prayed for, and patiently persuaded to consider that there is a better way. This is loving unto the end. It is loving unto the end of the person's fulfillment. It is loving unto the end of what your finite mind can see and with eyes of faith. Therefore, it is what the ancient Greeks called *agape*, and the late Kenneth Hagin referred to as the "God kind of love." *Agape* love knows no time nor space. St. Paul declared that the *agape* love of God suffers long and is not puffed up (see 1 Cor. 13:4). King Solomon declared that *"many waters [time and space] cannot quench love"* (Song 8:7a). Agape love is the only truly unconditional love. It leaves nothing undone, nothing unfinished, and nothing to the imagination.

—PROFOUNDLY SIMPLE—

The gospel of gracious love is profoundly simple and *simply profound.* It is multifaceted and multitasking. It is supernatural and naturally super. The love of God was embodied in the Lord Jesus, who epitomized and exemplified love, the more excellent way. The apostle John exhorts the believer with these words:

> *Beloved, let us love one another: for love is of God; and every one that loveth is born of God, and knoweth God. He that loveth not knoweth not God; for God is love. In this was manifested the love of God toward us, because that God sent His only begotten Son into the world, that we might live through Him* (1 John 4:7-9).

The Teacher's gracious love for His disciples was a many-splendored thing. He kept them. He never left them. He taught them. He was tender with them. He rescued them. He renewed them. He covered them. He calmed them. He encouraged them. He entrusted them. He protected them. He provided for them. He appreciated them. He celebrated them. He restored them. He was a faithful Shepherd to them. He was a friend to them. He loved them unto the end of their three-year preparation with one hundred-percent acceptation, and released them into a ministry without probation. Jesus loved them to the highest level that they could attain by virtue of His influence in their lives. When Peter reneged on Him, Jesus still loved him so much so that He restored him. Three times, this impetuous disciple denied Him; and three times, the Master Teacher deliberated with him.

> *...Peter was grieved because He said unto him the **third** time, Lovest thou Me? And he said unto Him, Lord, Thou knowest all things; Thou knowest that I love Thee. Jesus saith unto him, Feed My sheep* (John 21:17, emphasis added).

Restoration had finally come. *He had been restored back to his place in God.* Jesus loved Peter unto the end. It is the kind of love that we must have toward the homosexual. It is the kind of love that dares to dream the redemptive dream. It is a *restorative* and *radical* love that *transcends traditions* of men, and it is not afraid of the *tarnish that threatens* to attach itself to those who help others overcome their personal proclivities and internalized inclinations. The Church must love unto the end. Robert F. Kennedy once said, "Some men see things as they are and ask why? Others dream things that never were and ask why not?" The Church must ask the same. Why not believe God for special miracles for special people? Why not recognize that only as people reach out to others will they ever touch others? Laying on of hands is simply a personal touch. What the heart feels, the hand should touch, and the smile should embrace with passion. A wish is passive, a desire is assertive, but passion is aggressive.

—PASSION IN ACTION—

The gospel of gracious love puts passion into action. For the Church to save the homosexual from himself, we have to see him as Jesus sees us. Jesus looks through retinas of restoration, not seeing a person's present state, but his predestined divine design. He never simply saw people where they were, but where they could be and where they were going to be. The circumstances of life have in many instances *torn* and *worn* away the divine design of the mind, the emotions, the will, and the body of the person living in homosexuality. Those who promote and practice the gay and lesbian lifestyle are *"dead men walking."* Those who resist getting out of same-sex sin are *twice dead.* Those who exist to get out of it are half-dead. Those who persist in perverted pleasure are the *living dead* (see Jude 1:12). The Church has to be better than this. To see something and do nothing is informed apathy. It is not enough to know what needs to be done; the Church must do it.

> THOSE WHO PROMOTE AND PRACTICE THE GAY AND LESBIAN LIFESTYLE ARE "DEAD MEN WALKING."

Love Is Not Blind

Love is sometimes blind, but *gracious* love is not. It is double vision. When Jesus sees a soul, first He sees the person *deep* within, and then He sees the *damage* that is within. Jesus' love can also be likened unto tunnel vision.

He sees you and only you. If there was not a single soul alive but you, He would have given His life just for you. You ought to repeat to yourself, "I am loved." Luther Vandross' award-winning song, "Dancing With His Father" tells of when he was a child and how his father held him high and carried him up the stairs to the bed. And he knew for sure that he was loved. Surely after all that God has done for us, through the *passion of the Christ*, we ought to know that we are loved too! This is indeed a gracious word!

Jesus loved His disciples *unto the end.* The only acceptable end for any person, including the gay and lesbian, is *precious fellowship* and *perfected worship* of the heavenly Father. God's gracious love corresponds to man's divine design. We are creatures who are divinely designed to love and to be loved. When you love life, life will love you back. Only the love of God can effect such an incredible end. Simon Peter was reunited with Jesus after denying Him. He was *reunited* and, to use the old Peaches and Herb phrase, "It felt so good." Simon Peter became St. Peter because of *gracious love.* It really feels good to be understood, especially after erring. To err is human, to love is divine design. *Gracious love* renews, re-commissions, and rededicates the errant child of God. As a disciple or imitator of the Master Teacher, he became an apostle, a sent one, and a master teacher and maker of disciples in his own right. The master pattern of discipleship makes sense. It works. In Peter's case, the cycle was complete. Jesus had reached down and picked him up, and now he was to do the same. Like a renovated building or item of refurbished art, the former fisherman was lovingly restored, and he became a restorer of paths to dwell in and repairer of the breach (see Is. 58:12). The Savior's gracious love for Peter took him to a place that he had never been. Gracious love is able to take all the years that the *cankerworm*, the *palmerworm, caterpillar,* and the *locust* have eaten and restore them in manifold proportions, effecting a change beyond recognition (see Joel 2:25-26).

Saint Augustine tells the story of a former lover calling to him, but he did not answer. When she enquired why, he told her that the person she was calling was dead. Obviously, he was referencing the person he used to be. In essence, the love of God had effectually given him a new identity. His old person was passed away, revealing a new, better, and wiser creation in Christ.

If Jesus would have looked at His disciples as they were, He would have given up on them early in the ministry. These 12 fellows were not willing to lay down their *self-life* even in the slightest sense. Once the Word was explained, they had to be trained to reign, and groomed until *self* had no more room.

—PERCEIVES THE POTENTIAL—

The gospel of gracious love espouses the kind of love that perceives the potential in sinners and accentuates the positive while making a sincere attempt at eliminating the negative. It affirms the best in all men. It hopes and believes all things, and thinks no malicious thought of evil. It is the kind of love that makes you know that there is good in the worst of us, bad in the best of us, something in all of us, and therefore it behooves none of us to talk about the rest of us. St. Paul teaches that love *"beareth…believeth… hopeth…endureth all things"* (1 Cor. 13:7).

Seeing and Sensing

When you behold the gay person, what do you see and sense? *You should* see a fragmented soul in need of forgiveness and wholeness. Nathaniel was not a stereotypical synagogue altar boy per se; but when Jesus beheld him initially, He surmised that he had all the right stuff and a good heart. He had no guile, which means he had no gall, no bitterness, and no badness. He was the forgiving type. It is going to take the "forgiving type" to affect the world for Jesus. St. John records the encounter in John 1:47, *"Jesus saw Nathanael coming to Him, and saith of him, Behold an Israelite indeed, in whom is no guile!"*

When people sense your heart toward them, they will almost always respond favorably to you. This is to be expected. It has been said that, "People do not care how much you know until they know how much you care." If the believer seeks to minister to the bleeding and dying, it should either be done in gracious love, or he should keep his insensitive facial opening closed. That is a gracious way of saying that he really should shut up. *Exponents of the Bible can sometimes do more harm than the opponents of the Bible.* Disguised disciples can do more damage than the devil. *Mere Christianity* can assuage *authentic Christianity.* Accentuated negatives can eliminate positives. Gracious love sees the sinner, sees the situation, and sees the salvation of that soul. Christians deliver good news from God and not from the Bad News Bears. If a person's life does not manifest intentional love, which is a fruit of the Spirit, his commitment to Christ's cause should be seriously questioned. Any church that is not a loving church is not an "authentic" church, and the members are merely "playing

> THE HOMOSEXUAL CANNOT BE TOLD GOD LOVES HIM WHEN ALL OF THE CHURCH'S ACTIONS ARE AS IF THEY HATE HIM.

436

church." The homosexual cannot be told God loves him when all of the church's actions are as if they hate him. It is love that covers multitudinous sins—not hard looks, hate mail, and smear campaigns.

The Sinner's Soul

Jesus was known as a friend of sinners because He sought to restore their souls (see Mt. 9:10; 11:19). The Father is called a friend to the friendless. Although He was not of the *world* and He did not act like the *world*, yet He knew how to reach out to the *world* and cause sinners to leave their *worldly* ways and their old *world of activity*. Meeting Jesus was an automatic good day. Jesus is our example. We need to be sociable with sinners without the fear of "backsliding." *The Church must be delivered from homophobia.* We are helpers one of another and not hinderers to one another.

To be homo-friendly is not an endorsement of excess; it is an exercise in evangelism. Sinners need exposure to somebody who is right with God if they are to ever leave the wrong. They need to see living witnesses of them who show themselves friendly. They should leave the straight person's presence amazed that "we could call them friends." Think of it this way: Whenever you want to open up and talk about your personal problems, who do you choose? Obviously, you choose a friend. That's what friends are for. The secular songwriter says, "For good times, for bad times, they'll [friends] be on your side forever more...after all, that's what friends are for." Those who show the love of God to a sinner in "living color" will reap the actions of their investment multifold. Gracious love is not afraid to befriend the friendless and find common ground with what is uncommon to them (see Acts 10:28). The "oil and wine" Church is commissioned to care for the homeless and the homosexual. We are called to the liar and the lesbian. We are even called to the beggar and to the bi-sexual. We should always be picking up those who are put down.

There is no higher call, no greater goal, no loftier summit, no more prestigious position than to be known as a coworker with Christ, the Son of the living God. The call necessitates spending time and energy in intentional relational development with those of the gay and lesbian community, especially, if they are in your family. Insensitivity to others is always the result of isolation from others. People need the Lord, and people also need people. The gays boast of coming out of the closet in a parade down Main Street. The godly need to come out of the corner, while we preach about a street called "Straight." Being cloistered may be comfortable, but it is not being truly Christ-like (see Acts 26:26).

God With Skin On

The story is told of a little girl, who upon being put to bed by her parents, was frightened by the lightning flashes and rolling thunder of a breaking storm. She immediately got up and proceeded to casually get into her parents' bed. Her father took her by the hand and walked her back to her bedroom, explaining that there was nothing to fear. "God is in control," he said. Moments later, unconvinced, at the first sound of thunder and sight of lightning, she immediately got up again and this time she dove into her parents' bed. Her father was a little bothered by this and very sternly reminded her that "God is in control." She listened respectfully and properly replied, "Daddy, I know that God is in control, but I *need somebody with some skin on.*" Like the little girl, all human beings need to know that God is in control, but they also need to be ministered to by someone filled with God, with some flesh on.

The believer, in a limited sense, is God with skin on—not in a deified sense, but in a dignified one. The only God some people will ever know is the one who they see in the believer. The Master Teacher called His disciples, *the lights of the world* (see Mt. 5:14). Those with caring affection do not shun the same-sex attraction crowd, but they rise to the challenge to *let their light shine that men may see their good works and glorify the Father.* When the Church lights a candle, it illuminates the way of the gay out of his social stigma and spiritual status. When the Church curses the darkness, it is equivalent to turning an indifferent and indecent cold shoulder to them. When the Church throws out the lifeline to those in the misery of depravity, and the sea of captivity, in effect, it becomes a type of Moses leading people into the "promised land" of purpose and potential. When the Church guides a soul into self-awareness, it hastens the day that personal proclivities are dealt with as a destiny-destroying enemy. Deliverers will always find a way to reach the unreachable and to touch the untouchable. Those in need of deliverance will always seek out a deliverer.

Sex in the City

There is a popular HBO television show called *Sex in the City.* I have never seen it, because I believe that very often HBO is not a Home Box Office, but oftentimes it presents Hell-Bound Only television shows. HBO 3, 2, and 1 will make a person forget all about the Father, the Holy Ghost, and the Son. Reportedly, this sitcom has received wide acclaim. The Church must aggressively pursue the "Sex in the City" crowd. Their sadness makes them ripe for the harvest.

During the decade of the 50's, David Wilkerson, a great preacher and founder of Teen Challenge, resigned his pastorate from a small church in Virginia to do a work for God in the ghettos of New York City. He often stood on the corners of New York City, preaching "Jesus loves you" to the gang members and Harlem "hoodlums." In the classic writing, *The Cross and the Switchblade*, a notorious gang leader and violent son of a practicing witch approached this preacher one day, threatening to cut him up into a thousand pieces. David Wilkerson responded by affirming that what he said perhaps was true. He said, "Yes, son, you could cut me up into a thousand pieces, but every piece would still cry out that Jesus loves you!" The love expressed through David's words and spirit so broke this man's defenses down that, within days, he and others in his gang received Jesus Christ as Savior and Lord.

The gangs of New York City experienced multiple conversions to Christ; and over 50 years later, many thousands of people have been delivered through the ministry of Teen Challenge. Today, Nicky Cruz, the young man who was converted, and whose story is told in the autobiography entitled, *Run, Baby, Run,* is an internationally recognized prophet and great worldwide evangelist. *Everybody needs somebody to love anybody, when they are nobody.*

—PROCREATIVE AND RE-CREATIVE—

The Bar and the Backslider

The gospel of gracious love is procreative and re-creative. It is proficient and sufficient. It is prolonged, and it stretches with a long arm. Someday in the future, I will write a fiction novel that details church life. However, it will not be idealistic church life that I write about. It will be realistic street life that real Christians struggle with on a daily basis. I'm going to entitle it, *The Bar and the Backslider.* It will be the story of a man of God who grows into greatness because someone's love was procreative toward him and met his need. He is delivered from effeminacy. However, the local ministers do not want to be seen in a social setting with him, lest they become subjects of the gay rumor mill.

For a brief season, he discontinues any involvement in church. During this time, the outward indications evidence that he is not managing very well. His mannerisms bespeak that he is being pursued by the gay serpent. The enemy is seeking permanency in effeminacy. The people in the church scorn him and look down upon him while snubbing their noses at him. They say the most God-awful things about him. They chew him up, and they spit him out. They tred upon his reputation, and they bury him in the dirt of derogatory description. He is cursed by spiritual authorities and written off as too far gone to be re-gotten. His depression leads him into a lifestyle of sexual sin with both males and females. Since misery loves company, soon thereafter, the devil embraces what the church considers disgraced. Anyone with any experience in church life knows that the enemy is always glad to search through church garbage because he knows it is filled with things that should never have been discarded and thrown out. These individuals become known as trophies of satan and treasures of darkness.

Even the brother's friends shun him. They are ashamed of him. Christians tend to judge things harshly when they or their family are not personally affected by them. Only his family stands by him. His praying parents and interceding siblings never cease to make mention of his name in prayer. The novel will depict that people would probably have more compassion on homosexuals if they discovered that someone in their own family was a card-carrying member of the gay and lesbian closet community. The backslidden brother needs a shepherd, but the pastors and preachers who know his condition do not have time nor patience to deal with this pestilence of putrid perversion. Instead, they make comments like, "If he was real, he would never be doing what he is," or "I knew there wasn't anything to him."

> PEOPLE WOULD PROBABLY HAVE MORE COMPASSION ON HOMO-SEXUALS IF THEY DISCOVERED THAT SOMEONE IN THEIR OWN FAMILY WAS PREDISPOSED.

In the course of events, he goes out of town for a few days of rest and respite. He visits a church having a revival. He attends the first night, and he almost answers the altar call. Instead, he overhears some of the church people say, "Look at that sissy." A thousand thoughts pierce his tormented soul. A million voices scream, "Leave...leave now...there is no hope for you. You will never be changed! You will never be saved!" He leaves and gets in his car with tears running down his cheeks from a mixture of conviction and condemnation. The Spirit had done His part, but the devil was on his job as well. He bursts into the first bar he finds and buries himself in strong drink, which continues every day and night for the rest of the week.

Unbeknownst to him, the guest evangelist had noticed him in the back of the church and had felt an immense burden to pray for him. After missing him for the next few nights, he inquired, "Where is that brother who was sitting in the back on the first night of revival?" They tell the preacher that he has been seen frequenting the bar, nightly. The story of the Good Samaritan comes to the preacher's mind. The minister decides to visit the bar to go minister to the bent-wrist backslider. Out of concern that his good not be evil spoken of, he submits his action to his spiritual covering.

After searching fruitlessly for a while, the preacher locates him, sits on the barstool next to him, and shares the gracious love of Christ with him. As the preacher confronts him in a procreative manner, he releases a re-creative spirit of restoration. In so many words, this preacher says, "*What doest thou here, Elijah?*" (1 Kings 19:13) The brother is restored to God. Despite the archers having shot at him, his bow abides, and strength and his branches are going over the wall (see Gen. 49:22). The story details his deliverance.

The theme is that the malediction on his life could have been announced and his ministry could have been buried in a graveyard called "He Never Got to Be." God canceled the funeral arrangements and pronounced the benediction of blessing and favor. Procreative love graciously stretched forth its hand to the lowest of places, unafraid of getting dirty or misunderstood. As the story climaxes, this man will grow to be one of the mightiest men of God ever born of a woman. Because of the pain of his own personal saga with same-sex sin, he possesses an anointing to heal hurting hearts on every corner of the globe. He literally goes from a bent-wrist, backslidden brother, to a legend in his Christian time. He is used of God to completely restore others and help them to become one-hundred-percent *men!* Together they form an international men's ministry called the "Band of Brothers." Their evangelistic theme is "From the Bar to the Brotherhood." They dedicate their lives to helping brothers struggling with identity issues so that it will never be an issue again.

The closing song will be, "Love Lifted Me."

I was sinking deep in sin, far from the peaceful shore;

very deeply stained within, sinking to rise no more.

Then the Master of the seas heard my despairing cry,

from the waters lifted me, now safe am I.

LOVE LIFTED ME...LOVE LIFTED ME.

When nothing else could help, love lifted me!

When we were in sin, we were like a child or baby who makes a mess and cannot clean himself. We were like the alcoholic who cannot dry himself. We were like the prison inmate who cannot free himself. We were like the thief who cannot stop himself. We were like the drug user who cannot deliver himself. We were like the streetwalker who cannot change himself. We were like the gay or lesbian person who cannot rearrange themselves. But the Master of the sea heard our despairing cry. From the waters He lifted you and me, now safe are you and I. It was love…God's costly, caring procreative and re-creative gracious love. God's love slides on, but it should never be treated as something one can slip in and out of. Gracious love is never greasy.

—GRACIOUS LOVE VERSUS GREASY GRACE—

What shall we say then? Shall we continue in sin, that grace may abound? God forbid. How shall we, that are dead to sin, live any longer therein? (Romans 6:1-2)

Therefore we ought to give the more earnest heed to the things which we have heard, lest at any time we should let them slip (Hebrews 2:1).

The gospel of gracious love is compelling and expelling. It makes you do certain things that you ordinarily would not do. It makes you not do other things that you always used to do. The gospel of greasy grace is a sorry substitute for the gospel of gracious love. What the Savior says, is *gracious*. What satan says, is *greasy, grimy,* and *slimy*. Note the contrast.

GRACIOUS LOVE SAYS:	GREASY GRACE SAYS:
God commands repentance. He is not winking anymore.	"It's your thing; do what you want to do and I can't tell you who to sock it to" (60's song).
If a man sins, he has an advocate with the Father.	Not if, but when you sin, again and again; you're just a sinner saved by grace.
He loves his own unto the end.	God is love, so you should never be concerned about His wrath, justice, and righteousness.

Gays and lesbians can be changed by the power of the Holy Spirit.	Gays and lesbians are fine just like they are and they don't need to change.
There is a way without God that appears right, but it is really wrong.	There are many ways to one God, including ways to live.

The gospel of greasy grace is another gospel. St. Paul declares that whoever preaches it, shall be considered *"anathema"* or accursed (see 1 Cor. 16:22). St. John declared that they should not be bidden *God speed* (see 2 Jn. 1:10). The gospel celebrates diversity, but it does not tolerate diversion. Ancient Israel was instructed to show *"no mercy"* (see Deut. 7:1-3) to the inhabitants of the land. There was to be no covenant, because inevitably, it would end up becoming like *thorns in their side and pricks in their eyes* (see Num. 33:55). All of the -ite's and -tite's, Amorites, Jebusites, Canaanites, Girgashites, Perizzites, Hittites, Hivites, Uptites, Mosquito Bites, and Out of Sights had to know that God's way is the best way. The people could become proselytes and no longer simply be an *Ite* or *Tite*.

The German theologian, Dietrich Bonhoeffer, who was executed for leading the religious resistance to Hitler's Nazism, warned against the cheapening of the grace of God. He wrote these words:

> Cheap grace is the deadly enemy of our Church. We are fighting to-day for costly grace. Cheap grace means grace sold on the market like cheapjacks' wares. The sacraments, the forgiveness of sin, and the consolations of religion are thrown away at cut prices. Grace is represented as the Church's inexhaustible treasury, from which she showers blessings with generous hands, without asking questions or fixing limits. Grace without price; grace without cost! The essence of grace, we suppose, is that the account has been paid in advance; and, because it has been paid, everything can be had for nothing. Since the cost was infinite, the possibilities of using and spending it are infinite. What would grace be if it were not cheap?[14]

Free, But Not Cheap

Grace is free, but not cheap. Grace appeases and pleases, but it is not greasy. Grace eradicates sin, but it does not validate it. It is said that when the legendary D.L. Moody came to Christ, immediately thereafter, he ran outside

443

into the streets of Chicago attempting to witness to others. He stopped a woman, asking, "Do you know grace?" The woman responded, "Grace who?" In reality, grace is not just an attribute of God. It is the person of God Himself. The God of all grace is also the God of all comfort. God is love, and love is grace in caring affection. There is nothing greasy about the grace of love.

During the 70's, there was a popular Christian bumper sticker that read: "If you were arrested for being a Christian, would there be enough evidence to convict you?" Does the world believe that Christ was sent by the Father because of the love they see you expressing toward others? In Matthew 24:12, speaking about the last days, Jesus states *"because iniquity shall abound, the love of many shall wax cold."* Second Timothy 3:1-3 says in the last days, men shall be *lovers of themselves* and *"lovers of pleasures more than lovers of God."* St. Paul's three allusions to love teach a critical concept. The expression of God's true love will lift you out of soulish self-love, which is the by-product of self-seeking, self-will, and self-preservation.

The Color of Love

One of my favorite movies is Steven Spielberg's, *The Color Purple.* Biblically, the color *purple* represents royalty. The decor of All Nations Church in Columbus, Ohio, and Charlotte, North Carolina, is varying shades of purple. The robe that Jesus wore to His passion and that the Roman soldiers cast lots for was purple.

It was a preeminent color of choice for the tabernacle tapestry and the high priests' garments. Upon the breastplate that covered his garment, he wore 12 precious stones representing the 12 tribes of Israel. He was to always remember that though he was the high priest, those to whom he was called to minister were the *royal priests.* Purple kept him cognizant of this and the stones kept him mindful to keep the people he represented close to his heart. The color *purple* should remind all seekers of truth of the regal nature of the Righteous One and His royal subjects. These 12 chapters were specifically designed with this in mind.

In the blockbuster hit, *The Color Purple,* one of the most moving scenes is when the nightclub singer and loose-living woman reaches out to visit her father, who is the local pastor. Initially, he disdains her and turns his back on her. However, as the movie ends, she starts singing a song entitled, "God's Trying to Tell You Something." The scene starts in the local juke joint, but proceeds with a lengthy procession to the church house. All the people leave the place and follow her into the church. The choir is singing the same song. They merge voices and the audience erupts in passionate, expressive, pentecostal worship. The pastor, seeing the effect of redemption at work, turns to his daughter, and this time he does not shun her, but rather embraces her. Every time I see this scene, it deeply touches my fathering-pastoral heart. The Church needs to take a course entitled, "The Color Purple 101." We've had enough hate from the professors of the Word. What the world needs now is a gracious *hug*! Steve Gallagher's *Sexual Idolatry* describes vividly the true nature of the gracious love of God.

> The dangerous thing about savoring God's love while in a state of unrepentant sin is that a person can actually be deceived, thinking he is in true fellowship with the Lord. Notice in the story concerning the rich, young ruler that Jesus' love did not determine this man's eternal destiny. Yes, Mark tells us that Jesus did indeed love him. I am sure His love manifested itself as a powerful passion which emanated from His very Being. Nonetheless, this man's eternity depended upon *his response* to that ardent love. Would he obey the words of Jesus or not? As Jesus is faithful to do with all those who follow Him, He mercifully brought this man to a cross-road—Choose today whom you will serve…I am convinced that what many people today are accepting as grace is really nothing more than *the presumptuous license to sin.*[15]

These words are poignant reminders of the gravity of not confusing gracious love with greasy grace. Often on the music awards programs, a person, whose song has been heralded and chosen as the recipient of an award, will mount the stage giving praise to his or her "Lord and Savior, Jesus Christ." This is confusing, in light of the lyrics of their celebrated song. Recently, I saw an entertainer gyrate and continually grab his crotch area with sexual motions while performing. Then he proceeded to give glory to God in his acceptance comments. The Bible admonishes the believer to "*lift up holy hands.*" Holding oneself to provoke sensual response is not holy. It is ho-ley, however. This is what I mean by loosey-goosey living. Living loosely, lip-syncing praise while blowing kisses at someone else's lips may get you an award, and it may also get you in trouble with God. The spirit of loosey-goosey is all over Hollywood, and shamefully, it has built an altar in the believer's temple. How can one invoke God's name to sanction music that degrades women, glorifies illicit sex, and mercilessly spews profanity on every line. There are some things that do not mix. Praise and perversion are two of them. You cannot serve the Savior and sing songs to sedate the sinner in a headlong plunge to hell! When a sexually unclean person either sings or preaches, he unleashes that duplicitous demon upon the entire audience. It is satanic, seductive, and sensual; and it is belched from the pit of perversion's capital, a crater called hell. James 3:15 says, *"This wisdom descendeth not from above, but is **earthly, sensual, devilish"*** (emphasis added).

God's grace abounds, but no person has the liberty to willfully live out of bounds. God's grace is more than sufficient, but it is not silly and sin-laden. Too much grease renders greasiness. This results in slipperiness. A petition for God's grace in the continuation of sin renders presumption. Too much grease is unhealthy. To continue in sin that grace may abound is forbidden. Too much grease produces oil slicks. Too much grease on the wrong object ruins it. Greasy grace leads to a greasy life of scattered ruins in the form of broken relationships, strewn careers, and shattered dreams.

—ALWAYS ABOUNDING—

The gospel of gracious love is an abiding and always abounding assurance. It is not easy believism, nor is it mere intellectual assent. It is the unwavering, undiminished, and unmoving capacity to stand during the most tempting of times. John MacArthur writes:

> The contemporary church has the idea that salvation is only the granting of eternal life, not necessarily the liberation of a sinner from the bondage of his iniquity. We tell people that God loves them and has a wonderful plan for their lives, but that is only half the truth. God also hates sin and will punish unrepentant sinners with eternal torment. No gospel representation is complete if it avoids or conceals those facts. Any message that fails to define and confront the severity of personal sin is a deficient gospel. And any "salvation" that does not alter a life-style of sin and transform the heart of the sinner is not a genuine salvation.[16]

The gospel of gracious love neither accuses the sinner, nor does it excuse the sin. It diffuses the situation by delivering the soul of the sinful in the waiting embrace of Emmanuel, God with us. William Barclay, the legendary Bible expositor exhorts:

> Grace is not only a gift; it is a grave responsibility. A man cannot go on living the life he lived before he met Jesus Christ. He must be clothed in a new purity and a new holiness and a new goodness. The door is open, but the door is not open to the sinner to

come and remain a sinner, but for the sinner to come and become a saint.[17]

St. Paul says, *"That Christ may dwell in your hearts by faith…comprehend with all saints what is the breadth, and length, and depth, and height; and to know the love of Christ, which passeth knowledge, that ye might be filled with all the fullness of God* (Eph. 3:17-19). The love of Christ provides humanity with an ocean of grace. Whenever you swim in an ocean, you are warned against going out too far. One must always beware of the riptide of sin that seeks to pull you in.

> There is an ocean of grace waiting for us, inviting us to dive in and swim. There's no end to its depth or length, and even through endless ages of eternity, we will stand in awe at the wonder of it all. The tragedy is that many preachers and teachers today have unintentionally misrepresented God's grace, practically turning it into a license to sin. And in doing this, they have cheapened its power and demeaned its value. They have polluted the holy waters flowing from the heavenly throne.
>
> Can I be totally honest with you? I believe that grace is one of the most misunderstood subjects in the contemporary Church. On the one hand, there are legalists who seem to forget that salvation is by grace through faith and not by works. They turn Christianity into a lifeless religion plagued by futility and marked by always-failing human effort.
>
> On the other hand, there are leaders who seem to forget that salvation by grace includes freedom from sin as well as forgiveness of sin. They turn Christianity into a religion that "saves" but doesn't transform. Both positions are wrong. Dead wrong.[18]

Michael Brown
Go and Sin No More

—TARGETING THE TEMPTER—

The gospel of gracious love targets the tempter, just as the tempter targets all of God's children. That is his job, and he is on it every day. Just as he targeted me when I was a teenager, I have flipped the script and I am now targeting the tempter. You must do the same. You must measure the enemy as you meet him on life's battlefield. The Church must flip the script and target the tempter. There is no measure that he will not meet and no length to which he will not go. He is relentless and ruthless. He is determined and despicable. He does not discriminate. He will not be deterred. Age, gender, and disposition makes no difference to the devil. Heed the Mosaic call to show him, *No Mercy!* He has not shown the homosexual any mercy. He must reap what he has sown. He has sown to the wind; he must reap the whirlwind (see Hos. 8:7). God speaks through the whirlwind to the world, the flesh, and the devil (see Job 38:1). The "oil and wine" Church must cause him a storm of trouble.

He must pay for his mental madness. Coals of fire must be heaped upon him for molesting God-given moments and decimating divinely inspired dreams. He must pay for mishandling, misdirecting, and for causing misunderstanding, resulting in lifetime mismanagement of mission. He must pay for fiercely focusing on the gay and lesbian person and systematically unsettling their sexuality. He must be punished for consuming the homosexual from childhood to adulthood with a consciousness steeped in confusion concerning sexuality. His house of horrors must be spoiled of those held captive therein (see Mt. 12:29).

The human body contains no less than 600 muscles, 970 miles of blood vessels, and 20,000 hairs in the ear; and yet physiology alone does not determine identity and neither does the body part between the legs. Identity is more than physical; it is also spiritual. In the image of God, made He male and female (see Gen. 1:27). Divine design is masculine, and it is feminine. The confusion of the two is the recipe of catastrophe and the prescription of perversion.

Satan is no respecter of persons. Indiscriminately, he will take a very innocent child and make him his next victim. *He preys when people fail to pray or when they are not covered by prayers of the righteous.* All of mankind is just a means to his end of garnering worshipers from God the Father unto himself. The sound of a redeemed soul praising God of his own free will is a cacophony to satan. He will never have such a redemptive experience. Spitefully, he works to ensure that as many of mankind as possible does not either. The sound of a transformed former homosexual worshipping God as he remembers how the Father's love opened his eyes to the darkness of the demonic force of homosexuality, is particularly perturbing and defiantly disturbing to satanic fervor. Redeemed homosexuals have turned over the tables and turned the tide. Now, the tempter becomes the target. This is why homosexual activists will ferociously attack anyone who even remotely suggests that homosexuals can be delivered, transformed, and changed. Briar Whitehead says, "A great threat is implied by the word, 'change.' "[19]

Dr. M. Scott Peck, author of *People of the Lie,* says,

Evil human beings are those who refuse to change, who see no reason to change, who have built layer on layer of self-deception. We are led to believe that real evil does not have anything to do with the mother of three next door, or the deacon in the church down the street, but my own experience is that evil human beings are quite common and usually appear quite ordinary to the superficial observer.[20]

St. Paul says, "*Good overcomes evil*" (Rom. 12:21). The gospel of gracious love is the good news that as Christ has overcome the world, in like manner, the gay and lesbian can overcome homosexuality. The victory that overcomes evil is faith. Without it, it is impossible to please the Lord (see Heb. 11:6). Faith in God is the prescription for overcoming the diagnosis of the evil heart of unbelief. The Scripture states, "*Take heed, brethren, lest there be in any of you an evil heart of unbelief, in departing from the living God*" (Heb. 3:12). Those who say the homosexual either cannot change, or should not change, are exercising an evil heart of unbelief. With God, "*nothing shall be impossible*" (Luke 1:37). Any pro-gay apologist who states otherwise has committed high treason against the Holy One Himself. The good news is that Jesus paid it all and therefore, "*all things are possible to him that believes*" (Mt. 19:26). The debt for sin is wiped out at the cross. Calvary covers it all. This is a word that must be ministered graciously to the gay and lesbian community.

The Caring Affection: In Conclusion
The Gospel of Gracious Love

Tony Campolo, a great author and controversial liberal theologian, tells a story that illustrates "The Gospel of Gracious Love." While on an itinerant ministry engagement in Honolulu, Hawaii, he had jet lag upon arrival and had difficulty sleeping throughout the entire night. At 3:00 a.m. he ventured into an all-night diner. Within moments, several women walked in. It became apparent that they were women plying the ancient trade of "sex for sale." He overheard that one of the women of the night named Agnes was having her 39th birthday the next day. Upon the departure of the women from the diner, he (Tony Campolo) approached the owner of the eatery about allowing him to host an impromptu surprise birthday party for Agnes the following night. The owner and his wife thought it was a good idea, and they both agreed to it.

Decorations

The next day they ordered the decorations, the cake, and the trimming, including a festive birthday sign that they taped to the window. Later that evening, a large crowd had gathered in the establishment, awaiting the entrance of the birthday girl. Upon her entry, everyone loudly exclaimed, "Happy birthday, Agnes!" She stood there speechless and then she started to cry. The traditional "Happy Birthday" song began, and she cried even more. The tears flowed freely and forcefully. She was in a state of disbelieving shock. The candles were blown out, and she requested to be allowed to not simply cut the cake, but to keep it in her apartment for a couple of days. Of course, nobody refused her simple request and according to Campolo, she went grasping the cake "as if it were the Holy Grail!" Silence filled the room. Suddenly, he said, "Why don't we pray for Agnes that God will bless her on this birthday? That He will bring peace into her life and save her from all that troubles her." He prayed thusly and concluded with "Amen."

Demonstration

The owner looked at him and said, "Hey, you did not tell me you were a preacher. What kind of church do you preach at?" Campolo thought and then smiling he said, "I preach at the kind of church that throws birthday parties for whores at 3:00 in the morning." The owner replied, "No, you do not.

There is no church like that. If there were, I would join a church like that!" I truly believe that this kind of church would never have an empty seat. People need literal love and not belittling looks. People need acceptance and not accommodation. People need Jesus and not judgmentalism. People need to hope and not be hurt. People need a smile and not a frown. People need blessing and not cursing. People need salvation and not condemnation. People need a pastor and not a pimp. People need a pray-er and not a player. People need a church home and their own home. People need a family of faith and not foes with no faith. The Agnes company is waiting for decorations, the demonstration, and the celebration of their personhood. They are different, but they deserve dignity. They are deep in sin, but they do not know that they can change. Perhaps it will take three deeds of love before they dare to believe that it could really be true when you say, "Jesus loves you."

Application

The parable of the Good Samaritan shows an application of the compassionate approach. It is the crescendo in the symphony of all human relations parables. It reverberates through the corridors of time and confronts us in these latter times. It is the gold standard of the currency of the Kingdom of God. Every day, in cities across our land, *certain gay men and lesbian women fall among thieves*. The minute precious little ones are born; they are preprogrammed and prepackaged with a predisposition for predestination defined as purpose. On the way, there are always demonic dream-stealing thieves. Sometimes the thief is an abusive father, a molesting uncle, an experimental cousin, or the neighborhood bullies known as the big boys. Sometimes the thief is a disconnected dad, a misaligned mom, a perverted preacher, a perpetrating pastor, or a bi-curious person. Their sole goal is to sample somebody's sexual merchandise. The thief is always eager to slash and dash one's dreams to shreds, leaving open and exposed wounds in and around their heart, the place out of which flows the issues of your life and abundance. Satan is the chief thief and a master murderer (see Jn. 10:10).

Will the Real Christian *Please* Stand Up?

Many years ago, there was a famous television game show that was called, *To Tell the Truth*. At the conclusion of a brief question-and-answer time in which three different individuals each claimed to have the same identity, the contestant would have to guess which person was the real individual they claimed to be. The host would then say, "Will the real (he'd state the name) pleeease stand up." Inevitably, after a momentary hesitation and further chicanery, the real person would reveal himself by standing up. The "oil and wine" Church has come to a critical juncture. It is time to either stand up or close up. Many believers have been like the priest who went on *the way* and the Levite who came to the *way* of the man, but both chose to pass him by the *way* and leave him on the *wayside*. Only the Samaritan went to *where he was* and did not leave him the *way* he was. The Father is calling the Church to go beyond looking from afar to drawing near to where the hurting people are. The gay and lesbian persons in our midst are not "Gorillas in Our Midst." They are souls seeking salvation. The Father is seeking to save souls. Real Christians must rise up and amass a coordinate campaign that transcends cultural comfort zones. This will release and increase the radical revolution.

THE GAY AND LESBIAN PERSONS IN OUR MIDST ARE NOT "GORILLAS IN OUR MIDST." THEY ARE SOULS SEEKING SALVATION IN OUR MIDST.

—THE END—

The gospel of gracious love is the Father's post-card to a perilous post-modern world in a predicament of pent-up pain. There can be no more business as usual. Gracious love is the order of the day. It is a tough love that tenderly touches the tethered and tattered. The commission is complete only when we commit ourselves to compassionate, convicted concern. From the cradle to the grave, gracious love is the way. From infancy to eternity, gracious love is the order of the day. Jesus, the Master Teacher, exemplified the God-kind of gracious love in loving "us unto the end." When a movie says "The End," it means *the end*. It is not over until it is over. The salvation of a soul is a work in progress. There are different ages and different stages. Everyone's end is truly different. Whereas some respond to the gospel message *immediately, importunely,* and *expediently,* in many instances the homosexual person, because of the deep issues associated with being so inclined, may require more time to respond to the love of Christ. However, it is the Church's challenge to see him or her to the end. The end is a place of restoration and transformation. To bring a person to this state, could take a little love or a lifetime of love. Agape love will bring the *cessation* of all their shame, guilt, and pain. It is unto deliverance, despite the daily difficulties. It is a love unto a new life despite the nuances that have served as a nemesis. *"Therefore if any man be in Christ, he is a new creature: old things are passed away; behold, all things are become new"* (2 Cor. 5:17).

The gospel of gracious love is the gracious gospel of a loving God. Grace is without merit, and without qualification. *Grace* is not greasy; it is not loosy-goosey; nor is it legalistic. *Grace* is more than what you say before you eat. It is warm and wooing, and it is strong and steadfast. The grace of God teaches us to deny ungodly lusts and to dare to live godly lives. The grace of love is greater than the disgrace of life. The grace of God abounds where worldly sin abides. The darker the night, the brighter the light. The deeper the depths of sin, the higher the heights of holiness. The more shameful the act, the more hopeful the action. Graciousness is the battle cry of the "oil and wine" Church of the 21st century. God's grace is still amazing. It still looks beyond human faults and sees human needs. It still flows from the highest mountain and reaches into the lowest valley. It still gives strength from day to day, and it has never lost its power. Whenever the straight person sees the gay and lesbian person, he should say, "but for the grace of God, there go I." The gospel of gracious love is confrontive with sin, combative with satan, compassionate with the sinner, compelling with the saint, and comprehensive with the same-sex couple. The gospel of gracious love will tell the naked truth, and then clothe the naked. After all, as our brother's keeper, aren't we to be a cover for our brother and a security blanket for our sister?

The Father is the architect of gracious love. Jesus is the author of gracious love. The Holy Spirit is the accomplisher of gracious love. This writing in *gracious* love *is finished*. It is completed. Tetelastai. Grace, mercy, and peace be multiplied unto you. Maranatha. Even so, come, Lord Jesus. We expect You!

—THE PRAYER OF BENEDICTION—

The Prayer of *Gracious Love:* Dear heavenly Father, thank You for loving us while we were yet in our sins. Gracious God, we thank You for Your immeasurable, inimitable, indisputable grace. May it never be said of us that we received the grace of God in vain. Give us grace to finish this race. Thank You for *creating* a way back into Your presence. Thank You for *caring* enough to *condescend* even at the *cost* of the life of Your only begotten Son. Lord, what You have freely given us, may we freely give to others. May we never kick the fallen for falling; but help us to help someone else, including the *homosexual.* Help us to minister love and not legalism. Help us to heal their hurts, their hearts, and their haunting memories. Help us not be *prejudiced, presumptuous,* and *preconceived* in our notions.

Grant us to be *prepared* in our attitude and good in our *graciousness*. In the name of He who is the express image of living love, in Jesus' name we pray. Amen! Amen!

ENDNOTES

1. Edward T. Welch, *Blame It on the Brain* (Phillipsburg, NJ: 1998), 175.

2. Erwin W. Lutzer, *The Truth About Same-Sex Marriage* (Chicago, IL: Moody Publishers, 2004), 86.

3. Edythe Draper, *Draper's Book of Quotations for the Christian World*, (Wheaton, IL: Tyndale House Publishers, Inc., 1992), Entry 7164, Bible Illustrator 3.0 for Windows, Parsons Technology, Inc. 1990-1998, Illustrations Copyrighted at Christianity Today, Inc., 1984-1995, Faircom Corp.

4. Herndon L. Davis, *Black, Gay, and Christian* (Atlanta, GA: Creative Marketing & Book Publishing, 2004), 3.

5. Ibid., 151-153.

6. Ibid., 151.

7. Ibid., 151.

8. Ibid., 143.

9. Ibid., 134.

10. Ibid., 86.

11. Ibid., 280.

12. Ibid., 281.

13. Ibid., 152.

14. Dietrich Bonhoeffer, *The Cost of Discipleship* (New York: Simon & Schuster, 1959), 43.

15. Steve Gallagher, *Sexual Idolatry* (Dry Ridge, KY: Pure Life Ministries, 2000), 261 and 263.

16. John F. MacArthur, Jr., *The Gospel According to Jesus* (Panorama City, CA: 1988), 60.

17. William Barclay, as quoted in Michael Brown, *Go and Sin No More* (Ventura, CA: Gospel Light, 1999), 224.

18. Michael L. Brown, *Go and Sin No More*, 213-214.

19. Briar Whitehead, *Craving for Love* (Grand Rapids, MI: Monarch Books, 2003), 201.

20. Dr. M. Scott Peck as quoted by Whitehead, *Craving for Love*, 307.

BIOGRAPHICAL SKETCH
OF
Dr. Brian Keith Williams

◣ **THE MAN: Dr. BRIAN KEITH WILLIAMS** was born and raised in the city of Baltimore, Maryland. During the winter of 1978 he moved to Columbus, Ohio, where he has resided since. He attended the University of Maryland on a journalism scholarship and received his doctorate of divinity degree from St. Thomas Christian College in Jacksonville, FLA. He is the husband of Andria Williams. They have been married for twenty-five years and are the blessed parents of three children: Achea, Brian and Brandon.

◣ **THE MINISTRY:** Dr. Williams is the Apostle and founder of ALL NATIONS CHURCH, INC., located in Columbus, Ohio and in Charlotte, North Carolina. Additionally, he oversees approximately twenty churches throughout the USA as well as All Nations Church of the Harvest in Brazil and Global Life Church in St. Thomas, Virgin Islands. He is a prophetic ministry gift whose heartbeat is to bring believers into a lifestyle of true worship. He has traveled over four million miles throughout thirty years of active ministry. He has preached in over a thousand different settings, including hundreds of conferences, on topics ranging from eschatology to sexuality, and everything in between. He is consistently invited back over and again. Pastors testify, "their church will never be the same again." He is an avid reader and possesses nearly twenty thousand volumes in his personal library. He is affectionately called, an Apostle of Glory and Revelation.

◣ **THE MANDATE:** Dr. Williams is a revolutionary ministry gift known for revelatory preaching, relevant teaching and relentless worship. His revival meetings are characterized by enormous manifestations of God's glory. He has delivered the word of the Lord to major leaders, both spiritual and secular. His ministry is distinguished by his uncompromising boldness and cutting edge understanding of the times. He possesses an anointing for the new millennium and he is committed to planting and pioneering local All Nations Churches throughout the world, via the Apostolic Network of Churches, Inc. (A.N.C).

— THE MASSES: Dr. Williams is founder and president of the BKW Young Preachers' Institute. He has personally ordained nearly three hundred preachers. He has installed nearly two dozen pastors of local churches. Accordingly, he has also consecrated numerous pastors to the Bishopric. He has self-published several books and is currently working on a major release entitled, *Ministering Graciously to the Gay and Lesbian Community*. He is a much sought after conference speaker, whose travels have taken him to various parts of the world, the most recent being Brazil, England, Mexico, The Virgin Islands, Antigua, Jamaica and South Africa. Additionally, he has made guest appearances on TBN, CBN, Daystar, Word, Inspiration and a host of other networks. His ministry has featured a daily telecast called, *A Taste of Glory*, seen throughout the USA as well as Europe. His daily radio broadcast, *Midday Miracles*, is heard throughout the United States, and the continent of Africa, via radio, shortwave radio, and the internet.

— THE MERITS: Dr. Williams is a member of the One Church/One Child Adoption organization and the Charismatic Bible Ministries. The Mayor of Columbus and the Governor of the State of Ohio have recognized him for Outstanding Community Service. He has participated in White House briefings with two different Presidential administrations. He has been recognized for his activism as a member of the Coalition for the Restoration of the Black Family and Faith Based Initiative Summit Hearings on Capitol Hill. Those who hear him expound the Word of God testify of a truth, Dr. Brian Keith Williams was born for such a time as this.